# Household Energy Consumption in China: 2016 Report

Xinye Zheng · Chu Wei
Editors

# Household Energy Consumption in China: 2016 Report

中国人民大学出版社
CHINA RENMIN UNIVERSITY PRESS

Springer

*Editors*
Xinye Zheng
Department of Energy Economics,
School of Economics
Renmin University of China
Beijing, China

Chu Wei
Department of Energy Economics,
School of Economics
Renmin University of China
Beijing, China

Supported by fund for building world-class universities (disciplines) of Renmin University of China.

This book has received financial support from the Collaborative Innovation Center for China Economy with Chinese Characteristics, the National Natural Science Foundation of China (71273269, 71403285 and 71622014), the Humanity and Social Science Foundation of Ministry of Education of China (16YJA790049) and the National Social Science Foundation of China (15BJL099).

ISBN 978-981-13-7522-4 ISBN 978-981-13-7523-1 (eBook)
https://doi.org/10.1007/978-981-13-7523-1

Jointly published with China Renmin University Press, Beijing, China
The print edition is not for sale in China Mainland. Customers from China Mainland please order the print book from: China Renmin University Press.

Library of Congress Control Number: 2019936282



This Springer imprint is published by the registered company Springer Nature Singapore Pte Ltd.
The registered company address is: 152 Beach Road, #21-01/04 Gateway East, Singapore 189721, Singapore

# Preface

To understand the basic situation, characteristics, and influential factors in relation to residential energy consumption in China, the Department of Energy Economics of Renmin University of China (RUC) started the "Chinese Residential Energy Consumption Survey" (CRECS) in early 2013. In the first CRECS (i.e., CRECS 2012), a household survey questionnaire about the characteristics of household energy consumption in China was designed for the first time. It collected data from 1,450 urban and rural households in China about their energy consumption in 2012, including basic household information, expenditures on cooking and electrical appliances, space heating and air conditioning, transportation and traveling and energy consumption, as well as awareness of various energy policies. Based on the microdata of the CRECS 2012, we released and published the *Chinese Household Energy Consumption Report 2014* (Science Press) in 2014. In the same year, we focused on rural residents and carried out the second CRECS (i.e., CRECS 2013), in which we collected systematic data about energy consumption of 3,404 rural households in China in 2013 and developed a corresponding measurement module for estimation of biomass energy consumption by rural residents. The research results of this survey were released and published in the *Chinese Household Energy Consumption Report 2015* via the Science Press in 2016. These two reports on Chinese residential energy consumption attracted extensive attention from government agencies, academic institutions, media, and the public.

With strong support from the National Survey Research Center at Renmin University of China (NSRC), the third CRECS (i.e., CRECS 2014) was officially started in the summer of 2015 and conducted simultaneously with the Chinese General Social Survey (CGSS). It covered 3,863 urban and rural households in 28 provinces in China (including autonomous regions and municipalities, excluding Tibet, Hainan, Ningxia, Hong Kong, Macao, and Taiwan), aiming to provide reference for the subsequent data collection and scientific research. This book is a summary of the research, which is mainly based on data from the third CRECS while also considering the data from the first two rounds of surveys.

This household survey and the subsequent scientific research are the fruit of multiparty cooperation. The Department of Energy Economics in School of Economics, RUC was responsible for designing the questionnaire, training of investigators, preparation of the research report, etc. NSRC was responsible for sampling, questionnaire conduction, data verification, etc. We hereby express our heartfelt thanks to the National Academy of Development and Strategy, RUC, the School of Economics, RUC, and other organizations for funding the survey and the subsequent research and to the Collaborative Innovation Center for China Economy with Chinese Characteristics for funding the publication of this book.

Meanwhile, we received assistance and guidance from many experts in and outside RUC during the phases of questionnaire design, surveying, data collection and report drafting, and revision. Many scholars offered valuable advice on the research methodology and the draft report, including Researcher Tan Xianchun and Associate Researcher Liu Yu of Chinese Academy of Sciences, Professor Zhao Xiaoli of China University of Petroleum, Professor Wang Xiaohua of Nanjing Agricultural University, Associate Professor He Xiaoping of Xiamen University, Associate Professor Sun Yan of Dalian University of Technology, Professor Shi Minjun, Professor Qiu Huanguang, Associate Professor Wang Weidong, Associate Professor Tang Jie of RUC, etc. We are also grateful to students of the National Academy of Development and Strategy, RUC and the Department of Energy Economics of School of Economics, RUC for their assistance with conduction of the questionnaire.

Various authors have made substantial contribution to this book during the phases of drafting, revision, and perfection. Zheng Xinye and Wei Chu oversaw the data collection and report preparation, and the contributors of the specific chapters are, respectively, as follows:

Chapter 1, written by Wei Chu, is a brief introduction of the research background, main findings, and policy implications. The section about smart family is the joint contribution of Wu Shimei, Wang Dan, Hu Jingqiu, and Wei Chu.

Chapter 2 is an introduction of the sampling methods and the specific implementation of the household investigation as well as a descriptive analysis of the data in different questionnaire modules. Contributors of this chapter include Wei Chu (Sect. 1), Chen Zhanming and Zeng Shipei (Sect. 2), Xia Xiaohua (Sect. 3), Song Feng and Wu Jieqi (Sect. 4), Huang Ying (Sect. 5), Qin Ping and Miao Wenjie (Sect. 6), and Zhang Xiaobing (Sect. 7).

Chapter 3, written by Wu Shimei, describes the "bottom-up" calculation method of the residential energy consumption based on energy consumption of appliances.

Chapter 4 is comparative analysis of data about Chinese residential energy consumption from various perspectives. It is written by Hu Jingqiu, Wu Shimei, and Bi De.

Chapter 5 studies the Chinese residential energy consumption in the international context. Contributors of this chapter are Zhao Yutong and Wang Dan.

Chapter 6, written by Xie Lunyu and Zhang Shuhan, is a quantitative analysis of the residential energy consumption in urban and rural areas.

Chapter 7 studies the household appliance ownership and income inequality. It is written by Hu Naiyuan, Wang Qitong, Zhang Xiaobing, and Qin Ping.

Chapter 8, written by Yu Yihua and Ma Ben, studies the factors that may affect the rural residents' choice of water heaters.

Chapter 9 analyzes the correlation between air pollution and residents' happiness. It is written by Qin Ping, Miao Wenjie, Zhang Yang, and Chen Shuai.

Chapter 10 is a systematic description of the status quo of residential demand-side management in China and the chances and challenges in this regard. It is written by Song Feng and Wu Jieqi.

Wei Chu and Hu Jingqiu oversaw the compilation of this book. Despite our efforts, if there is any deficiency in this book, please do not hesitate to let us know.

February 2017

The Editorial Team of the Report
Zheng Xinye, Wei Chu, Yu Yihua
Qin Ping, Xie Lunyu, Song Feng
Zhang Xiaobing, Wu Shimei, Hu Jingqiu
Wang Dan, Zhao Yutong, Chen Zhanming
Xia Xiaohua, Huang Ying

# Introduction

To further study the characteristics and the inherent law of residential energy consumption in rural and urban areas in China, the Department of Energy Economics of Renmin University of China started the "Chinese Residential Energy Consumption Survey" in early 2013. The third survey, started in the summer of 2015, covered 3,863 households in 28 provinces and aimed to provide reference for the subsequent data collection and scientific research. This book is a summary of the research, which is mainly based on the data from the third CRECS while also considering the data from the first two rounds of surveys.

# Contents

# Chapter 1
# Research Background and Main Conclusions

**Shimei Wu, Dan Wang, Jingqiu Hu and Chu Wei**

## 1 Research Background

While the world is going through tremendous changes brought about by informatization, China is also undergoing rapid development driven by urbanization and industrialization, as if it is taking a high-speed train. In the past over 30 years, China has achieved development in economy, society and ecological environment which took advanced economies centuries to achieve. In such a compressed period, the living environment, living conditions and consumption patterns of Chinese residents have also undergone unprecedented changes.

To track the trends in change of Chinese residential consumption patterns, understand the intrinsic dynamic mechanism and study the behavior patterns of Chinese residents, the Department of Energy Economics of School of Economics, Renmin University of China (RUC) started the "Chinese Residential Energy Consumption Survey" (CRECS) in early 2013, with focus on residential energy consumption. So far, we have finished three rounds of household surveys in the form of questionnaires. Through systematic and comprehensive collection of data about residential energy consumption, we hope to identify and extract scientific issues of major theoretical value, provide open and basic data for scientific research at home and abroad, and provide advice on how to solve important practical problems and improve people's life.

The motivation for our research on Chinese residential energy consumption, or our aim and focus in the research, is to explore the following three basic issues: 1. What kind of change has taken place to Chinese residential energy consumption pattern and what is the underlying driving mechanism? 2. What characteristics, commonalities and heterogeneities are presented in the current residential energy consumption pattern in China? 3. What will be the trend in future development of

S. Wu · D. Wang · J. Hu · C. Wei (✉)
Renmin University of China, Beijing, China
e-mail: xiaochu@ruc.edu.cn



X. Zheng and C. Wei (eds.), *Household Energy Consumption in China: 2016 Report*, https://doi.org/10.1007/978-981-13-7523-1_1

Chinese residential energy consumption pattern? The previous two reports, i.e., *Chinese Household Energy Consumption Report 2014* and *Chinese Household Energy Consumption Report 2015*, mainly focused on analysis of the historical background and status quo in China. In this book, we attempt to expand the scope of research to the whole world and study the future development of residential energy consumption from a global perspective. We hope to identify general commonalities and different characteristics by comparison and to envisage the future through observation and review of historical experience. In this regard, we have noted the following points.

## *1.1 Demand for Power and Energy that is "Stronger, Faster and Brighter"*

Figure 1 presents the historical development of power generation from energy by mankind during the past over 3,000 years. It is apparent that in a fairly long period, mankind could only rely on working animals as a source of power. Around 200–300 B.C., Europeans began to use water energy for irrigation and as a source of power.[1] However, in the following 1,000-plus years, the power of prime mover did not show any obvious improvement. The invention of steam engine in the 18th century brought about a more efficient and stronger form of power for human, which resulted in extensive use of coal and the power necessary for the industrial revolution. It also enabled qualitative improvement in human's ability to generate power from energy and facilitated new heights one after another.

With significant improvement in power of prime movers, the transportation also went through rapid changes during the past over 300 years. As shown in Fig. 2, from walking at a speed of several kilometers per hour without any vehicle to automobiles and ships powered by steam engines with a speed of dozens of kilometers per hour, from trains with a speed of over 100 km per hour to airplanes with a speed of nearly 1,000 km per hour, the maximum speed of vehicles has been setting new record high one after another, significantly shortening the time required to travel from one place to another.

Since humans learnt to make fire by drilling wood, our pursuit for brightness has never ceased. The development of lighting devices and fuels goes along with the development of human beings. As shown in Fig. 3, during the period from 1700 to 2000, people used lamps powered by five kinds of fuels in the United Kingdom. But the average lighting efficiency of candles and oil lamps remained less than 100 lumens in the period. While the use of kerosene and gas lamps marks a significant progress in the history of lighting, these lamps burnt certain material to give light.

[1]The earliest record of water wheel is probably found in the Mediterranean region or Greece. In China, water wheel has been used for grain production since the Han dynasty. See Oleson, J. P. (1984). *Greek and Roman mechanical water-lifting devices: the history of a technology.* Toronto: University of Toronto Press.

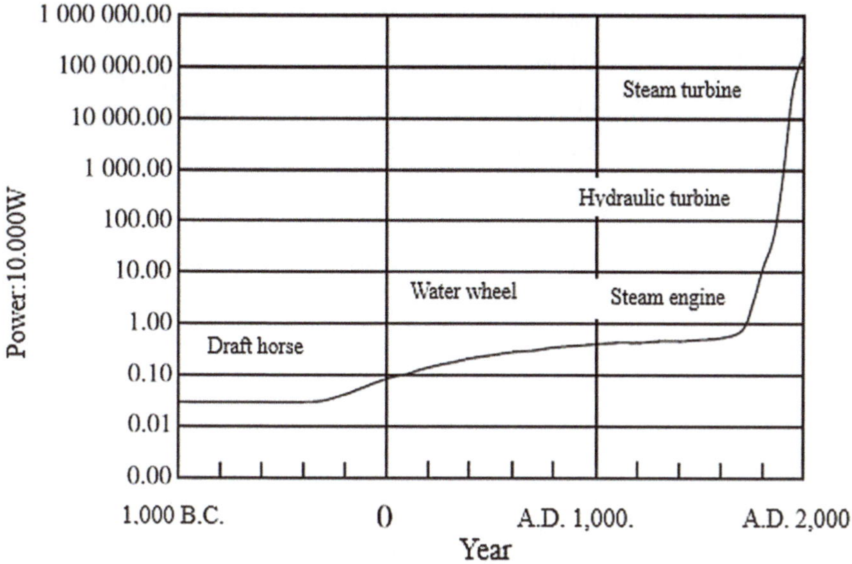


**Fig. 1** Maximum power of prime movers used by human (1,000 B.C.–2,000). *Source* Smil, V. (2004). World history and energy. In *Encyclopedia of Energy.* 6, 549–561

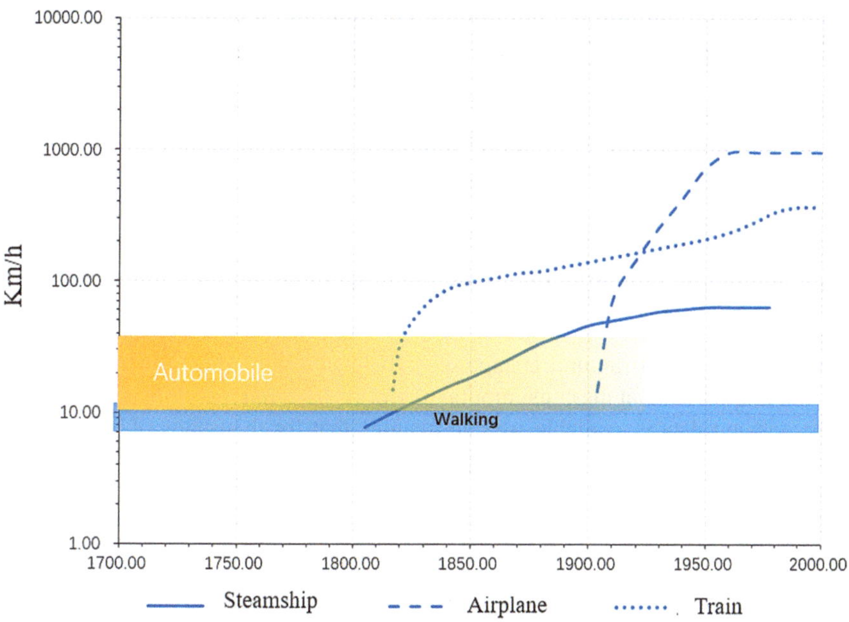


**Fig. 2** Maximum speed of vehicles used by mankind from 1700 to 2000. *Source* Smil, V. (2004). World history and energy. In *Encyclopedia of Energy.* 6, 549–561

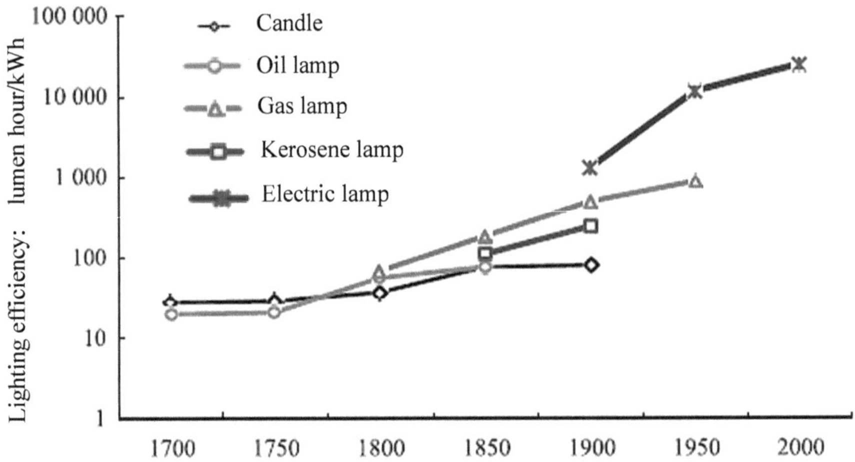


**Fig. 3** Average lighting efficiency of lamps powered by different fuels in the United Kingdom from 1700 to 2000. *Source* Fouquet, R. & Pearson, P. J. G. (2006). Seven centuries of energy services: the price and use of light in the United Kingdom (1300–2000). *The Energy Journal, 27*(1), 139–177

It wasn't until Thomas Edison's invention of the electric light bulb in 1879 that mankind was able to enjoy a "brighter" world with electric lighting.

Lumen refers to the luminous flux of light produced by one cd (Candela, abbreviated as cd, is a unit of luminous intensity. The light emitted by a common candle is roughly 1 cd luminous intensity) over a solid angle (angle represented by the sphere cone corresponding to 1 $m^2$ of spherical cap on a unit sphere with a radius of 1 m. The central angle of its corresponding middle section is approximately 65°).

## 1.2 *On the Eve of the Third Energy Transition*

Figure 4 shows the structural change of global energy consumption from 1800 to 2008. It is apparent that the consumption of biofuel has been declining in this period-if the relevant data is available-we can imagine that for thousands of years before 1800, humans only used natural energy, especially wood.

As the futurist Jeremy Rifkin put it, "the great economic revolutions in history occur when new energy regimes emerge". Each major energy transition leads to revolution in productivity, way of life and production. In the early eighteenth century, steam engines were developed and used in the United Kingdom to help coal mines deal with underground water. In the second half of the eighteenth century, steam engines powered by coal replaced most of the other sources of power and served as a vigorous support in the first Industrial Revolution. The first energy transition in the history of mankind appeared in the second half of the nineteenth century. Coal accounted for only 13% in the global primary energy consumption in 1860,

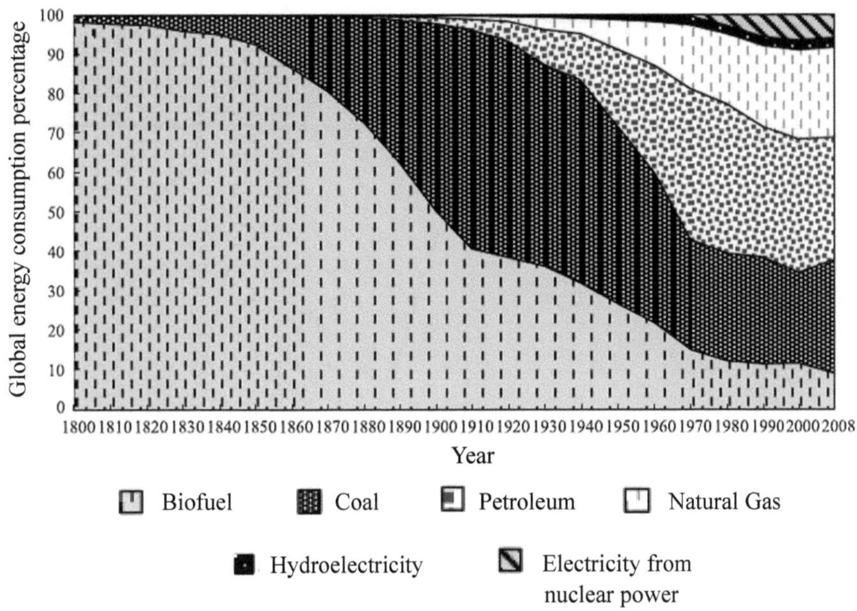


**Fig. 4** Historical trends in world energy consumption from 1800 to 2008. *Source* Smil, V. (2010). *Energy transitions: history, requirements, prospects*. New York: Praeger Publishers

but the figure rose to 55% in 1910 when coal replaced biofuel to be the leading energy. Since the 1870s, the invention and use of petroleum-powered internal combustion engines and electricity led to another revolution in production technologies and directly started the automobile era and the electric era while facilitating the upgrading of other industrial sections. Thanks to the second Industrial Revolution, coal was no longer the leading energy and petroleum became the main energy across the world. Petroleum consumption accounted for 38% of the global primary energy consumption in 1970, while coal consumption provided only 28%. The replacement of coal by petroleum as the main energy marks the completion of the second energy transition.

The process of energy transition in major developed countries is highly consistent. As shown in Figs. 5 and 6, before the Industrial Revolution, humans mainly used natural energy such as wood, water, wind and other biomass as well as humans and livestock living on food. In the United Kingdom, coal was used extensively as substitute of other energy sources in the seventeenth century. In the United States, the extensive use of coal started in mid-nineteenth century. By the twentieth century, the shares of coal consumption in the United Kingdom and the United States reached a historical high, marking the conclusion of the first energy transition from wood to coal. Afterwards, petroleum and natural gas accounted for increasingly higher proportions in energy consumption and replaced coal as the main energy. Petroleum

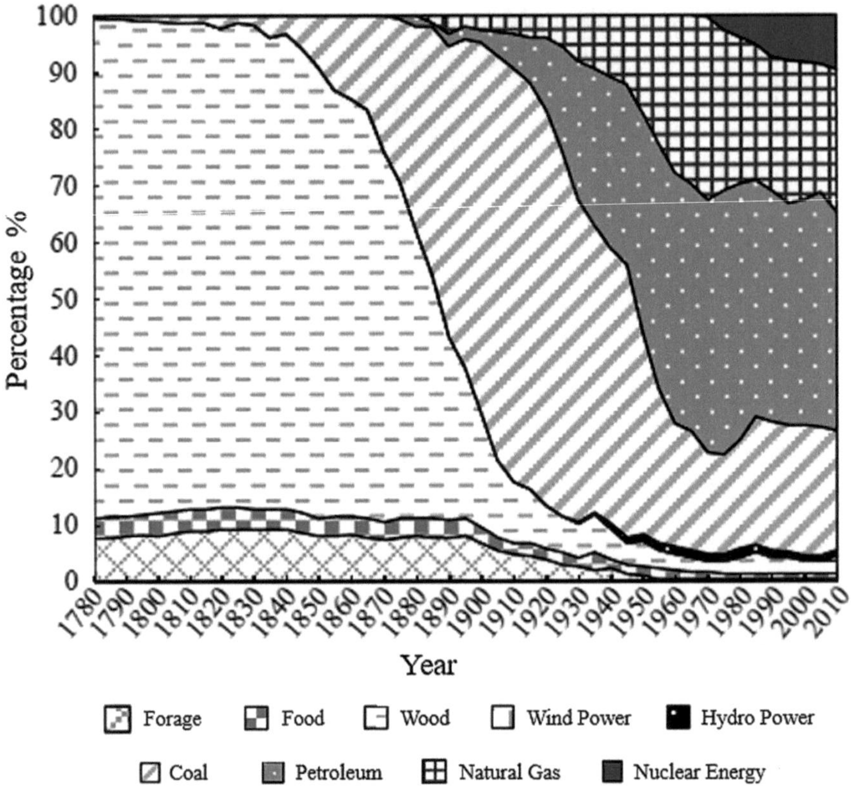


**Fig. 5** Energy consumption structure in the U.S. from 1780 to 2010. *Source* O'Connor, P.A., & Cleveland, C.J. (2014). U.S. energy transitions 1780–2010. In *Energies*, 7, 7955–7993

consumption hit a new all-time high in the 1970s, marking the completion of the second energy transition.

Each energy transition also brings revolution in people's way of living. Take the fuel for home heating in the United States as shown in Fig. 7 as an instance. During the period from 1940 to 2008, the percentages of wood and coal as heating fuels in average American households continued to drop. Fuel oil was popular for some time, but its percentage quickly declined around 1960. The percentage of LPG (liquefied petroleum gas), with minor changes, was small in household use. It is noteworthy that natural gas was extensively used and over 50% of American households used natural gas as the main fuel for home heating after 1970. Meanwhile, with more and more households turning to electric heating, over 30% of American households used electricity as the main energy for home heating by the end of 2007.

The world is now on the eve of a new energy transition. The third energy revolution, replacement of petroleum, is around the corner. Energy consumption is diversified, so, it remains unknown what will be the next leading energy across the world. Natural

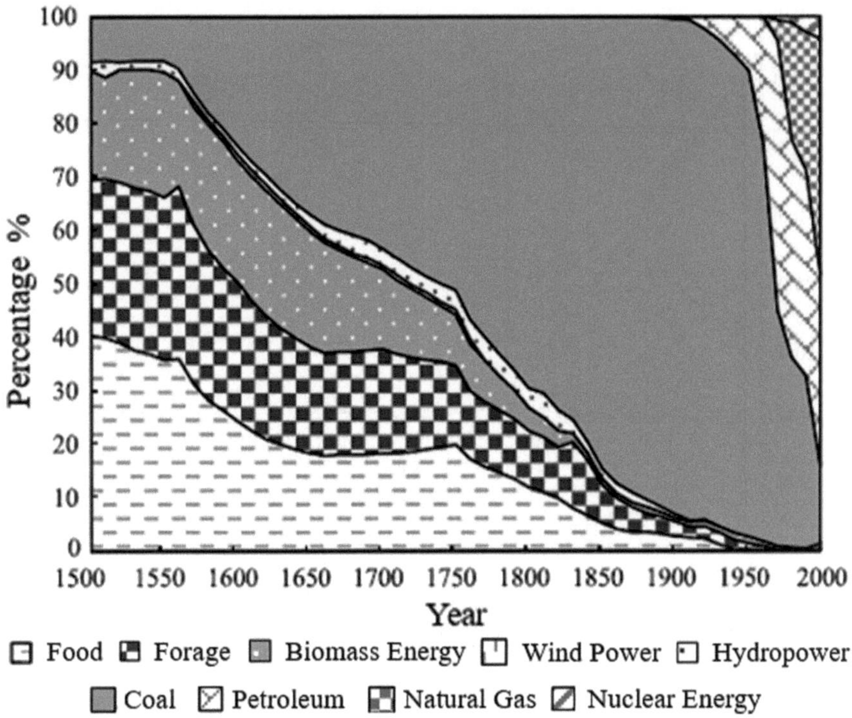


**Fig. 6** Energy consumption structure in UK from 1500 to 2000. *Source* Fouquet, R. (2010). The slow search for solutions: lessons from historical energy transitions by sector and service. In *Energy Policy.* 38, 6586–6596

gas may play a more important role, renewable energy and nuclear energy are likely to become the dominant primary energy while electricity will be the basic platform of energy.[2] Despite uncertainties in existing new energy technologies and development paths, it is possible that the main objective of the approaching third energy transition is to replace fossil energy and to combine with new communication networks and intelligent information technologies.

## *1.3 Energy Becomes an Important Indicator of Welfare*

Undoubtedly, energy has become a major driving force for progress of human society. Indicators such as amount, intensity and structure of energy consumption, etc. are extensively used for measurement of social welfare.

[2]See World Energy Outlook 2016 issued by the International Energy Agency.

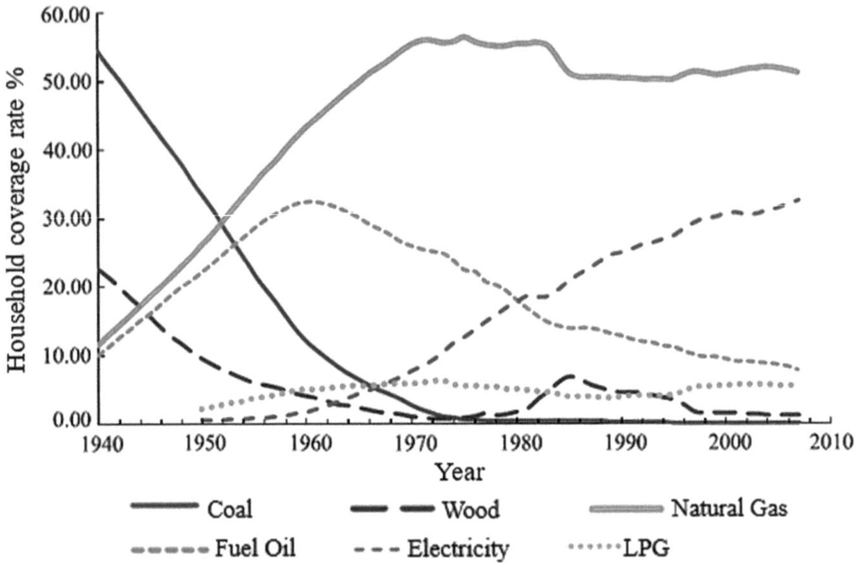


**Fig. 7** Historical transition of fuel for home heating in the U.S. from 1940 to 2008. *Source* O'Connor, P. A. (2010). Energy transition. In *The Pardee Papers, No.12.* Boston University

Energy consumption per capita is often used for monitoring variation in human development and comparison of development in different regions. Figure 8 shows the relation between energy consumption per capita in different countries and the human development index (HDI). HDI is a comprehensive index created by the United Nations Development Programme in 1990 to replace the conventional index of Gross National Product (GNP). It accesses human development of member countries from the perspectives of life expectancy, education and quality of life. We can see from Fig. 8 that a strong positive correlation exists between energy consumption per capita and HDI of these countries. To be specific, for countries with comparatively lower energy consumption per capita, the fitting curve shows steeper slopes. With increase of the per-capita energy consumption, the variation in HDI becomes moderate.

If we divide the diagram into four quadrants based on a standard of energy consumption per capita of 6000 kgoe (kgoe) and HDI of 0.8, we will note that most of the developing countries and countries in transformation including the BRICS countries, i.e., Brazil, India, China, South Africa and Russia, fall into the lower left quadrant, which means that they are in a stage of "low energy consumption and low development index". In contrast, the developed economies in the upper right quadrant, including the United States and Canada in North America, Luxemburg and Iceland in Europe and Qatar and Kuwait in the Middle East, enjoy "high energy consumption and high development index". Trinidad and Tobago falls into the lower right quadrant of "high energy consumption and low development index", indicating that its high level of energy consumption does not lead to high level of development. In contrast,

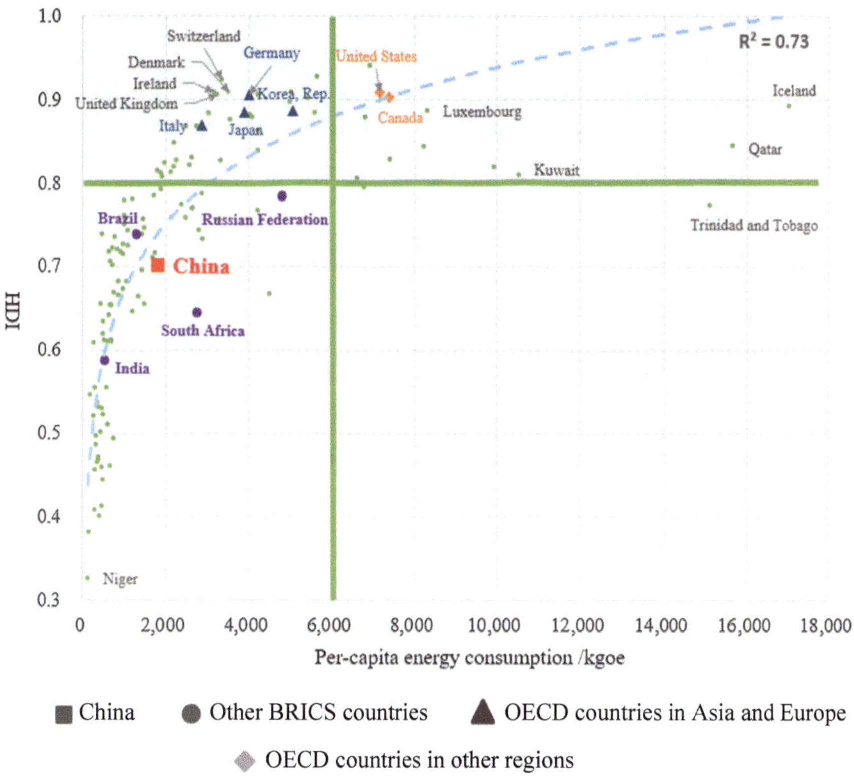


**Fig. 8** Scatter diagram of HDI: energy consumption per capita in 134 countries in 2010. *Source* World Development Indicators, World Bank; Human Development Reports, UNDP

the upper left quadrant with "low energy consumption and high development index" shows characteristics of "low-carbon" development to some extent. In another word, countries in the upper left quadrant have achieved a comparatively higher level of development with lower energy consumption. These countries include major European countries like Germany, the United Kingdom, Sweden, Denmark, Ireland and Italy and some Asian countries like Japan and the Republic of Korea. Decision-makers may prefer the combination of energy consumption and development index as shown in this quadrant.

Energy intensity is also an important indicator that has attracted much attention from researchers and decision-makers. An interesting illustration in this regard is a nighttime light image based on satellite data as shown in Fig. 9. Through quantitative measurement, scientists found that both on global and regional scales, the remote sensing of nighttime lights provides abundant spatial information about human habitat. In addition, such data of nighttime lights has a significant quantitative correlation with socio-economic variables. Therefore, they can be used for measurement and monitoring of urbanization process and regional economic development and to cor-

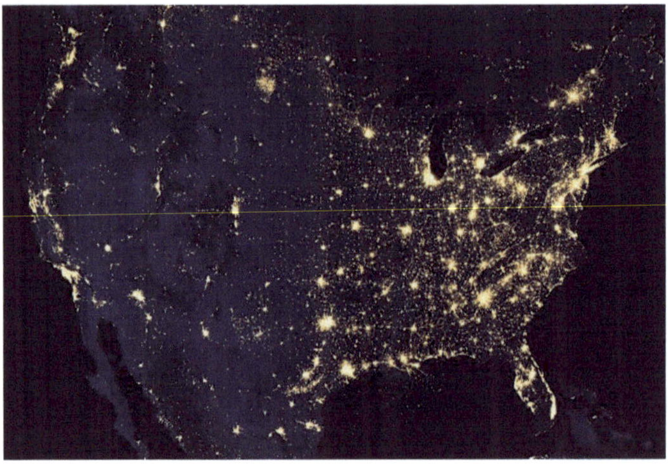

**Fig. 9** The United States of America at night in 2012. *Source* NASA/NOAA. The United States of America at night. https://www.nasa.gov/mission_pages/NPP/news/earthat-night.html, 2012-12-05

rect errors in statistics of economic and social activities. The research in relation to Fig. 10 is based on satellite data, which reveals a significant correlation between the nighttime light intensity in various countries across the world and Gross Domestic Product (GDP), the common indicator of economic development. Consequently, the data from remote sensing satellites can be used for estimation of economic activities in some under-developed regions without necessary statistics and rectification and prediction of existing GDP statistics. Meanwhile, the nighttime light intensity data is also used in researches of some other fields, including estimation of population spatial distribution, changes in utilization of land, measurement of unbalanced development, identification of the impoverished, etc.[3]

Moreover, the energy consumption structure is often used for assessment of development process and difference in development of different regions. Figure 11 shows the correlation between the percentage of population with access to electricity and the development index of the relevant countries in 2010. As shown in Fig. 11, for developing countries suffering from electricity shortage, access to and use of electricity is vital to people's living standard. The rising electrification level shows a significant positive correlation with the improvement in development level. However, when the percentage of population with access to electricity approaches 100%, the difference in development of countries is no longer dependent upon the change in electrification level. China is at a higher level in developing countries in terms of electrification. The percentage of Chinese population with access to electricity reached 94.2% in 1990 and increased to 99.7% in 2010, which is much higher than

[3]For application of such data, see *Overview of researches based on DMSP/OLS nighttime light data*. Wang, H. R., Zheng, X. Q. & Yuan, T. (2012). Overview of researches based on DMSP/OLS nighttime light data. *Progress in Geography*, *31*(1), 11–18.

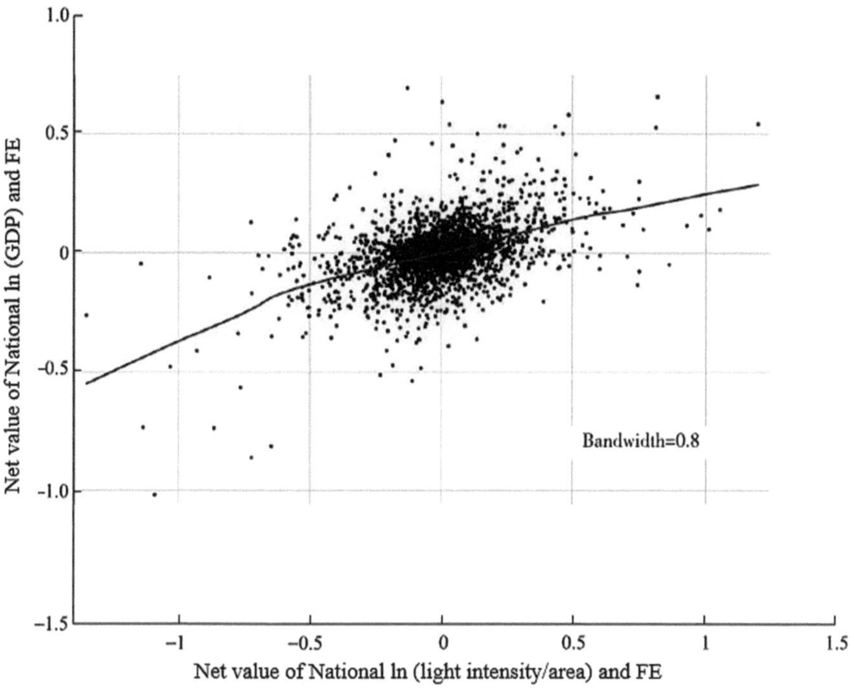


**Fig. 10** Fitting diagram of GDP and light in countries. *Source* Henderson, J.V., Storeygard, A., & Weil, D.N. (2012). Measuring economic growth from outer space. *American Economic Review, 102*(2), 994–1028

the figure in India (75%) and South Africa (82.7%) and a bit higher than the figure in Brazil (98.9%). Though, the figure in China is still lower than that of Russia and developed economies which have achieved 100% electricity coverage.

In addition to use of new clean energy (e.g., electricity), the use of solid fuel (e.g., briquette, firewood and straw) also reflects the structure of fuel and development level. Figure 12 shows the correlation between the percentage of population with access to non-solid fuel and the HDI. Similarly, we note that countries with a larger solid-fuel-consuming population usually have lower development indexes. Take the African country Niger in the lower left as an example. 3% of its population had access to non-solid fuels including petrol, natural gas or electricity and the remaining 97% had to rely on solid fuels of lower thermal efficiency. That means, the family members of these households, usually women and children, spend more time collecting, transporting and storing solid fuels. On one hand, this cuts down the time these members should have spent on study or working, thus leading to low income and poverty. On the other hand, these family members are usually responsible for cooking and other household chores consuming solid fuels, resulting in in-door air

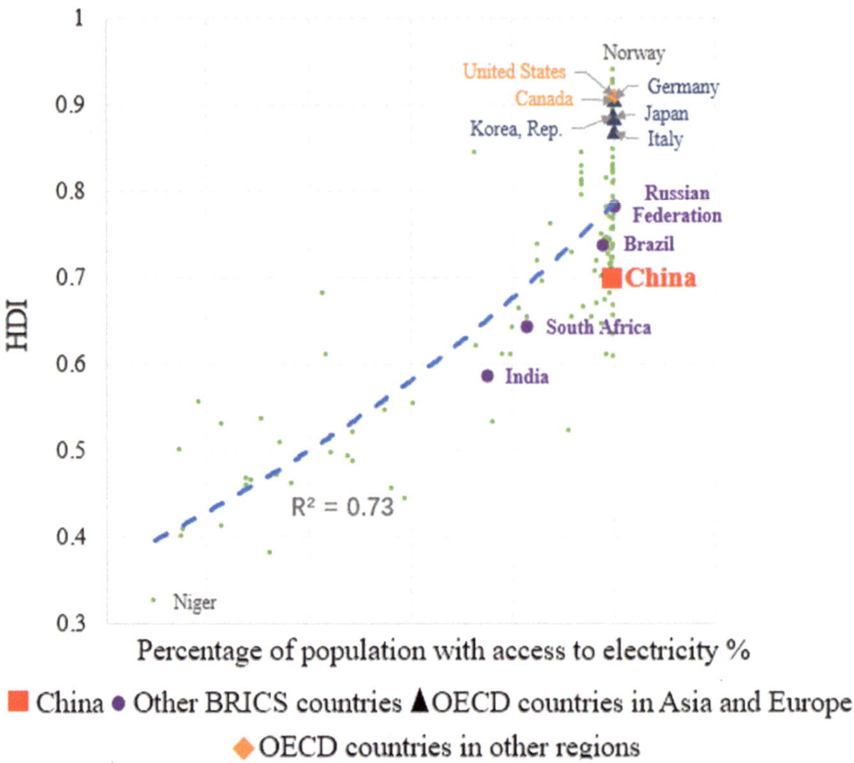


**Fig. 11** Scatter diagram of percentage of population with access to electricity and HDI in 134 countries in 2010. *Source* World Bank. World Development Indicators. Global Consumption Database

pollution that may harm their health and increase medical expenditure.[4] As a result, the HDI of Niger is only 0.33, ranking the last in all countries.

As revealed in Fig. 12, the extensive use of non-solid fuel is closely and positively correlated with the development level. However, like the case in Fig. 11, when the percentage of population with access to non-solid fuels approaches 100%, the difference in HDI of countries is no longer influenced by the fuel structure. China has made remarkable progress in its energy infrastructure. In 1990, only 35.8% of the Chinese population had access to non-solid fuels, but this figure rose to 46.5% in 2000 and 54.3% in 2010. Though the percentage in China is higher than that of another big developing country, India (42.4%), there remain wide discrepancies with developed countries or even other developing countries. For example, the percentage of population with access to non-solid fuels in South Africa rose from 61% in 1990

[4]For multiple effects of solid fuels on the impoverished population, please refer to the report of World Health Organization (WHO), Fuel for life: household energy and health, 2006.

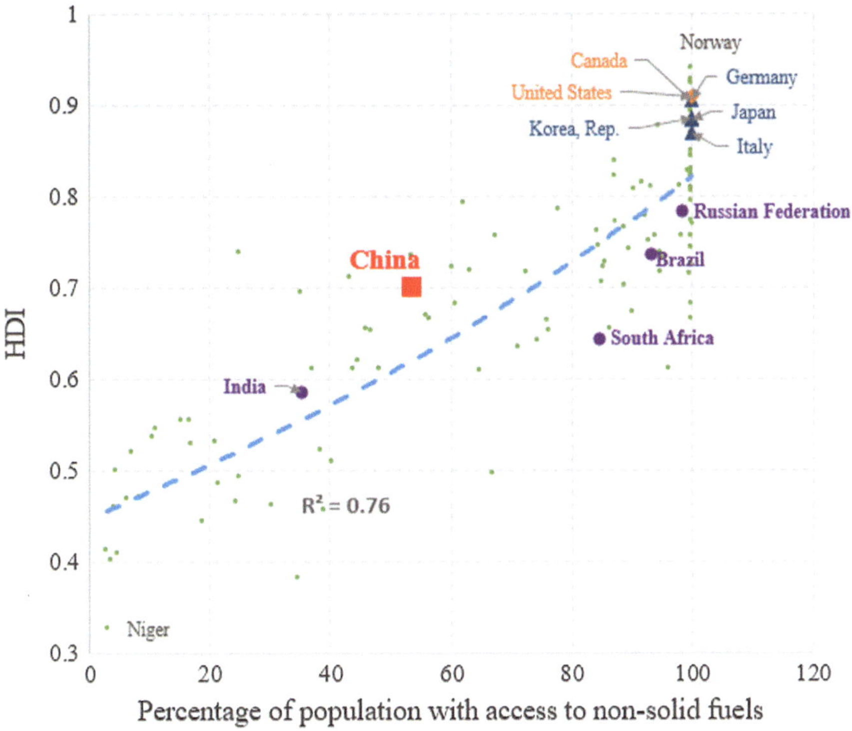


**Fig. 12** Scatter diagram of percentage of population consuming non-solid fuels and HDI in 134 countries in 2010. *Source* World Bank. World Development Indicators. Global Consumption Database

to 85% in 2010 and the figure in Brazil and Russia reached about 95% in 2010, which played an important role in improving people's living standard.[5]

## *1.4 Economic Growth is the Main Driving Force of Energy Consumption*

Throughout the world, we found that economic growth is the main driving force of energy consumption. As shown in Fig. 13, there is a significant positive correlation between GDP per capita measured by purchasing power parity (PPP) and energy consumption per capita in various countries in 2010. It demonstrates that residents'

[5]According to the latest estimation of WHO, in 2013, there was still 45% of Chinese population using solid fuels. 14% of its urban population use solid fuels and 79% of its rural population use solid fuels. See WHO: Global health observatory data repository, public health and environment-household air pollution-exposure.

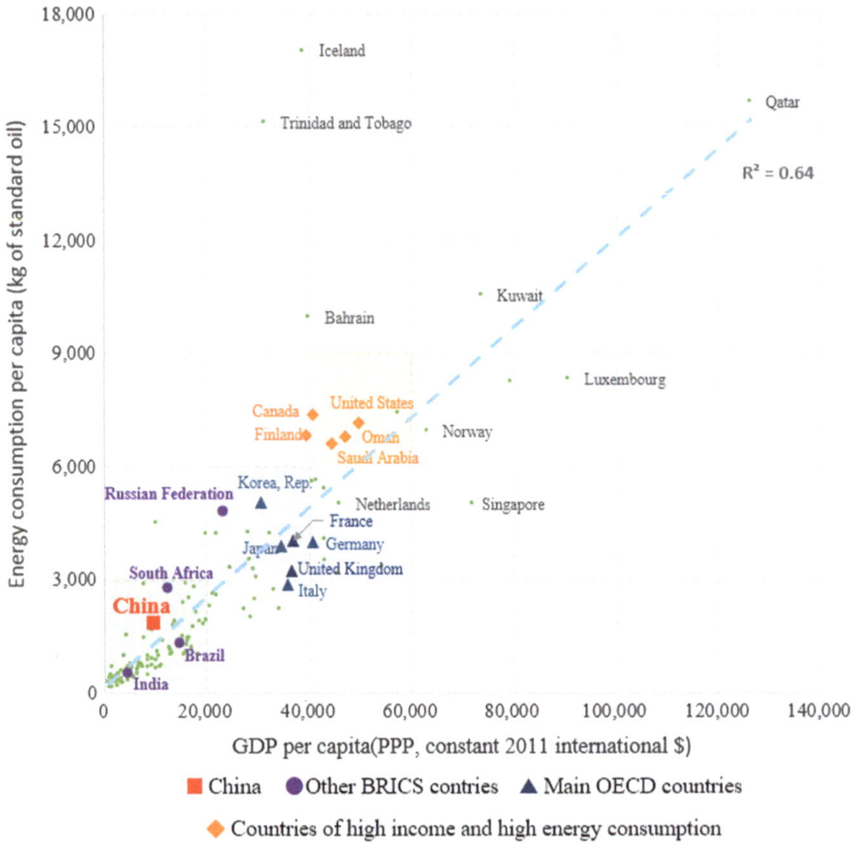


**Fig. 13** Scatter diagram of GDP per capita and energy consumption per capita in 2010 in 134 countries GDP per capita (PPP, international dollar in 2011). *Source* World Bank. World Development Indicators

demand for energy rises with the increase in GDP per capita. We may divide the countries into three main clusters based on their distribution in the diagram. As shown in Fig. 13, the cluster with "low income and low energy consumption" includes 86 countries with GDP per capita no more than USD20,000 and energy consumption per capita no more than 3,000 kgoe. Four of the BRICS countries, Brazil, China, India and South Africa, fall into this cluster. Another BRICS country, Russia, falls into the second cluster along with other OECD economies including Republic of Korea, Japan, France, Germany, the United Kingdom and Italy, etc.[6] The GDP per capita of these countries is between USD20,000–40,000 and the energy consump-

[6]Countries falling into this cluster have high income and low energy consumption. As shown in Fig. 13, the energy consumption per capita is less than 3,000 kg of oil equivalent in Italy and less than 4,000 kg of oil equivalent in Germany, while both countries enjoy higher income per capita. So, Italy and Germany both fall into this cluster.

tion per capita is between 3,000 and 6,000 kgoe. The third cluster represents even higher income (GDP per capita between USD40,000 and 60,000) and even higher energy consumption (energy consumption per capita between 6,000–9,000 kgoe). This cluster includes a total of five countries, namely, the United States and Canada in North America, Finland in Europe[7] and Saudi Arabia and Oman in the Middle East.

Meanwhile, all the countries are divided into two types according to the fitting curve in Fig. 13. For countries above the curve, it is considered that their energy consumption per capita has exceeded the average energy demand corresponding to their own income. According to the globally-fitted income-energy correlation, the energy consumption of countries below the curve is lower than the average level. The proximity of a country to the fitting curve shows that the income-energy relationship of that country is consistent with the general global features. As revealed in Fig. 13, when the income level is low, most countries are close to the fitting curve, but when the income exceeds a certain figure, say, USD40,000, the energy consumption pattern of various countries show great discrepancies. Iceland and Canada have similar income levels, but due to different locations and other factors, the energy consumption per capita of the former is 2.3 times that of the latter. Luxembourg and Singapore are outliers of another type. Take Singapore as an example. Its energy consumption per capita is close to that of the Republic of Korea, but its income is 2.4 times that of the latter. Such differences can be attributed to differences among countries in other aspects.[8]

Figure 13 depicts the correlation between level of economic development and energy consumption at the macro level. For further study of residential energy consumption, more detailed statistics are required. So far, there has not been any comprehensive comparison of residential energy consumption in different countries. Some researchers have compared the statistics in some countries, and in Chap. 5 of this book, we will compare the microdata of countries in the same period. Figure 14 depicts the correlation between the GDP per capita and the energy consumption per capita in 88 developing countries in 2010 from the perspective of residential consumption expenditure. The energy expenditure of residents mainly refers to consumption of three kinds of commercial energy, including electricity, gas and other fuels (e.g., coal). It is noted that there is a positive correlation between the level of economic development and residential expenditure on commercial energy in these countries. If we use the points on the fitting curve to represent the average level of these developing countries, we can see that India, China and South Africa are close to the fitting curve, which means that they, like other developing countries, have a high degree of consistency in "economic development-residential energy expenditure pattern". Brazil and Russia are above the fitting curve, which means that their

[7]Finland has a high GDP per capita of nearly USD40,000 and high energy consumption. So, theoretically, it falls into the cluster of countries with high income and high energy consumption.

[8]For research on differences in energy consumption, further information can be obtained from: Sun, J.W. (1998) Changes in energy consumption and energy intensity: a complete decomposition model. In: *Energy Economics 1998, 20*(1): 85–100; Ang, B.W., Zhang, F.Q. (2000) A survey of index decomposition analysis in energy and environmental studies. In: *Energy 25*(12): 1149–1176.

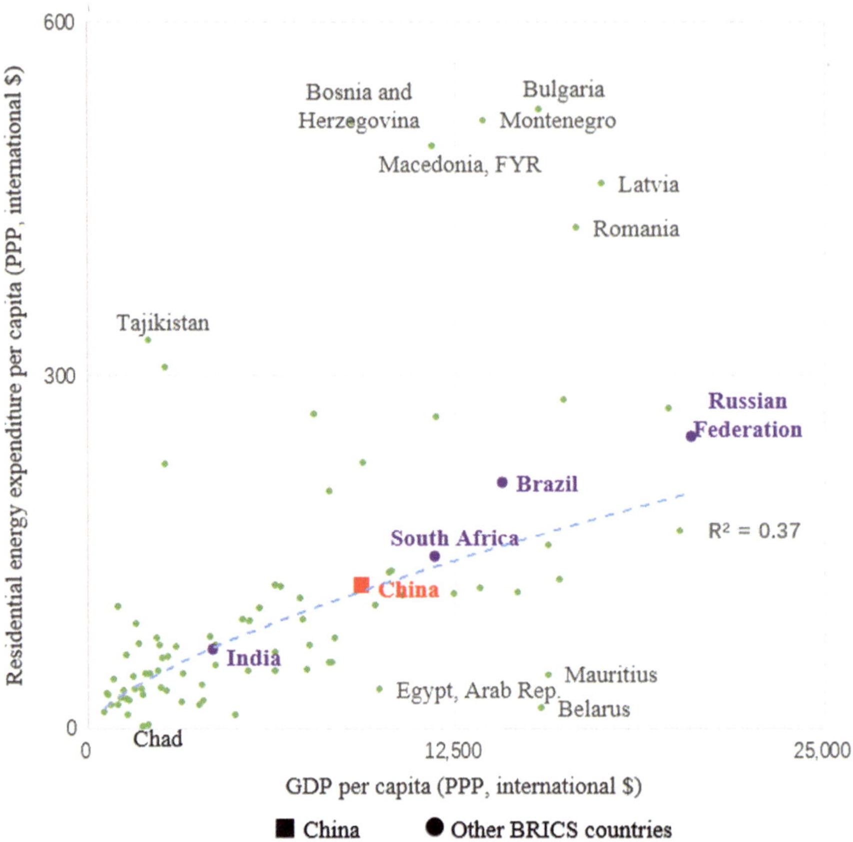


**Fig. 14** Scatter diagram of GDP per capita and residential energy expenditure per capita in 88 developing countries in 2010 (GDP per capita and residential energy expenditure per capita measured by PPP). *Source* World Bank. World Development Indicators. Global Consumption Database

energy consumption per capita is higher than the average level corresponding to their income level. Some developing countries show strong heterogeneity, such as countries in the Balkan Peninsula including Bulgaria, Bosnia and Herzegovina, Montenegro, Macedonia, Latvia and Romania, etc., having great difference from other developing countries. On average, with the same income per capita, the residential energy consumption per capita in these Balkan countries is significantly higher than that of other regions. For example, the GDP per capita in Bosnia and Herzegovina is close to that of China, but its residential expenditure on commercial energy is 4.3 times that of Chinese residents. In addition, we note some countries below the fitting curve, including Belarus, Mauritius and Egypt, etc., which means that the energy expenditure per capita in these countries is significantly lower than the average level corresponding to their income level.

## 1.5 Different Effects of Urbanization

Urbanization is obviously another main factor leading to differences in energy consumption in different countries. Due to multiple differences between the rural and urban areas in construction features, public transportation, energy infrastructure and access to energy service, etc., there are considerable discrepancies in people's way of using energy for production and consumption in these areas.[9] Figure 15 is a scatter diagram depicting the percentages of urban population and energy consumption per capita for 166 countries respectively in 1990 and 2012. We can note from the diagram that the fitting curves at two different time points are very close and go upward, which means that countries with higher urbanization ratios tend to have higher level of energy consumption per capita. The urbanization ratio and energy consumption per capita in China in 1990 were close to the figures of India in the same period, but in 2012, China achieved a rapid increase in urbanization ratio and energy consumption, with the highest growth rate in the BRICS countries. In 2012, the energy consumption per capita and urbanization ratio in China were both close to the figures of South Africa in 1990. In contrast, India, with nearly the same starting point as China, was slow in progress and its urbanization ratio only increased from 25% in 1990 to 32% in 2012, a bit higher than the urbanization ratio in China (26%) in 1990. The energy consumption per capita in India in 2012 (623 kgoe) was less than that of China in 1990 (767 kgoe). During this period, due to institutional reasons, Russia made no progress and even retrogressed in terms of urbanization and energy consumption. Compared with its performance in 1990, the urbanization ratio in Russia in 2012 was slightly higher, but the energy consumption per capita dropped. The performance of South Africa and Brazil in urbanization and energy consumption were similar, both having significant increase in urbanization ratio and minor growth in energy consumption per capita. However, among the BRICS countries, only Brazil remained below the fitting curve, which means that its energy consumption per capita was lower than the average level of energy consumption fitted according to the same urbanization ratio as in Brazil.

Figure 15 reveals the general correlation between urbanization and energy consumption in various countries. However, comparing the statistics of the five BRICS countries, we have already noted significant differences. We will conduct a detailed study and make comparison of the five BRICS countries based on the macro-level urbanization indicator characterized by percentage of urban population. Figure 16 shows the percentages of energy consumption expenditure to overall consumption expenditure in rural and urban areas of the BRICS countries in 2010. The countries are divided into groups according to their level of income for comparison. First, we study the urban residents in Fig. 16a and note that the five countries share similar "income-energy consumption" features. To be specific, the urban residents of

[9]For more information about the effect of urbanization on demand for energy, please refer to: Glaeser, E. (2011) Cities, productivity, and quality of life. In: *Science 333*(6042): 592–594; Wei, C. (2017) Will urbanization increase residential energy demand-a literature review. In: *Economic Theory and Business Management V36*(1): 95–109.

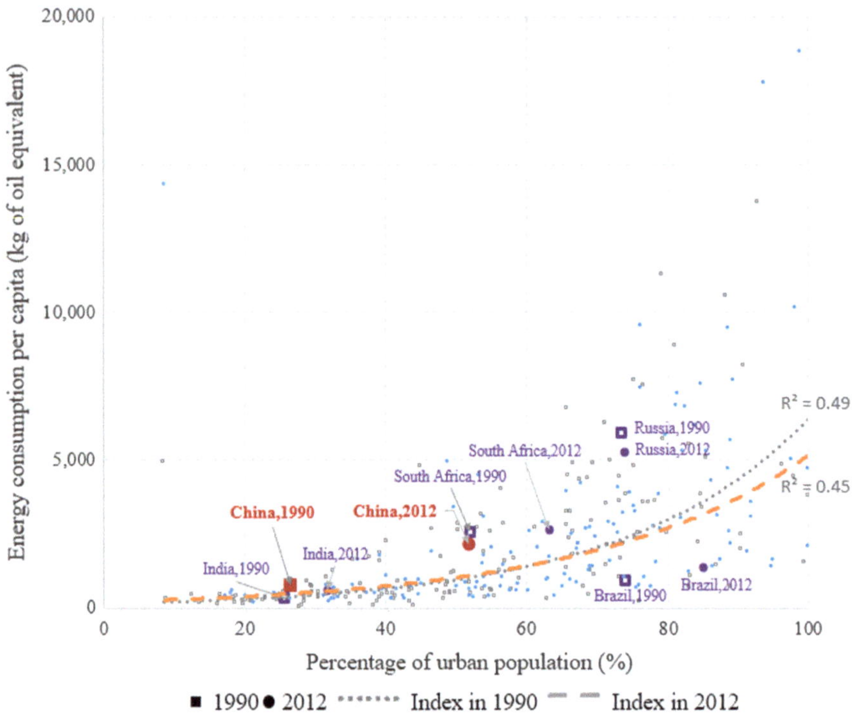


**Fig. 15** Scatter diagram of urban population percentage and energy consumption per capita in 166 countries respectively in 1990 and 2012. *Source* World Bank. World Development Indicators

the group with the lowest income had the highest percentage of energy expenditure among all the groups in the country. In contrast, the urban residents of the group with high income (according to the standards of the World Bank, high-income population refers to 10% of the population with the highest income per capita) had the smallest percentage of energy expenditure. Another feature is that though middle- and high-income groups (both around 3%) of urban residents had similar percentages of energy expenditure, there were great discrepancies among urban residents of the lowest income group. For instance, in Brazil, the urban residents of the lowest-income group spent 13.4% of their total consumption expenditure on energy, while the percentage of energy consumption in total consumption expenditure was only 2.5% for the high-income group. Excessive energy expenditure will hinder people's consumption of commercial energy and relevant durable goods, encroach on their expenditure on the consumption of other goods and service and reduce the consumption welfare. It may also cause people to use traditional energy instead of commercial energy. Unlike the situation in Brazil, the percentage of energy expenditure for urban residents does not show dramatic difference in Russia. Urban residents of different income groups in China, India and South Africa had similar percentages of energy expenditure.

The World Bank uses four levels of consumption to segment the residential consumption data in countries based on global distribution of the income per capita. The lowest consumption segment corresponds to the 50th percentile and below; the low consumption segment to the 51th–75th percentiles; the middle consumption segment to the 76th–90th percentiles; and the higher consumption segment to the 91st

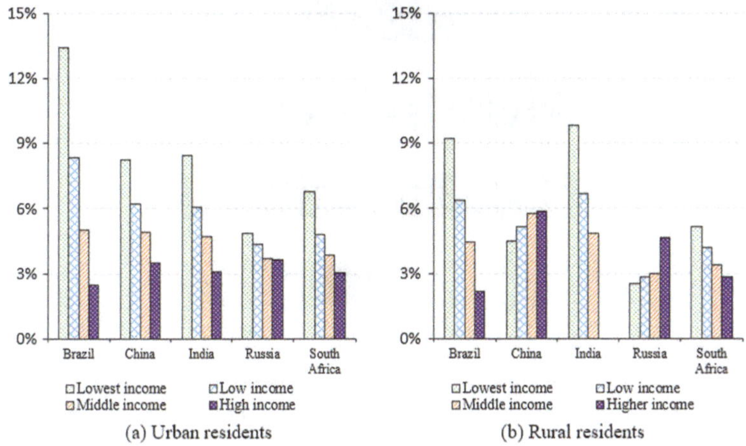


percentile and above.

**Fig. 16** Percentage of expenditure on energy consumption in overall consumption expenditure in groups of residents with different income levels in rural and urban areas in BRICS countries in 2010. *Source* World Bank. Global Consumption Database

Figure 16b shows the different expenditure on energy consumption for rural residents of different income levels. The rural residents in Brazil, India and South Africa are similar to their urban counterparts: the higher income, the lower percentage of expenditure on energy consumption. The statistics of China and Russia, however, show a positive correlation between income and energy expenditure: as the income rises, the rural residents in these two countries will spend more on the consumption of commercial energy. It is especially the case in Russia, where the percentage of energy expenditure rose from 3 to 4.7% when rural residents moved from middle-income group to high-income group. Comparatively speaking, the Chinese rural residents do not show much difference in percentage of energy consumption expenditure, being respectively 4.5, 5.2, 5.8 and 5.9% for rural residents of groups of the lowest, low, middle and high income. In addition, by comparison of groups of the same level of income in rural and urban residents as shown in Fig. 16, we note that in general, urban residents spend a higher percentage on energy consumption than their rural counterparts. However, there are two obvious exceptions: one is that the rural residents of the lowest-income group in India spend significantly more on energy consumption (the percentage being 9.8%) than their urban counterparts (the percentage being 8.5%), and the other is that the rural residents of high-income group in china and Russia spend a higher percentage on energy consumption than their urban counterparts.

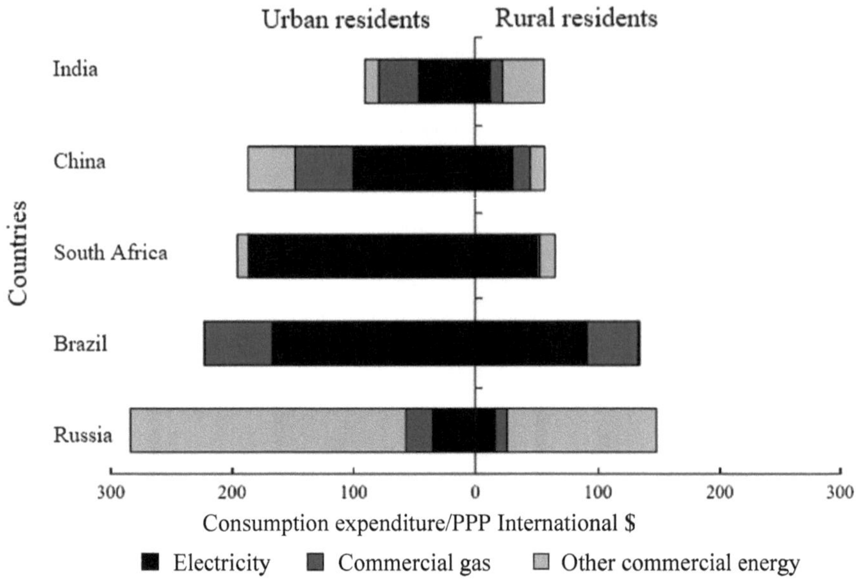


**Fig. 17** Expenditure on different commercial energy of rural and urban residents in BRICS countries in 2010. *Source* World Bank. Global Consumption Database

Figure 17 compares the structure of expenditure on commercial energy in rural and urban areas of BRICS countries. The commercial gases include natural gas, gas conveyed by pipelines, etc. Other commercial energy includes coal, etc. The five BRICS countries are ranked according to the urban residents' total expenditure on energy consumption.

First, let's look at the left part of Fig. 17. We note that the urban residents' expenditure on energy consumption in 2010 was the lowest in India, amounting to international $90 (PPP. The same applies in the following sections). China and South Africa were close with respectively international $187 and international $196. The energy expenditure of urban residents as the highest in Russia, amounting to international $284. In terms of the energy consumption structure, India and China were similar, since their energy expenditure of urban residents was mainly on electricity (accounting for about 50% of the energy expenditure) and commercial gas (accounting for 26–36% of the energy expenditure), with some expenditure on other commercial energy like coal, etc. 3/4 of the urban residents' energy expenditure in Brazil was for electricity and 1/4 was for commercial gas. In South Africa, the urban residents' energy expenditure was mainly for electricity (95%). In Russia, the main expenditure on energy consumption of urban residents was used to purchase other commercial energy like coal, etc. (80%) and the electricity consumption accounted for only 12% of the total energy expenditure.

The ranking in the right part of Fig. 17 is consistent with the left part about urban residents. The rural residents in India spent only international $56 on commercial energy, which is the lowest in the five countries. The second and the third are China (international $57) and South Africa (international $65). The annual energy expenditures of rural residents in Brazil and Russia were similar, respectively being international $134 and international $148. In terms of the energy consumption structure, the energy expenditure of rural residents in India and Russia was mainly on other commercial energy like coal, etc., while expenditure on electricity accounted for a small percentage. In China, the energy consumption structures of rural and urban residents were very similar, with more than half of their energy expenditure on electricity, and the expenditure on commercial gas and other commercial energy respectively accounted for 26 and 21% of the total. The rural residents' expenditure on energy in South Africa was also mainly for electricity, but unlike their urban counterparts, they consumed more coal and other energy. 2/3 of the rural residents' energy expenditure in Brazil was for electricity, and the remaining was mainly for commercial gas.

Comparing the statistics about urban and rural residents in Fig. 17, it can be seen that the energy expenditures in rural and urban areas of India and Brazil are the most similar. The urban residents' expenditure on commercial energy in these two countries were 1.6 and 1.7 times of the expenditure of their rural counterparts respectively. By comparison, the widest discrepancy between urban and rural energy expenditure is in China, with the former being 4.3 times of the latter. This may be considered as an illustration of the wide discrepancy between rural and urban areas due to different policies in China. Of course, further data study and explanation is required to understand the reasons underlying the specific heterogeneity as revealed in Figs. 16 and 17.

## 1.6 The Future Trends of Energy Consumption in China

What will the future energy consumption be like in China? Will it show convergence or grow more and more discrepant? Figure 18 may provide us with some clues based on the development of different countries. We mainly drew the trajectories of GDP per capita-energy consumption per capita from 1960 to 2014 of main developed economies, BRICS countries and some transformational and developing countries. It can be seen that these countries can be divided into two types according to the development level.

Statistics about Brazil, China, India, Republic of Korea, South Africa, Argentina and Mexico are about the period from 1971 to 2013. Russian statistics are about the period from 1990 to 2013. Statistics about other countries are about the period from 1960 to 2014.

The development trend of energy consumption per capita in developed economies is basically an inverted U shape: go upward, and then remain steady and even fall. If we particularly look at the downward trend, we will note three different patterns in the falling energy consumption per capita.

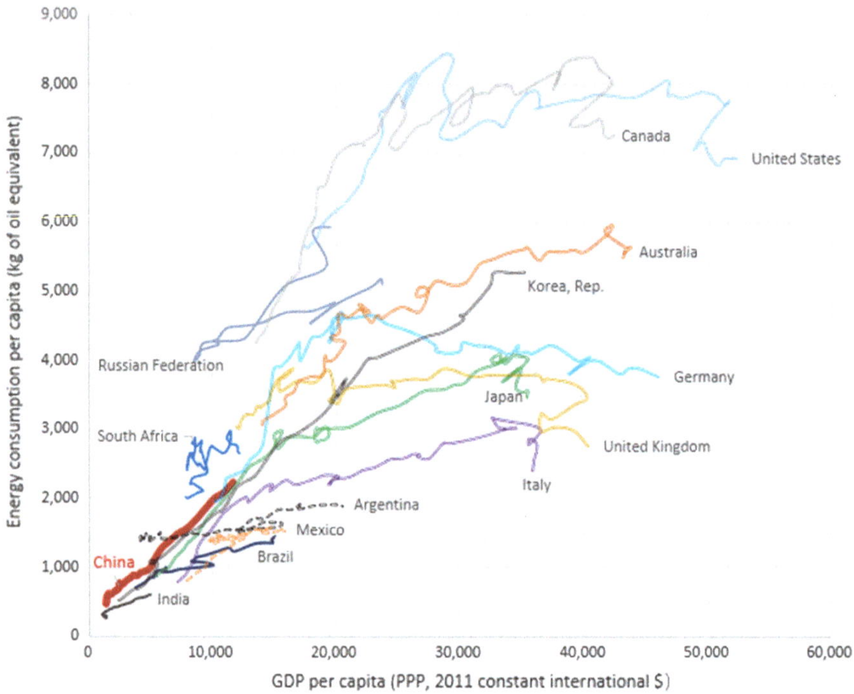


**Fig. 18** Trajectories of GDP per capita-energy consumption per capita from 1960 to 2014 in main countries. *Source* Data about energy consumption per capita is World Bank. Data about GDP and population are from Penn World Table 9.0 and Feenstra, R. C., Inklaar, R. and Timmer, M. P. (2015). The next generation of the penn world table. In: *American Economic Review, 105*(10), 3150–3182

(1) Rapid growth followed by mild fluctuation and downward trend in both economic development and energy consumption. The United States and Canada are typical of this pattern, with energy consumption per capita significantly higher than other countries. Meanwhile, the development trends in these two countries are very similar, especially in mid and late 1990s, when their energy consumption per capita suffered from stagflation and remained at a steady level for a long period. In 2007 and 2008, with the decrease of GDP per capita, their energy consumption per capita also showed apparent decline.
(2) Rapid growth followed by sharp fall in energy consumption per capita due to slowdown in economic growth or sluggish economy. The curves of countries with such characteristics, including Australia, Japan and Italy, resemble an inverted V shape. The difference lies in the time point when the downward trend begins to occur. The energy consumption per capita in Australia did not show apparent decline until 2008, while the figure nearly fell off cliff since 2005 in Italy and began to fall since 2000 in Japan after reaching the peak value.

(3) Countries with inverted U-shaped curves are noteworthy, as they show a trend of economic growth accompanied with continuous decline in energy consumption, of which Germany and the United Kingdom are the most typical. Germany experienced a rapid growth in energy consumption and reached the peak value of its energy consumption per capita before 1988, showing an apparent downward trend since then. By 2014, the energy consumption per capita in Germany was 3,749 kgoe, slightly lower than its consumption level in 1970 (3,861 kgoe), while its GDP per capita increased from international $14,921 in 1970 to international $45,961 in 2014. In the United Kingdom, the energy consumption per capita reached its peak value in 1973 and had been falling slowly since then. In 2014, the energy consumption per capita in the United Kingdom (2,752 kgoe) dropped to the lowest level of this period, lower than the figure in 1960 (3,033 kgoe), while the GDP per capita in the same period showed an overall growth trend.

The situation in the Republic of Korea is similar to that of Germany and the United Kingdom. Its energy consumption per capita reached the peak in 2012 and began to decline since then, though its economy continued to develop. However, based on the existing data, it is not yet possible to decide whether the Republic of Korea has reached a turning point like Germany and the United Kingdom and will continue to achieve decoupled economic growth and energy consumption, or whether it will show a long-term fluctuation in energy consumption per capita like Canada and the U.S.

Most developing countries show a growing trend toward the upper right corner. In another word, with the increase in GDP per capita, the energy consumption per capita also increases. However, it is clear that the current and future changes in developing countries may be the trajectories that the developed countries experienced in the past. The slope of the curves in developing countries shows three types of characteristics:

(1) The energy consumption per capita grows at a slow rate with the improvement of economic growth. Typical countries include Brazil, Mexico, Argentina and India, etc., all having a gentle slope in their curves.
(2) The energy consumption per capita experiences rapid increase with the development of economy. The most typical country is China. The trend of its curve is nearly the same as the curves of Germany, Italy, Japan and the Republic of Korea in the early stage, and the slope of its curve is also similar to those of Australia and the United Kingdom in the early stage. For example, in 2013, the GDP per capita and energy consumption per capita in China were respectively USD11,673 and 2,226 kgoe, close to the figures of Germany in 1963 (USD11,092 and 2,281 kgoe), of Japan in 1969 (USD11,834 and 2,194 kgoe), of Italy in 1970 (USD12,684 and 2,026 kgoe) and of the Republic of Korea in 1990 (USD12,048 and 2,167 kgoe). It seems to indicate that China is now undergoing a process of economic development and energy consumption which is similar to and consistent with the historical trends in the above-mentioned industrial countries.

(3) Countries like South Africa and Russia have experienced more fluctuations in their development. South Africa experienced economic stagnation in the early stage while its energy consumption increased with fluctuations. Afterwards, with minor economic recovery, its energy consumption showed multiple fluctuations. Russia had two curves of development. In early 1990s, its development trend was similar to that of the United States and Canada, with a level close to that of the United States in early 1960s and Canada in early 1970s. However, due to the historical transformation, its development showed an inversion with declining economic growth and energy consumption. It wasn't until 1998 that Russia was able to reverse the downward trend and went back to normal development, but the following development curve had been comparatively gentle.

To predict the future development trend in China, there is no doubt that we should pay more attention to countries that are similar to China in terms of the curves. With a close look at the development trend in China, we note that the curves of Germany, Japan, the Republic of Korea and Italy all closely intersect the curve of China at some time. Due to the limitations of data, we did not draw the curves of the United Kingdom and Australia in the early stage, though their early slopes are also similar to that of China. However, what drew our attention was that the above-mentioned industrialized countries had differentiated their development paths after exceeding a GDP per capita of USD12,000–15,000. Countries represented by Australia and the Republic of Korea continue to develop with the previous slope of GDP per capita-energy consumption per capita while countries as represented by Germany and Canada have steeper slopes of growth. Japan and Italy experienced economic growth along with milder increase in energy consumption, showing moderate slopes on the curves. This may indicate that China is likely to be confronted with three development path choices after further development in the future: The first is to continue with the current pattern of economic development and energy consumption and maintain the growth momentum. The second is to enter a fast lane of super high-speed increase in energy consumption, as Germany and Canada experienced in the early stage of development. The third is to gradually reduce the growth rate of energy consumption while pursuing economic development, as Japan and Italy experienced in the early stage of development, hoping to achieve the turning point where economic growth can be decoupled from energy consumption. Of course, we cannot learn from international experience by simply relying on the observation of a single diagram. Instead, we shall also consider various factors in the development of different countries, such as the international context, resource endowment, development goals, technology levels, policy tools and other factors. Though, undoubtedly, Fig. 18 may serve as a reference and shed light on research of future patterns of energy consumption in China.

## 1.7 Future Family Lifestyle and Energy Consumption Patterns

In 1830, when the industrial revolution in the United Kingdom was about to be completed, the famous British historian Thomas Babington Macaulay made the following prediction about human life in 100 years: in 1930, the British will have more food, garments and better living environment than we have now…High-tech machines made according to theories that had not been discovered until now will enter every household…most people will think we may be crazy.[10] History shows that his prediction is completely correct.

As an academic research report, we aim to conduct scientific analysis based on facts and data. It is not in our comparative advantage or appropriate for us to predict the family models and lifestyle of the next 50 or even 100 years. With continuous technological progress in the fields of biology, medical and space science, etc., people are undoubtedly curious about the future life. But this also increases the uncertainty in the study and prediction of future residential energy consumption. Therefore, we shall cautiously look ahead at the future family lifestyles.

Figures 19 and 20, taking the historical development of the American family as an example, reveal some rules. It is apparent that since the twentieth century, household electrical appliances have been put into extensive use and replaced a large part of manual work. Refrigerators make it possible to freeze foods, significantly reducing the time spent on purchasing, storing and processing foods. Vacuum cleaners improve the house cleaning efficiency and reduce the time spent on cleaning and tidying up. The use of washing machines and clothes dryers significantly reduces the time spent on laundry and drying clothes. The use of home appliances such as electric stoves, microwave ovens and dish washers, etc. reduces the time spent on cooking. Replacement of manual work with such electrical appliances improves the household productivity: while satisfying the same and even more demands of family members, they reduce the time spent on housekeeping. The average hours of American women spent on housekeeping dropped from 58 h each week in 1900 to 14 h each week in 2011. The reduction in time spent on housework made it possible for these people to receive better education or enter the labor market.

According to our observation of the historical trends in Figs. 19 and 20, we believe that in future, most functions of families will be outsourced, more and more smart home appliances will replace repetitive manual housework (e.g., sweeping, laundry) and satisfy personal needs (e.g., heating and air conditioning) while specialized division of labor will be able to satisfy some of the complex, different needs (e.g., medical service, food service). People will have more time available for innovation and reflection. Let's envisage the future family life from the perspectives of clothing, food, housing and transportation, which we may refer to as the "smart family".

---

[10]Thackeray, F. & Findling, J. (2015). *Events that changed Great Britain since 1689* (Shi, L. Trans.) Beijing: New World Press (original work published in 2002).

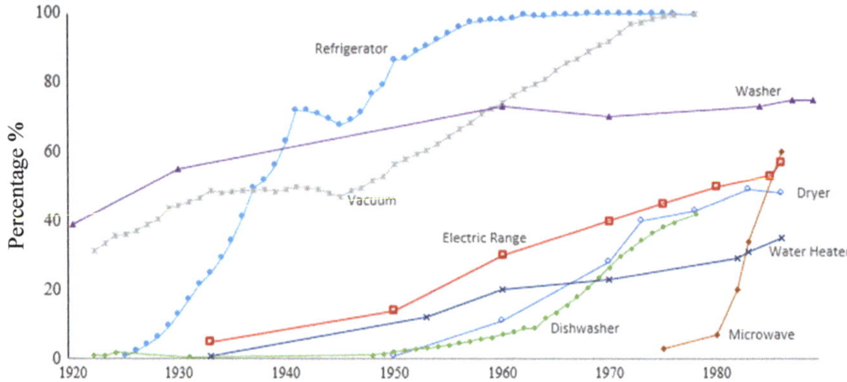


**Fig. 19** Percentage of American households with different electrical appliances from 1920 to 1989. *Source* Greenwood, J., Seshadri, A. & Yorukoglu, M. (2005). Engines of liberation. *Review of Economic Studies,* 72 (1), 109–133

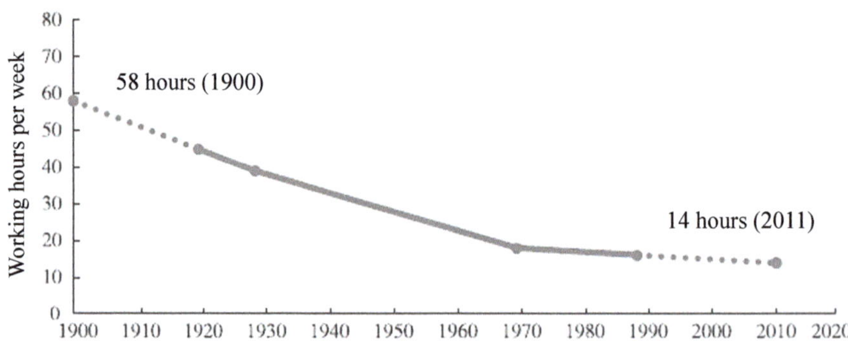


**Fig. 20** Working hours of American women spent on housework (including cooking and laundry, etc.) each week. *Source* Bureau of Labor Statistics. American time use survey; Roser M. Figure 2 in section "Working Hours", Our World in Data

Extended Reading:

(1) Housing

The development trends of future family are smart, energy-saving and systemized. Smart home devices are important carriers for smart family in the future. The control system of smart home devices can control all the household electrical devices including television, lamps, thermostat and security devices, etc. Consumers can operate the control system through vocal commands and set different scenes of use. Adaptive and self-learning, the smart control system can learn about people's life habits, then adjust their behavior. It can automatically decide the scene of use and conduct associated and coordinated operation through several connected sensors, thus achieving self-learning and human-computer interaction and the overall optimum status in terms of energy consumption and comfort.

The future households will use smart partitions. The living room will be more flexible in functions as the major space for leisure and recreation. Residents can send command through the control system to adjust the temperature, light and space of the living room into various models including party model, film-watching model and guest-receiving model, etc. When the owner is out of home, the housekeeping robot will clean the house as is necessary and set all the devices to an optimum status. As soon as the owner walks into the house, unlike the existing voice control lamps, the lighting devices will automatically switch to the most suitable brightness, color and angle according to the indoor and outdoor brightness, heart rate and mood of the owner, etc. Meanwhile, the central control system will automatically decide whether to open the shutters according to the outdoor brightness. It will also automatically adjust the color and texture of walls and furniture like sofa according to the owner's needs and satisfy their various requirements. The digital photo frame on the wall will loop display the owner's photos and refresh their memories, making life fresh every day.

The future smart thermostat will be able to sense the specific location of the occupant and, based on its knowledge of the occupant's requirement of comfortable temperature, analyze data of the house such as the temperature, humidity and air condition and other information to start, adjust and stop the device automatically. Accordingly, the temperature in the area where the occupant stays is kept stable, while energy consumption caused by air conditioning or heating the empty area is reduced and it can also have real-time monitoring of the air quality for automatic purification of the indoor air.

When the occupant washes up and is ready to go to bed, the mattress will automatically adjust to the occupant's body and needs, in addition to recording his or her sleep length and depth, heart rate and so on. The occupant can access and visualize such data through a smart device. If you find it difficult to sleep because of the snore from your partner, the smart earplug will block the noise according to your needs and play soothing music. Once you are awake, the robot will choose an outfit for you according to the weather, your preference and schedule, saving you from having to make a choice or deciding on a matching outfit.

When the occupant is out of home, the security device in the house will automatically determine the scene of security and check for possible security threats through cameras and sensors, etc. It can also send alarms to the occupant through a smart phone or wristband.

(2) Clothing

Once the occupant enters the cloakroom, the robot housekeeper will remove the dust on his or her clothing and disinfect the exposed skin and change the occupant to loungewear. After the occupant takes a shower, the robot housekeeper will put the occupant's clothes in a washer & dryer combo, which can automatically choose the most appropriate washing and drying mode according to the color and material of the clothes. Then, the robot housekeeper will fold the laundry and put them away in a proper place. If new clothes are needed, it's not necessary to go to a mall, as virtual shopping is possible through VR devices. The system can recommend the best choice for the occupant based on his or her height, size, preference and the fashion. When the online shopping is completed, the clothes will be sent to your home by express companies.

(3) Food

In smart families, both cooking and dining are enjoyable, because they are made easy by the robot housekeeper and smart systems for food storage and cooking. Different kinds of foods are stored in categories by the robot housekeeper in cooperation with the food storage system according to the temperature, humidity and oxygen content of the foods. The system keeps daily record of the consumption and remaining value of vegetables, meat, fruits and cereals, and sends diet recommendations to the occupant's mobile according to his or her health condition, helping the occupant maintaining a balanced diet while avoiding waste. Of course, in case of no interest in the recommendation given by the system, the occupant may also choose dishes as he or she likes and the food storage system will prepare the proper amount and proportion of nutrient in advance.

If the occupant is a cooking enthusiast, the ingredients will be ready whenever he or she arrives home. Want to learn a new dish? No problem. The audio-visual system will automatically switch on and play a video demonstrating the cooking skills of Michelin star chefs. The occupant may follow the tutorial step by step. Of course, the robot housekeeper also gives advice as necessary. Without having to worry about the timing or seasoning, everyone can learn to cook like a five-star chef at home. In case cooking is considered as a burden by the occupant, there is also an option for such lazy people. The robot housekeeper can cook for the occupant, including pickling fish, cutting onions and garlics, all according to the occupant's preference. The occupant can just take a rest and wait for the meal.

If the occupant likes natural and organic food, planting at home is a choice. The smart robot will consider the space available in the house and the occupant's preference before choosing a suitable place for vegetables and spices which are planted and harvested at a fixed rate. With a wall of green plants, the occupant not only enjoys a living environment, but also have ready access to the freshest vegetables. The occupant may also share the harvest with friends. The highly smart life could also be idyllic.

Want to lose some weight or build muscle? Just tell the robot housekeeper, then the system will automatically conduct analysis and work out a diet plan based on the occupant's current weight, target body fat percentage and level of physical activities. It will arrange your meals automatically every day and adjust the plan according to the occupant's health condition. Can't restrain yourself? You may choose the compulsory mode under which the system sets a warning line. Once the occupant has had more food than the standard, the food storage system will refuse to offer any snack or dessert. People no longer need to worry about overeating that could result in failure of weight loss.

If the occupant wants to invite some friends for dinner, the system will purchase the necessary items if they send the menu to the robot housekeeper in advance. It will be no problem whether you want to show off your cooking skills or simply enjoy the treat prepared by the smart system.

In a smart family, people do not need to worry about defrosting fish, shrimps or other meat, because the classified storage system ensures that all food is kept fresh. There will not be any fruit or ice cream sitting too long in the fridge, because the system automatically keeps record of the food availability and sends reminders to the occupant according to the freshness of food. People will not have to go to supermarkets every week but often forget to buy something like sauce or garlics, because the system can generate a shopping list based on the food consumption rate and purchase online, which only requires your confirmation with a click on mobile.

(4) Transportation

If the occupant intends to go on vacation, simply tell the control system to "switch to vacation mode" and the system will switch all devices in the house to vacation mode. Each device will be in energy-saving mode or cut off the power supply as is necessary. The robot housekeeper will also adjust the operation modes of devices according to the situation in the house. Before the occupant leaves, the automatic scanning system in the backpack or suitcase will remind him or her of any item that has not been packed based on your routine and practice.

Meanwhile, tell the control system in advance where you are going and your schedule, then your mobile will be connected with the system to generate optimum traveling and path plans. Whether you are going to the airport or driving to a certain place, it will automatically avoid traffic congestion and save time as much as possible, providing you with the best possible traveling experience.

(5) Work and recreation

In future, the whole household will be controlled by the control center, which can adjust the parameters to realize completely smart and personalized settings. Each family member is allocated an account. Considering the different preferences and habits of each member, the household devices will learn and adjust their settings in different accounts according to the family members' habits to satisfy their various needs. Parents can control children's accounts and restrain their use of recreational facilities like video games, computers, television, etc., even monitoring their sitting and writing habits.

The future smart control system in the household can efficiently arrange the time allocated to individual and family recreation. It will adjust the time for recreation in each member account, arrange time for family recreation and send reminders to family members through the central control system. Meanwhile, the future smart family system can detect the emotion and health condition of each family member and form corresponding recreation plans. In future, family members may be able to maintain better relationship through the smart family system, because the smart family will help create a harmonious family atmosphere in its smart way.

In future families, there will be fewer screens while walls are used in a flexible manner. By setting adjustment, the future walls will break through the limit of material and have more functions in addition to partitions. Walls will be able to realize automatic adjustment and replacement, serving multiple functions such as screen of live TV, streaming media, PSP (PlayStation Portable, a handheld game console developed by Sony) and system interface of VR games and memo pad, etc. The mode conversion will be implemented by the control center. The control center is installed on the occupant's mobile as an individual APP and can monitor and adjust the modes in real time via the internet. The recreation system and rest system are connected, so, if the sofa senses that the person who was watching TV has fallen asleep, the television will automatically lower its voice and the lights will be dimmed. Meanwhile, the control center will respond in a certain period and wake up the person who will then go to bed.

VR technologies will find even more extensive use in a wide variety of recreational activities. Occupants will not only be able to experience VR games through smart walls, but also enjoy an immersive experience of live shows or concerts without leaving home. Relevant performance production companies may make this a reality through expansion of industrial chains.

When the occupant sits down, the smart robot will offer him or her a cup of coffee, tea or cola based on its knowledge of the occupant's preference. The television can detect the occupant's mood through a built-in camera and play his or her favorite TV programme with the most appropriate voice, brightness and contrast, etc. If the occupant feels bored playing games alone, the robot housekeeper will join and play together just like a friend. If the occupant is addicted to soap operas and games and neglects his or her work or procrastinates, the control system will send a reminder based on the occupant's schedule. Depending on the degree of tardiness, the system can send different levels of reminders, such as turning off the recreational devices automatically or sending repeated voice reminders till the occupant starts to work. When the occupant wants to contact parents or friends after work, the occupant will be able to see them through wearable devices as if they were near you.

(6) Health condition monitoring and diagnosis

The smart fitness system is connected with the smart diet system and works out the most effective fitness plan for the occupant based on its observation of the occupant's BMI (body mass index) and knowledge of the occupant's preference. The household fitness equipment comes with energy recycling devices and the recycled energy is completely used for household consumption.

While the occupant is washing up before bed, the smart toothbrush will send brushing feedback to him or her via a mobile App, informing the occupant of the proper brushing force and sending data of the teeth to the occupant's designated dentist. When the occupant looks into the mirror or is about to take a shower, the smart mirror or the shower equipment will first measure and test his or her weight, BMI and breath and send the BMI data and health condition to the central control system, which in turn sends the same to the kitchen, fitness equipment, sleep devices, etc. The kitchen equipment will automatically adjust menus to control the occupant's calorie intake, and the fitness equipment will automatically adjust the occupant's exercise intensity and specific activities. The sleep devices will remind the occupant to have regular sleep and avoid staying up late.

When the occupant walks into the bathroom and sits on the toilet, the toilet will analyze a wide variety of data including the occupant's digestive ability, etc. based on the feces to see whether there is any malnutrition or health problem. The analysis results are sent to the central control system which will make a medical appointment if necessary.

(7) Energy management

In the future, the distributed energy Internet will be in extensive use.[11] Depending on the energy endowment in specific areas, each household will have a smart power generation system through photovoltaic or wind energy, or a geothermal system. The energy consumed by all the household devices will be solely generated from the clean solar energy, geothermal energy or electricity generated from solar energy or wind power. These distributed energy systems are connected to the traditional power system. When a family has a surplus of power supply, for better efficiency in energy use, it may sell the extra power generated from photovoltaic device or wind energy to the traditional power system or store the extra power via energy storage devices. On the other hand, when a family does not have sufficient power supply from its own power generating device, it may purchase power supply from the grid through the two-way power meter or use the power supply from energy storage devices.

The central control system can control the operation of various devices and set the optimum switch-on/off timing and dynamic adjustment according to energy-consumption curves and real-time power price. The occupant can also have remote-control through different devices. When the demand for power is low at night, the system will automatically charge the batteries of electric cars and other electric devices in the garage. The energy pay system is linked with the occupant's financial system. In addition to real-time display of energy consumption and cost of different devices, it will also keep you informed of the monthly energy income or bill through the Internet. With well-developed distributed energy facilities and energy storage devices as well as meticulous energy demand management, the future electricity is likely to be very cheap or even free of charge[12] if renewable energy is used sufficiently.

In addition, the data about residential energy load is sent to the dispatching center of energy supply in real time for proper adjustment of energy supply and pricing. Other parameters including the overall energy consumption and $CO_2$ emission of the community and city will also be planned in demand-side management depending on weather and incidents for optimal performance.

[11] For the definition and explanation of energy Internet: Rifkin, J. (2012) *The third industrial revolution* (Zhang, T.W. & Sun, Y.N. Trans.) Beijing: CITIC Press.

[12] For more on this idea, please refer to: Rifkin, J. (2014) *The zero marginal cost society the internet of things, the collaborative commons, & the eclipse of capitalism* (CCID experts group, Trans.) Beijing: CITIC Press.

## 2 Main Research Findings

This book is mainly based on the data acquired from the CRECS 2014, while some chapters also refer to data from the CRECS 2012 and CRECS 2013 for comparison. Through statistical analysis of the micro data, this book describes the basic patterns and main characteristics of residential energy consumption in China. It compares the amount, type, end uses and cost of energy consumption in different regions of China and in rural and urban areas. It also compares the results of residential energy consumption surveys, the relevant energy consumption data, consumption structure and expenditure, etc. of various countries. Based on such description and comparison, we made quantitative analysis of the factors leading to the differences in residential energy consumption, then we studied the ownership and choice of different electric devices and the residents' happiness. Finally, we summarized the existing policy instruments for residential demand-side management (DSM) and envisaged the future development of smart family. These studies not only provide fundamental supportive parameters for academic research, but also provide a detailed and specific picture for the public to understand the patterns of residential energy use and the necessary fundamental data and approaches for decision makers.

To be specific, the main findings of this book are as follows:

1. We made quantitative estimation of the gross residential energy consumption and its structure in China. The results show that in 2014, the average energy consumption of a standard Chinese family based on weighted sample was 1,087 kg of coal equivalent (kgce), and 1,208 kgce (including transportation) if transportation was considered. Biomass energy and electricity were the dominant sources of energy, accounting for 27.8% and 21.4% of the total respectively, followed by district heating (20.0%) and pipeline gas. The main end uses of energy were cooking and space heating, accounting for 39.8% and 36.9% of the terminal energy consumption respectively, followed by heating water (12.0%) and household electrical appliances (10.5%).
2. Significant differences exist between northern and southern China in residential energy consumption. The differences mainly lie in consumption of gas, biomass energy and coal. In terms of the end uses, it is mainly cooking in southern China and space heating in northern China.
3. Significant differences exist between rural and urban areas in residential energy consumption. The main difference is in the use of biomass energy and pipeline gas. Due to accessibility of firewood and straw in rural areas, rural households use a lot of firewood and straw as fuel. In urban areas, residents tend to use pipeline gas and bottled liquid gas.
4. The residential energy consumption expenditure was RMB2,341 for each household. From the perspective of energy cost, the average household consumption expenditure in China in 2014 was RMB39,029. In 2014, the residential energy

consumption expenditure for each household was RMB2,266[13] in rural areas and RMB2,786 in urban areas. Expenditure on electricity accounted for the highest percentage in both rural and urban areas.

5. The carbon emission incurred from residential energy consumption was 3,706 kg of $CO_2$. In 2014, the weighted carbon emission (transportation excluded) of each Chinese household was about 3,465 kg of $CO_2$. The $CO_2$ emission was 6,006 kg of $CO_2$ from each urban household and 2,759 kg from each rural household in 2014. In terms of the types of energy, electricity and coal were the main sources of carbon emission. In terms of the end uses, space heating caused the most carbon emission.
6. The residential energy consumption in China is at a lower level in the world, only 1/3 of that in the United States and 1/2 of that in the United Kingdom. Most of the energy consumption surveys in developed countries are conducted through household survey for data collection and independent algorithm. Concerning energy consumption, a major difference between developed countries and developing countries is 100% access to electricity. In addition, natural gas and liquified petroleum gas are used efficiently in developed countries, while China uses more diesel and coal. Overall, there is not much difference between the energy consumption structures in rural and urban areas, but there are differences in the consumption percentages of various types of energy sources. This is related to the lifestyle, living habits, access to energy, etc. Space heating and air conditioning are main end uses in residential energy consumption. The extensive use of electrical appliances is also an important feature of household energy use in developed countries. It is worth mentioning that many developed countries have conducted further surveys and researches based on the residential energy consumption surveys. For example, the United States included a survey about assistance to low-income families in its energy consumption survey. This may serve as reference to our future surveys concerning residential energy consumption. Concerning the energy consumption reports of developing countries, most of the developing countries face greater difficulties than developed countries in data collection and are inferior to the latter in terms of data transparency and survey preciseness. For example, India only listed the percentages of families using certain energy sources, but did not contain any statistics about the specific amount. We also found it difficult to locate data about specific consumption expenditure in similar reports of African countries. Due to underdeveloped economy in these countries, energy use depends on regional energy endowment to a large extent. Meanwhile, due to wealth gap and urban-rural gap, there are significant differences between regions in energy use in developing countries. It is obvious from the reports that in nearly every underdeveloped country, cooking and illumination are the primary end uses of energy in residential energy consumption, which are also the focus in energy

---

[13]While calculating the rural residential energy consumption expenditure, the accessible firewood and charcoal are converted based on market price (It is possible that the rural residents collect such energy for free and do not have to pay).

consumption survey in developing countries. The biggest difference in terms of energy use between these countries and developed countries and even China is the frequent use of firewood, paraffin wax and candles. Concerning the residential energy use in underdeveloped regions, burning questions include poor access to electricity, low efficiency in energy use, etc.

7. We compared the residential energy consumption in rural and urban areas and identified the factors and mechanisms contributing to their differences. Study shows that after urbanization, if the new urban residents consume energy in the same manner as the original urban residents, the new urban households will have the following changes in energy consumption: the power consumption and the total energy expenditure will double; these people will no longer use coal and significantly reduce the use of biomass energy; they will use district heating or electric heating and use natural gas or electricity for cooking. Main observable factors contributing to the differences between energy consumption in rural and urban areas are household income, family size and education level. Non-observable factors such as differences in energy conservation awareness and living habits also have great impact on the differences between rural and urban areas in energy consumption. Urbanization changes rural families into urban families, whose income and housing conditions change accordingly. The energy consumption behavior of the households will also change, leading to increase in energy consumption amount and energy expenditure. In the long run, the rural residents will become more and more similar to their urban counterparts in energy conservation awareness and living habits, resulting in further increase in energy consumption amount and energy expenditure. Therefore, the increasing demand for energy due to urbanization will maintain in a fairly long period.
8. We studied the correlation between income inequality and ownership of household electrical appliances. We used micro survey data to create statistics about income distribution of various provinces, based on which we studied the impact of income inequality on household electrical appliance ownership. In addition, we conducted a systematic study of the possible factors that may affect such ownership from the perspectives of ownership and numbers of electrical appliances. The results of empirical study show that in most cases (except for television), income inequality has a negative influence on household electrical appliance ownership. This is probably because of the nonlinear correlation between electrical appliance ownership and household income. People with extremely high or extremely low income has minor influences on the electrical appliance ownership, and main consumers of electrical appliances are the middle-income group. Therefore, in the case of high income inequality, there are many people with extremely high or low income and a low level of household electrical appliance ownership. Another possible reason is that high income inequality leads to rising savings rate among the high-income population and low disposable income among the low-income population, thus leading to decline in consumption. In addition, our research shows that even with controlled income distribution, the household and personal characteristics of the respondents still

had significant influences on household electrical appliance ownership. To be specific, the household location, year of construction of residence, number of permanent residents, housing space, disposable household income and education level, etc. had significant positive influences on household electrical appliance ownership.

9. We conducted quantitative identification of the factors contributing to the differentiation in choice of water heaters among the rural residents. Through empirical analysis of personal data on the micro level, we noticed the differentiation in rural residents' choice of water heaters. For various types of water heaters and households, the significance of the crucial factor varies. Thus, purchasing a water heater is a complicated decision-making process. Results reveal that the different driving factors in choice of water heaters are mainly the following ones: (1) The demographic variable has a significant influence in the first stage of decision-making concerning residents' choice of water heaters, i.e., whether it is necessary to purchase a water heater, but does not have any influence on the choice in the second stage, i.e., which type of water heaters is to be bought. (2) In addition to sociodemographic characteristics (such as income, household size and age), information availability is found to be a decisive factor in the decision-making process of household water heater choice. Exchange of information plays an important role both in the first and the second stage. Households close to downtown are more likely to install solar water heaters. (3) An innovative finding in in this chapter is that factors such as income, household size and owner's age only determine whether a household will install a water heater but cannot determine the type of water heater. In rural China, due to strict control of electricity price, the electricity price does not have a significant role in speeding up the green transformation of the energy system. (4) In the effort to promote solar water heaters in rural China, the subsidy policy included in the "Home Appliances Going to the Countryside" project does not have any effect in the first stage, and contributes more to the decision on purchasing electric water heaters instead of solar water heaters in the second stage. In another word, the government subsidization fails to have an effect as is expected. It shall be more prudent to promote use of low-carbon solar water heaters and green transformation of the energy system in further policies.
10. We conducted an in-depth study of the correlation between air pollution and the self-evaluation of personal health and happiness of the rural and urban residents. Based on the relevant data of subjective sense of happiness and self-evaluation of health of the respondents, we matched with the hourly air pollution data of the corresponding period and used the maximum wind speed of the day of interview as the instrumental variable to conduct an in-depth study of the correlation between air pollution and self-evaluation of personal health and happiness of the rural and urban residents. Results show that air pollution significantly undermined the rural and urban residents' self-evaluation of health and subjective well-being. To be specific, with each increment of 10 units in AQI (air quality index), the residents' self-evaluation of health declined by 3.2% and their sub-

jective well-being declined by 2.1%. With each increment of 10 units (μg/$m^3$) in PM2.5 concentration, the residents' self-evaluation of health declined by about 3.5% and their subjective well-being declined by 2.3%. However, the influences of different pollutants on people's subjective well-being varies. A significant negative correlation existed between residents' happiness and the common pollution indexes such as $PM_{2.5}$ density, AQI and $SO_2$, density, etc. In addition, the influences of air pollution on residents' health self-evaluation and subjective well-being vary depending on people's income level, gender and geographical location (i.e., rural and urban areas).

11. We reviewed and commented on the residential demand-side management policies in light of the *Several Opinions on Further Deepening Electricity System Reform* approved in an executive meeting of the State Council of China in December 2014. Researches show that China is currently in the initial stage of demand-side management, with room for improvement in terms of regulation, technology and public awareness. Demand-side management techniques cover efficiency management and demand-side response. Concerning energy efficiency management, so far, China still needs to make efforts to improve its energy label administration and to promote energy-efficient products. Concerning demand-side response, the government shall foster the growth of electricity load integrators and electricity service agencies to serve the residential sector, further develop and promote power and information technologies and formulate an effective time-of-use (TOU) pricing system for peak-load shifting. The Central Committee of the Communist Party of China released *Several Opinions on Further Deepening Electricity System Reform* [(2015) No. 9] on March 15, 2015, which draw up plans on fostering new market entities in the electricity market, optimizing electrical and information technologies and further developing demand-side response. This is a great opportunity for residential demand-side management in China. However, the long-standing disturbing problem of cross subsidization in the electricity market is not thoroughly solved through this round of electricity system reform and the potential of residential demand-side management in China does not receive sufficient attention strategically either. They are barriers to development and further efforts are required to solve these problems.

The other chapters of this book are organized as follows: Chap. 2 is an introduction of the sampling methods of the household survey and a descriptive analysis of various sections of the questionnaire. Chapter 3 describes the calculation methods of the residential energy consumption and the setting of relevant parameters. In Chap. 4, we make the balance of energy consumption and energy flow chart, conduct analysis and comparison of the amount, structure and cost of residential energy consumption in different regions and in the rural and urban areas, and calculate the carbon footprint incurred from residential energy consumption. Chapters 5–10 are researches on specific issues, including comparison with other countries in terms of residential energy consumption, comparison of residential consumption in urban and rural areas, identification of influential factors, correlation between residents' electrical appliance ownership and income inequality, identification of factors contributing to rural residents' choice of water heaters, correlation between air pollution and residents' happiness as well as a systematic study of the residential energy demand-side management.

# Chapter 2
# Descriptive Statistics of Questionnaire Data

**Chu Wei, Zhanming Chen, Shipei Zeng, Xiaohua Xia, Feng Song, Jieqi Wu, Ying Huang, Ping Qin, Wenjie Miao and Xiaobing Zhang**

## 1 Design and Implementation of Questionnaire

Several organizations of RUC helped with the third CRECS (CRECS 2014). The most significant difference between this survey and the previous two rounds of surveys is that the CRECS 2014 was completed as a part of the Chinese General Social Survey (CGSS).

The CGSS is a major social survey programme in China which is the earliest of its kind and lasts the longest, with the most significant influence and fruitful achievements. It is a joint programme of NSRC of RUC and a research center of Hong Kong University of Science and Technology (HKUST) and conducted by NSRC of RUC. Following the international standard, the continuous cross-sectional surveys were conducted annually since 2003 in over 10,000 households in various provinces, municipalities and autonomous regions in China. The CRECS 2014 is a formal module of the CGSS. To be specific, the design of questionnaire, training of researchers, data collection and verification and preparation of the research report were completed by the Department of Energy Economics, RUC. NSRC was responsible for sampling of the overall CGSS, researcher training for other modules, implementation of questionnaire and data recovery, etc.

### *1.1 Sampling*

The questionnaire was conducted from July 2015 to October 2015 focusing on the basic characteristics of Chinese households and their energy consumption in 2014. The sampling of this CRECS consisted of two stages:

C. Wei (✉) · Z. Chen · S. Zeng · X. Xia · F. Song · J. Wu · Y. Huang · P. Qin · W. Miao · X. Zhang
Renmin University of China, Beijing, China
e-mail: xiaochu@ruc.edu.cn

 
X. Zheng and C. Wei (eds.), *Household Energy Consumption in China: 2016 Report*, https://doi.org/10.1007/978-981-13-7523-1_2

(1) The first stage: sampling for the CGSS

So far, the CGSS has used three sets of sampling schemes. The sampling for the CGSS this time was designed based on the sampling scheme of 2010.[1] The targeted population was all the urban and rural households in 31 provinces, autonomous regions and municipalities (excluding Hong Kong, Macau and Taiwan) in China for all-round reflection of the situation in China.

In the on-site survey in the CGSS in 2015, Ominisurvey, a questionnaire system developed by NSRC, was first put into use and significantly improved the timeliness of data collection and the data quality compared with paper questionnaire. As in previous surveys, the CGSS in 2015 used the sampling method based on addresses on maps on village and household level, which was well recognized in large-scale social and economic surveys in China. We also conducted mapping and sampling checking in 478 communities across the country. In the sampling process, stratified three-stage probability sampling was used and sampling units of different stages varied according to the situation of each specific stratum. During the first stage of sampling, prefectures (prefecture-level cities, province capitals, municipalities and areas under their administration) and counties were selected as the primary sampling unit. During the second stage, residential districts, villages and towns were selected as the secondary sampling unit. During the third stage, the neighborhood committees and village committees were selected as the tertiary sampling units. During the fourth stage, individuals of each household were used as the last level of sampling unit.

The target sample size for the sampling design in 2010 was 12,000 households across the country, including 2,000 households in the required stratum and 10,000 in the selective stratum. The total sample size for the required stratum was 20,000 households, among which 40 primary sampling units (sub-districts) were selected, followed by 2 secondary sampling units (neighborhood committees) selected from each primary sampling unit and 25 households selected from each secondary sampling unit. The total sample size for the selective stratum was 10,000 households, among which 100 primary sampling units (prefectures, county-level cities and counties) were selected, followed by 4 secondary sampling units (neighborhood and village committees) selected from each primary sampling unit and 25 households selected from each neighborhood or village committee. As a result, 100 county-level organizations, 5 metropolises, 480 village and neighborhood committees and 12,000 individuals were selected as samples.

The distribution of the primary sampling units is as shown in Fig. 1.

Meanwhile, to ensure consistency with the practical situation in terms of sample distribution in rural and urban areas, the households under the administration of neighborhood committees were hypothesized as urban residents and those under the administration of village committees were hypothesized as rural residents, while the proportion of urban and rural samples was determined as 6:4. Based on the distribution of samples in the first stage, 80 neighborhood committees were selected from the required stratum, covering 2,000 households. To ensure the proportion of urban

[1]For details, please consult "sampling design" for the second phase of the CGSS (2010–2019) on the website http://cgss.ruc.edu.cn/ run by the NSRC.

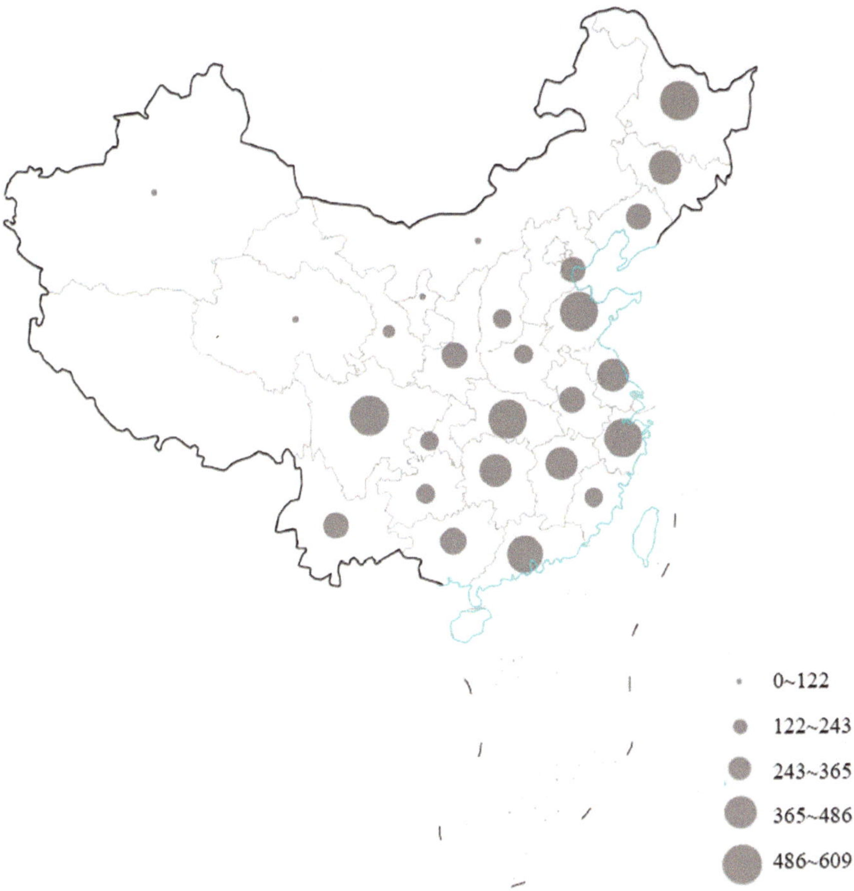


**Fig. 1** Distribution of primary sampling units in sampling design of the CGSS

and rural samples, the proportion of neighborhood committees to village committees in the selective stratum was approximately 13:12. To maintain the same proportion of 13:12 in the secondary sampling units, urbanization level (percentage of non-agricultural population) of the primary sampling units shall be considered to set the number of sample village committees and sample neighborhood committees. For this purpose, the primary sampling units at the prefecture and county level were divided into several sections according to urbanization level (represented in percentage of non-agricultural population). Then, the number of village and neighborhood committees in the sample prefectures and counties was allocated according to the situation in different sections to maintain the required proportion of neighborhood committees and village committees.

The CGSS 2015 covered 478 neighborhood and village committees in 28 provinces, autonomous regions and municipalities (excluding Tibet, Hainan,

Ningxia, Hong Kong, Macau and Taiwan) in China. Effective questionnaires were received from 11,559 individuals.

(2) The second stage: sampling for the CRECS

Besides the core module and the 10-year retrospective module concerning economic attitudes and behavior, the CGSS 2015 contained four other modules including the CRECS. Considering that the questionnaire for normal modules of the CGSS could take a long period, questions in the CRECS module were significantly optimized. As a result, the questionnaire for the CRECS 2014 contained 115 key questions about energy consumption. Other economic and social variables of households were integrated with general questions of the CGSS.

In view of the time required for completion of the CGSS questionnaire and the CRECS module, the CRECS questionnaire did not cover all the sampling units for the CGSS. Instead, 1/3 of the CGSS sampling units, i.e., 4,000 households, were randomly selected. Since a computer-aided questionnaire system was adopted for all the questionnaires in this round of CGSS, and researchers conducted the questionnaires with tablets, the system was designed in such a manner that once a researcher completed a questionnaire about the basic module of the CGSS, probability was 1/3 that the following one was a CRECS module. In another word, the sampling of this round of CRECS was conducted through random sampling on the basis of general sampling for the CGSS. All the household sampling documents and household survey registration forms were recorded electronically, so that the whole household sampling process was automatic, which also kept a detailed record of the household survey process.

The sampling for the CRECS 2014 covered 28 provinces, autonomous regions and municipalities (excluding Tibet, Hainan, Ningxia, Hong Kong, Macau and Taiwan), 85 prefectures and cities and 127 counties and districts in China. Altogether 3,863 households were involved, 54.75% of which were rural residents. The geographical distribution of the sampling residents is as shown in Fig. 2.

## 1.2 *Questionnaire Implementation and Quality Control*

The CRECS questionnaire was conducted by NSRC along with the CGSS questionnaire. NSRC cooperated with 53 universities in China and formed the Chinese Social Survey Net (CSSN), responsible for the CGSS and other large-scale and long-term panel surveys. 25 universities and scientific institutes across China participated in the field survey in 2015.

Besides designing the questionnaire for household survey, the CGSS team also completed the revision and compilation of the *2015 Manual for Mapping and Sampling* and the *2015 Survey Manual* during the period from February 2015 to June 2015. For better quality control, the project team designed the questionnaire for household survey and application form for additional samples for supervision during the field survey to ensure the smooth progress of the project. Before the field

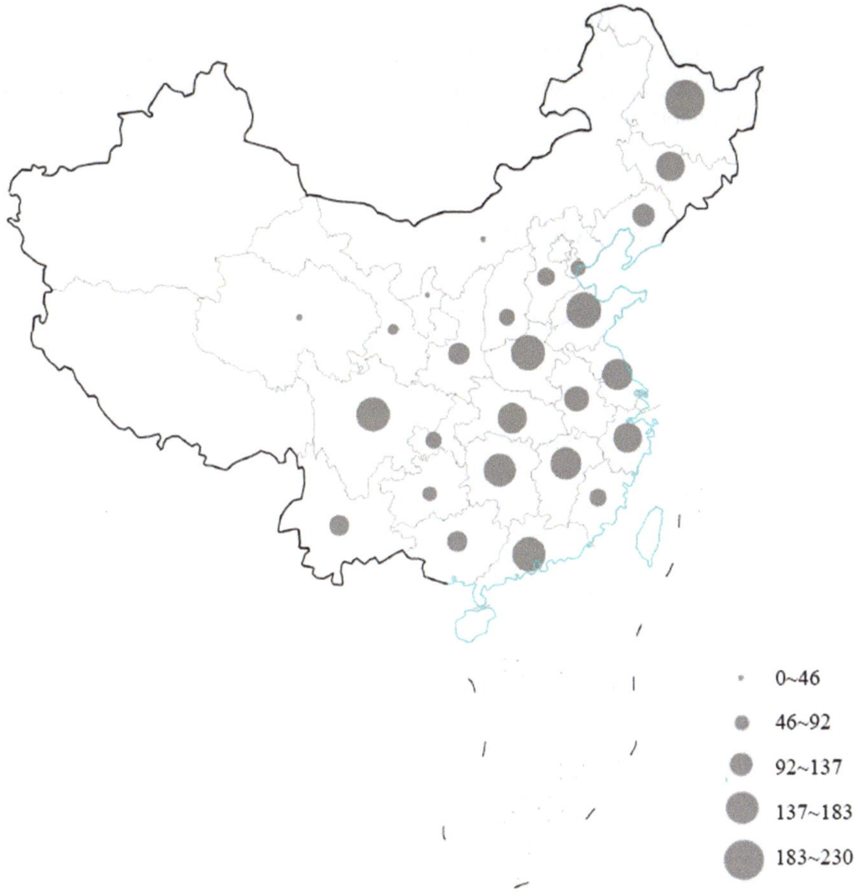


**Fig. 2** Geographical distribution of sampling residents in the CRECS 2014

survey started, the project team counted, printed and mailed all the paper materials based on the sample size in different regions and the number of researchers of the cooperating organizations.

To guarantee the quality of field survey, in the CGSS 2015, 27 people were recruited and trained in 3 phases for supervision of field survey. Each supervisor was strictly screened and interviewed, followed by an 8-day training about mapping and survey and field research at NSRC. After the training, the trainees were examined and qualified ones were allocated to different places to work with local researchers. They were responsible for technical guidance to the local researchers and quality control. On average, each supervisor spent about one month in the field. Besides on-site supervisors, the remote quality control for questionnaires in the CGSS 2015 was mainly based on real-time data that was uploaded to the server. Through real-time statistical analysis of data and subsequent telephone interview, any problem in the field survey was spotted immediately, then feedbacks and supplementary training were provided as necessary. Meanwhile, a better interaction between on-site supervision and remote quality control played an important role in the real-time quality control with support of the questionnaire system.

## 2 Household Characteristics

### *2.1 Household Demographics*

(1) A large proportion of the households consist of 3 family members.

The effective samples of residents (Effective samples of residents after removing the missing value. Hereinafter referred to as the effective samples) about household size in this survey amounted to 3,863 households. As shown in Fig. 3, among the respondents, households consisting of 2 or 3 members were the most common. 1,000 households consisted of 3 members, accounting for 25.89% of the effective samples. 997 households consisted of 2 members, accounting for 25.81% of the effective samples. Households consisting of 4 and 5 members were 745 and 442 respectively, accounting for 19.29% and 11.44% of the effective samples respectively. 1-member and 6-member households were fewer, accounting for less than 7% of the effective samples respectively. Households consisting of 7 or 8 members or more members accounted for less than 3% of the effective samples respectively. According to the data of the 6th national population census in China, among the households of different

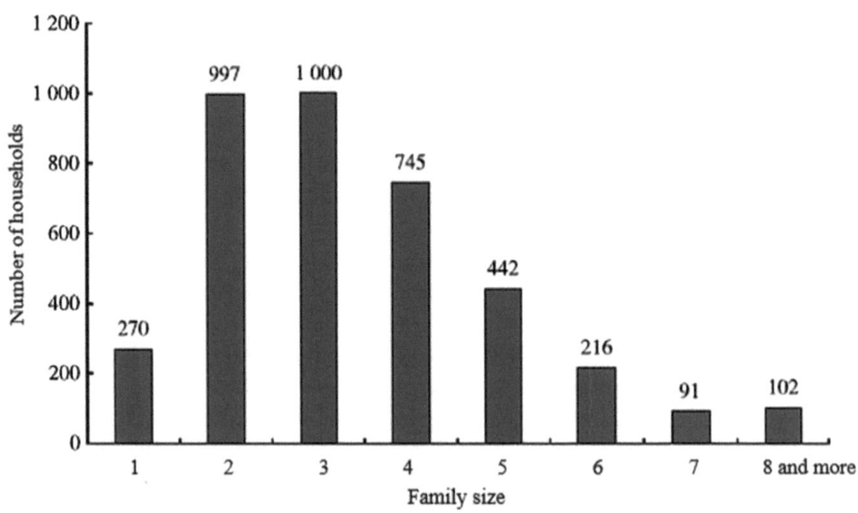


**Fig. 3** Household size

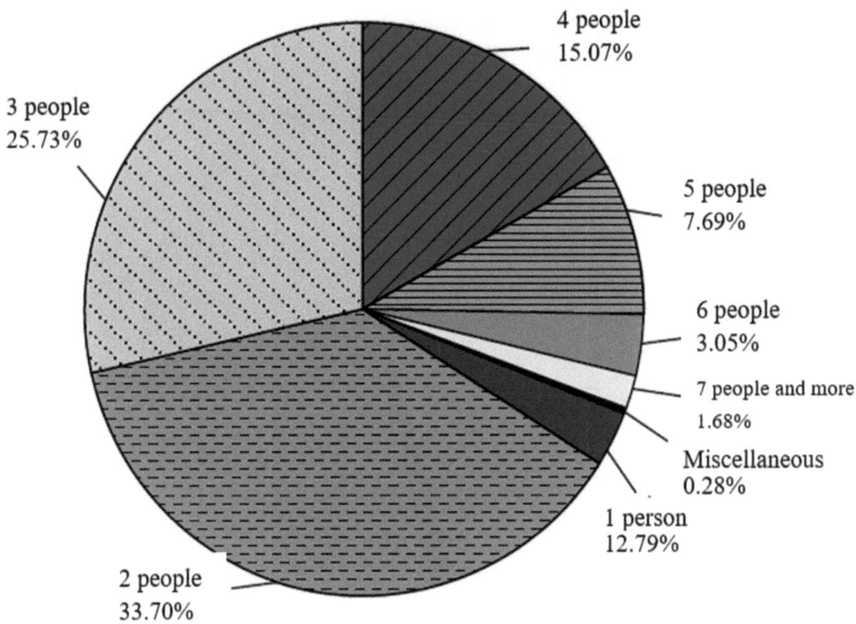


**Fig. 4** Permanent residents in households

sizes in China, the largest proportion is 3-member households, followed by 2-member and 4-member ones. Therefore, the statistics about household size in this survey is consistent with the result of the national population census.

(2) A large proportion of the households have 2 permanent residents.

According to the definition in the questionnaire of this survey, different from household size, the permanent residents in a household refer to residents staying for over 6 months in households, excluding visitors, servicemen or servicewomen and boarding students. The effective samples about permanent residents in households in this survey also amounted to 3,863 households. As shown in Fig. 4, the largest proportion of the samples had 2 permanent residents, amounting to 1,302 households and accounting for 33.70% of the effective samples. The second and the third largest proportions had 3 and 4 permanent residents, accounting for 25.73% and 15.07% of the effective samples respectively. A small proportion of the households had 1 or 5 and more permanent residents, each accounting for 13% of the respondents.

(3) Family members mainly include heads of households and their spouses and children.

Among the respondents, 13,329 people were related with the heads of households. As shown in Fig. 5, the heads of households accounted for 28.98% of the respondents, while their spouses and children accounted for 23.20% and 21.16% of the respondents respectively. So, the heads of households accounted for the largest proportion.

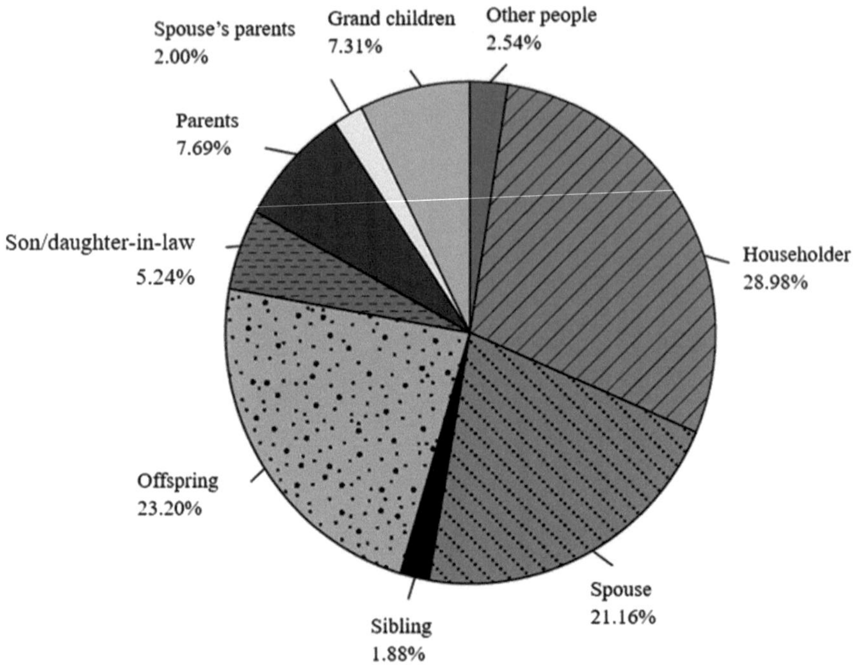


**Fig. 5** Family relationship of permanent residents in households

Meanwhile, parents, grandchildren and sons- or daughters-in-law of the heads of households also accounted for a large proportion of the total, but each accounted for no more than 10%. Parents-in-law, siblings and other relatives accounted for a small percentage of no more than 3% respectively. Therefore, the household residents covered in the survey mainly consisted of the heads of households and their spouses and children. The share of the heads of households was slightly higher than that of their children and the share of spouses was slightly lower than that of the children, but there was no significant difference between the shares of these three parties. This is consistent with the general structure of Chinese households.

(4) The share of male respondents is slightly higher than that of female respondents.

The gender-related modules in this survey are in the sections about social demographics and family relationships which are considered as an integrity for the time being. 13,329 respondents were covered in the survey, including 6,699 males and 6,630 females, accounting for 50.26% and 49.74% of the total respectively. According to the statistics of the Ministry of Human Resources and Social Security of the People's Republic of China, in 2014, males totaled 700,790,000 and accounted for 51.23% of the total Chinese population, while females totaled 667,030,000 and accounted for 48.77% of the total. The sex ratio of respondents in this survey is consistent with that in the total population.

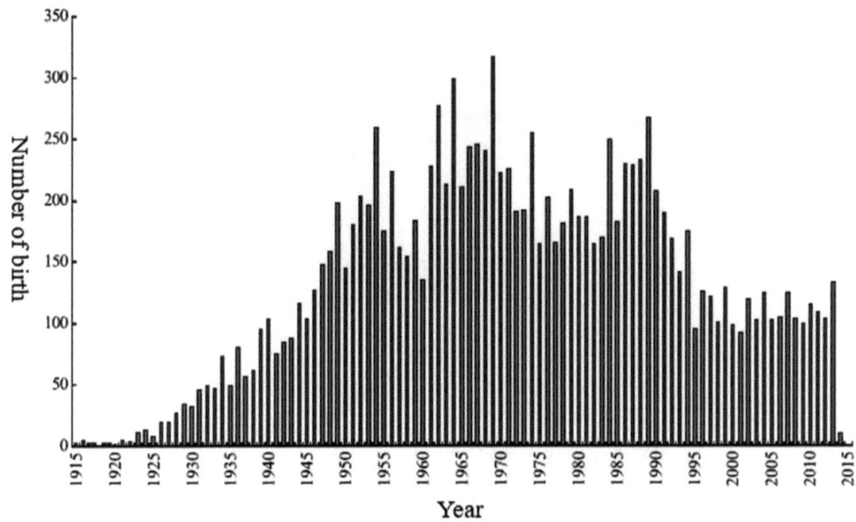


**Fig. 6** Year of birth of household members

(5) The largest proportion of household members were born in the 1960s.

Figure 6 shows the distribution of year of birth of the household members in this survey. As revealed in Fig. 6, a large proportion of the samples were born in the 1960 s, showing a multimodal distribution. Before the year 1950, the number of births increased over time and reached the peak value in the mid-1950s. By the end of the 1950s, the number of births first declined and then rose. In the mid- and late 1960s, the number of births peaked again and declined afterwards. The number of births began to increase in the early 1980s and peaked in the early 1990s. Since then, the annual number of births has been declining and maintains at the level in the late 1990s.

## *2.2 Information About the Head of Household*

(1) The majority of the heads of households have only completed elementary and junior secondary education.

The heads of 3,863 households in this survey generally had low educational level. Most of them only completed junior secondary education at the best. Moreover, many people did not receive any formal education. As shown in Fig. 7, people who have only completed junior secondary and elementary education accounted for the largest percentage, 28.19% and 21.93% of the total respectively. People who have only completed senior secondary education (including secondary schools for specialized purposes and vocational schools) accounted for 18.04% of the total. People without

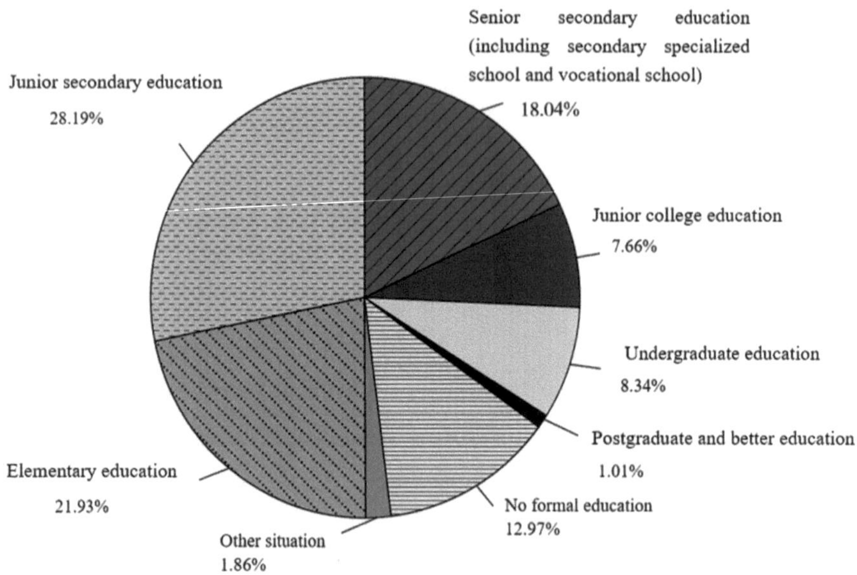


**Fig. 7** Education background of respondents

formal education accounted for 12.97% of the effective samples. A small percentage of the respondents have completed junior college or undergraduate education, accounting for 8.34% and 7.66% of the effective samples respectively. In addition, an extremely small percentage of the respondents have received postgraduate and better education. Evidently, the respondents had low educational level in general.

(2) Most of the respondents are Han people.

The number of effective samples for survey about ethnic group is the same as that of education background. Among the heads of 3,863 households answered the questionnaire, the majority were Han people, accounting for 92.44% of the total. Among the respondents of ethnic minority groups, there were comparatively more Hui and Zhuang people, 79 people and 44 people respectively, accounting for 2.05% and 1.14% of the total respondents, while the respondents of other ethnic minority groups accounted for less than 1% of the effective samples respectively. The data of the 6th national population census is cited here for comparison. Compared with the percentages of people of various ethnic groups in China, the percentages of Han, Hui, Mongolian, Daur, Hani, Russian and Salar people in this survey were higher than the national level, while the other ethnic groups accounted for lower percentages than the national level (Table 1).

**Table 1** Comparison of percentages of some ethnic groups (unit: %)

| Ethnic group | Percentage in the current survey | Percentage in the 6th census |
|---|---|---|
| Han | 92.44 | 91.60 |
| Hui | 2.05 | 0.79 |
| Zhuang | 1.14 | 1.27 |
| Mongolian | 0.85 | 0.45 |
| Manchu | 0.70 | 0.78 |
| Uygur | 0.70 | 0.76 |
| Tujia | 0.49 | 0.63 |
| Daur | 0.36 | 0.01 |
| Hani | 0.31 | 0.12 |
| Tibetan | 0.23 | 0.47 |
| Bai | 0.03 | 0.15 |
| Bouyei | 0.03 | 0.22 |
| Korean | 0.03 | 0.14 |
| Dong | 0.03 | 0.22 |
| Russian | 0.03 | 0.0012 |
| Miao | 0.03 | 0.71 |
| Salar | 0.03 | 0.01 |

## 2.3 *Employment Information of Household Members*

(1) Respondents are mainly engaged in full-time jobs.

In this survey, we conducted questionnaire concerning the employment information of household members among the heads of households and their spouses, but we did not enquire other household members about their jobs in recent years. Consequently, we had a small number of effective samples. Results show that the effective samples concerning nature of jobs in 2014 amounted to 2,645 people, including 1,432 heads of households and 1,213 spouses. As the questions about job nature of spouses were answered by the heads of households, there were less spouses than householders due to omission in answering the questions. As shown in Fig. 8, in 2014, approximately 85.67% of the effective samples of householders and their spouses were engaged in full-time jobs. As for jobs of other natures, 309 respondents were engaged in part-time jobs and accounted for 11.68% of the effective samples. A small percentage of respondents, 2.65% of the total, could not answer the relevant questions.

(2) Respondents are mainly employed by others.

The survey about employment included questions concerning the nature of employer of the householders and their spouses. Statistics show that more than half of the householders and their spouses were employed by others. As shown in Fig. 9, among the

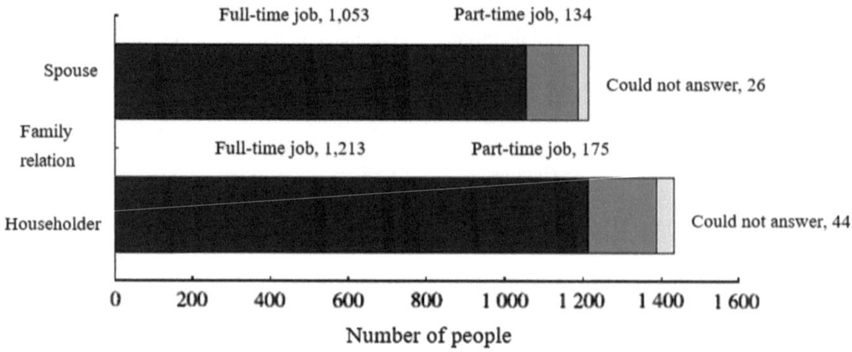


**Fig. 8** Nature of jobs of household members

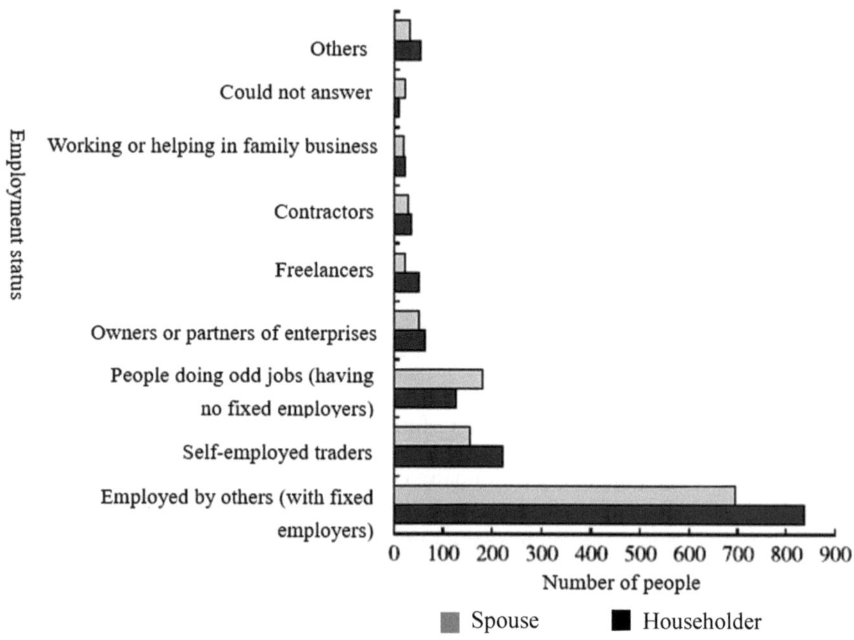


**Fig. 9** Employment status of household members

2,626 effective samples, 1,534 were employed by others (with fixed employers), accounting for 58.42% of the effective samples. Self-employed traders and people doing odd jobs (people with no fixed employers) accounted for the second and third largest percentages, 14.28% and 11.77% of the total respectively. People of other employment status were of small percentages. To be specific, 4.34% of the effective samples were owners (or partners) of enterprises and 2.78% were freelancers. Contractors and people working or helping in one's family business accounted for about 2% of the total respectively.

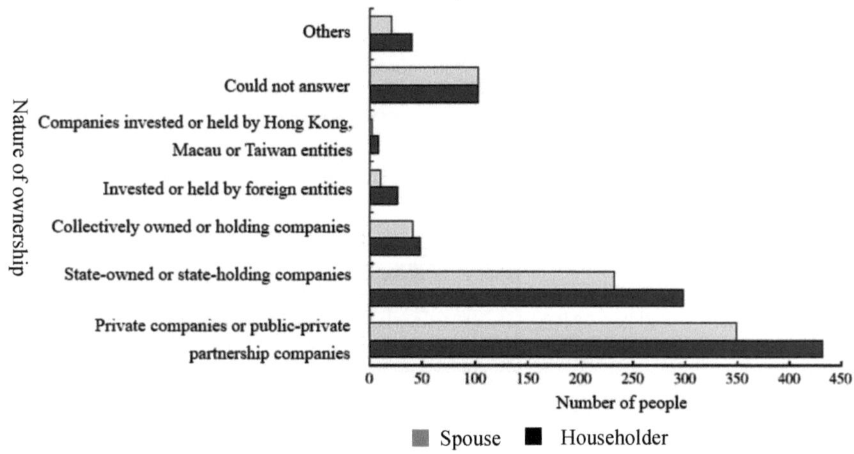


**Fig. 10** Nature of ownership of respondents' employers

(3) Respondents' employers are mainly private companies or privately held companies in terms of the nature of ownership.

By nature of ownership, we refer to the ownership of means of production in economic activities, through which the ownership of asset appreciation and profits of enterprises can be determined. The question concerning the nature of employer implies that the respondent has an employer. So, there were only 1,714 effective samples. As shown in Fig. 10, not considering the private companies and public-private partnership companies which accounted for nearly half of the total, 530 people were employed by state-owned or state-holding companies, accounting for the second largest proportion (30.92%). 89 people were employed by collectively owned or collectively holding companies, accounting for the third largest percentage (5.19%), much inferior to the second. Other forms of ownership such as companies invested or held by foreign entities or Hong Kong, Macau and Taiwan entities accounted for small proportions, each with a percentage of no more than 3%. Meanwhile, some respondents could not answer this question or chose the option of "others". Overall, the employers of the respondents were mainly private companies or privately held companies.

(4) Respondents mainly work for companies.

In the survey about types of employers of the householders and their spouses, the options of self-employment (including self-employed traders) and having no employers were also included. Therefore, we had more effective samples for types of employers than the samples for nature of ownership, amounting to 2,645 people. As shown in Fig. 11, people employed by companies accounted for the largest percentage, about 4/10 of the effective samples. 842 people were self-employed or had no employer, accounting for 31.83% of the effective samples, taking up the second largest percentage. The other types of employers, including public institutions, official departments, social organizations, neighborhood/village committees

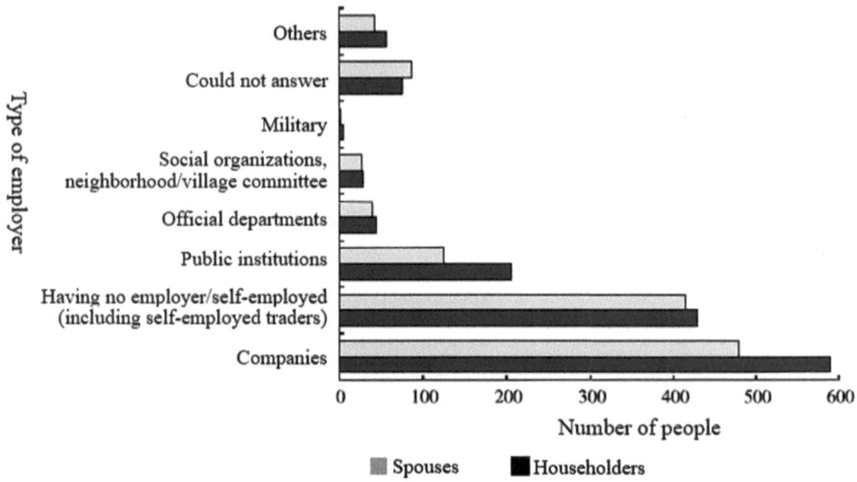


**Fig. 11** Type of employers

and military force, etc., respectively accounted for 12.48, 3.14, 2.04 and 0.23% of the total, all with a small percentage. In addition, some respondents chose "could not answer" or "others". Overall, the householders and their spouses were mainly employed by companies.

# 3 Housing Characteristics

## *3.1 Residences*

Out of the 3,863 households in the survey, 1,748 lived in urban areas, accounting for 45.2% of the total samples, and 2,115 lived in rural areas, accounting for 54.8% of the total samples. Concerning the time of moving into the current residences, 126 households moved in in 2015, 801 households moved in during 2010–2014 and 1,172 households moved in during 2000–2009.

In 2014, 90.9% of the respondents spent 7 days of each week in their residences. In another word, these buildings were mainly for residential purpose for these people. Concerning the time of construction (Fig. 12), most of the residential buildings were built from 1980 to 2010. It is understandable since the said 30 years have been a crucial period of development for China.

We enquired the respondents about the average sunshine duration in summer and winter in their residences (Figs. 13 and 14). We found wide discrepancies in the average sunshine duration and no concentration in any range in winter, but in summer, the sunshine duration was generally more than 8 h, accounting for 33.83% of the total.

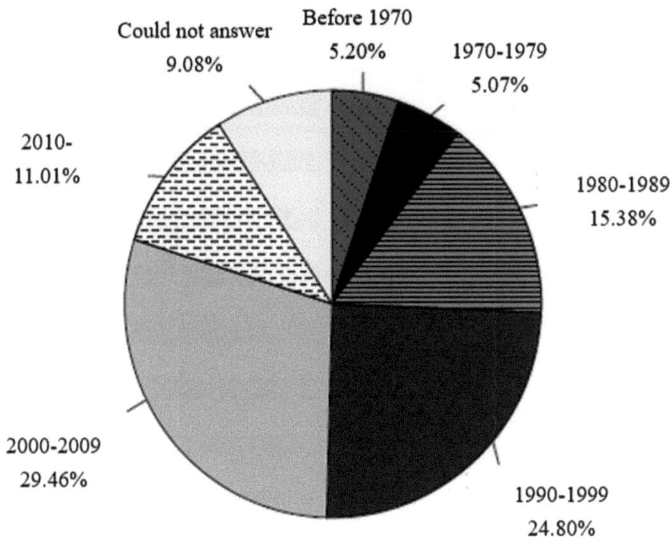


**Fig. 12** Construction time of residential buildings

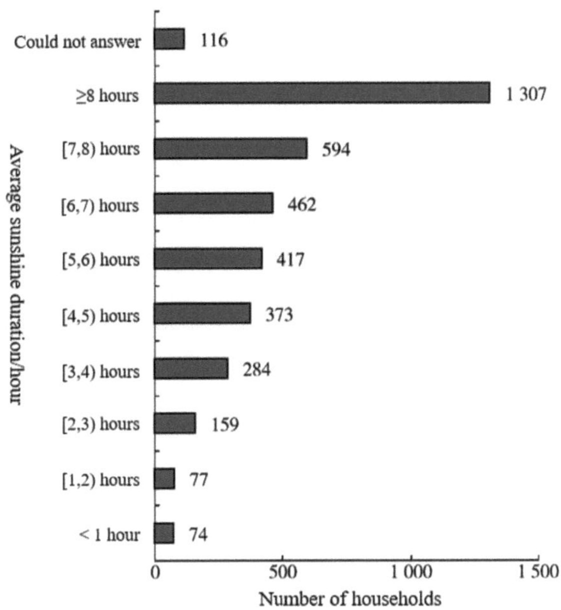


**Fig. 13** Average sunshine duration in summer

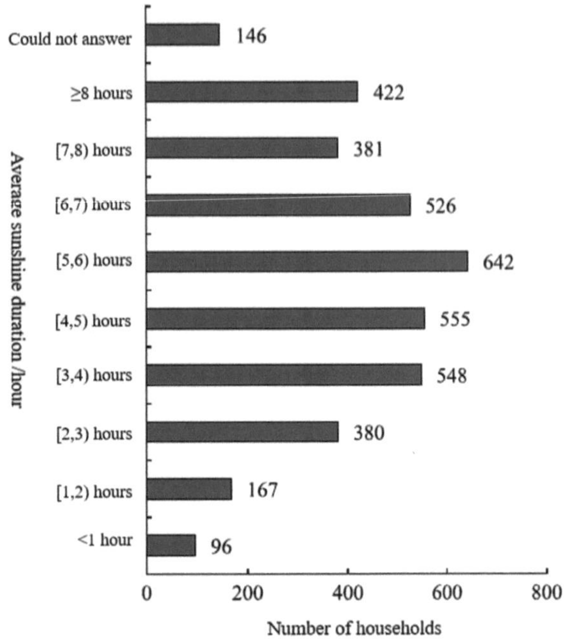


**Fig. 14** Average sunshine duration in winter

## 3.2 *Windows*

Through enquiry about window frames (Fig. 15), we found that the main material of window frames was aluminum, accounting for 41.00% of the total samples. The second and the third most used material were UPVC and wood, accounting for 22.00% and 28.00% of the total respectively. Regarding the window glass (Fig. 16), 72.00% of the respondents used single-glazed windows, accounting for the largest proportion. The second largest proportion was double-glazed windows, accounting for 23.00% of the total.

## 3.3 *Energy-Saving Transformation of Existing Residences*

Concerning the recent replacement of windows or glasses and the number of households engaging in such transformation (Fig. 17), most of the respondents, 66.34% of the total, did not replace any of their windows or glasses. 14.85% and 6.93% of the respondents replaced their windows or glasses during the period from 2010 to 2015 and the period from 2005 to 2009 respectively. In another word, the survey results show that the percentage of window/glass replacement has been on the rise in the past ten years.

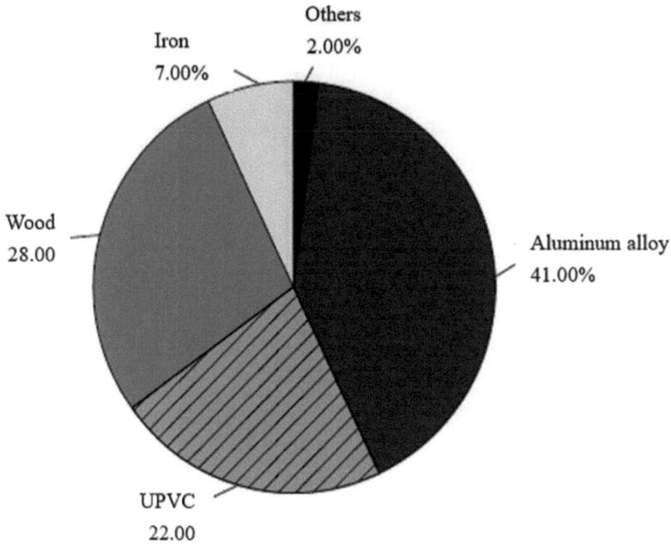


**Fig. 15** Types of material for window frames

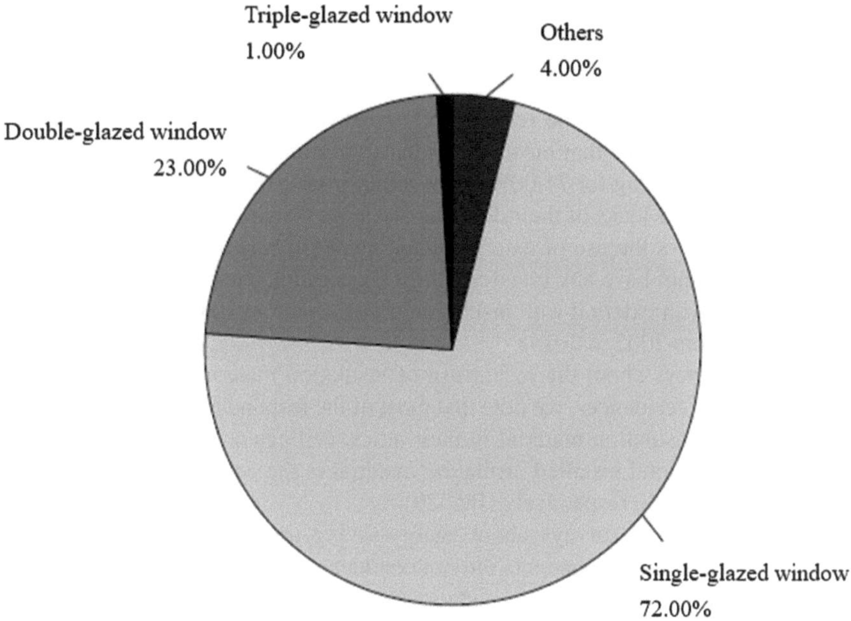


**Fig. 16** Types of window glasses

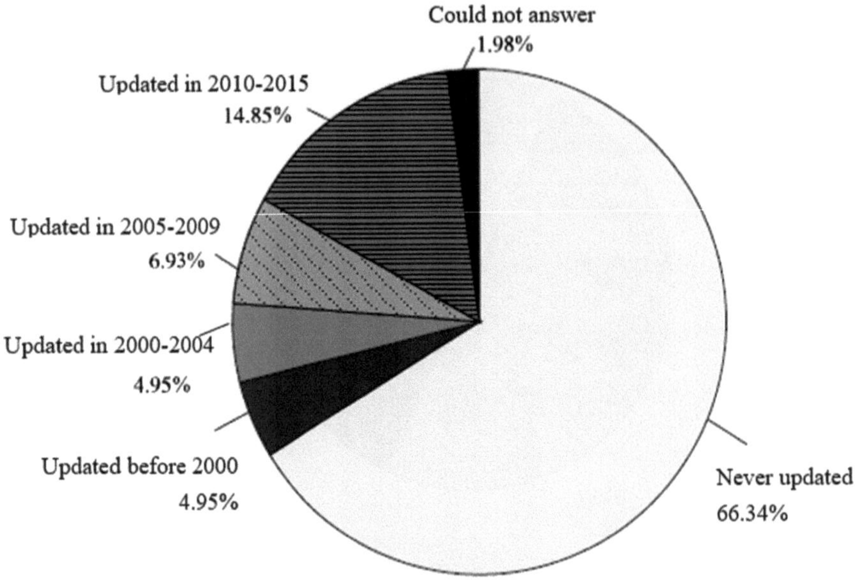


**Fig. 17** Distribution of time and number of households relating to recent update of windows or glasses

Through surveys about the respondent's most recent seal of window and door leaks (Fig. 18), we note that most respondents did not seal the gaps of their doors or windows, accounting for 71.00% of the total. From 2005 to 2015, 20.00% of the respondents had the leaks of their doors and windows sealed.

Figure 19 shows the use of external cladding. Results show that 85.00% of the respondents did not have any transformation concerning external cladding. Among the residences with external wall insulation transformation, 10.00% was conducted in the period from 2005 to 2015.

Through surveys about the recent use of insulation material in attics, ceilings, pipelines, etc. of residences, we note that most of the respondents (85% of the total) never used any insulation material in their attics, ceilings or pipelines, etc. 6.00% and 4.00% of the total installed insulation material in the period between 2010 and 2015 and before 2000 respectively (Fig. 20).

Statistics from the surveys about energy-saving transformation of residences show that most of the respondents did not conduct any transformation. The second largest proportion of respondents made such transformation in the recent 10 years (2010–2015 and 2005–2009), which illustrates the increase in demand of such transformation. Users of energy-saving transformation of residences are expected to increase.

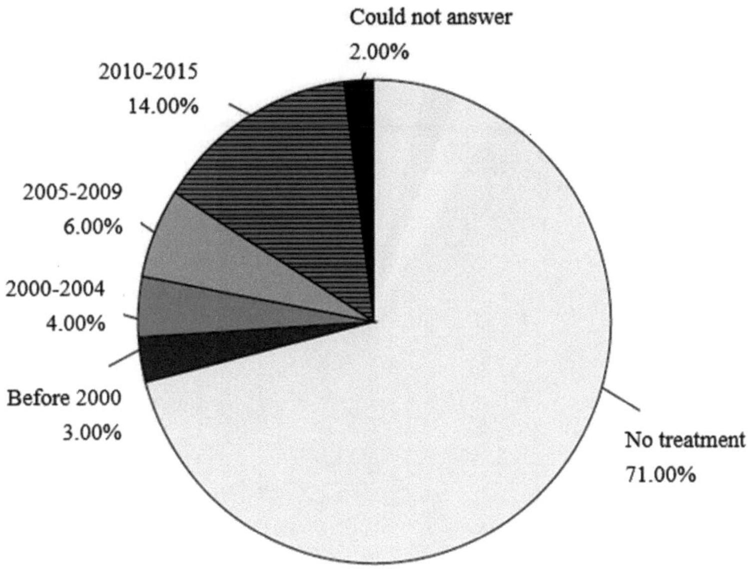


**Fig. 18** Survey of residents concerning the most recent seal of window and door leaks

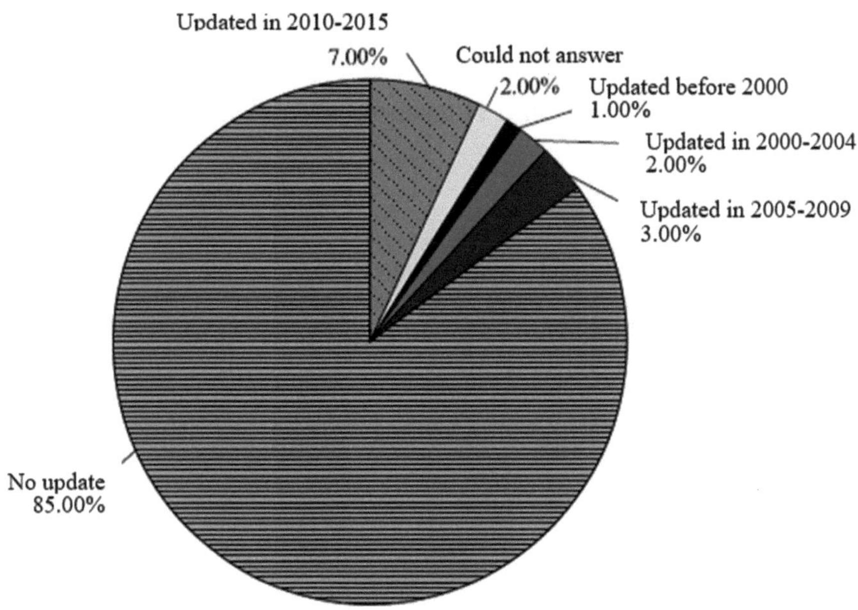


**Fig. 19** Recent transformation concerning external wall insulation

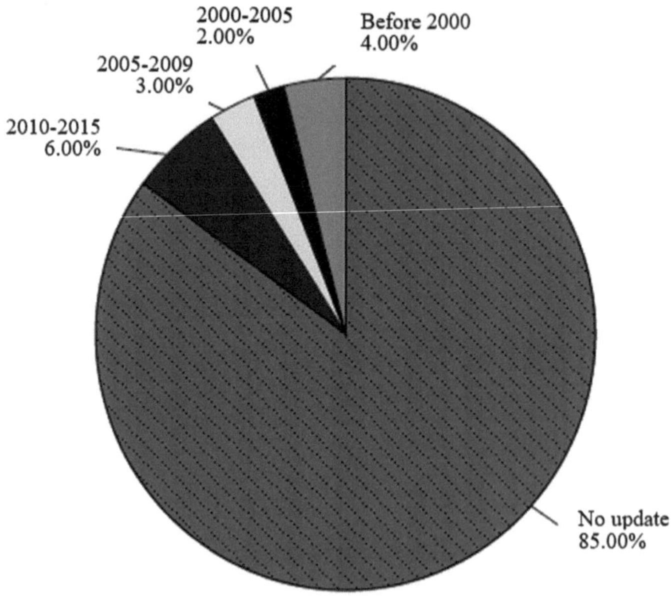


**Fig. 20** Survey about the most recent use of insulation material in attics, ceilings, pipelines, etc. in residential buildings

# 4 Kitchen Equipment and Household Electrical Appliances

## *4.1 Kitchen Equipment*

The energy-consuming kitchen equipment involved in this survey mainly include cooking appliances such as various stoves, electric rice cookers, pressure cookers, etc. The 3,863 households owned 4,925 burners in total, 1.27 burners per household on average. The largest proportion of respondents used gas ranges, accounting for 50.25% of the total. The second and third largest proportion used induction cooktops and wood-burning/clay stoves, accounting for 23.65% and 22.76% of the total respectively. 2.46% of the respondents used stoves burning honeycomb briquettes. A small percentage of households used stoves fueled by biogas, solar energy or oil (Fig. 21). Urban households showed a higher percentage of using induction cooktops and gas ranges than rural households, while rural households had a higher percentage of using stoves burning wood and honeycomb briquettes.

Concerning the fuel for gas stoves, 50.91% of the respondents used bottled LPG, 43.03% used pipeline natural gas and 6.06% used pipeline coal gas (Fig. 22). Among the respondents using wood-burning stoves and clay ovens, 78.14% used firewood, 21.41% used straw and 0.45% used livestock and fowl excrement (Fig. 23).

In addition to stoves, the respondents owned 4,539 pieces of other kitchen equipment, among which electric rice cookers had the largest share, accounting for 53.36%

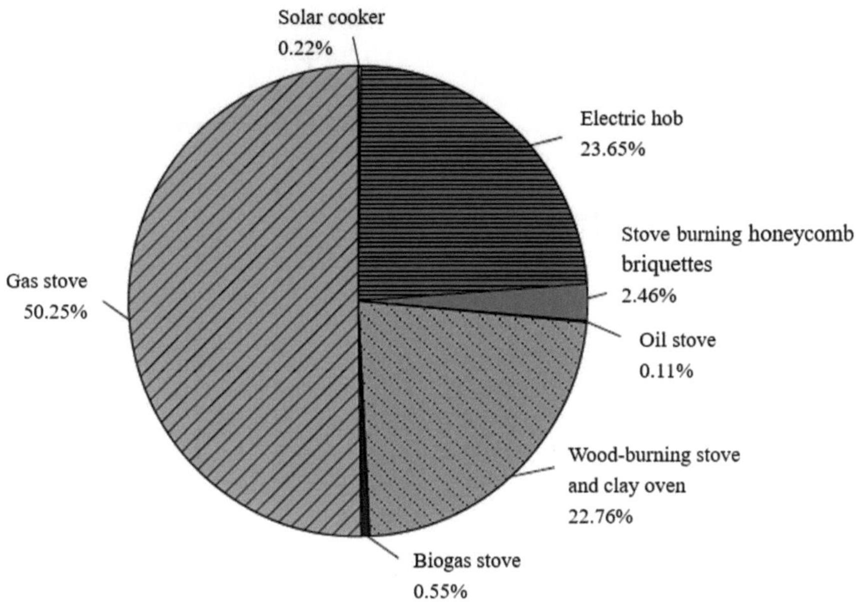


**Fig. 21** Main types of stoves

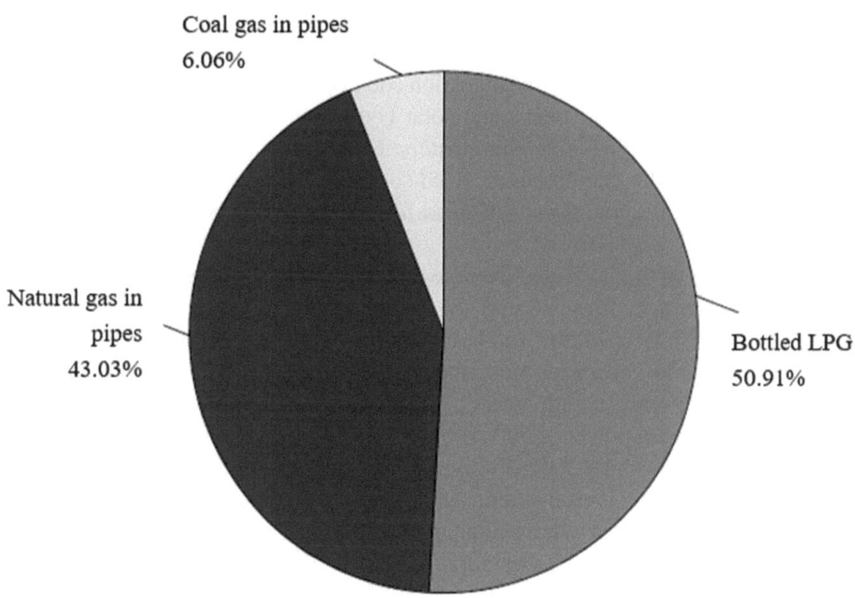


**Fig. 22** Types of fuel for gas stoves

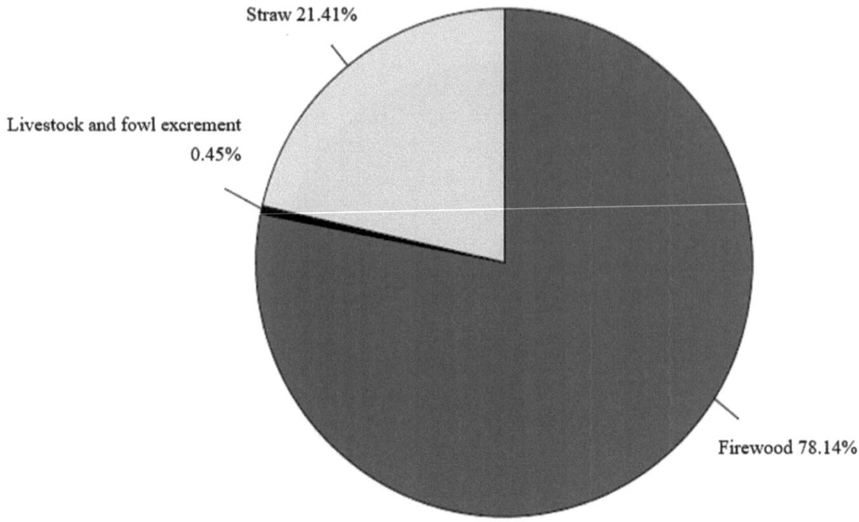


**Fig. 23** Types of fuel for wood-burning stoves and clay ovens

of the total. Electric kettles, pressure cookers, microwave ovens and ovens accounted for 18.18%, 13.31%, 11.68% and 0.68% of the total respectively (Fig. 24).

In the questionnaire, we enquired about the types of subsidies received while purchasing kitchen equipment like induction cooktops, electric rice cookers, pressure cookers, microwave ovens, ovens and solar cookers, etc. The survey results show that 97.81% of the energy-consuming equipment did not enjoy any subsidies. 1.06, 0.51 and 0.62% of the equipment received subsidies for rural residents to purchase household electrical appliances, subsidies for energy-saving products and trade-in subsidies (Fig. 25) respectively.

The distribution of power and average power of the respondents' kitchen equipment are as shown in Figs. 26 and 27. Equipment with power of over 1,500 w accounted for 16.76% of the total. Equipment with power of 1,000–1,500 w accounted for the largest proportion, about 22.07% of the total. The second largest proportion was equipment with power of 700–1,000 w, accounting for 21.66% of the total. Equipment with power of 500–700 w, 300–500 w and below 300 w accounted for 18.46%, 13.46% and 7.59% of the total respectively. Concerning the power of different types of energy-consuming equipment, the average power of induction cooktops was the highest (approximately 1,189.85 w) and the average power of electric rice cookers was the lowest (approximately 739.60 w).

Concerning the frequency of use, 86.22% of the burners were used at least once per day, 48.22% were used no less than 3 times per day and 6.04% were used less than once in a week (Fig. 28). Concerning the duration of use, 34.73% of the burners were used for 15–30 min each time and 34.07% were used 30–45 min each time (Fig. 29).

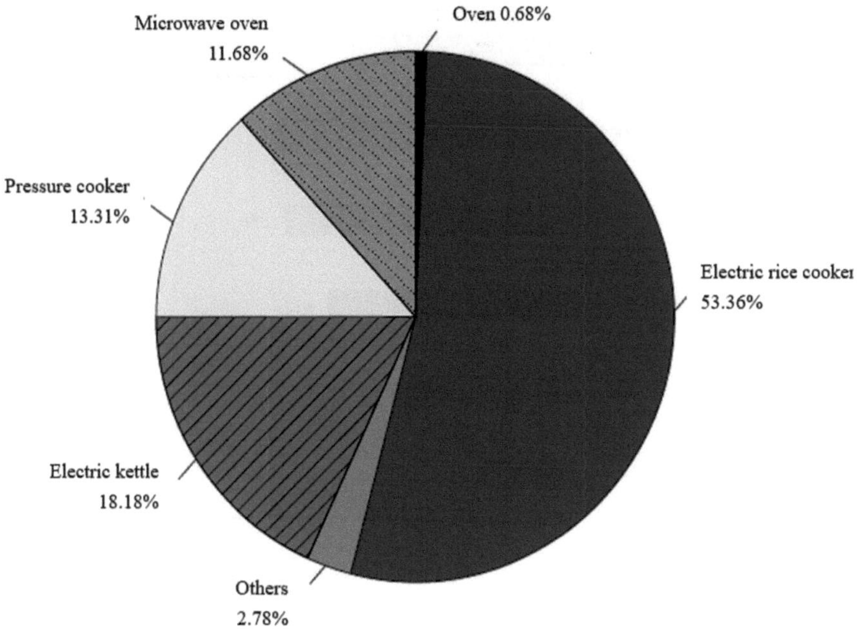


**Fig. 24** Other kitchen equipment

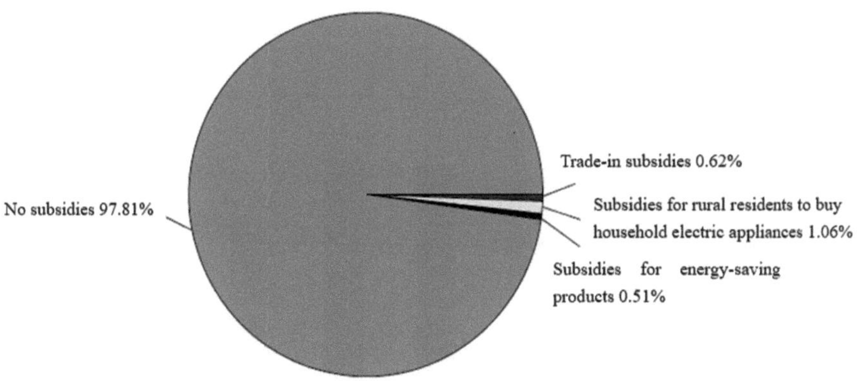


**Fig. 25** Types of subsidies for kitchen equipment

The frequency and duration of use of other energy-consuming kitchen equipment are as shown in Figs. 30 and 31. 40.8% of the electric rice cookers were used twice per day and the duration of use each time for 45.99% of the total was 15–30 min. 39.17% of the electric kettles were used no less than 3 times per day and the duration of use each time for 64.92% of the total was less than 15 min. 31.05% of the pressure cookers were used 1–3 times every week and the duration of use each time for 38.98% of the total was 15–30 min. 38.71% of the ovens were used 2–3 times per month

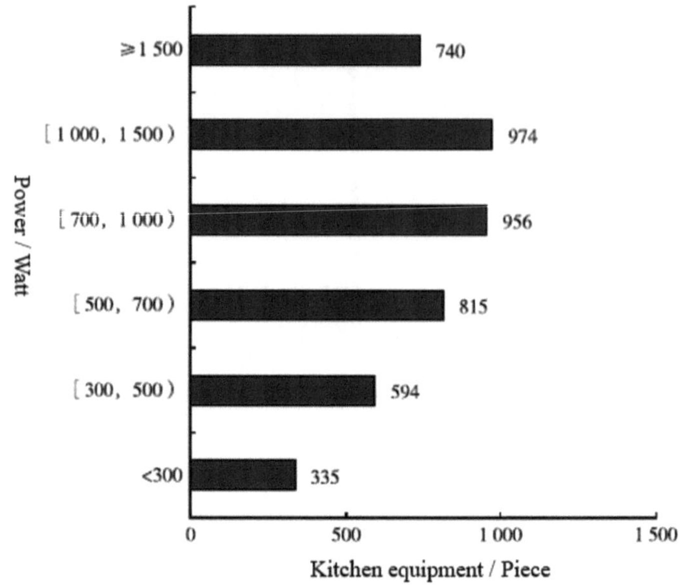


**Fig. 26** Distribution of power of kitchen equipment

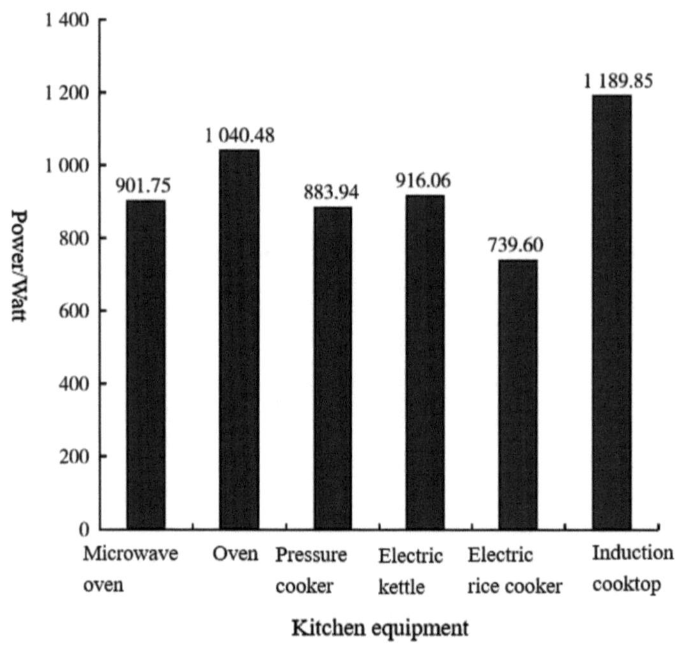


**Fig. 27** Average power of kitchen equipment

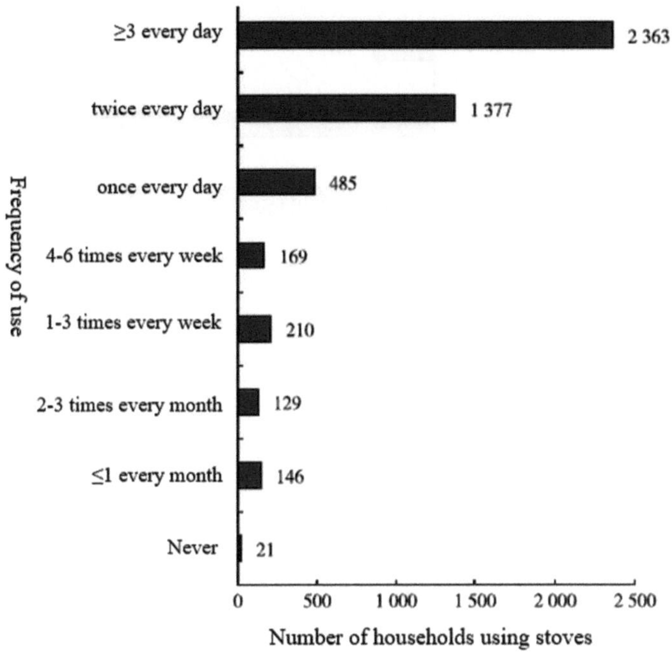


**Fig. 28** Frequency of use of stoves

and the duration of use each time for 30.00% of the total was 30–45 min. 24.1% of the microwave ovens were used once per day and the duration of use each time for 76.86% of the total was less than 15 min.

## *4.2 Household Electrical Appliances*

The 3,863 households in this survey owned 3,509 refrigerators (including freezers) in total. The average number of refrigerators per 100 households was 90.8. 14.22% of the refrigerators and freezers were of small volume (less than 75 L), 62.64% were of medium volume (75 L or more to 150 L), 21.19% were of large volume (150 L or more to 250 L) and 1.95% were of extra-large volume (250 L or more).

The households in this survey owned 3,104 washing machines in total. The average number of washing machines per 100 households was 80.4. 7.99% of the washing machines had capacities of less than 3 kg, 46.34% had capacities of 3 kg (included)–5 kg (excluded), 33.91% had capacities of 5 kg(included)–7 kg (excluded), and 11.76% had capacities of 7 kg and more.

The households in this survey owned 4,420 television sets in total. The average number of television sets per 100 households was 114.44. 35.09% of the total had smaller than 29-in. screen (1 in. = 2.54 cm), 28.93% had 29-in. (included) to 33-in.

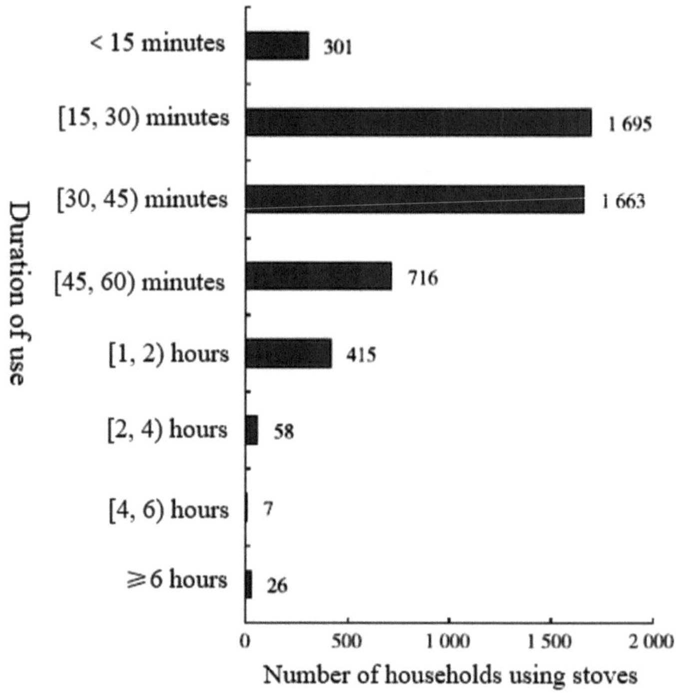


**Fig. 29** Duration of each use of stoves

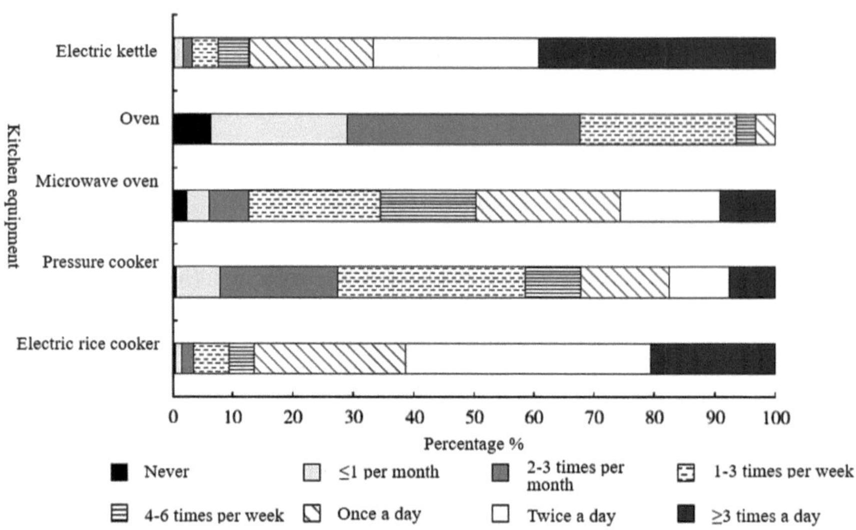


**Fig. 30** Frequency of use of other kitchen equipment

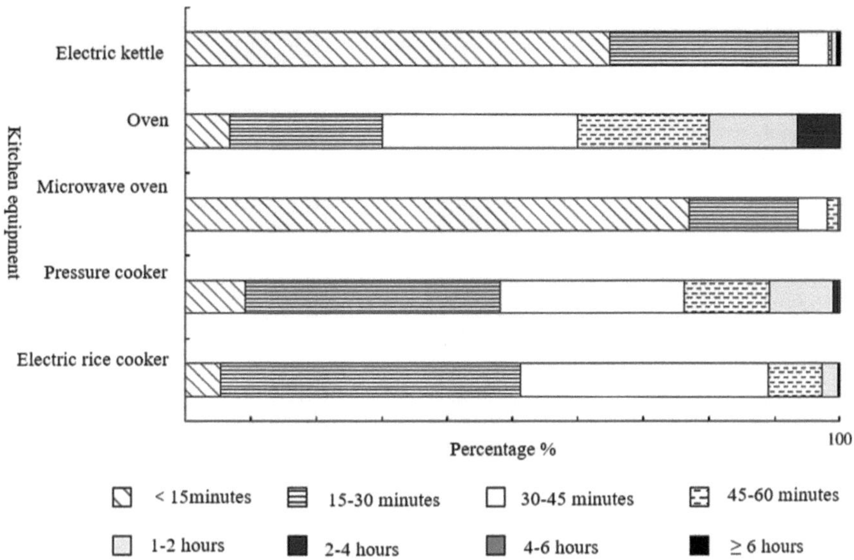


**Fig. 31** Duration of use of other kitchen equipment

(excluded) screen, 23.10% had 33-in. (included) to 43-in. (excluded) screen, 11.53% had 43-in. (included) to 55-in. (excluded) and 1.35% had 55-in. screen or larger one. Concerning the way of receiving signals, 45.07% used set-top boxes, 26.77% used cable TV, 20.09% used satellite dishes, 4.72% used antennae and 3.34% used the internet. This survey also enquired the respondents about the way the television was turned off. 42.92% of the respondents chose "pressing the power button", 40.03% chose "turning it off with the remote control" and 17.05% chose "turning off the television and cutting off the power".

The households in this survey owned 2,116 computers in total. The average number of computers per 100 households was 54.78. 60.07% of the total were desktops, 35.09% were laptops and 4.84% were tablets. Concerning the screen size, 2.87% of the total were smaller than 10 in., 9.88% were between 10 in. (included) and 13 in. (excluded), 41.3% were between 13 in. (included) and 16 in. (excluded), 30.19% were between 16 in. (included) and 20 in. (excluded) and 15.76% were 20 in. or larger. More than half of the computers were connected to the internet via cable broadband, 25% used wireless internet and 13% used ADSL (asymmetric digital subscriber line) or optical fiber. A small number of computers used dial-up internet access. While the computers were not in use, 95% of the households turned it off, among which the households "turning off the computer and cutting off the power" and those "turning off the computer without cutting off the power" accounted for 50% of the total respectively.

In summary, the electrical appliance ownership per 100 households is as shown in Fig. 32.

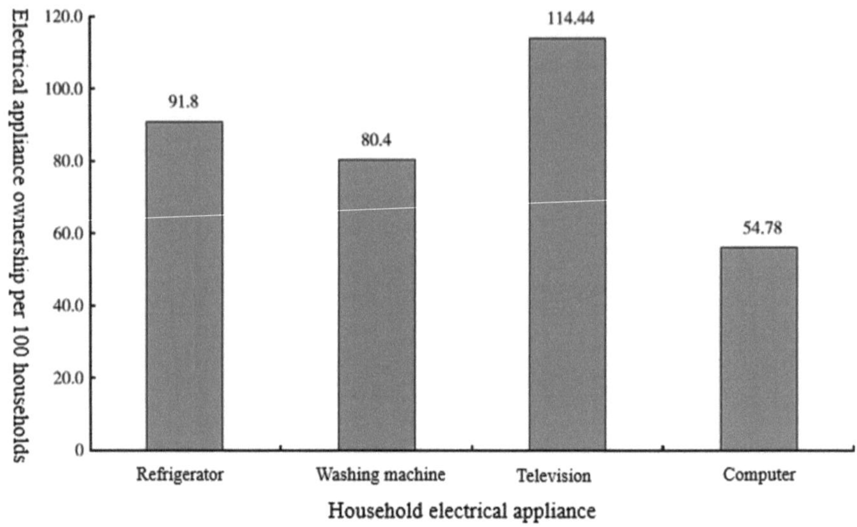


**Fig. 32** Electrical appliance ownership per 100 households

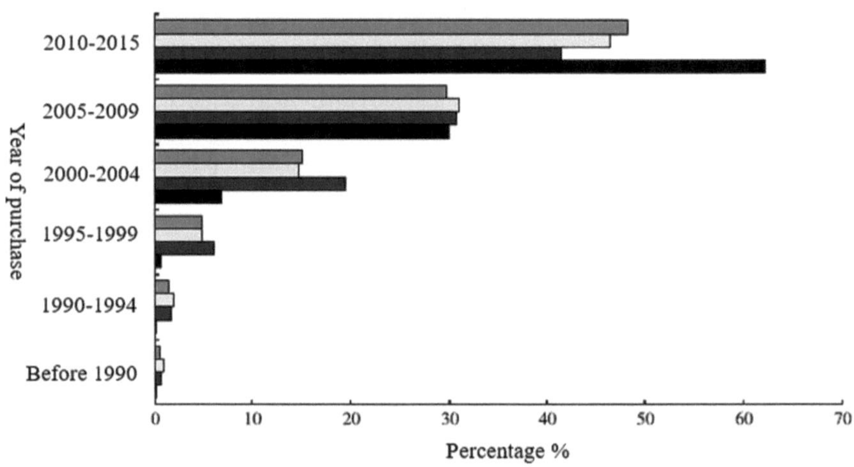


**Fig. 33** Distribution of year of purchasing electrical appliances

The year of purchase of the respondents' electrical appliances is as shown in Fig. 33. 49.62% of the electrical appliances were purchased between 2010 and 2015 and only 6% were purchased before 2000. Concerning the specific type of electrical appliances, the year of purchase of refrigerators and washing machines were close in each interval while television sets were generally purchased earlier. 8.46% of the television sets were purchased before 2000 and 41.42% were purchased after 2010. Computers were generally purchased later, with only 0.96% of the total purchased before 2000 while 62.21% were purchased after 2010.

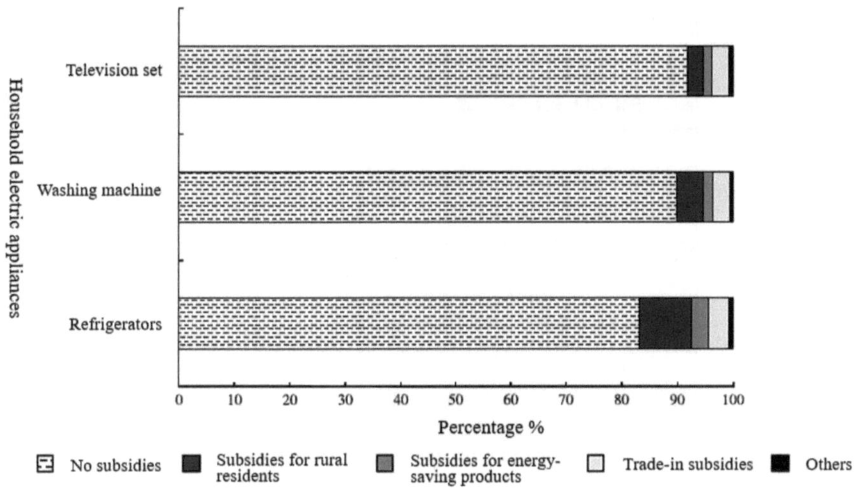


**Fig. 34** Types of subsidies for household electrical appliances

Most of the respondents did not enjoy any subsidies while purchasing electrical appliances. While purchasing refrigerators, 9.36% of the respondents received subsidies for rural residents to buy electrical appliances, 3.73% and 3.09% received trade-in subsidies and subsidies for energy-saving products respectively. While purchasing washing machines, 4.69% of the respondents received subsidies for rural residents to purchase electrical appliances, 3.20% and 1.68% received trade-in subsidies and subsidies for energy-saving products respectively. While purchasing television sets, the percentage of receiving the above-mentioned subsidies are 2.92%, 3.25% and 1.44% respectively (Fig. 34).

Concerning the power of household electrical appliances, the numbers of refrigerators running on 300–500 w of power, 500–700 w of power and 700–1,000 w of power were similar, accounting for 21.67%, 20.15% and 19.27% of the total respectively. The majority of washing machines were running on 300–500 W of power and 500–700 W of power, accounting for 26.42% and 25.33% of the total respectively. The power of 38.4% of the television sets was below 300 w, taking up the largest percentage, followed by those running on 300–500 and 500–700 w, accounting for 21.90% and 18.78% of the total respectively (Fig. 35). On average, the power of refrigerators was the highest and the power of television sets was the lowest.

Concerning the energy efficiency, a large proportion of the television sets and computers did not have any energy efficiency label, accounting for 71.08% and 67.94% of the total respectively. Refrigerators of Grade-1 energy efficiency accounted for a large proportion, 43.66% of the total, and Grade-2 and Grade-3 refrigerators accounted for 23.32% and 9.14% of the total respectively. Among washing machines with energy efficiency labels, Grade-2 ones accounted for the largest proportion, 23.42% of the total, followed by Grade-1 and Grade-3 ones, accounting for 18.57% and 11.44% of the total respectively. Grade-1 and Grade-2 TV sets both accounted for approxi-

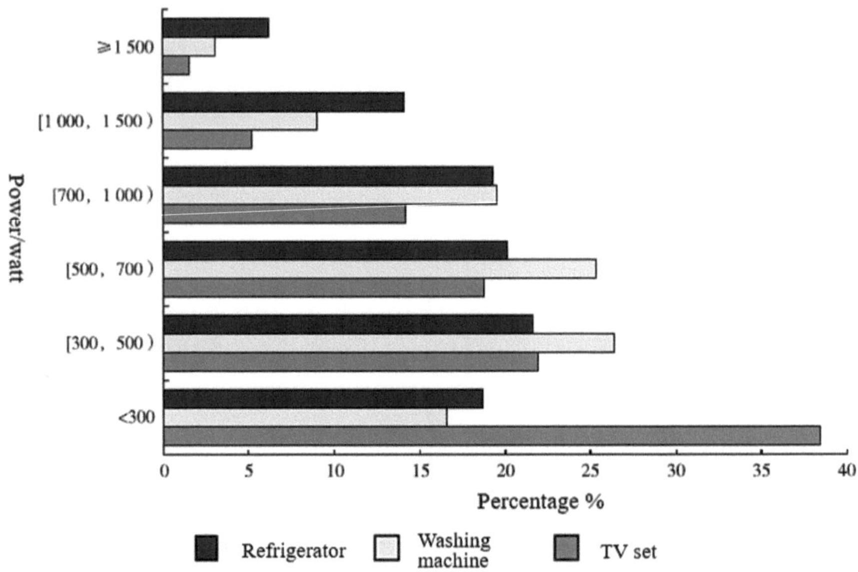


**Fig. 35** Distribution of power of household electrical appliances

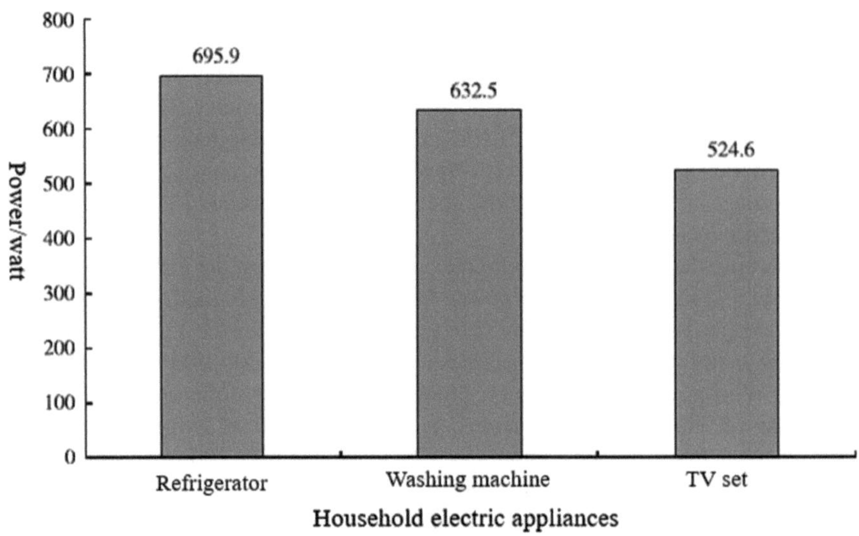


**Fig. 36** Average power of household electrical appliances

mately 12% of the total. 14.18% of the computers were of Grade-1 energy efficiency and 11.85% were of Grade-2 (Figs. 36 and 37).

In the survey, we also enquired about the duration of use of various electrical appliances. For refrigerators, 81.33% of the total were in use for [10, 12) months

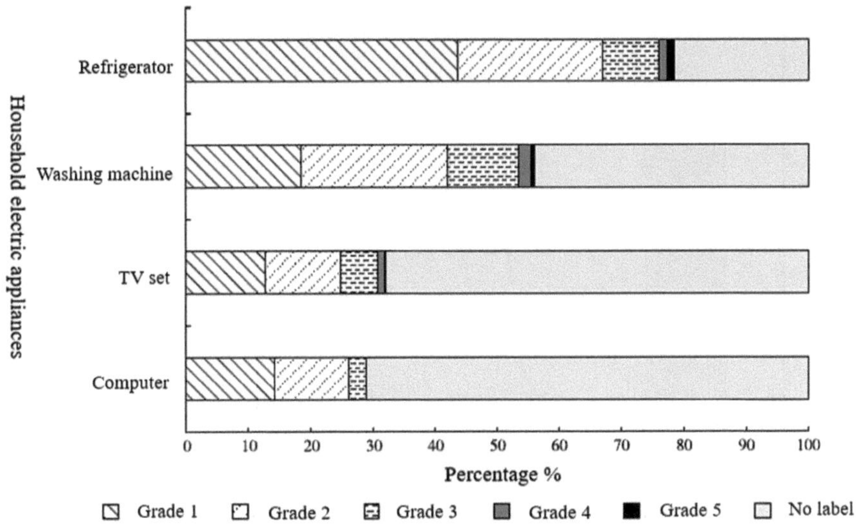


**Fig. 37** Distribution of energy efficiency of household electrical appliances

each year, 6.6% and 6.37% of the total were in use for [4, 7) months and [7, 10) months respectively. For washing machines, 40.38% of the respondents used it 2–3 times a week, 20.03% used it once a day. The average duration for each operation of washing machine was [30, 45) min for 37.8% of the respondents, and [45, 60) min for 22.99% of the respondents. For television sets, 29.42% of the respondents used it for [2, 3) h every day, 26.91% used it for [3, 5) h every day. For computers, 24.39% of the households used it for [2, 3) h every day and 20.65% used it for [3, 5) h every day. The average duration of use for various household electrical appliances is as shown in Fig. 38.

## *4.3 Light Bulbs*

Among the 3,863 respondents, 1,722 households used fluorescent lights, 976 households used incandescent bulbs and 2,921 households used energy-efficient light bulbs. In the households using fluorescent lights, the average number of fluorescent lights per household was 4.11; in the households using incandescent bulbs, the average number of incandescent bulbs per household is 3.46; and in the households using energy-efficient light bulbs, the average number of energy-saving bulbs was 4.7. 31.46% of the respondents used each lamp for [2, 3) h/day, 30.98% used each lamp for [3, 5) h/day. Among the 5,134 lamps with known service life, the service life for 57.87% was less than 3 years and 22.01% was between 3 and 6 years.

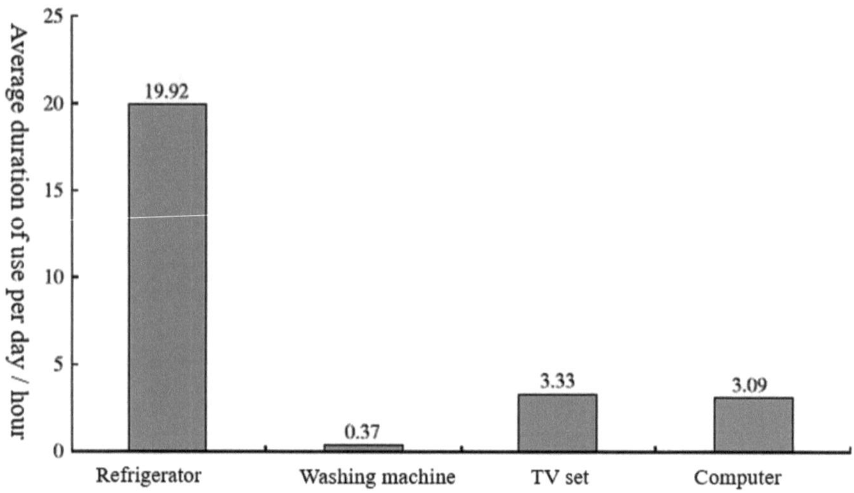


**Fig. 38** Average duration of use of electrical appliances per day

# 5 Space Heating and Air Conditioning

There are two major types of residential heating system: district heating and household heating. In district heating, the central heat source is conveyed to users through pipelines, while household heating mainly uses pipelines of household boilers, air conditioners and electrical radiator heaters.

## *5.1 Space Heating in Winter*

Among the 3,863 effective samples, 17.84% used district heating, 27.72% used household heating, 0.78% used both (district heating + household heating) and 53.66% had no space heating service.

(1) District heating

Among the 719 households using district heating (including those using both district heating and household heating), 45.90% were supplied with heat from the public heat supply network. The other major sources of heat included regional (neighborhood) boiler (28.09%), regional thermal power station (15.30%), regional (neighborhood/building) central air conditioning (1.11%) and regional surplus industrial heat (0.14%), as shown in Fig. 39. Concerning the media of heat transfer, as shown in Fig. 40, 78.86% of the respondents used hot water, 11.27% used steam and a small percentage used hot air and other media.

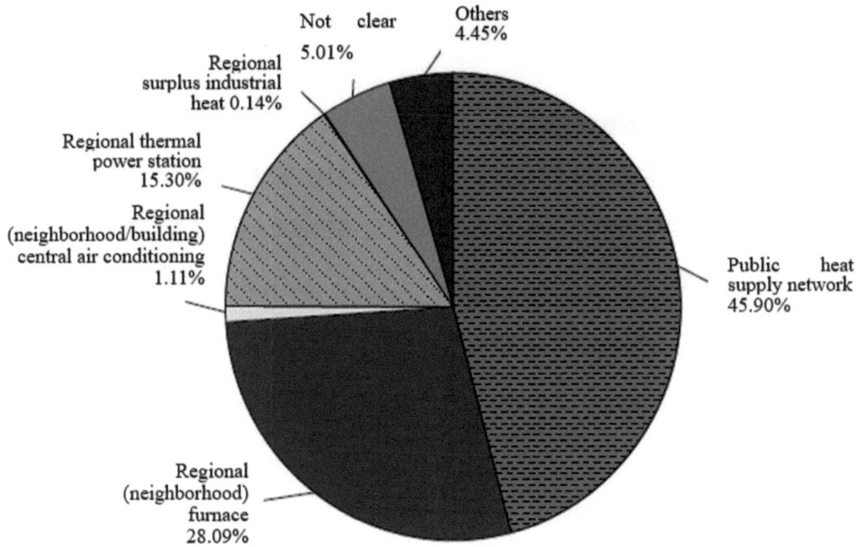


**Fig. 39** Heat sources of district heating

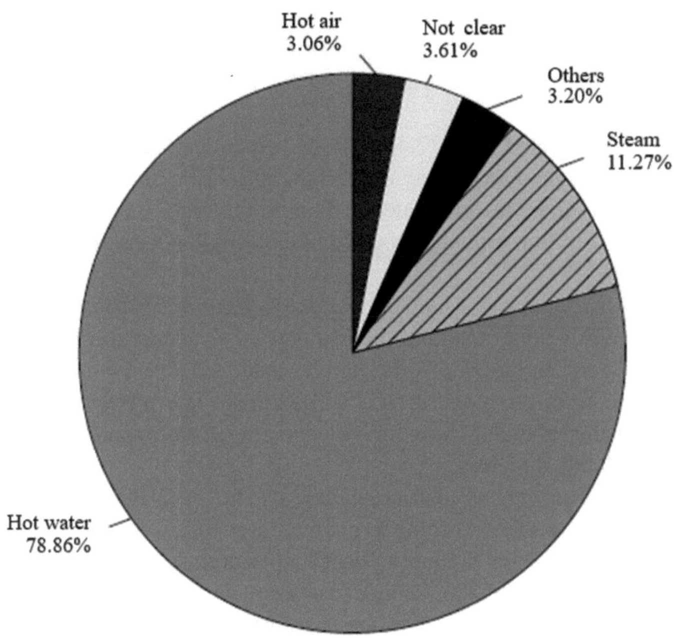


**Fig. 40** Media for district heating

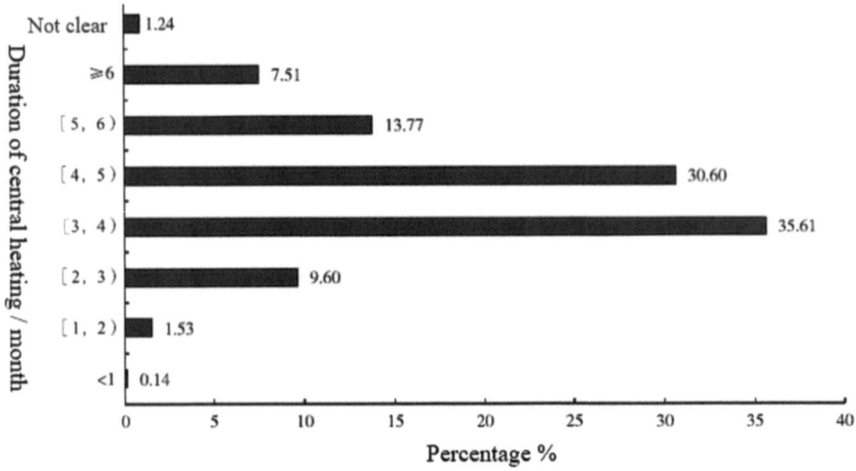


**Fig. 41** Duration of district heating

The duration of district heating varies in regions (Fig. 41). Most respondents enjoyed district heating for [3, 4) months (35.61% of the total) or [4, 5) months (30.60% of the total). 9.60% of the respondents had district heating for [2, 3) months and a small percentage had district heating for less than 2 months or more than 6 months.

Concerning the heated area, 72.46% of the respondents had heating in all rooms and a small percentage had heating only in the master bedroom. Most respondents had more than 50 square meters heated in their households (accounting for 66.9% of the total). 86.23% of the respondents said that they could not control the temperature as they wished.

In 2003, in the *Guiding Opinions on Pilot Reform of District Heating System*, eight ministries in China including the Ministry of Construction requested that to promote energy conservation, efforts shall be made to advance the pricing system based on heat consumption and individual metering. The survey results show that 86.37% of the samples did not have individual meters for heat consumption and only 10.57% had individual meters.

Concerning the pricing of district heating, as shown in Fig. 42, 75.66% of the respondents were charged according to the floor area of residence and 13.77% were charged according to actual amount of heat supply or duration of heating. It is noteworthy that only 4.73% of the respondents were charged according to the actual amount of heat supply, far less than the share of households with individual heat meters (10.57%). Obviously, for some households, the individual heat meters failed to play a role in household-based pricing or energy conservation.

Among the 719 households with district heating, 82.48% bore the heating cost. Among the households which partially bore the heating cost, 43.72% received sub-

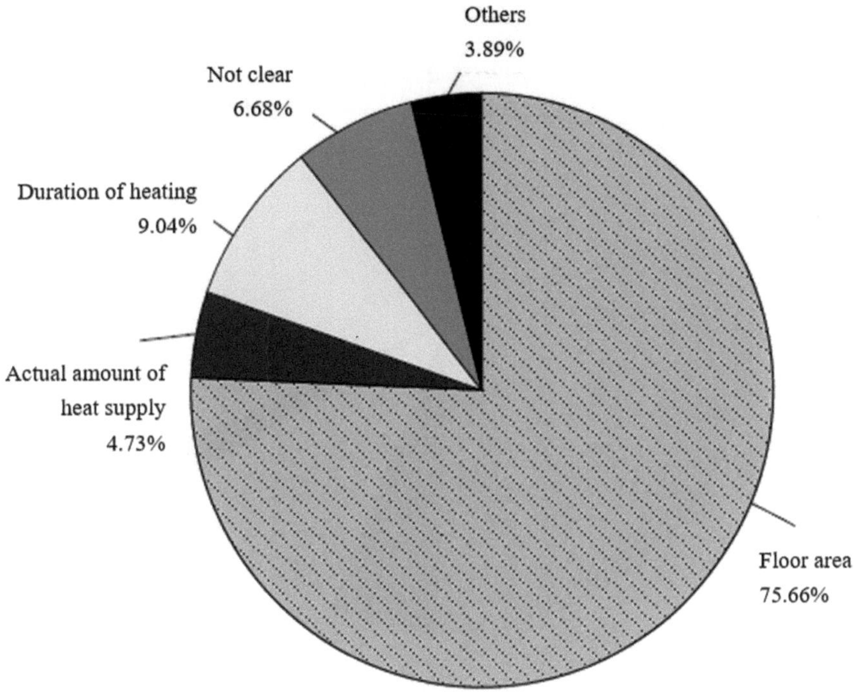


**Fig. 42** Pricing of district heating

sidies from the government, neighborhood or employer of household members and 25.58% received support from relatives, friends or others (Fig. 43).

(2) Household heating

1,101 samples used household heating (including those using both central and household heating) and claimed to own 1,532 pieces of household heating equipment in total, 1.39 piece per household on average. 97.55% of the households owned 0–3 pieces of household heating equipment and 2.45% had no such equipment. In our survey, we requested information for a maximum of 3 pieces of household heating equipment from each household and obtained the detailed information of 1,485 pieces of such equipment. As shown in Fig. 44, the main household heating equipment was (wood/coal) burners and heatable brick beds, accounting for 28.75% and 23.70% of the total respectively. The other commonly used household heating equipment included electric radiator heaters, household air conditioners and boilers. Electric heating equipment (e.g., air conditioners) accounted for 31.85% of the total, while non-electric ones accounted for 68.15%.

The major fuel for household heating was firewood and coal. 29.73% of the household heating equipment used firewood and 51.05% used coal, as shown in Fig. 45. It's noteworthy that although over 30% of the respondents owned electric

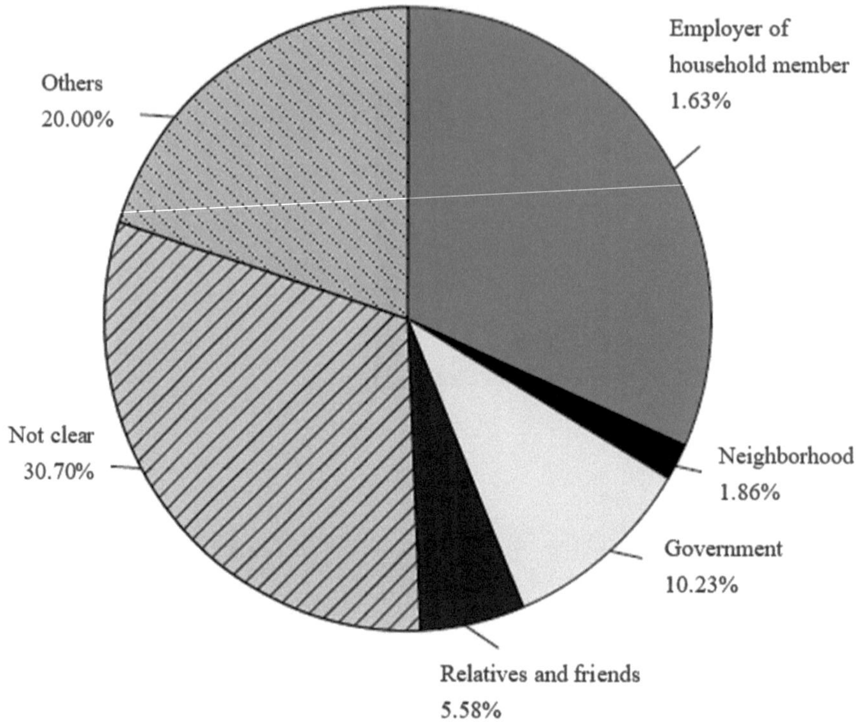


**Fig. 43** People or entities responsible for payment of district heating fee

heating equipment, only 1.60% of the total used them for space heating, which meant that the usage of electric heating equipment in many households was very low.

The duration of heating per year and the hours of use per day for household heating was as shown in Figs. 46 and 47. It can be seen that the heating duration for a major proportion of these households was 2–4 months, slightly shorter than the duration of district heating. The hours of use per day was polarizing, no more than 10 h for 64.57% of the households using household heating and more than 16 h for 22.90% of them.

In terms of the heated area, among the families using household heating, only 19.1% had heating for all the rooms, while 55.6% had heating only in the master bedroom. The heated area was largely 10–70 $m^2$, accounting for 72.5% of the total.

## 5.2 *Water Heaters*

45.09% of the 3,863 sample households did not have any water heater. The other 2,121 households owned 2,189 water heaters in total. Most of the households owned 1 water heater per household (accounting for 97.08% of the households with water

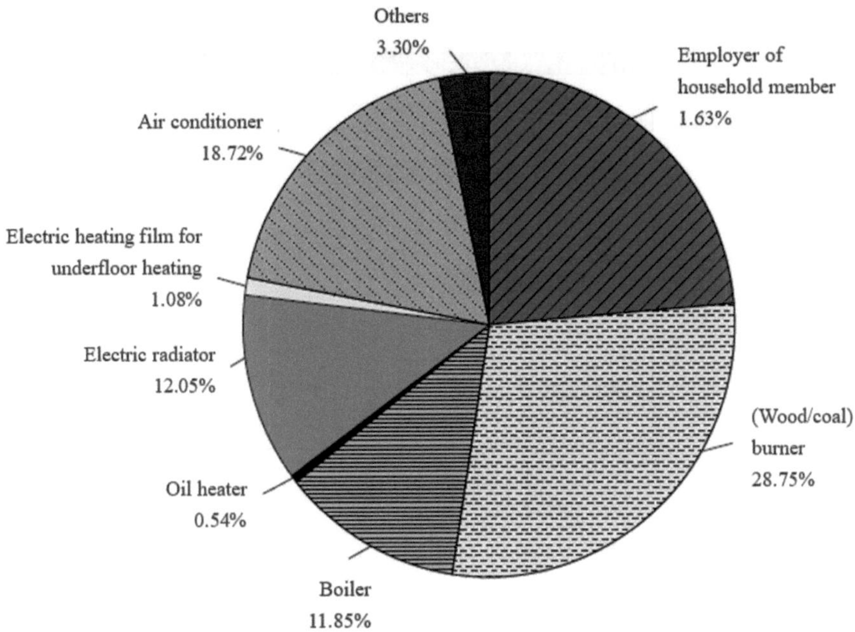


**Fig. 44** Distribution of household-based heating equipment

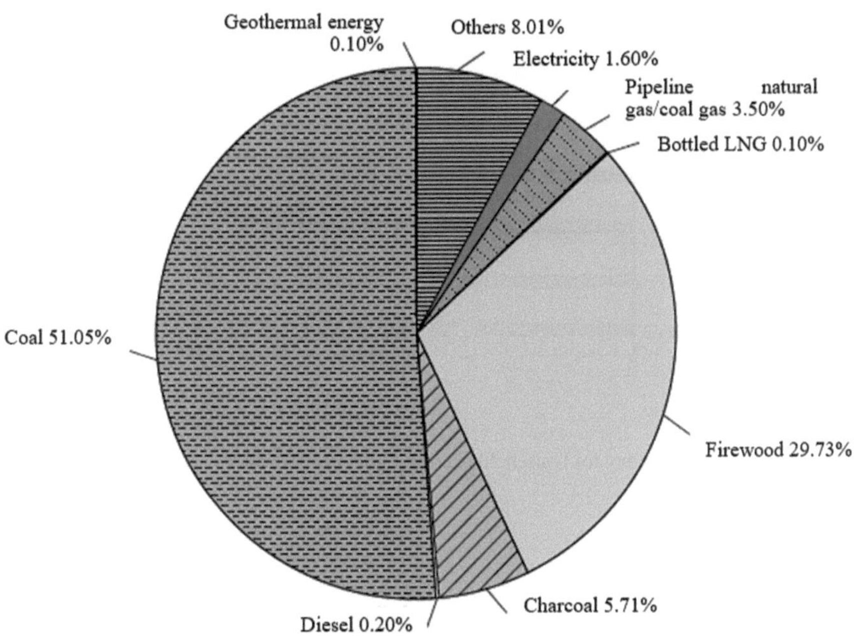


**Fig. 45** Distribution of fuel for household heating

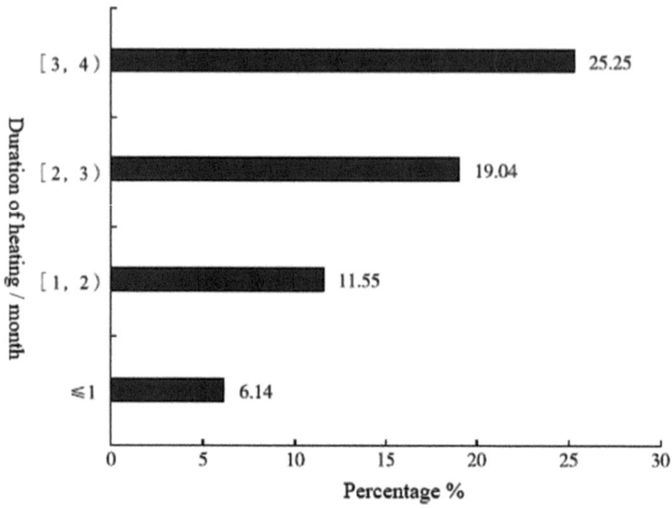


**Fig. 46** Duration of household heating

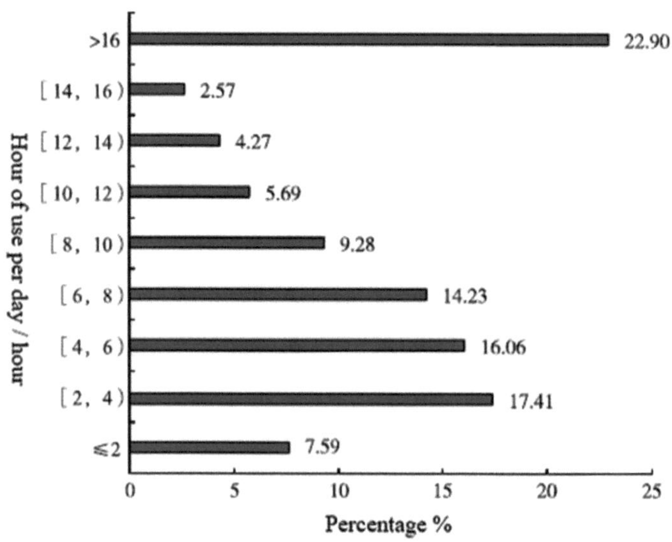


**Fig. 47** Hour of use per day for household heating

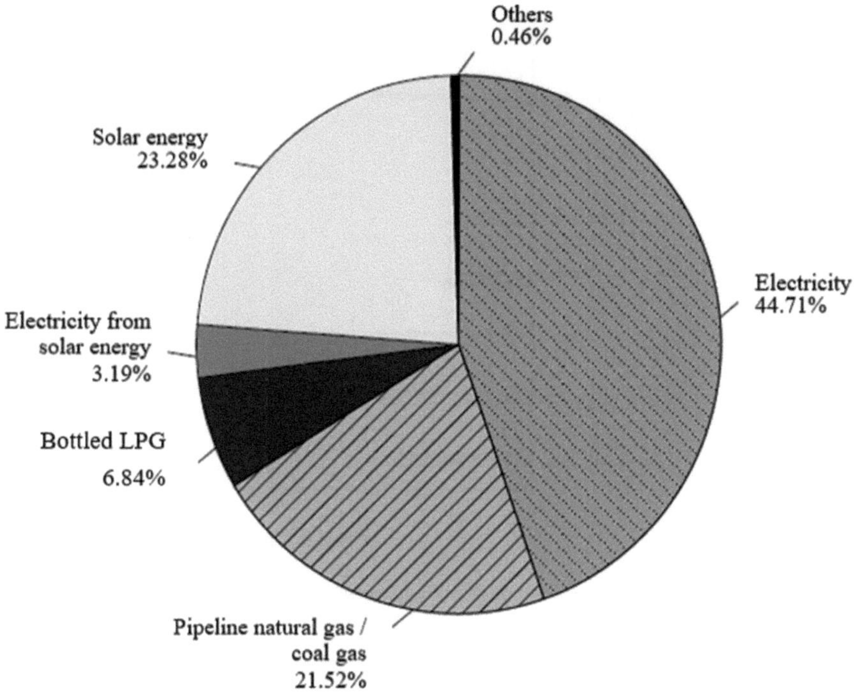


**Fig. 48** Types of fuel for water heaters

heater) and very few owned several. Since we requested information for a maximum of two water heaters from each household, we gathered data of 2,183 water heaters, 55.7% of which were storage water heaters and 44.3% were demand-type. 44.71% of the water heaters of the respondents were powered by electricity, 26.47% by solar energy or electricity from solar energy and 28.36% by bottled LPG or pipeline natural gas/coal gas (Fig. 48).

The distribution of frequency and duration of use of water heaters are as shown in Figs. 49 and 50. Concerning the frequency of use, most of the water heaters were used at least once per day. Concerning the duration of use, 91.81% of the total were used for no more than 60 min each time. Concerning the energy efficiency labelling, 51.26% of the total did not have energy efficiency label, 39.11% were of Grade 1–2 and 8.87% were of Grade 3–4.

## 5.3 *Air Conditioning*

The air conditioning equipment we covered in the survey was mainly air conditioners and electric fans. 55.94% of the 3,863 samples did not have air conditioners. The

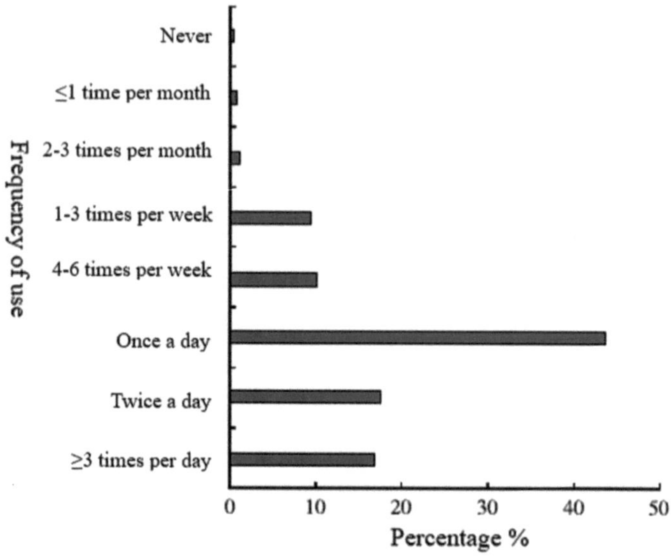


**Fig. 49** Distribution of frequency of use of water heaters

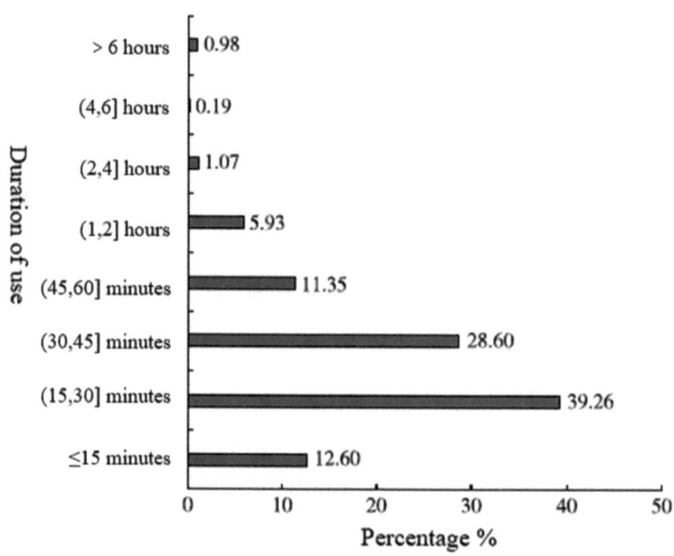


**Fig. 50** Duration of each use of water heaters

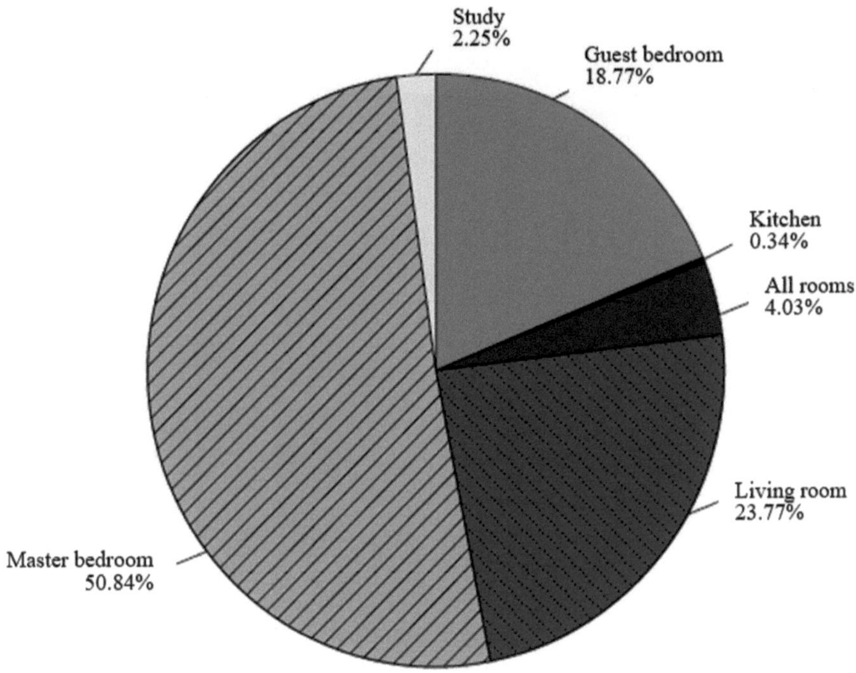


**Fig. 51** Working area of air conditioners

other 1,702 households, 63% of which had only one air conditioner, owned 2,626 air conditioners in total. We obtained data about 2,618 air conditioners, 95.38% of which were split type, 85.84% had power of no more than 3,600 w (1.5 HP), 56.76% had variable frequency and 43.24% had fixed frequency. 79.6% of the air conditioners were purchased after 2005. As shown in Fig. 51, 69.61% of the air conditioners were used in bedrooms (including master bedrooms and guest bedrooms) and 23.77% were used in living rooms.

As shown in Fig. 52, 90.76% of the air conditioners were used for air conditioning for no more than 4 months per year, and many were used for 2–3 months. Since most of the air conditioners were used for cooling bedrooms, they were seldomly used for more than 8 h/day. 80.73% of the total were used for cooling for no more than 6 h/day (Fig. 53).

A large proportion of the air conditioners had energy efficiency labels and 60.64% of the total were of Grade 1–3. 91.84% of the air conditioners were purchased without any subsidies and only 3.39% of the total were purchased with subsidies for rural residents to purchase electrical appliances.

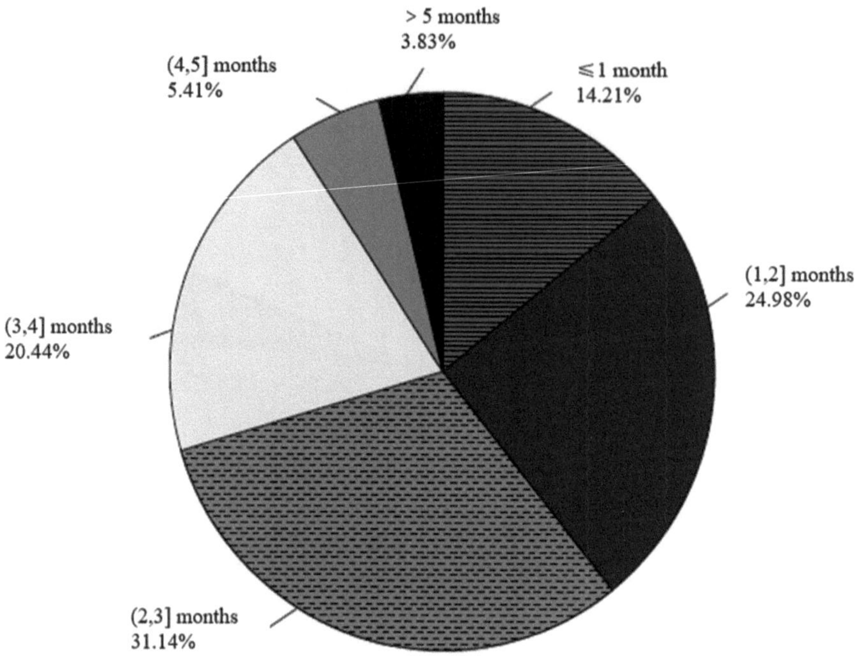


**Fig. 52** Duration of use of air conditioners

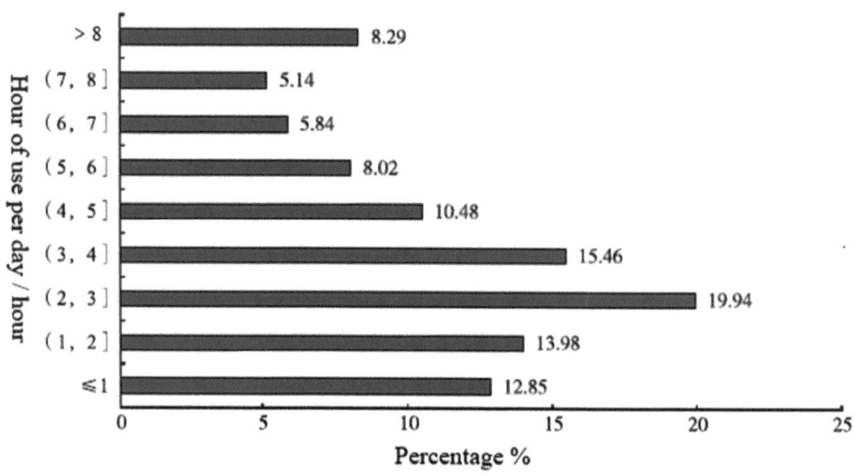


**Fig. 53** Average hour of use per day of air conditioners

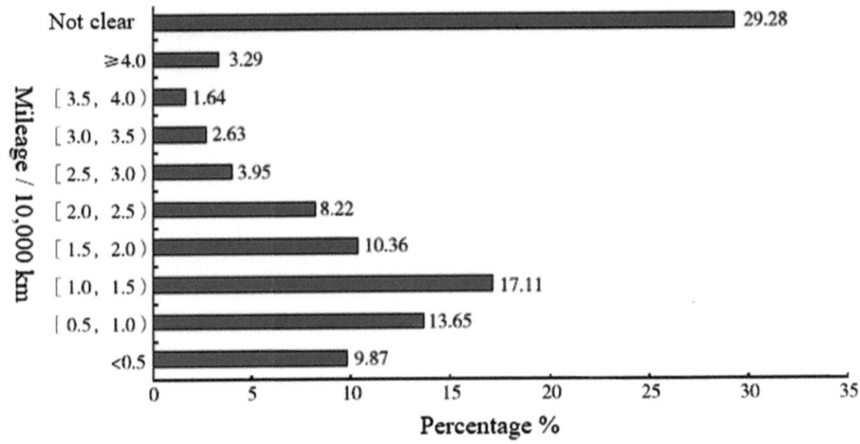


**Fig. 54** Mileage of households in 2014

# 6 Statistical Description of Transport

17.2% of the 3,863 respondents purchased vehicles, including 478 sedans, 9 pickup trucks, 20 SUVs, 64 vans, 24 trucks, 6 agricultural trucks and 4 other vehicles. If sedans, pickup trucks and SUVs are all considered cars, the number of car samples would be 507, meaning 13.1 cars per 100 households and 0.054 cars per capita on average. The car ownership in general is low.

Rapid increase in car ownership and mileage causes pressure on transport. According to the mileage covered by the households in 2014 (Fig. 54), the mileage of 9.87% of the cars was no more than 5,000 km, 13.65% was 5,000–10,000 km and 17.11% was 10,000–15,000 km. In addition, around 30.1% of the cars had mileage of more than 15,000 km. On average, the average mileage of the sample households in 2014 was 10,943 km.

As shown in Fig. 55, the accumulated mileage up to 2014 was evenly distributed. The accumulated mileage for 8.22% of the cars was less than 10,000 km, 9.05% was 10,000–20,000 km, 11.02% was 20,000–30,000 km, 12.83% was 30,000–50,000 km, 12.50% was 50,000–80,000 km and 16.29% was over 80,000 km. Meanwhile, the owners of 183 cars (approximately accounting for 30.10% of the total) did not know the accumulated mileage of their cars.

Concerning the age of cars (from the date of manufacture to the end of 2014), 36.35% of the total were less than 3 years old, 40.62% were 3–6 years old, 14.47% were 6–10 years old and 6.09% were older than 10 years. In addition, owners of 20.47% of the cars did not know the age of their cars. If cars with engine capacities of less than 1.6 L were considered small-displacement cars, 34.21% of the total (608 sample observations) were small-displacement ones. Meanwhile, 145 respondents did not know the engine capacity of their cars. Concerning the type of fuel for cars, 565 effective samples (43 respondents did not know the type of fuel of their cars)

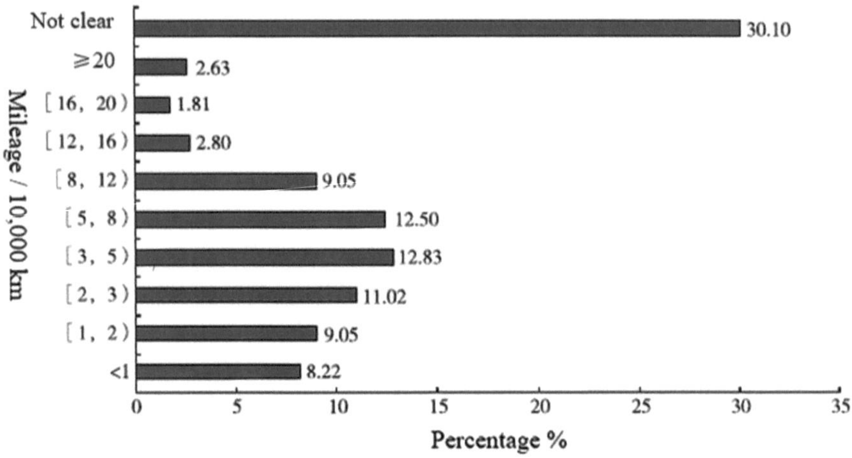


**Fig. 55** Accumulated mileage of households up to 2014

used electricity, hybrid fuel, diesel, ethyl fuel and natural gas, but the main type of fuel was#93 gasoline. 406 of these cars used #93 gasoline, accounting for 66.78% of the total. 115 cars used #97 gasoline, accounting for 18.91% of the total. 3 cars used ethyl fuel, 29 cars (mainly agricultural trucks (tricycles) and trucks (quadricycles)) used diesel, 2 cars used hybrid fuel (gasoline and natural gas) and 10 cars used electricity.

Figure 56 shows the actual fuel consumption per 100 km of vehicles, which was below 6 L for 7.00% of the cars, 6–8 (excluded) L and 8–10 (excluded) L for 20.00 and 19.00% of the cars, 10–12 (excluded) liters for 12.00% of the cars and more than 12 L for 4.00% of the cars.

Concerning payment of the fuel cost, 399 households had such expenditure in 2014, 96.7% of which bore all the cost, 1.3% did not bear any, 1% bore 0–1/3 of the cost, 0.5% bore 1/3–2/3 and 0.5% bore more than 2/3. For households that did not bear any such cost, 54% had the cost covered by employers, 31% by relatives and friends and the remaining by anonymous sources.

# 7 Household Income and Expense and Energy Consumption

## *7.1 Basic Information About Household Income and Expense*

For household income, 3,541 effective samples were collected, the sample mean of which was RMB69,788. It included 1,937 effective samples of rural households,

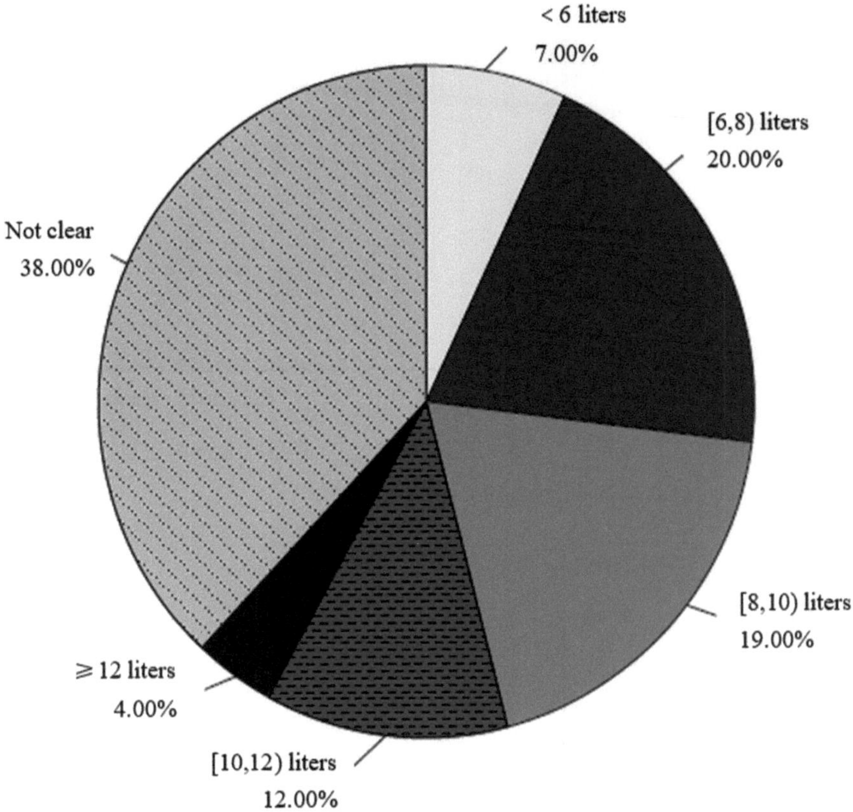


**Fig. 56** Fuel consumption per 100 km of household vehicles

the sample mean of which was RMB50,154, and 1,604 effective samples of urban households, the sample mean of which was RMB93,497. For household expense, 3,243 effective samples were collected, the sample mean of which was RMB36,080. It included 1,797 effective samples of rural households, the sample mean of which was RMB28,136, and 1,446 effective samples of urban households, the sample mean of which was RMB45,960 (Fig. 57).

The survey results show that among the rural respondents, the annual income of 487 households, 25.1% of the total, was less than RMB10,000 in 2014. The annual income for more than half of the rural respondents in 2014 was RMB10,000–50,000. Only 6.5% had annual income of more than RMB100,000 and 1.8% had more than RMB200,000 (Fig. 59). Concerning the household expense, among the 1,797 rural households, 32.6% of the respondents had household expense of no more than RMB10,000 in 2014, 42.0 and 15.5% of them had annual household expense of RMB10,000–30,000 and RMB30,000–50,000. Only 2.3% of the rural respondents had annual household expense exceeding RMB100,000 and 0.8% had more than RMB200,000 (Fig. 58).

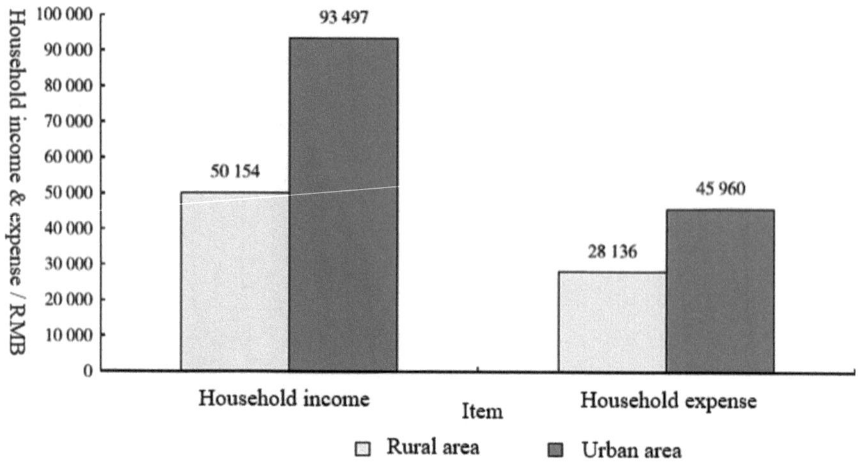


**Fig. 57** Household income and expense in 2014

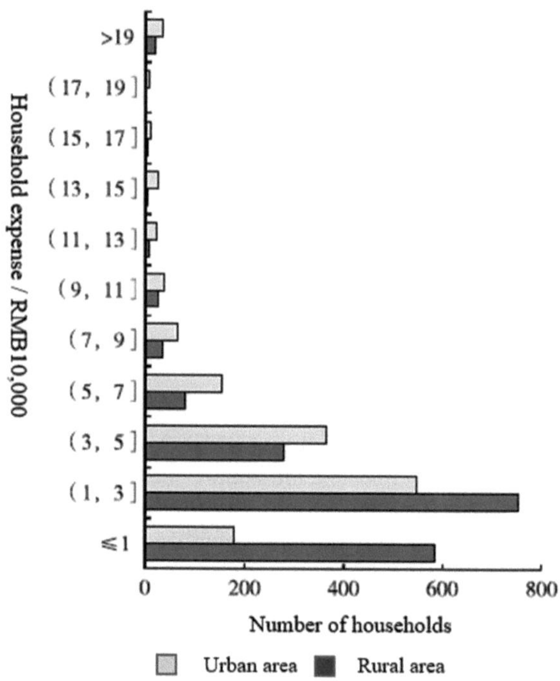


**Fig. 58** Household expense in 2014

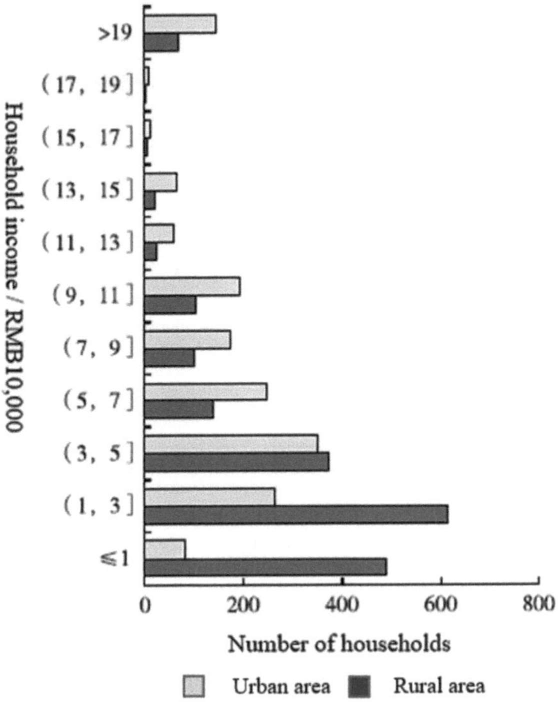


**Fig. 59** Household income in 2014

Among the 1,604 urban households, the annual income of 81 households was no more than RMB10,000, accounting for 5% of the total. 38.4% of these respondents had annual income of RMB10,000–50,000, 19.4% had annual income of more than RMB100,000 and 5.2% had more than RMB200,000. Concerning the household expense, among the 1,446 urban households, 12.4% of the total had household expense of no more than RMB10,000 in 2014, 38 and 25.2% of these respondents had annual household expense of RMB10,000–30,000 and RMB30,000–50,000. 7.4% of these respondents had annual household expense exceeding RMB100,000 and 1.8% had annual expense of more than RMB200,000.

In terms of the components of household expense (Figs. 60 and 61), the expenditure on food and housing accounted for large proportions, 32.89% and 16.30% of the total respectively. The expenditure on health care and education was 13.53% and 12.16% of the total respectively. The expenditure on clothing, household supplies and transport did not have great differences, accounting for 7–10% of the total respectively.

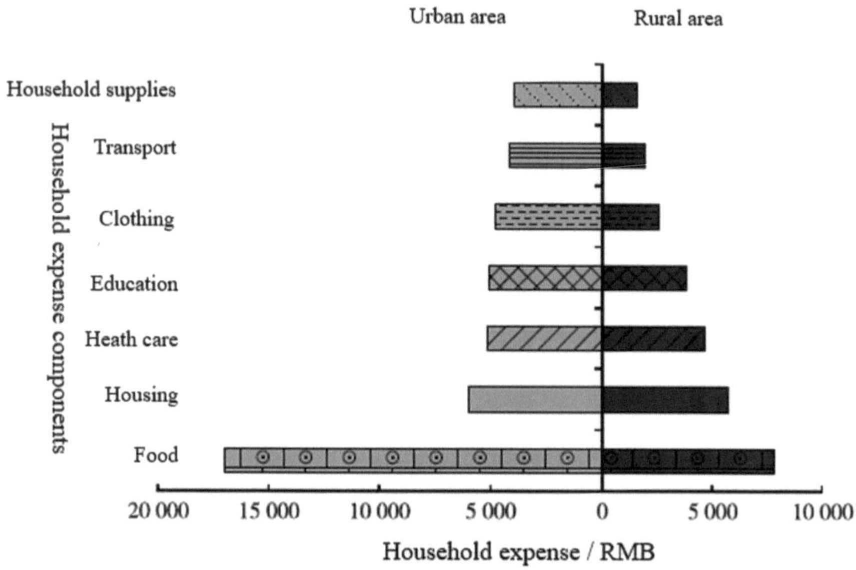


**Fig. 60** Components of household expense in rural and urban areas

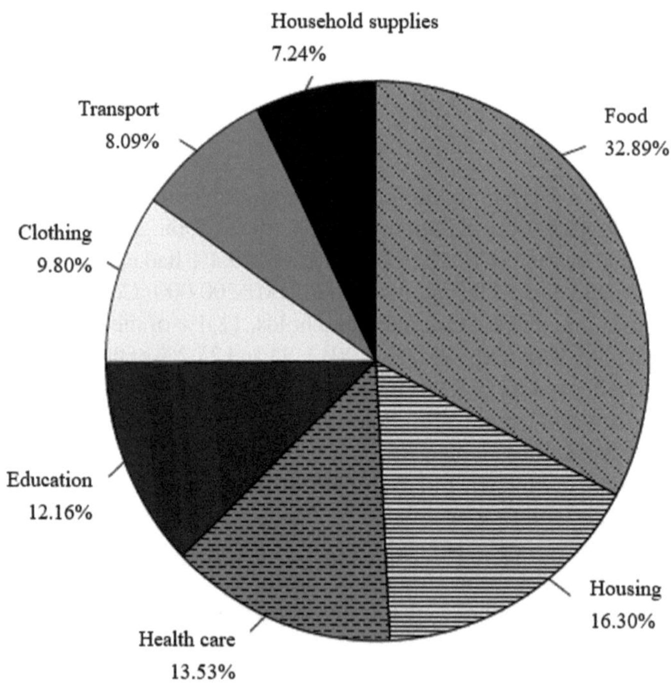


**Fig. 61** Components of household expense

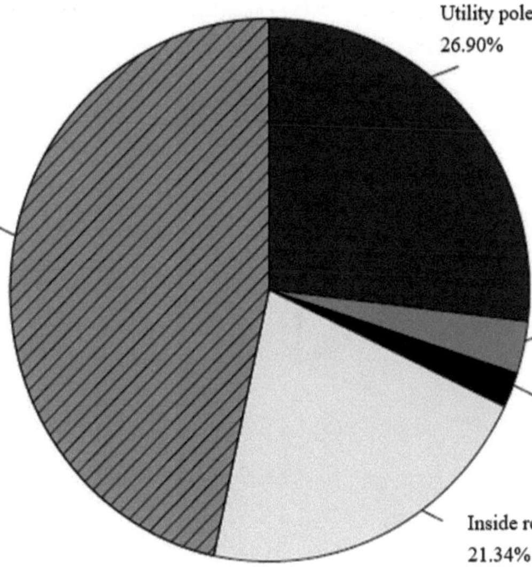


**Fig. 62** Installation position of electricity meters

## *7.2 Basic Information of Electricity Consumption*

The survey results show that 99.8% of the respondents had electricity consumption, 6 rural households and 1 urban household had no electricity consumption. 95.1% of the respondents had individual electricity meters for each household, 46.64% of which were installed in corridors, 26.90% on utility poles outside residence, 21.34% inside the residence and 3.06% in the respondents' communities, village or neighborhood committees (Fig. 62).

Concerning the types of electricity meters, 44.1% of the respondents used smart meters, 33.8% and 11.9% used mechanical meters and smart card meters respectively and 10.2% did not know the type of their meters.

In this survey, 95.5% of the 3,856 effective samples knew the amount of electricity consumption and electricity expense per month. Among the 3,682 effective samples of collecting information about electricity consumption, the main channels for them to learn about electricity consumption were bills from power companies or property companies and inquiring meter readers, accounting for 36.51% and 33.45% of the total samples respectively (Fig. 63).

Concerning payment of the electric bills, among the 3,856 effective samples, 64.7% of the respondents paid their bills after consumption and 34.1% pre-paid through smart cards. Concerning the payment options (Fig. 64), the majority were payment at offices of power companies and doorstep payment collection (by meter readers, electricians, village committees, property companies or landlords), accounting for 53.58% and 18.52% of the total respectively. In addition, 14.86% of the respondents used automatic payment service of banks to settle the electric bills.

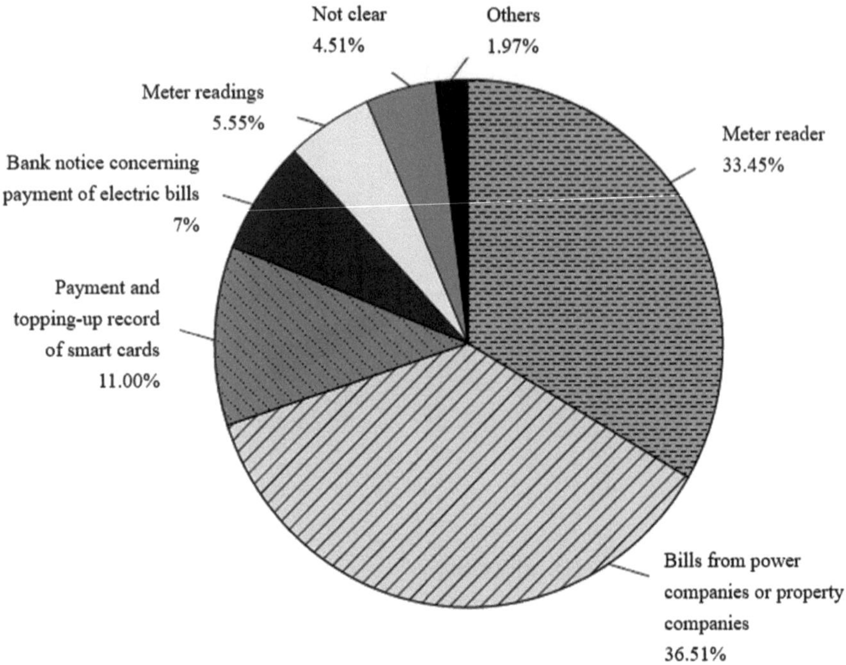


**Fig. 63** Ways to obtain information about electricity consumption

Concerning the frequency of payment, 61.7% of the respondents settled the electric bills monthly, 27.1% quarterly, 6.8% half-yearly and 4.4% paid by others.

## *7.3 Household Electricity Consumption*

The sample observation of annual electricity consumption totaled 2,898, the annual electricity consumption of which amounted to 1,628.2 kWh. 15.5% of the samples consumed no more than 500 kWh through the year and 63.8% consumed less than 1,500 kWh. 5% of the respondents consumed more than 4,000 kwh annually (Fig. 65).

Regarding the seasonal data about 2,873 effective samples, the average electricity consumption per household was 474.7 kWh in summer and 371.8 kWh per household in winter. Concerning the expenditure on electricity, the average annual expenditure on electricity of the respondents was RMB1,793.0, accounting for 2.6% of the annual expenditure. 98.0% of the respondents bore all the expenditure on electricity.

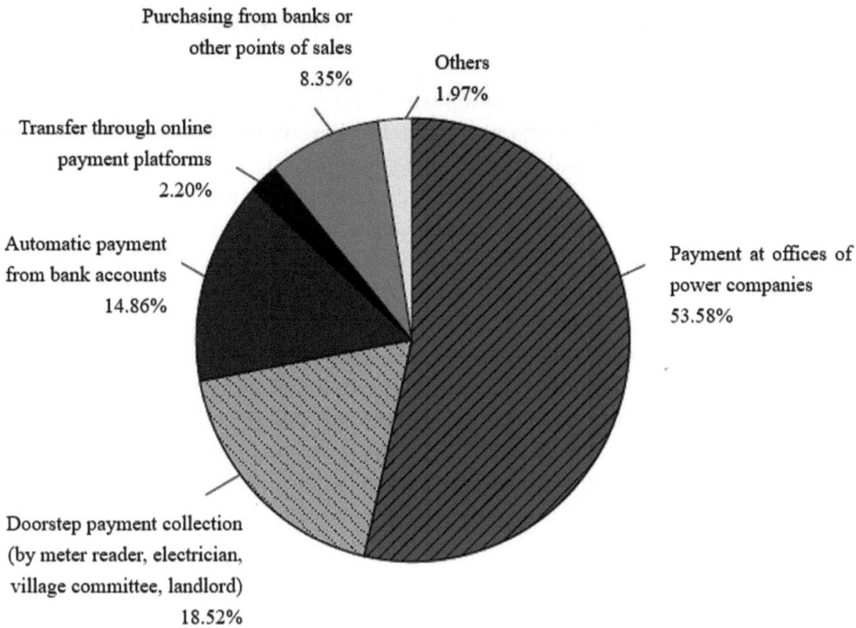


**Fig. 64** Payment of electric bills

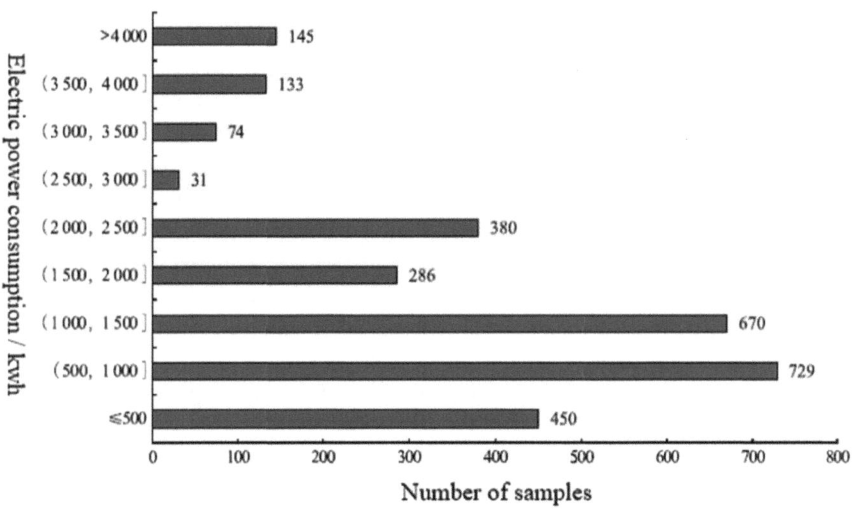


**Fig. 65** Household electricity consumption

## 7.4 Respondents' Knowledge of Electricity Pricing Policies

Compared with electricity prices for industrial and commercial sectors, the residential electricity price in China has been low. To alleviate the tension between electricity demand and supply and promote energy conservation and emission reduction in China, it is important to manage electricity demand using pricing policies and direct residents to use electricity rationally and implement electricity conservation. At present, there are two main residential electricity pricing policies for demand-side management, tiered pricing and peak-valley TOU pricing. For tiered electricity pricing, tiered prices are fixed based on the amount of electricity consumed and the price increases to a higher level with the increase in consumption of electric power. Peak-valley TOU electricity pricing is a form of time-based electricity pricing system, in which 24 h are divided to many sections of peaks and valleys and the electricity price varies depending on the time of day: high at the peak and low at the valley.

China enacted the tiered electricity pricing system nationwide since July 1st, 2012. During our survey, however, only several provinces and municipalities adopted tiered electricity pricing and peak-valley electricity pricing. We enquired the residents about their knowledge of the two pricing policies. Results show that among the 2,897 effective samples, 25.75% of the respondents were aware of the peak-valley pricing policy, 74.9% of which knew whether the peak-valley pricing system was effective in their provinces, and 40.2% of the respondents had received notices from power companies about such pricing system. The peak-valley electricity pricing is generally not enacted without application of the consumers, so, the householders shall take valid identity documents and submit applications at the local office of power companies to start using such pricing system. According to the survey, 61.9% of the respondents were willing to submit such applications and 32.6% were not. Concerning the reasons for unwillingness to submit applications for peak-valley electricity pricing (Fig. 66), 7.4% of these respondents were concerned that it might lead to rising electricity tariff because their household electricity consumption was largely during peak hours and it was difficult to adjust the time of electricity use; 18.3% considered it troublesome to adjust their electricity consumption behavior despite the possibility of cutting down electricity tariff; 18.2% were doubtful whether peak-valley electricity pricing could cut down electricity tariff.

Unlike peak-valley electricity pricing, tiered electricity pricing was comparatively in wide use. In this survey, 39.2% of the respondents knew tiered electricity pricing, 72.2% of which knew whether the tiered electricity pricing policy was effective in their provinces, 39.8% of the respondents had received notices from power companies about such pricing system. Concerning the acceptance of tiered electricity pricing, 49.0% of the respondents had adopted tiered electricity pricing and 36.9% had not. The first tier of electricity consumption can be adapted to the family size as shown in the household register (the larger the family, the more electricity consumption allowed in the first tier), but the householders shall take valid identity documents and submit applications at the local office of power companies. 68.5% of the respondents were willing to submit such applications. The reasons for unwillingness to submit

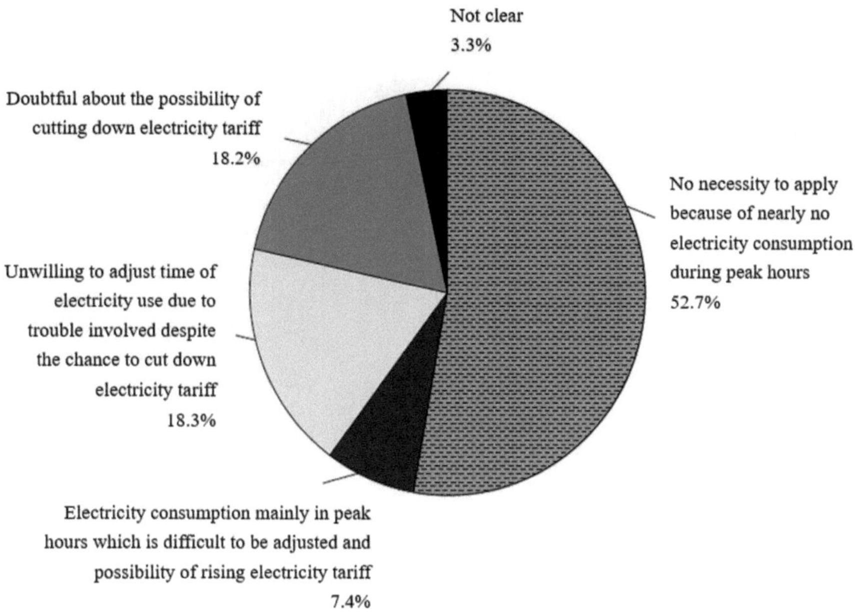


**Fig. 66** Reasons of unwillingness to apply for peak-valley pricing

applications for tiered electricity pricing were similar to the case of peak-valley pricing. 40.22% of the respondents unwilling to submit such applications considered it unnecessary, because their electricity consumption had been within the range of the first tier; 22.01% considered it troublesome to go through the procedures to increase the maximum electricity consumption of the first tier despite the possibility of cutting down electricity tariff; 33.82% were doubtful whether increased electricity in the first tier could cut down electricity tariff (Fig. 67).

## *7.5 Household Consumption of Other Energy Sources*

Figure 68 depicts the residential consumption of other energy sources. Not considering electricity, the most-used energy source of the respondents was bottled LPG and pipeline natural gas, accounting for 33.2% and 24.8% of the total respectively. Respondents consuming coal blocks and honeycomb briquette accounted for 10.8 and 4.8% of the total. Straw was also common energy source consumed by the respondents, but excrements of livestock and poultry was only used by a small percentage of the respondents, around 0.6% of the total.

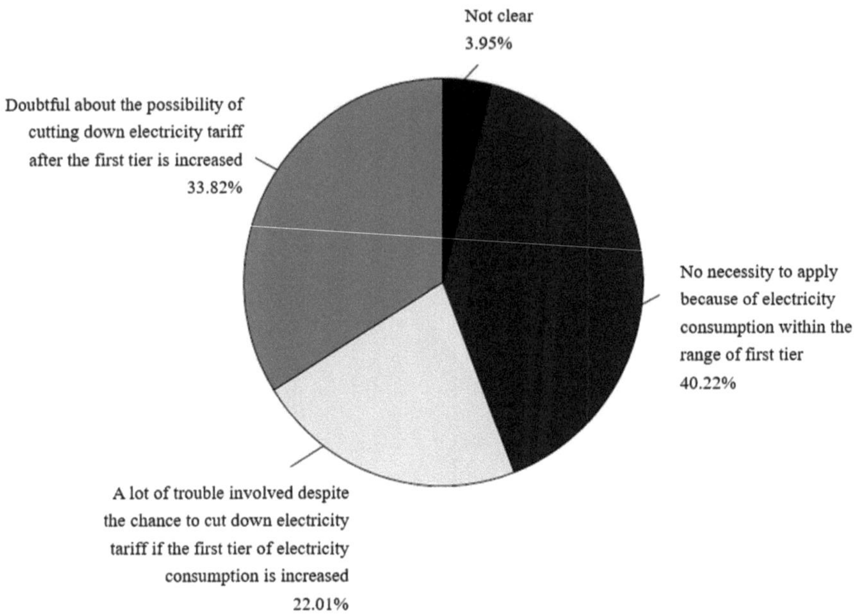


**Fig. 67** Reasons of unwillingness to apply for increase of the amount of electricity consumption in the first tier

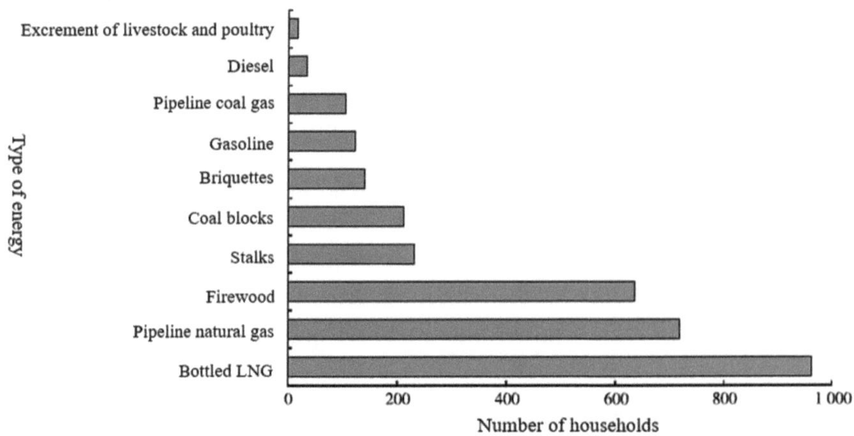


**Fig. 68** Household consumption of other energy

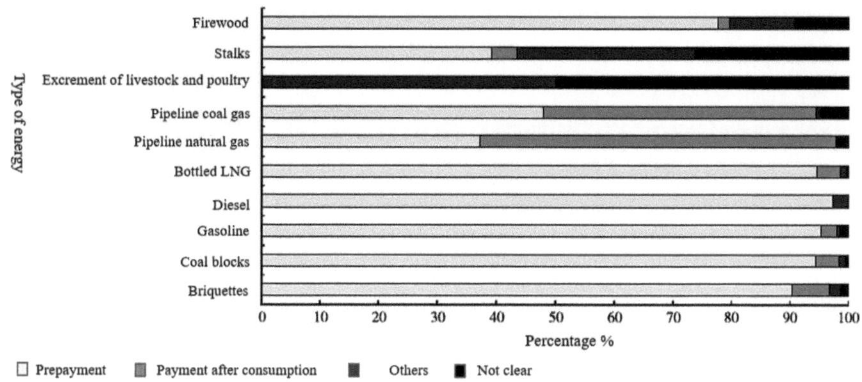


**Fig. 69** Payment options for energy cost

Figure 69 shows the payment options of various energy consumption. On average, 73.1% of the respondents prepaid before consumption and 24.1% paid after consumption. Meanwhile, 64.2% of the respondents prepaid for electricity before consumption. In terms of the payment collection options, 54.2% of the respondents said that they would pay at the local office of energy suppliers and 18.4% said that the suppliers offered payment collection service at doorstep. Concerning the frequency of payment, 61.5% of the respondents paid monthly and 27.3% paid every 2–3 months. 6.9% of the respondents said that the interval between two payments of electricity tariff was more than 6 months.

# Chapter 3
# Methods for Estimating Residential Energy Consumption

**Shimei Wu**

## 1 Basic Approaches and Methods

Daily life of households incurs energy consumption to various degrees. Different activities require different energy sources and more than one type of energy sources may be consumed in a single activity. Moreover, due to differences in accessibility and cost of energy sources in different regions and households, the energy sources involved in energy-consuming activities of households vary in regions. The energy consumption amount also varies in households due to differences in activity frequencies. Therefore, in calculation of household energy consumption, the energy sources consumed in each energy-consuming activity of each household shall be specified and the tested energy consumption shall be calculated based on characteristics of the activities (e.g., frequency of use, duration of use, etc.). Based on calculation of the various energy sources consumed in household activities, the total household energy consumption can be obtained.

Supposing that $i$ households consume $n$ types of energy sources (such as coal, natural gas, LPG and electricity, etc.) for $m$ types of energy-consuming activities (such as cooking, use of household electrical appliances, space heating and air conditioning, etc.), the consumption of the $n$th type of energy in the $m$th type of activity by the $i$th household is expressed as $\text{Energy}_{i,m,n}$, which can be converted to standard energy consumption measured in kilogram of coal equivalent based on the coefficient $\text{coef}_n$ of converting to coal equivalent for each energy source.

The annual energy consumption of the $i$th household is calculated according to Formula 1.

$$\text{Energy}_i = \sum_{m=1}^{M}\sum_{n=1}^{N} \text{Energy}_{i,m,n} \times \text{coe}f_n \tag{1}$$

S. Wu (✉)
Renmin University of China, Beijing, China
e-mail: wushimei@ruc.edu.cn



X. Zheng and C. Wei (eds.), *Household Energy Consumption in China: 2016 Report*, https://doi.org/10.1007/978-981-13-7523-1_3

The *n*th type of energy consumed by the *i*th household is calculated as follows:

$$\mathrm{Energy}_{i,n} = \sum_{m=1}^{M} \mathrm{Energy}_{i,m,n} \times \mathit{coef}_n \tag{2}$$

Similarly, the energy consumption of the *i*th household in the *m*th type of activity is as follows:

$$\mathrm{Energy}_{i,m} = \sum_{n=1}^{N} \mathrm{Energy}_{i,m,n} \times \mathit{coef}_n \tag{3}$$

This survey covered 15 energy sources, namely honeycomb briquettes, charcoal, gasoline/diesel/kerosene, other fuel oil, LPG, pipeline natural gas, pipeline coal gas, biogas, excrement of livestock and poultry, firewood, straw, electricity, district heating, solar energy and geothermal heat.

The residential energy-consuming activities were divided into five categories, namely cooking, space heating, air conditioning, household electrical appliances and water heating. For comparison with other researches in this field, we calculated the energy consumption of transportation for personal purpose in households, but we only gave it a descriptive statistical analysis in Chap. 5 and did not include it in the total household energy consumption. The energy consumption of cooking equipment and household electrical appliances is mainly determined by their energy consumption per hour (such as output power of electrical appliances and fuel consumption per hour of non-electric cooking equipment) and frequency and duration of use. Based on calculation in the first and second household energy consumption surveys, the energy efficiency and technical characteristics of the equipment covered in the first and second surveys will be considered and serve as references while estimating the parameters to be used. To guarantee the validity of comparison between the calculation results of the three household energy consumption surveys, the same methods of choosing parameters and calculation as used in the first and second surveys were used in relation to the parameters of equipment in the third survey. The energy consumption of residential space heating is influenced by means of heating. In district heating system, energy consumption of space heating is listed as a separate type of energy consumption. Due to inaccessibility of technical features of heat sources, information about fuels and heat loss rate in pipelines in regions where the households were located, we estimated the energy consumption of district heating by calculating the insulation of residences. In household heating system, the energy consumption of space heating is influenced by energy consumption per hour (such as the output power of air conditioners and consumption rate of firewood) and duration of heating.

After calculating the energy consumption based on the survey results of samples, we adjusted the weights of the calculation results according to the percentage of household numbers in various provinces to the national figure as revealed in the data of the 6th national population census in China. $\mathrm{Energy}_{\mathrm{national}}^{w}$ represents the weighted annual energy consumption of an average Chinese household. $N_k$ represents the number of households in $k$ province and $N$ represents the number of households in China. $\text{Energy}_{i,k}$ represents the annual energy consumption of the $i$th household in samples of $k$ province. $I_k$ represents the number of households covered in the survey in $k$ province. $\frac{\sum_{i=1}^{I_k} \text{Energy}_{i,k}}{N_{I_k}}$ represents the average energy consumption per household in $k$ province obtained from our calculation according to the questionnaire data.

$$\text{Energy}^{w}_{\text{national}} = \sum_{k=1}^{K} \frac{N_k}{N} \times \frac{\sum_{i=1}^{I_k} \text{Energy}_{i,k}}{N_{I_k}} \tag{4}$$

In the following sections, the energy consumed in different categories of energy-consuming activities of households will be estimated according to their characteristics.

## 2 Estimation of Energy Consumption of Kitchen Equipment

The kitchen equipment covered in the survey included main stoves such as wood-burning stoves, clay ovens, stoves burning honeycomb briquettes, oil stoves, induction cooktops, kerosene stoves, biogas stoves and solar cookers, etc., and other cooking equipment such as electric rice cookers, pressure cookers, microwave ovens, ovens and electric kettles, etc. Fuel for cooking equipment included honeycomb briquettes, gasoline, diesel, kerosene, bottled LPG, pipeline natural gas, pipeline coal gas, biogas, excrement of livestock and poultry, firewood, straw, electricity, solar energy and geothermal heat, etc.

The following factors shall be considered in calculation of energy consumption of kitchen equipment: energy consumption per hour of equipment (e.g., output power of electrical appliances), frequency of use per day, average duration per use and number of days in use per year. The number of hours in use per year of cooking equipment is calculated by multiplying its frequency of use per day, average duration per use and number of days in use per year. The number of days in use per year refers to the number of days the residents spent in their residences (when the survey was conducted) per year. The annual energy consumption of kitchen equipment is calculated according to Formula 5:

$$\begin{aligned}\text{Energy}_{\text{kitchen equipment}}\ (\text{kgce/year}) &= \text{energy consumption per hour}_{\text{kitchen equipment}}\ (\text{kgce/hour}) \\ &\times \text{number of hours in use}_{\text{kitchen equipment}}\ (\text{hours/year})\end{aligned} \tag{5}$$

Except for electrical equipment for which the output power was adopted as the energy consumption per hour, the energy consumption per hour of other types of stoves was determined according to the relevant literature and technical standards of the industry. The consumption rate is 0.33 kg/h for coal stoves, 2.00 kg/h for stoves burning firewood and straw, 0.40 $m^3$/h for stoves burning pipeline natural gas, coal gas and biogas and 0.31 kg/h for stoves burning bottled LPG.

# 3 Estimation of Energy Consumption of Household Electrical Appliances

The household electrical appliances covered in the questionnaire mainly included refrigerators, freezers, washing machines, drying machines, televisions sets, personal computers and light bulbs, all powered by electricity. The following factors shall be considered in calculation of energy consumption of household electrical appliances: output power, capacity, frequency of use per day, average duration per use, number of days in use per year and energy efficiency, etc. of the equipment.

## *3.1 Method for Estimating Energy Consumption of Refrigerators and Freezers*

While estimating the power consumption of refrigerators and freezers, due to absence of data about the output power and duration of use of such equipment, we calculated the power consumption based on their capacities, baseline of power consumption and energy efficiency. First, the refrigerators were divided into several types depending on their capacities and an average capacity was determined for each type: 50 L for small refrigerators, 112.5 L for medium-sized refrigerators, 200 L for large refrigerators and 250 L for extra-large refrigerators (with capacities of more than 250 L). Second, according to the calculation method prescribed in the *Maximum Allowable Values of Energy Consumption and Energy Efficiency Grades for Household Refrigerators* (GB 12021.2-2008), we estimated the baseline of electricity consumption of refrigerators. The calculation formula is as follows:

$$\text{Eenergy}_{\text{base}} = \left(M \times V_{\text{adj}} + N + \text{CH}\right) \times S_r/365$$
$$V_{\text{adj}} = \sum_{c=1}^{n} V_c \times W_c \times F_c \times \text{CC} \tag{6}$$

Energy$_{\text{base}}$ in Formula 6 represents the baseline of electricity consumption measured in kWh/24 hours. $M$ represents the parameter measured in kWh/liter (values shown in Table 1). $N$ represents the parameter measured in kWh (values shown in Table 1). CH represents the correction coefficient of the variable temperature compartment. $S_r$ represents the correction coefficient of the transmitting automatic refrigerating function. $V_{adj}$ represents the adjusted volume measured in liters.

**Table 1** Energy consumption parameters of refrigerators

| Type | *M*/(kWh/liter) | *N*/kWh |
|---|---|---|
| 0-star refrigerator compartment | 0.221 | 233 |
| 1-star refrigerator compartment | 0.611 | 181 |
| 2-star refrigerator compartment | 0.428 | 233 |
| 3-star refrigerator compartment | 0.624 | 223 |
| Refrigerator-freezer | 0.697 | 272 |
| Frozen food compartment | 0.530 | 190 |
| Freezer compartment | 0.567 | 205 |

*n* represents the number of various compartments in refrigerators. $V_c$ represents the tested effective volume of compartments measured in liters. $F_c$ represents the parameter, which is 1.4 for compartments of frost-free refrigeration and 1.0 for other compartments. CC represents the correction coefficient of climate and $W_c$ represents the weighted coefficients of types of compartments.

We were unable to obtain detailed data about the type of refrigerator compartments to determine the values of *M* and *N*. Currently, most of the refrigerators use 2-star and 3-star refrigerator compartments. So, we used their mean values, namely, $M = 0.526$ and $N = 228$.

Finally, the energy efficiency of refrigerators was considered. According to the calculation method of energy efficiency index prescribed in the *Maximum Allowable Values of Energy Consumption and Energy Efficiency Grades for Household Refrigerators* (GB 12021.2-2008), the tested power consumption of a refrigerator is its baseline power consumption multiplied by the energy efficiency index. Since we could not determine the types of refrigerator compartments, we used the mean values of energy efficiency indexes for refrigerators of grade 2–5 energy efficiency. A low energy efficiency index 0.4 was determined for grade-1 refrigerators and 1 for refrigerators with no energy efficiency labels which are not subject to energy efficiency adjustment. The intervals of parameters after adjustment are as shown in Table 2.

**Table 2** Energy efficiency index (EEI) of refrigerators

| Energy efficiency grade | EEI (refrigerator-freezer) | EEI (other types) | EEI after adjustment |
|---|---|---|---|
| 1 | [0, 40%] | [0, 50%] | 0.4 |
| 2 | (40, 50%] | (50, 60%] | 0.5 |
| 3 | (50, 60%] | (60, 70%] | 0.6 |
| 4 | (60, 70%] | (70, 80%] | 0.7 |
| 5 | (70, 80%] | (80, 90%] | 0.8 |
| No energy efficiency label | / | / | 1 |

Therefore, the tested electricity consumption of refrigerators and freezers is calculated according to the following formula:

$$\text{Energy}_{test} = \eta \times (M \times V + N)/365 \quad (7)$$

$\text{Energy}_{test}$ in Formula 7 represents the tested electricity consumption measured in kWh/24 hours. $M$ represents the parameter measured in kWh/L, the value of which is 0.526 (for refrigerators) or 0.567 (for freezers). $N$ represents the parameter measured in kWh, the value which is 228 (for refrigerators) or 205 (for freezers). $V$ represents the volume of refrigerators measured in liters, the value of which was obtained from the survey. $\eta$ represents the adjusted energy efficiency index.

The calculation formula of tested electricity consumption for freezers is the same as that for refrigerators. While calculating the annual energy consumption of refrigerators and freezers, the number of days in use per year refers to the number of days the residents spent in their residences (when the survey was conducted) per year. The formula for calculating the annual tested energy consumption (measured in kilogram of coal equivalent) is as follows:

$$\begin{aligned}&\text{Energy}_{refrigerator/freezer}\ (\text{kgce/year}) = \text{Energy}_{refrigerator/freezer}\ (\text{kWh/day})\\&\quad \times \text{number of days in use}_{refrigerator/freezer}\ (\text{days/year})\\&\quad \times \text{coefficient for converting electricity consumption to coal equivalent (kgce/kWh)}\end{aligned} \quad (8)$$

## 3.2 *Method for Estimating Energy Consumption of Washing Machines and Drying Machines*

While estimating the electricity consumption of washing machines and drying machines, since data about power of these machines were obtained from the questionnaire, we may calculate the energy consumption according to their power and number of hours in use.

In calculation of the annual energy consumption of washing machines and drying machines, the number of days in use per year refers to the number of days the residents spent in their residences (when the survey was conducted) per year. The calculation formula is as follows:

$$\begin{aligned}&\text{Energy}_{washing\ machine/dring\ machine}\ (\text{kgce/year})\\&= \text{power of equipment}_{washing\ machine/drying\ machine}\ (\text{kWh})\\&\quad \times \text{number of hours in use}_{washing\ machine/dying\ machine}\ (\text{hours/year})\\&\quad \times \text{coefficient for converting electricity consumption to coal equivalent (kgce/kWh)}\end{aligned} \quad (9)$$

## 3.3 *Method for Estimating Energy Consumption of Television Sets*

While estimating the electricity consumption of television sets, since data about their power were obtained from the questionnaire, we can calculate the energy consumption of television sets according to their power and number of hours in use.

The electricity consumption of television sets is the reference power multiplied by average number of hours in use, which is subsequently corrected with the energy consumption efficiency. However, despite the data about availability of energy efficiency labels of television sets in the survey results, we failed to obtain data about their energy efficiency. Therefore, we were unable to consider the influence of their energy efficiency on electricity consumption. The formula for calculating electricity consumption of television sets is as follows:

$$\begin{aligned}&\text{Average energy consumption}_{\textit{television sets}}\ (\text{kWh/day})\\&=\text{number of hours in use}_{\textit{television sets}}\ (\text{hours/day})\\&\quad\times\text{power}_{\textit{television sets}}\ (\text{kWh})\end{aligned} \tag{10}$$

In calculation of annual energy consumption of television sets, the number of days in use per year refers to the number of days the residents spent in their residences (when the survey was conducted) per year. The calculation formula is as follows:

$$\begin{aligned}&\text{Energy}_{\textit{television sets}}\ (\text{kgce/year})=\text{average energy consumption}_{\textit{television sets}}\ (\text{kWh/day})\\&\quad\times\text{number of days in use}_{\textit{television sets}}\ (\text{days/year})\\&\quad\times\text{coefficient for converting electricity consumption to coal equivalent (kgce/kWh)}\end{aligned} \tag{11}$$

## 3.4 *Method for Estimating Energy Consumption of Computers*

While estimating the electricity consumption of computers, as we failed to obtain data about power of computers and types of computer screens, we could only determine their power depending on the type of computers, including desktops, laptops and tablets. Generally, according to the technical specifications of various types of computers, their power is as shown in Table 3.

**Table 3** Reference power of computers

| Type of computer | Reference power/kW |
|---|---|
| Desktop (LCD) | 0.275 |
| Laptop | 0.080 |
| Tablet | 0.015 |

The electricity consumption of computers is the reference power multiplied by average number of hours in use, which is subsequently corrected with the energy consumption efficiency. However, though we obtained data about availability of energy efficiency labels of computers in the survey, we failed to obtain the corresponding data about energy efficiency index. Consequently, we were unable to consider the influence of energy consumption efficiency of computers on their electricity consumption. The number of days in use per year of computers refers to the number of days the residents spent in their residences (when the survey was conducted) per year. The formula for calculating the annual electricity consumption of computers is as follows:

$$\begin{aligned}\text{Energy}_{computer}\ (\text{kgce/year}) &= \text{power}_{computer}\ (\text{kW}) \times \text{number of hours in use}_{computer}\ (\text{hours/day})\\ &\times \text{number of days in use}_{computer}\ (\text{days/year})\\ &\times \text{coefficient for converting electricity consumption to coal equivalent (kgce/kWh)}\end{aligned} \tag{12}$$

## 3.5 *Method for Estimating Energy Consumption of Light Bulbs*

In estimation of electricity consumption of household light bulbs, we considered the consumption in different situations based on the number of hours in use per day and the type of light bulbs, namely, energy-efficient light bulbs and non-energy-efficient ones. Generally, the power is 8 W for energy-efficient bulbs and 40 W for non-energy-efficient ones. The electricity consumption of light bulbs is the sum of electricity consumption of energy-efficient bulbs and non-energy-efficient ones. The formulae for calculation of electricity consumption of lighting are as follows:

$$\begin{aligned}\text{Electricity consumption}_{energy-efficient\ bulb}\ (\text{kWh/day}) &= \text{power}_{energy-efficient\ bulb}\ (\text{kW})\\ &\times \text{number of hours in use}_{energy-efficient\ bulb}\ (\text{hours/day}) \times \text{number}_{energy-efficient\ bulb}\ (\text{piece})\end{aligned} \tag{13}$$

$$\begin{aligned}\text{Electricity consumption}_{non-energy-efficient\ bulb}\ (\text{kWh/day}) &= \text{power}_{non-energy-efficient\ bulb}\ (\text{KW})\\ &\times \text{number of hours in use}_{non-energy-efficient\ bulb}\ (\text{hours/day})\\ &\times \text{number}_{non-energy-efficient\ bulb}\ (\text{piece})\end{aligned} \tag{14}$$

$$\begin{aligned}\text{Electricity consumption}_{lighting}\ (\text{kWh/day}) &= \text{electricity consumption}_{energy-efficient\ bulb}\\ &+ \text{electricity consumption}_{non-energy-efficient\ bulb}\end{aligned} \tag{15}$$

In calculation of the annual energy consumption of light bulbs, the number of days in use per year refers to the number of days the residents spent in their residences (when the survey was conducted) per year. The calculation formula is as follows:

$$\begin{aligned}\text{Energy}_{lighting}\ (\text{kgce/year}) &= \text{electricity consumption}_{lighting}\ (\text{kWh/day})\\ &\quad \times \text{number of hours in use}_{lighting}\ (\text{days/year})\\ &\quad \times \text{coefficient for converting electricity consumption to coal equivalent (kgce/kWh)}\end{aligned} \tag{16}$$

# 4 Estimation of Energy Consumption of Space Heating, Air Conditioning and Water Heaters

The residential space heating systems covered in the survey included district heating and household heating. The residential air conditioning equipment included electric fans and air conditioners. Fuels for space heating are various, including electricity, pipeline natural gas or coal gas, bottled LPG, diesel, other fuel oil, fire wood, charcoal, coal, geothermal heat, etc. Air conditioning equipment is powered by electricity. In calculation of energy consumption from space heating, in addition to factors such as frequency of use per day, average duration per use, number of days in use per year and energy consumption per hour (e.g., output power of electrical appliances) of the equipment, we also need to consider the effective heating area, insulation characteristics of buildings, etc. The calculation of energy consumption of household air conditioning shall consider the power and energy efficiency of equipment as well as their average duration of use per day and number of days in use in summer.

## *4.1 Method for Estimating Energy Consumption of District Heating*

The energy consumption of residential space heating can be calculated by estimating the consumption of source energy or site energy of residences. The consumption of source energy refers to the total amount of processed and unprocessed energy required to provide certain amount of heating energy for residences, including loss in production and transmission of energy. The consumption of site energy refers to the amount of energy consumed by end users of residences for space heating. While estimating the energy consumption of district heating, due to inaccessibility of data about technical specifications of heat sources, fuels and heat loss in pipeline transmission in places where the households were located, we calculated the site energy consumption of residences indirectly according to Formula 17.

$$\begin{aligned}&\text{Energy}_{district\ heating}\ (\text{kgce/year})\\ &= \text{energy consumption baseline of buildings per unit area}_{district\ heating}\left(\text{kgce/m}^2\text{/heating season}\right)\\ &\quad \times \text{adjustment coefficient for buildings}\\ &\quad \times \text{usable area of residence (m}^2)\\ &\quad \times \text{standard heating season}_{district\ heating}\ (\text{heating season/year})\end{aligned} \tag{17}$$

First, the baseline of energy consumption for residences was determined according to the year of construction. In accordance with the heating requirement in China (which provides that indoor temperature shall not be below 18 °C in heating seasons) and relevant technical specifications about energy consumption, the energy consumption baseline for heating per unit area is as shown in Table 4. Concerning the correlation between age of buildings and their insulation effect, the basic characteristic is: the younger, the better.

Second, considering that building transformation influences the loss of heat and consequently the energy consumption of space heating, the corresponding adjustment coefficients were set. For instance, sealed doors and windows lead to 10% reduction in energy consumption; insulation treatment of external wall leads to 30% reduction in heat loss and insulation treatment of attics, ceilings and pipelines leads to 10% reduction in energy consumption.

Since the district heating system heats the complete area of residences, the usable area of residences was considered the heating area. If data for the said variable was not available, the heating area was considered 116.4 $m^2$ (the average usable area of households using district heating).

The duration of heating seasons varies in regions and shall be adjusted for comparison based on the same length of heating seasons. The duration of heating seasons was adjusted according to "duration (number of months) of heating" in the questionnaire data and the mean value, 4.15 months, of samples using district heating. If data about "duration (number of months) of heating" was not available, the duration of heating season was considered 4.15 months. Supposing that a heating season lasts 4.15 months, the duration of heating season for each household is "duration (number of months) of heating/4.15".

**Table 4** Energy consumption baseline per unit area of residences built in various ages

| Year of construction | Energy consumption per unit area/kgce |
|---|---|
| Before 1980 | 31.68 |
| 1980–1989 | 25.30 |
| 1990–1999 | 20.60 |
| 2000–2009 | 18.60 |
| 2010 and later | 12.50 |
| Data not available | 25.00 |

*Note* The energy consumption per unit area is calculated subject to the condition of indoor temperature at 18 °C/heating season

## 4.2 *Method for Estimating Energy Consumption of Household Heating*

Unlike district heating, household heating does not supply heat to the whole residence area throughout the day. Considering the various equipment and fuels for heating used in different households and the difference in duration of heating, we estimated the annual energy consumption of household heating depending on different types of heating equipment and fuel. The consumption of various fuels was converted to energy consumption measured in kilogram of coal equivalent.

(1) Electric heating equipment

For electric heating equipment such as air conditioners, electric radiator heaters and electric heating film, the annual energy consumption of heating can be calculated according to the nominal power of electrical appliances, energy efficiency grades of air conditioners, average number of hours in use per day and number of days in use per year.

Heating with air conditioners: In accordance with the *Minimum Allowable Value of Energy Efficiency and Energy Efficiency Grades for Residential Air Conditioners* (GB 12021.3-2010), the actual output power of air conditioners is the output power multiplied by adjusting coefficient for fixed and variable frequencies, then divided by energy efficiency ratio (EER). The rated power of air conditioners is considered the output power. Fixed and variable frequency air conditioners are calculated separately, the converting coefficient of which is 1 and 0.7 respectively and the air conditioner is considered fixed-frequency type when such data is not available. The EER of air conditioners reflects their energy efficiency grades. The EER for air conditioners of grade-1, grade-2, grade-3 and higher grades is 3.6, 3.4 and 3.2 respectively, and considered 3.2 when such data is not available. The annual electricity consumption of air conditioners can be calculated based on number of hours in use per day and number of days in use per year.

Heating with electric radiator heaters and electric heating films: The power of electric radiator heaters and electric heating films is both considered 1,200 W and their annual electricity consumption can be calculated by multiplying the power with number of hours in use per day and number of days in use per year.

(2) Non-electric heating equipment

For non-electric heating equipment powered by fuels (e.g., natural gas, firewood, charcoal and coal etc.), such as heatable brick beds, pipes of boilers, stoves for heating (burning firewood and charcoal, etc.) and oil heaters, etc., the annual consumption of fuels shall be calculated according to the heat load per unit area of fuels, usable area of residences, average number of hours in use per day and number of days in use per year.

Energy consumption of heating equipment burning firewood, including heatable brick beds, boilers and heating stoves: In the case of heating by boilers, supposing that the heat load per unit area of firewood is 0.1 kg/day, the energy consumption of boilers burning firewood for heating can be calculated by multiplying the said coefficient with usable area of residences, based on which the hourly firewood consumption can be obtained. In the case of heating with heatable brick beds or heating stoves, supposing that 2 kg of firewood is burnt per hour for heating, the annual energy consumption from heating stoves burning firewood can be calculated by multiplying the said coefficient with the number of heating hours per day and number of heating days per year.

Energy consumption of non-electric heating equipment powered by fuels other than firewood: If other fuels instead of electricity or firewood is used to power the non-electric heating equipment, the household energy consumption of heating per day from burning such fuels can be obtained by multiplying the heat load per unit area per day of each type of fuel with the usable area of residences, based on which the annual consumption of fuel can be obtained. The heat load coefficient of various fuels per unit area per day is as shown in Table 5.

(3) General formulae for estimation

The general estimation formulae are as follows:

$$\begin{aligned}\text{Energy}_{\textit{household heating:air conditioner}}\ (\text{kgce/year}) &= \text{output power}_{\textit{household heating:air conditioner}}\ (\text{kW}) \\ &\times \text{adjustment coefficient for type and energy efficiency}_{\textit{household heating:air conditioner}} \\ &\times \text{number of hours in use per day}_{\textit{household heating:air conditioner}}\ (\text{hours/day}) \\ &\times \text{number of days in use per year}_{\textit{household heating:air conditioner}}\ (\text{days/year}) \\ &\times \text{coefficient for converting electricity consumption to coal equivalent (kgce/kWh)}\end{aligned} \tag{18}$$

$$\begin{aligned}\text{Energy}_{\textit{household heating:others}}\ (\text{kgce/year}) &= \text{load per unit area}_{\textit{household heating:others}}\ (\text{kgce/day}) \\ &\times \text{usable area of residence}\ (\text{m}^2) \\ &\times \text{number of days in use per year}_{\textit{household heating:others}}\ (\text{days/year})\end{aligned} \tag{19}$$

**Table 5** Heat load coefficient per unit area per day of various space heating fuels

| Space heating fuel | Heat load coefficient per unit area per day |
|---|---|
| Pipeline natural gas/coal gas | 0.0632 $m^3$ |
| Bottled LPG | 0.048 $m^3$ |
| Diesel | 0.0576 L |
| Other fuel oil | 0.0576 L |
| Charcoal | 0.1 kg |
| Coal | 0.1 kg |

### 4.3 *Method for Estimating Energy Consumption of Water Heaters*

Water heaters include storage water heaters and demand-type water heaters. Storage water heaters mainly use electricity and pipeline natural gas/coal gas as fuel. For convenient calculation, storage water heaters burning gas were adjusted to demand-type ones. Fuels for demand-type water heaters include electricity, pipeline natural gas/coal gas, bottle LPG and solar energy. While estimating the energy consumption of water heaters, due to lack of data about their energy consumption per hour (e.g., output power of electrical appliances) and capacity, we used the mean value of data from the CRECS 2012. In the first questionnaire, the mean value of heating coefficient was 1.6, the average capacity of water heaters was 75.3 l and the average power was 1.5 kW. The power of storage water heaters was determined based on the capacity, while the energy consumption per hour of demand-type water heaters was determined according to the type of fuel. The reference energy consumption per hour of water heaters is as shown in Table 6. Generally speaking, the energy consumption of water heaters is the product of multiplying the energy consumption per hour of water heaters by the number of hours in use. Considering the significant difference in number of hours in use between storage water heaters and demand-type ones, we calculated the energy consumption of the two types of water heaters respectively.

(1) Storage water heaters

The number of hours in use of storage water heaters is calculated as follows: If the water heater works throughout the day, the actual number of hours in use is considered 3 h. If the water heater only works when hot water is needed, the actual number of hours in use is considered 0.5 h. The hot water supplied by a storage water heater in one operation can meet the need for hot water of a common household for a day, and a common household uses water heaters 1.025 times per day on average. We adjusted with the number of times the households use their water heaters per day on average. If a household uses a water heater more than 1.025 times per day, the water heater would re-heat the water, in which case, the frequency of use of water heaters per day is considered the average number of times in use of water heaters divided by 1.025. For energy efficiency indexes of storage water heaters, we adopted the maximum value as provided in the *Minimum Allowable Values of Energy Efficiency and Energy Efficiency Grades for Electrical Storage Water Heaters* (GB 21519-2008), as shown in Table 7.

**Table 6** Reference energy consumption per hour of water heaters

| Type of fuel for water heater | Energy consumption per hour |
|---|---|
| Electricity | 5 kW |
| Pipeline natural gas/coal gas | 2 $m^3$ |
| Bottled LPG | 1.8 kg |
| Solar energy | 0.4514 kgce/90 L |

**Table 7** Energy efficiency indexes of storage water heaters

| Energy efficiency grade | Energy efficiency index |
|---|---|
| 1 | 0.6 |
| 2 | 0.7 |
| 3 | 0.8 |
| 4 | 0.9 |
| 5 | 1.0 |
| No energy efficiency label | 1.0 |

The electricity consumption of storage water heaters is the product of energy efficiency index multiplied by power, number of hours in use, coefficient for converting electricity consumption to kgce and frequency of use per day. For storage water heaters powered by solar energy, the energy consumption is estimated according to the capacity of water heaters. In another word, the solar energy consumed for heating 90 L of water equals to 0.4514 kgce.

$$\begin{aligned}&\text{Electricity consumption}_{\textit{storage water heater}}\ (\text{kgce/day}) = \text{power}_{\textit{storage water heater}}\ (\text{kW})\\&\quad\times \text{number of hours in use}_{\textit{storage water heater}}\ (\text{hours/time})\\&\quad\times \text{frequency of use}_{\textit{storage water heater}}\ (\text{times/day})\\&\quad\times \text{energy efficiency index}_{\textit{storage water heater}}\\&\quad\times \text{coefficient for converting electricity consumption to coal equivalent (kgce/kWh)}\end{aligned} \tag{20}$$

$$\begin{aligned}&\text{Solar energy consumption}_{\textit{storage water heater}}\ (\text{kgce/day})\\&\quad= \text{energy consumption per unit of hot water (kgce/90 L)}\\&\quad\times \text{volume of hot water supplied (90 L/day)}\end{aligned} \tag{21}$$

While calculating the annual energy consumption of storage water heaters, the number of days in use per year shall be considered:

$$\begin{aligned}&\text{Energy}_{\textit{storage water heater}}\ (\text{kgce/year}) = \text{energy consumption}_{\textit{storage water heater}}\ (\text{kgce/day})\\&\quad\times \text{number of days in use}_{\textit{storage water heater}}\ (\text{days/year})\end{aligned} \tag{22}$$

(2) Demand-type water heaters

The number of hours in use of demand-type water heaters is calculated as follows: For electric demand-type water heaters, pipeline natural gas/coal gas and bottled LPG, the average duration of use is considered the number of hours in use each time. In addition, there is no data about their energy efficiency. Therefore, the energy consumption of demand-type water heaters is the product of energy consumption per hour multiplied by number of hours in use and frequency of use per day. The calculation formulae are as follows:

$$\begin{aligned}&\text{Electricity consumption}_{demand-type\ water\ heater}\ (\text{kgce/day})\\&=\text{power}_{demand-type\ water\ heater}\ (\text{kW})\\&\quad\times\text{number of hours in use}_{demand-type\ water\ heater}\ (\text{hours/day})\\&\quad\times\text{coefficient for converting electricity consumption to coal equivalent (kgce/kWh)}\end{aligned}\tag{23}$$

$$\begin{aligned}&\text{Gas consumption}_{demand-type\ water\ heater}\ (\text{kgce/day})\\&=\text{Gas consumption per hour}_{demand-type\ water\ heater}\ (\text{m}^3/\text{hour})\\&\quad\times\text{number of hours in use}_{demand-type\ water\ heater}\ (\text{hours/day})\\&\quad\times\text{coefficientfor converting gas consumption to coal equivalent}\ (\text{kgce/m}^3)\end{aligned}\tag{24}$$

$$\begin{aligned}&\text{LPG consumption}_{demand-type\ water\ heater}\ (\text{kgce/day})\\&=\text{LPG consumption per hour}_{demand-type\ water\ heater}\ (\text{kg/hour})\\&\quad\times\text{number of hours in use}_{demand-type\ water\ heater}\ (\text{hours/day})\\&\quad\times\text{coefficient for converting LPG consumption to coal equivalent (kgce/kg)}\end{aligned}\tag{25}$$

While calculating the annual energy consumption of demand-type water heaters, the number of days in use per year shall be considered:

$$\begin{aligned}&\text{Energy}_{demand-type\ water\ heater}\ (\text{kgce/year})\\&=\text{energy consumption}_{demand-type\ water\ heater}\ (\text{kgce/day})\\&\quad\times\text{number of days in use}_{demand-type\ water\ heater}\ (\text{days/year})\end{aligned}\tag{26}$$

## 4.4 *Method for Estimating Energy Consumption of Air Conditioning*

The equipment used for household air conditioning is air conditioners. According to the *Minimum Allowable Value of Energy Efficiency and Energy Efficiency Grades for Residential Air Conditioners* (GB 12021.3-2010), the actual output power of air conditioners is the output power multiplied by the adjustment coefficient of fixed and variable frequencies and then divided by the EER. The rated power of air conditioners is considered the output power. Fixed and variable frequency air conditions are calculated separately, the converting coefficient of which is 1 and 0.7 respectively and the air conditioner is considered fixed frequency if data about its type is not available. The EER reflects the energy efficiency grades of air conditioners. The EER for air conditioners of grade-1, grade-2, grade-3 and higher grades is 3.6, 3.4 and 3.2 respectively, and considered 3.2 when such data is not available. Based on the number of hours in use per day and number of days in use per year in summer, the electricity consumption of air conditioners for air conditioning can be calculated according to formula 27:

$$\begin{aligned}&\text{Energy}_{\textit{air conditioner for air conditioning}}\ (\text{kgce/year})\\&=\text{output power}_{\textit{air conditioner for air conditioning}}\ (\text{kW})\\&\quad\times\text{adjustment coefficient for type and energy efficiency}_{\textit{air conditioner for air conditioning}}\\&\quad\times\text{number of hours in use}_{\textit{air conditioner for air conditioning}}\ (\text{hours/day})\\&\quad\times\text{number of days in use in summer}_{\textit{air conditioner for air conditioning}}\ (\text{days/year})\\&\quad\times\text{coefficient for converting electricity consumption to coal equivalent (kgce/kWh)}\end{aligned} \quad (27)$$

## 5 Estimation of Energy Consumption of Household Transportation

The survey concerning means of household transportation only covered transportation by personal vehicles. The factors to be considered in calculation of energy consumption of household transportation include annual mileage of common vehicles and actual fuel consumption per 100 km.

The actual fuel consumption of vehicles is calculated by multiplying the actual fuel consumption per 100 km with annual mileage of common vehicles in 2014. The formula is as follows:

$$\begin{aligned}&\text{Energy}_{\textit{vehicle}}(\text{kgce/year})\\&=\text{actual fuel consumption}_{\textit{vehicle}}\ (\text{liter/100 km})\\&\quad\times\text{mileage}_{\textit{vehicle}}\ (100\ \text{km/year})\\&\quad\times\text{coefficient for converting fuel consumption to coal equivalent(kgce/liter)}\end{aligned} \quad (28)$$

Fuels for vehicles include No. 93 gasoline (No. 92 gasoline according to Beijing gasoline octane rating), No. 97 gasoline (No. 95 gasoline according to Beijing gasoline octane rating), ethanol-added gasoline, diesel, electricity, natural gas, hybrid power (gasoline and electricity, or, gasoline and natural gas). For converting consumption of No. 93 gasoline, No. 97 gasoline and ethanol-added gasoline to coal equivalent, the coefficient for converting fuel consumption to coal equivalent is adopted. For hybrid fuels, supposing the consumption proportion of each type of fuel is 1/2, the sum of such consumption multiplied with the corresponding converting coefficient is the energy consumption of hybrid fuel in kilogram of coal equivalent. For example, for hybrid cars consuming gasoline and electricity, the fuel consumption is considered the sum of 1/2 of gasoline and 1/2 of electricity.

**Table 8** Annual energy consumption of household transportation for personal purpose

| Variable | Unit | Observation | Average value | Standard deviation | Minimum value | Maximum value |
|---|---|---|---|---|---|---|
| Household vehicle energy consumption (sample value) | Kgce/year | 3,863 | 128.81 | 544.98 | 0 | 9,269.82 |
| Household vehicle energy consumption (weighted value) | Kgce/year | 3,863 | 121.46 | – | – | – |

According to our calculation, the average energy consumption of household vehicles is 128.81 kgce/year, which is 121.46 kgce/year after weight adjustment. The descriptive statistics of energy consumption of household vehicles is as shown in Table 8.

# Chapter 4
# Analysis and Comparison of Residential Energy Consumption

**Jingqiu Hu, Shimei Wu and De Bi**

This chapter describes and analyzes the residential energy consumption in China in terms of amount and cost of energy and carbon footprint using energy balance and energy flow charts, and compares the residential energy consumption in different regions of China. The analysis and comparison of residential energy consumption in China aims to identify its patterns and influential factors, help decision-makers and the public understand the basic characteristics and geological distribution of residential energy consumption in China and find out the potential, obstacles and influential factors for energy conservation in daily life. The energy sources for household consumption covered in this survey included coal, gasoline, diesel, kerosene, LPG, pipeline natural gas and coal gas, electricity and heat (steam, hot water and hot air for district heating), firewood, straw, solar energy and biogas, etc. Residential energy-consuming activities included cooking, use of household electrical appliances, space heating, water heating and air conditioning. The coefficients for converting consumption of various energy sources to coal equivalent are from the *China Energy Statistical Yearbook*. In addition, except for the energy balance, energy flow charts and carbon emission tables, the analysis in other sections is based on the calculation results of electrothermal equivalent.

Main findings of this chapter: (1) The annual energy consumption (excluding transportation) of a standard Chinese household in 2014 which was weighted according to the proportion of provincial household numbers to the national figure was 1,086.57 kgce, while the available energy was 620.65 kgce, merely accounting for more than half of the actual energy consumption. The primary sources of energy were biomass energy and electricity, and the main end uses of energy were cooking and space heating. (2) Concerning the regional differences, the difference between the northern and southern parts of China mainly lied in the consumption of LPG and coal. Concerning the differences in end uses, the primary end use was cooking in the south and space heating in the north. (3) The differences between urban and rural house-

J. Hu (✉) · S. Wu · D. Bi
Renmin University of China, Beijing, China
e-mail: jingqiu.hu@ruc.edu



X. Zheng and C. Wei (eds.), *Household Energy Consumption in China: 2016 Report*, https://doi.org/10.1007/978-981-13-7523-1_4

holds mainly lied in the consumption of biomass energy and pipeline gas. Thanks to availability of firewood and straw in rural areas, the rural households consumed a large amount of firewood and straw, while urban households used more pipeline gas and bottled LPG. (4) Concerning the cost analysis of energy, the residential energy expenditure for each household in China in 2014 was RMB2,341: RMB2,266 per household in rural areas and RMB2,787 per household in urban areas. Expenditure on electricity accounted for the largest proportion in both rural and urban areas. (5) The weighted residential carbon emission (excluding transportation) per household in China in 2014 was approximately 3,465 kg of $CO_2$. The annual carbon emission per household was 5,063 kg of $CO_2$ for urban residents and 3,038 kg of $CO_2$ for rural residents. Electricity and coal were the primary sources of carbon emission by energy sources, space heating produced the most carbon emission among all end uses.

## 1 Balance of Residential Energy Consumption in China

Energy balance is a kind of table compiling data about supply, processing, conversion and terminal consumption energy sources in the form of a matrix. Energy balance is a vivid depiction of demand for energy and end use of energy in the reporting period. Energy flow chart shows a systematic view of the sources and end uses of energy in a region in a visual manner, which is a powerful supplement to energy balance. Based on the survey results, due to lack of data about energy processing, conversion and supply, in this section, a 2D matrix consisting of energy sources and end uses is created according to the converting coefficients as shown in Tables 1 and 2. In Tables 3 and 4, we calculate the residential energy balance in China in 2014, which is weighted according to the provincial household numbers based on electrothermal equivalent and coal consumption of power generation respectively, and draw the energy flow charts as shown in Figs. 1 and 2.

**Table 1** Coefficients for converting energy consumption to kgce

| Energy | Coefficient | Unit |
|---|---|---|
| (Honeycomb) briquettes | 0.35715 | Kgce/kg |
| Charcoal | 0.3584 | Kgce/kg |
| Gasoline | 1.4714 | Kgce/kg |
| Kerosene | 1.4714 | Kgce/kg |
| Diesel | 1.4571 | Kgce/kg |
| Fuel oil | 1.4286 | Kgce/kg |
| Bottled LPG | 1.7143 | Kgce/kg |
| Pipeline natural gas | 1.3300 | Kgce/m$^3$ |

(continued)

**Table 1** (continued)

| Energy | Coefficient | Unit |
|---|---|---|
| Pipeline coal gas (water gas) | 0.3571 | Kgce/m$^3$ |
| Biogas | 0.7140 | Kgce/m$^3$ |
| Excrement of livestock and poultry | 0.4710 | Kgce/kg |
| Firewood | 0.5710 | Kgce/kg |
| Straw | 0.5000 | Kgce/kg |
| Electricity (electrothermal equivalent) | 0.1229 | Kgce/kWh |
| Electricity (coal consumption of power generation) | Depending on standard coal consumption of the specific province | Kgce/kWh |

*Note* The calorific value of briquettes for residential consumption is lower than that of industrial coal. So, the coefficient for converting consumption of residential briquettes into kgce is considered half of the coefficient for raw coal, namely 0.7143 kgce/kWh $\times$ 0.5 = 0.35715 kgce/kWh
*Source China Energy Statistical Yearbook*, National Energy Administration of the People's Republic of China

**Table 2** Coal consumption of power generation in some provinces and municipalities in 2014 (Unit: kgce/kWh)

| Region | Standard coal consumption of power generation | Region | Standard coal consumption of power generation |
|---|---|---|---|
| Beijing | 0.231 | Shandong | 0.304 |
| Tianjin | 0.296 | Henan | 0.299 |
| Hebei | 0.305 | Hubei | 0.293 |
| Shanxi | 0.305 | Hunan | 0.295 |
| Inner Mongolia | 0.314 | Guangdong | 0.296 |
| Liaoning | 0.295 | Guangxi | 0.298 |
| Jilin | 0.287 | Chongqing | 0.305 |
| Heilongjiang | 0.308 | Sichuan | 0.302 |
| Shanghai | 0.288 | Guizhou | 0.307 |
| Jiangsu | 0.293 | Yunnan | 0.312 |
| Zhejiang | 0.285 | Shaanxi | 0.306 |
| Anhui | 0.294 | Gansu | 0.309 |
| Fujian | 0.294 | Qinghai | 0.331 |
| Jiangxi | 0.298 | Ningxia | 0.324 |

*Source China Electricity Yearbook 2015*

**Table 3** Residential energy consumption balance in 2014: electrothermal equivalent (Unit: kgce)

| Energy consumption | | Firewood/straw | Charcoal | Coal | Diesel/gasoline/kerosene/ethanol-added gasoline | Electricity | Bottled LPG | Pipeline natural gas | Pipeline coal gas | Biogas | Solar energy | Heat | Sum |
|---|---|---|---|---|---|---|---|---|---|---|---|---|---|
| Cooking | Stoves burning firewood | 201.58 | | | | | | | | | | | 201.58 |
| | Stoves burning honeycomb briquettes | | | 3.56 | | | | | | | | | 3.56 |
| | Oil stove | | | | 0.02 | | | | | | | | 0.02 |
| | Induction cooktop | | | | | 34.76 | | | | | | | 34.76 |
| | Gas stove | | | | | | 79.92 | 63.45 | 2.34 | | | | 145.71 |
| | Biogas stove | | | | | | | | | 0.81 | | | 0.81 |
| | Electric rice cooker | | | | | 33.67 | | | | | | | 33.67 |
| | Pressure cooker | | | | | 3.50 | | | | | | | 3.50 |
| | Microwave oven | | | | | 1.76 | | | | | | | 1.76 |
| | Oven | | | | | 0.06 | | | | | | | 0.06 |

(continued)

**Table 3** (continued)

| Energy consumption | | Firewood/straw | Charcoal | Coal | Diesel/gasoline/kerosene/ethanol-added gasoline | Electricity | Bottled LPG | Pipeline natural gas | Pipeline coal gas | Biogas | Solar energy | Heat | Sum |
|---|---|---|---|---|---|---|---|---|---|---|---|---|---|
| | Solar cooker | | | | | | | | | | | | |
| | Electric kettle | | | | | 7.06 | | | | | | | 7.06 |
| | Others | | | | | | | | | | | | |
| Electrical appliance | Refrigerator | | | | | 15.48 | | | | | | | 15.48 |
| | Freezer | | | | | 1.59 | | | | | | | 1.59 |
| | Washing machine | | | | | 8.29 | | | | | | | 8.29 |
| | Drying machine | | | | | 0.11 | | | | | | | 0.11 |
| | Television set | | | | | 72.38 | | | | | | | 72.38 |
| | Computer | | | | | 11.54 | | | | | | | 11.54 |
| | Lamps and light bulbs | | | | | 4.23 | | | | | | | 4.23 |
| Residential heating | District heating | | | | | | | | | | | 217.04 | 217.04 |
| | Heatable brick bed | 78.64 | 0.28 | 9.06 | | | | | | | | | 87.98 |

(continued)

**Table 3** (continued)

| Energy consumption | | Firewood/ straw | Charcoal | Coal | Diesel/gasoline/ kerosene/ ethanol-added gasoline | Electricity | Bottled LPG | Pipeline natural gas | Pipeline coal gas | Biogas | Solar energy | Heat | Sum |
|---|---|---|---|---|---|---|---|---|---|---|---|---|---|
| | Residential air conditioner for space heating | | | | | 0.83 | | | | | | | 0.83 |
| | Boiler pipe for space heating | 1.93 | 0.15 | 14.88 | 0.05 | 0.10 | | 3.34 | | | | | 20.45 |
| | Heating stove (burning wood and coal, etc.) | 12.96 | 5.91 | 52.63 | | | | | | | | | 71.51 |
| | Electric radiator heater | | | | | 2.93 | | | | | | | 2.93 |
| | Oil-filled radiator heater | | | | | | | | | | | | |
| | Electric heating film | | | | | | | | | | | | |
| | Others | | | | | | | | | | | | |
| Heating water | Water heater | | | | | 24.79 | 26.71 | 56.41 | | | 21.93 | | 129.84 |

(continued)

**Table 3** (continued)

| Energy consumption | | Firewood/ straw | Charcoal | Coal | Diesel/gasoline/ kerosene/ ethanol-added gasoline | Electricity | Bottled LPG | Pipeline natural gas | Pipeline coal gas | Biogas | Solar energy | Heat | Sum |
|---|---|---|---|---|---|---|---|---|---|---|---|---|---|
| Air conditioning | Air conditioner | | | | | 9.87 | | | | | | | 9.87 |
| Total (transportation excluded) | | 295.11 | 6.34 | 80.13 | 0.06 | 232.97 | 106.63 | 123.20 | 2.34 | 0.81 | 21.93 | 217.04 | 1086.57 |
| Transportation | Automobile | | | | 121.46 | | | | | | | | 121.46 |
| Total (transportation included) | | 295.11 | 6.34 | 80.13 | 121.52 | 232.97 | 106.63 | 123.20 | 2.34 | 0.81 | 21.93 | 217.04 | 1208.03 |

*Note* (1) The energy consumption is calculated in electrothermal equivalent (coefficient for converting electricity consumption to coal equivalent is 0.1229 kgce/kWh). In the calculation result, the sample value is considered 0 if any question is left unanswered. To be specific, all questions concerning energy consumption of solar cooker, other cooking equipment not included in Table 3, electric radiator heater, oil-filled radiator heater, electric heating film and other heating equipment not included in Table 3 were not answered, which was consequently considered 0 and not included in Table 3

(2) Weight adjustment in accordance with percentage of household numbers of various provinces in the national figure. The provincial number of households is from the sixth national population census in China

**Table 4** Residential energy consumption balance in 2014: coal consumption of power generation (Unit: kgce)

| Energy consumption | | Firewood/straw | Charcoal | Coal | Diesel/gasoline/kerosene/ethanol-added gasoline | Electricity | Bottled LPG | Pipeline natural gas | Pipeline coal gas | Biogas | Solar energy | Heat | Sum |
|---|---|---|---|---|---|---|---|---|---|---|---|---|---|
| Cooking | Stoves burning firewood | 201.58 | | | | | | | | | | | 201.58 |
| | Stoves burning honeycomb briquettes | | | 3.56 | | | | | | | | | 3.56 |
| | Oil stove | | | | 0.02 | | | | | | | | 0.02 |
| | Induction cooktop | | | | | 85.33 | | | | | | | 85.33 |
| | Gas stove | | | | | | 79.92 | 63.45 | 2.34 | | | | 145.71 |
| | Biogas stove | | | | | | | | | 0.81 | | | 0.81 |
| | Electric rice cooker | | | | | 81.76 | | | | | | | 81.76 |
| | Pressure cooker | | | | | 8.43 | | | | | | | 8.43 |
| | Microwave oven | | | | | 4.20 | | | | | | | 4.20 |
| | Oven | | | | | 0.15 | | | | | | | 0.15 |

(continued)

**Table 4** (continued)

| Energy consumption | | Firewood/ straw | Charcoal | Coal | Diesel/gasoline/ kerosene/ ethanol-added gasoline | Electricity | Bottled LPG | Pipeline natural gas | Pipeline coal gas | Biogas | Solar energy | Heat | Sum |
|---|---|---|---|---|---|---|---|---|---|---|---|---|---|
| | Solar cooker | | | | | | | | | | | | |
| | Electric kettle | | | | | 17.02 | | | | | | | 17.02 |
| | Others | | | | | | | | | | | | |
| Electrical appliance | Refrigerator | | | | | 37.39 | | | | | | | 37.39 |
| | Freezer | | | | | 3.91 | | | | | | | 3.91 |
| | Washing machine | | | | | 20.08 | | | | | | | 20.08 |
| | Drying machine | | | | | 0.28 | | | | | | | 0.28 |
| | Television set | | | | | 175.39 | | | | | | | 175.39 |
| | Computer | | | | | 27.78 | | | | | | | 27.78 |
| | Lamps and light bulbs | | | | | 10.24 | | | | | | | 10.24 |
| Residential heating | District heating | | | | | | | | | | | 217.04 | 217.04 |
| | Heatable brick bed | 78.64 | 0.28 | 9.06 | | | | | | | | | 87.98 |

(continued)

**Table 4** (continued)

| Energy consumption | | Firewood/ straw | Charcoal | Coal | Diesel/gasoline/ kerosene/ ethanol-added gasoline | Electricity | Bottled LPG | Pipeline natural gas | Pipeline coal gas | Biogas | Solar energy | Heat | Sum |
|---|---|---|---|---|---|---|---|---|---|---|---|---|---|
| | Residential air conditioner for space heating | | | | | 1.99 | | | | | | | 1.99 |
| | Boiler pipe for space heating | 1.93 | 0.15 | 14.88 | 0.05 | 0.23 | | 3.34 | | | | | 20.58 |
| | Heating stove (burning wood and coal, etc.) | 12.96 | 5.91 | 52.63 | | | | | | | | | 71.51 |
| | Electric radiator heater | | | | | 7.14 | | | | | | | 7.14 |
| | Oil-filled radiator heater | | | | | | | | | | | | |
| | Electric heating film | | | | | | | | | | | | |
| | Others | | | | | | | | | | | | |

(continued)

**Table 4** (continued)

| Energy consumption | | Firewood/straw | Charcoal | Coal | Diesel/gasoline/kerosene/ethanol-added gasoline | Electricity | Bottled LPG | Pipeline natural gas | Pipeline coal gas | Biogas | Solar energy | Heat | Sum |
|---|---|---|---|---|---|---|---|---|---|---|---|---|---|
| Hot water | Water heater | | | | | 59.59 | 26.71 | 56.41 | | | 21.93 | | 164.64 |
| Air conditioning | Air conditioner | | | | | 23.56 | | | | | | | 23.56 |
| Total (transportation excluded) | | 295.11 | 6.34 | 80.13 | 0.06 | 564.47 | 106.63 | 123.20 | 2.34 | 0.81 | 21.93 | 217.04 | 1418.07 |
| Transportation | Automobile | | | | 121.46 | | | | | | | | 121.46 |
| Total (transportation included) | | 295.11 | 6.34 | 80.13 | 121.52 | 564.47 | 106.63 | 123.20 | 2.34 | 0.81 | 21.93 | 217.04 | 1539.53 |

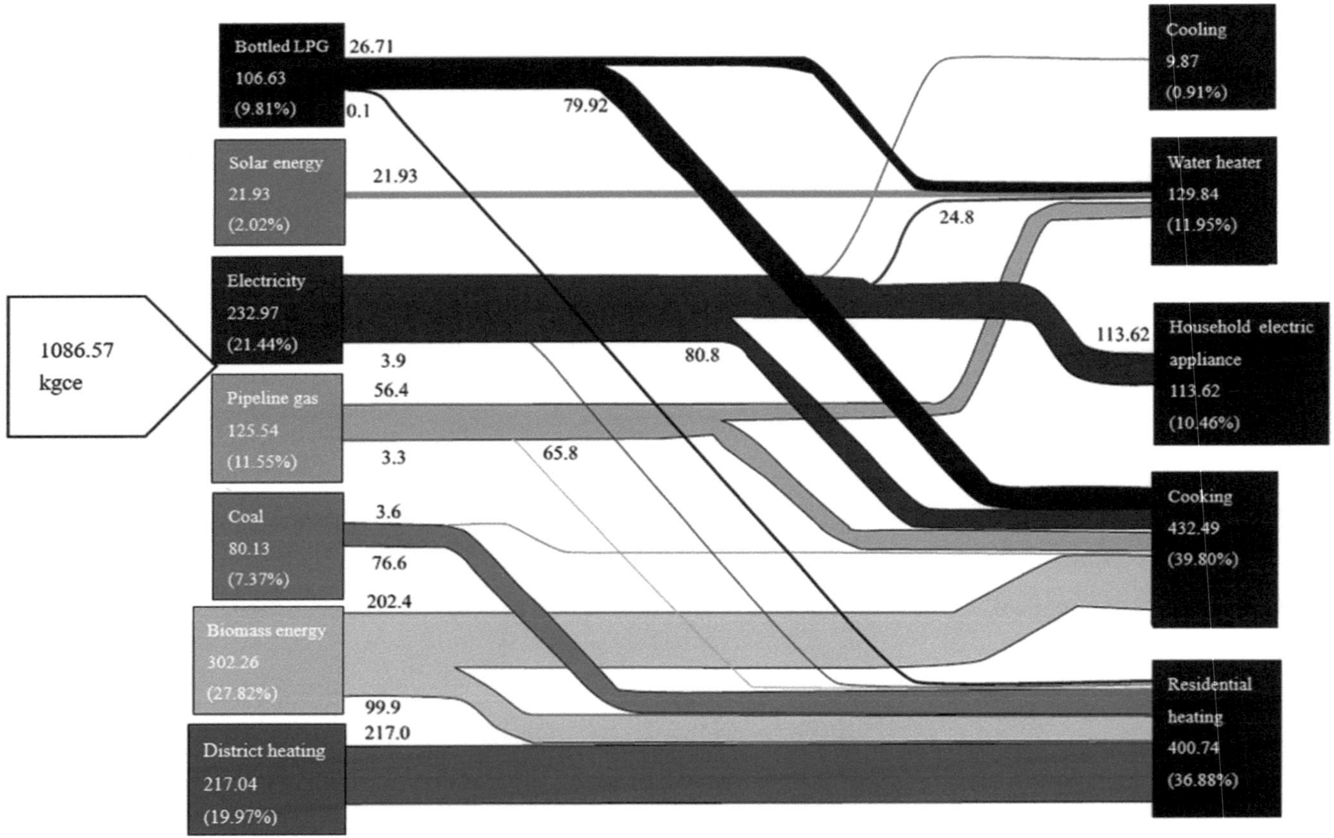


**Fig. 1** Energy flow chart of standard Chinese households in 2014 (electrothermal equivalent)

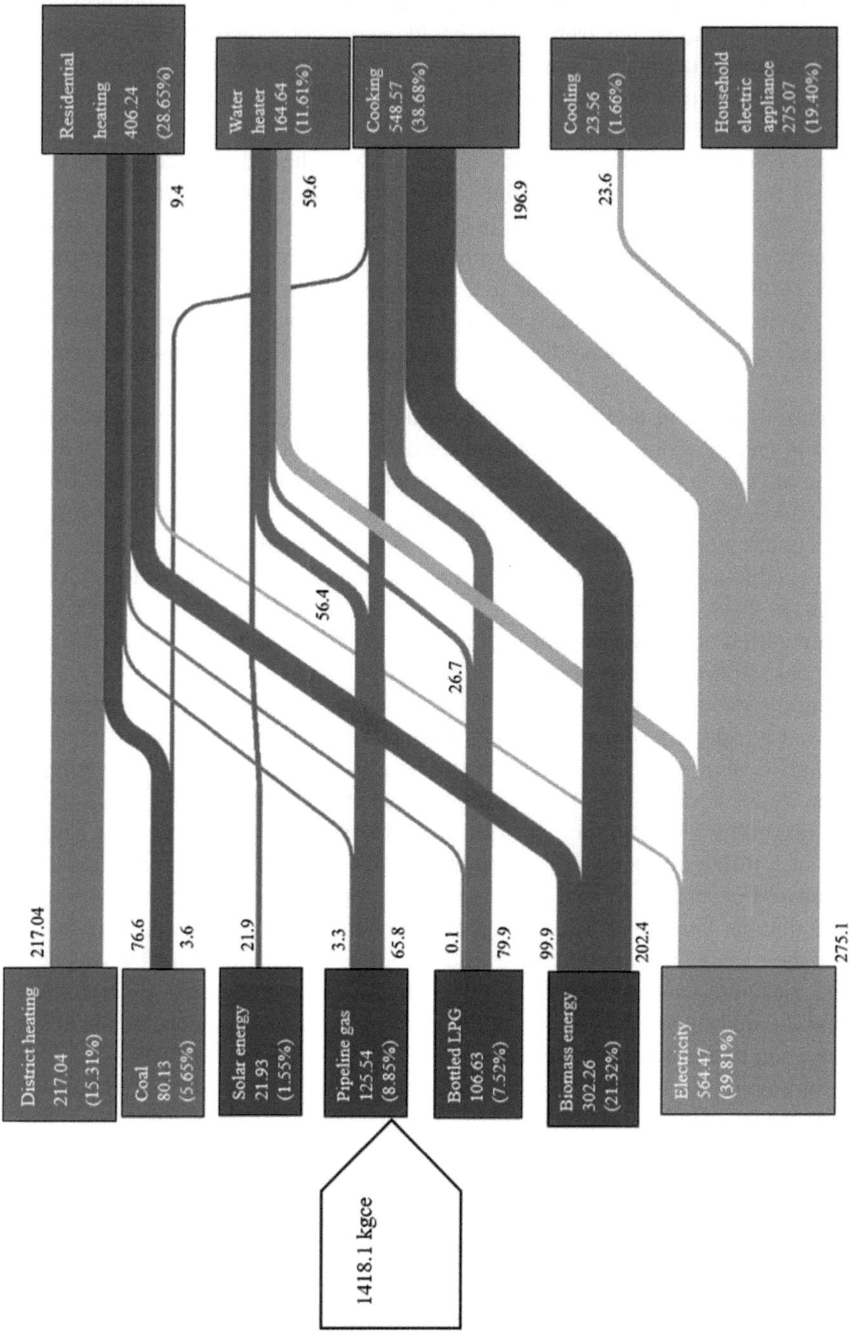


**Fig. 2** Energy flow chart of standard Chinese households in 2014 (coal consumption of power generation)

According to our estimation based on the coefficient for converting electrothermal equivalent to coal equivalent and weight adjustment according to the provincial household numbers, the average household energy consumption per household (excluding transportation) in China in 2014 was 1,086.57 kgce (Table 3). Overall, the primary energy sources for household consumption were firewood/straw, electricity and gas (including bottled LPG, pipeline natural gas and pipeline coal gas). In 2014, the annual electricity consumption was 232.97 kgce per household, accounting for 21.44% of the total energy consumption. The annual consumption of firewood and straw per household was 295.11 kgce in 2014, accounting for 27.16% of the total. The annual gas consumption per household was 232.17 kgce in 2014, accounting for 21.37% of the total. The annual coal consumption per household was merely 80.13 kgce in 2014. Though, since coal is mainly used for heat supply and power generation, we cannot estimate the indirect coal consumption per household accurately.

Concerning the end uses of energy, cooking and space heating consumed the majority of energy, including 432.49 kgce for cooking, accounting for about 39.8% of the total, and 400.74 kgce for space heating, accounting for 36.88% of the total. Besides, household electrical appliances consumed 113.62 kgce per household, accounting for a small percentage (10.46%) of the total energy consumption. Fuel oil (including gasoline and diesel) was the main energy consumed in transportation. In 2014, the consumption of fuel oil for transportation was 121.46 kgce per household. If energy consumption of transportation was considered, the average energy consumption per household in China in 2014 would be 1,208.3 kgce.

According to our calculation (Table 4) based on coal consumption of power generation and weight adjustment according to the provincial household numbers, the average residential energy consumption per household (excluding transportation) in China in 2014 was 1,418.07 kgce, which is 331.5 kg more than the result calculated according to electrothermal equivalent. Considering the different types of energy, such difference is mainly caused by calculation of electricity consumption. In calculation according to coal consumption of power generation, the electricity consumption per household was the highest, amounting to 564.47 kgce, more than twice of the energy consumption calculated according to electrothermal equivalent; the coal consumption was 80.13 kgce, identical with the result calculated according to electrothermal equivalent; the consumption of firewood and gases had no obvious differences in both calculation methods.

According to the energy balance, we drew the energy flow chart of energy consumption of standard Chinese households based on electrothermal equivalent. To make it simple and clear, we combined biogas, firewood, straw and charcoal as biomass energy and combined pipeline natural gas and pipeline kerosene as pipeline gas. Since oil consumption accounted for a very small proportion of the total household energy consumption, it is not presented in Fig. 1.

As shown in Fig. 1, in calculation based on electrothermal equivalent, among the energy consumed in residential energy consumption in China in 2014, 27.82% was from biomass energy, 21.44% was from electricity, 19.98% was from heat of district heating, 11.55% was from pipeline gas, 9.81% was from bottled LPG, 7.37%

was from coal and the remaining 2% was from solar energy. Concerning the end uses of energy, 36.88% was for space heating, mainly using heat of district heating, biomass energy and coal, 39.8% was for cooking, mainly using biomass energy, various gases and electricity, 11.95% was for water heating, mainly using various gases, solar energy and electricity, while the remaining electricity was mainly for use of household electrical appliances and air conditioning.

As shown in Fig. 2, the calculation result based on coal consumption of power generation is slightly lower than the result based on electrothermal equivalent. The difference in energy consumption by energy sources mainly lies in the estimation of electricity consumption, as electricity consumption per household is the highest, more than twice of the consumption calculated based on electrothermal equivalent, accounting for 39.81% of the total energy consumption. Concerning the other types of energy consumed, 21.32% was biomass energy, 15.31% was heat from district heating, 8.85% was pipeline gas, 7.52% was bottled LPG, 5.65% was coal and 1.55% was solar energy, all showing decline in proportions compared with the calculation results based on electrothermal equivalent. However, the consumption of firewood and gas did not have any obvious difference in both methods of calculation.

Concerning the end uses of energy, the proportion of energy consumption for space heating in households fell to 28.65%, mainly using heat from district heating, coal and biomass energy; the proportion of energy consumption for cooking rose to 38.68%, with the percentage of electricity consumption increasing significantly, mainly using biomass energy, various gas and electricity; 11.61% of the energy consumed was for water heating, mainly using pipeline gas, solar energy and electricity; the proportion of energy consumption of household electrical appliances increased from 10.46 to 19.4%. The remaining electricity consumption was mainly for use of household electrical appliances and air conditioning.

## 2 Analysis of Available Energy in Residential Energy Consumption

Generally, available energy is a concept in study of thermal energy. Whatever energy or equipment is doing work, only part of it is useful. In another word, only part of the thermal energy is utilized. In China, the research on available energy in residential energy consumption is scarce, and the existing studies mainly cover Jiangsu and the western region of China. Wang and Wu (1999) are the earliest to propose that the same consumption of different energy sources cannot meet the need for the same amount of available energy; moreover, with the increasing percentage of commercial energy, based on the available energy per capita, the residential energy demand can be predicted in a more accurate and reliable manner. Afterward, based on the situation in Jiangsu, Wang and Di (2002) calculated that the available energy per capita for cooking in rural households of Jiangsu in 1997 was 60.1 kgce. Wang and Hu (2010) also proposed that effective heat per capita, electricity consumption per capita and the proportion of commercial energy may serve as characteristic indexes of rural residential energy consumption. In their opinion, effective heat per capita referred to the available energy for cooking per capita obtained from consumption of various types of energy. Through analysis of three rural areas in Jiangsu, Wang (2012) calculated the proportions of commercial energy to effective heat in rural households of southern, northern and central Jiangsu, from which he found that the proportion of commercial energy to effective heat was 18% higher in southern Jiangsu than in northern Jiangsu. Wang et al. (2014) further claimed that effective heat reflected the practical consumption level of effective heat in residential cooking, water heating and animal husbandry, etc., which did not include demand of effective heat for space heating in winter and air conditioning to avoid the influence of factors like climate on the comparability of the said indexes. The average residential energy consumption per capita was 26.7 GJ and the effective heat was 2.86 GJ, showing a very low thermal efficiency. Concerning study of the western area of China, Niu et al. (2012) also mentioned that the thermal efficiency of different energy varied in use, therefore, effective heat may reflect the residential energy consumption more accurately than physical quantity. Niu et al. (2013) conducted calculation based on questionnaire data and found that the energy consumption per household in rural areas in the west of the Huangtu Plateau was 1,978.2 kgce, while the effective thermal energy per household was only 430 kgce, showing a thermal efficiency of 21.7%. In contrast, the energy consumption per household in Lanzhou city was 1,598.7 kgce and the effective thermal energy per household reached 1,054 kgce, showing a high thermal efficiency of 65.9%. The difference in thermal efficiency between rural and urban areas is significant. Sun et al. (2015) calculated that the energy consumption per capita of farmers and herdsmen in the southern part of Gansu province was 996.05 kgce, but the comprehensive thermal efficiency was only 18.77%, showing that the quality of energy was poor.

Generally, available energy is a concept in study of thermal energy. Whatever energy or equipment is doing work, only part of it is useful. In another word, only part of the thermal energy is used. This section focuses on the thermal efficiency of various fuels in calculation of the effective thermal energy of households in China, aiming to identify the amount of energy that is converted to available energy for residential consumption during use of energy. As shown in Table 5, the thermal efficiency is the lowest when biomass energy and coal are directly burnt as fuel, while the heat-supply units of cogeneration or combined heat and power and large heating boilers (running on thermal energy) of regional boiler rooms have the highest thermal efficiency.

As shown in Fig. 3, when converted to coal equivalent, the weighted available energy (excluding transportation) of Chinese households in 2014 was 620.57 kgce, accounting for about half of the practical energy consumption. Of the total, consumption of heat and electricity accounted for the largest proportion, and their conversion efficiencies were also the highest. For thermal energy, the physical amount consumed was 217.04 kgce and the practical available energy was 184.49 kgce, resulting in its proportion in total energy consumption rising from 20.0 to 29.7%. For electricity, the physical amount consumed was 232.97 kgce and the practical available energy was

**Table 5** Thermal efficiency of fuel (Unit: %)

| Fuel | Thermal efficiency | Fuel | Thermal efficiency |
|---|---|---|---|
| Heat | 85 | Biogas | 50 |
| Biomass energy | 20 | Electricity | 80 |
| Coal (direct burning) | 28 | Natural gas | 75 |
| Coal (boiler) | 65 | Gasoline | 30 |
| Liquefied gas | 60 | Solar energy | 40 |

*Source* Wang X. H. & Wu, Z. M. (1999). On estimation methods of rural residential energy consumption. *Renewable Energy Resources, 4*, 1–3. [In Chinese]. Niu, Y. Z., Niu, S. W., Zhang, X. & Zhao, C. S. (2013). Policy options on fuel use, energy conservation and emission reduction in household sector. *China Soft Science*, *5*, 45–55. [In Chinese]

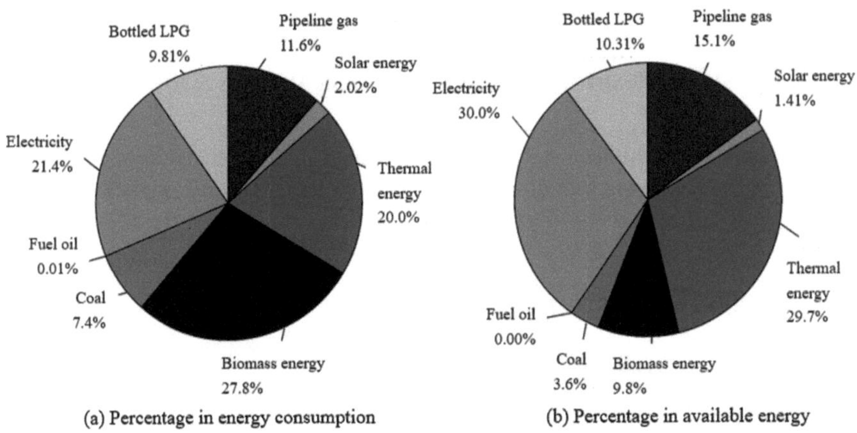


**Fig. 3** Proportions of various energy sources in energy consumption per household and available energy

186.38 kgce, resulting in its proportion in total energy consumption rising from 21.4 to 30.0%. Pipeline natural gas also had a high conversion efficiency, with the physical amount consumed being 123.20 kgce and the practical available energy being 92.40 kgce, the proportion of which in total energy consumption rising from 11.6 to 15.1%. For bottled LPG, the physical amount consumed was 106.63 kgce and the practical available energy was 63.98 kgce, leading to minor change in its proportion in total energy consumption. As for biomass energy including firewood, straw, charcoal and biogas, the conversion efficiency was the lowest: the physical amount consumed was 301.45 kgce and the practical available energy was 60.29 kgce, the proportion of which in total energy consumption declining from 27.8 to 9.8%. The conversion efficiency of coal was also low, as the physical amount consumed was 80.13 kgce and the practical available energy was 22.44 kgce, the proportion of which in total energy consumption declining from 7.4 to 3.6%. Concerning other types of energy such as solar energy and fuel oil, etc. which are not extensively used, their proportions in energy consumption in terms of both physical quantity and practical available energy were no more than 2%, so we shall not comment on them in this section.

It can be seen from the energy flow chart (Fig. 4) which is created according to Tables 3 and 6 that in 2014, the residential energy consumption efficiency in China was 57.11%. Space heating and cooking remained the dominant end uses of energy, accounting for 76.68% of the total energy consumption. In the meantime, space heating and cooking were also the main causes of energy loss. The energy loss per household incurred during space heating and cooking amounted to 833.23 kgce, and the available energy was only 413.4 kgce, which means that the energy consumption efficiency was 49.6%, slightly lower than efficiency of the system. The energy efficiency of household electrical appliances was the highest at nearly 80%. Hot water had the second highest energy efficiency of about 67%.

# 3 Analysis of Residential Energy Consumption Amount

To keep consistent with the data of the CRECS 2012, unless otherwise specified, the analysis in the following section is based on electrothermal equivalent (Table 3).

## *3.1 Comparison of Structures of Energy Types and Energy Demand*

(1) Structure of energy types in residential energy consumption

The average energy consumption (excluding transportation) per household in China in 2014 was 1,086.57 kgce (Table 3). The annual consumption of firewood and straw per household was 295.11 kgce, accounting for 27.16% of the annual energy consumption. The annual electricity consumption per household was 232.97 kgce, accounting for 21.44% of the annual energy consumption. The annual consumption of heat per household was 217.04 kgce, accounting for 19.98% of the annual energy consumption. The annual consumption of pipeline natural gas per household was 123.2 kgce, accounting for 11.34% of the annual energy consumption. The annual consumption of bottled LPG per household was 106.63 kgce, accounting for 9.81% of the annual energy consumption. The annual coal consumption per household was 80.13 kgce, accounting for 7.37% of the annual energy consumption. The other types of energy such as solar energy and biogas, etc. accounted for small proportions of the total (Fig. 5).

In general, the main energy sources used in residential energy consumption were biomass energy such as firewood, straw, charcoal, etc., electricity and gas. Despite

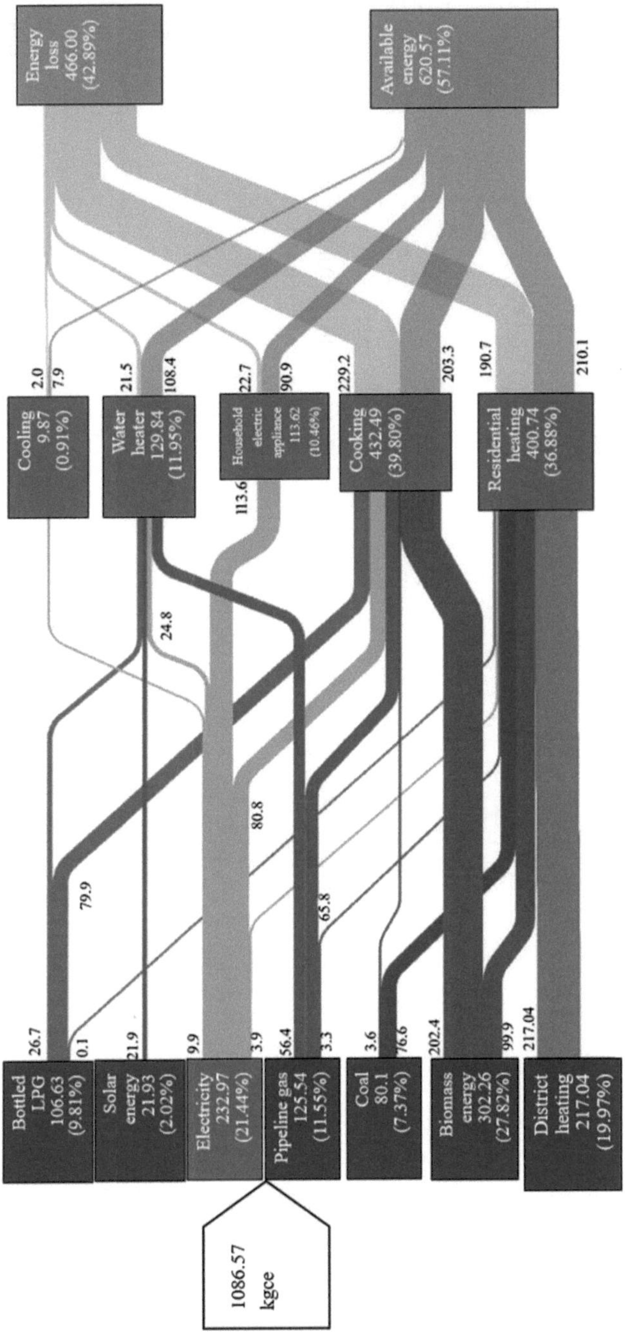


**Fig. 4** Flow chart of available energy of standard Chinese household in 2014: electrothermal equivalent

**Table 6** Available energy balance of households after weight adjustment in 2014: electrothermal equivalent (Unit: kgce)

| Energy consumption | | Firewood/ straw | Charcoal | Coal | Diesel/gasoline/ kerosene/ ethanol-added gasoline | Electricity | Bottled LPG | Pipeline natural gas | Pipeline coal gas | Biogas | Solar energy | Heat | Sum |
|---|---|---|---|---|---|---|---|---|---|---|---|---|---|
| Cooking | Stoves burning firewood | 40.32 | | | | | | | | | | | 40.32 |
| | Stoves burning honeycomb briquettes | | | 1.00 | | | | | | | | | 1.00 |
| | Oil stove | | | | 0.01 | | | | | | | | 0.01 |
| | Induction cooktop | | | | | 27.80 | | | | | | | 27.80 |
| | Gas stove | | | | | | 47.95 | 47.58 | 1.40 | 0.00 | 0.00 | 0.00 | 96.94 |
| | Biogas stove | | | | | | | | | 0.41 | | | 0.41 |
| | Electric rice cooker | | | | | 26.94 | | | | | | | 26.94 |
| | Pressure cooker | | | | | 2.80 | | | | | | | 2.80 |
| | Microwave oven | | | | | 1.41 | | | | | | | 1.41 |
| | Oven | | | | | 0.05 | | | | | | | 0.05 |

(continued)

**Table 6** (continued)

| Energy consumption | | Firewood/ straw | Charcoal | Coal | Diesel/gasoline/ kerosene/ ethanol-added gasoline | Electricity | Bottled LPG | Pipeline natural gas | Pipeline coal gas | Biogas | Solar energy | Heat | Sum |
|---|---|---|---|---|---|---|---|---|---|---|---|---|---|
| | Electric kettle | | | | | 5.65 | | | | | | | 5.65 |
| Electrical appliance | Refrigerator | | | | | 12.38 | | | | | | | 12.38 |
| | Freezer | | | | | 1.27 | | | | | | | 1.27 |
| | Washing machine | | | | | 6.63 | | | | | | | 6.63 |
| | Drying machine | | | | | 0.09 | | | | | | | 0.09 |
| | Television set | | | | | 57.91 | | | | | | | 57.91 |
| | Computer | | | | | 9.23 | | | | | | | 9.23 |
| | Light bulbs | | | | | 3.38 | | | | | | | 3.38 |
| Residential heating | District heating | | | | | | | | | | | 184.49 | 184.49 |
| | Heatable brick bed | 15.73 | 0.06 | 2.54 | | | | | | | | | 18.32 |
| | Residential air conditioner for space heating | | | | | 0.67 | | | | | | | 0.67 |

(continued)

**Table 6** (continued)

| Energy consumption | | Firewood/ straw | Charcoal | Coal | Diesel/gasoline/ kerosene/ ethanol-added gasoline | Electricity | Bottled LPG | Pipeline natural gas | Pipeline coal gas | Biogas | Solar energy | Heat | Sum |
|---|---|---|---|---|---|---|---|---|---|---|---|---|---|
| | Boiler pipe for space heating | 0.39 | 0.03 | 4.17 | 0.01 | 0.08 | | 2.51 | | | | | 7.18 |
| | Heating stove (burning wood and coal, etc.) | 12.96 | 5.91 | 52.63 | | | | | | | | | 18.51 |
| | Electric radiator heater | | | | | 2.34 | | | | | | | 2.34 |
| Hot water | Water heater | | | | | 19.84 | 16.02 | 42.31 | | | 8.77 | | 86.94 |
| Air conditioning | Air conditioner | | | | | 7.89 | | | | | | | 7.89 |
| Total (transportation excluded) | | 59.02 | 1.27 | 22.44 | 0.02 | 186.38 | 63.98 | 92.40 | 1.40 | 0.41 | 8.77 | 184.49 | 620.57 |
| Transportation | Automobile | | | | 36.44 | | | | | | | | 36.44 |
| Total (transportation included) | | 59.02 | 1.27 | 22.44 | 36.46 | 186.38 | 63.98 | 92.40 | 1.40 | 0.41 | 8.77 | 184.49 | 657.00 |

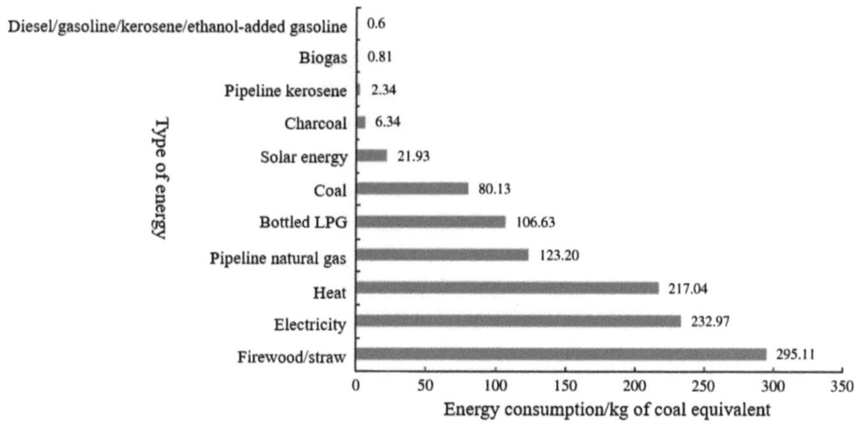


**Fig. 5** Residential energy consumption in China in terms of types of energy

the annual coal consumption per household of 86.47 kgce, coal was mainly used for heat supply and power generation and heat supply accounted for a large proportion in such use. Therefore, the indirect coal consumption per household could not be estimated accurately.

(2) Structure of energy demand in residential energy consumption

In terms of the end uses of energy, cooking and space heating accounted for the most consumption. The energy consumption of cooking was 432.49 kgce, accounting for about 39.8% of the total. The energy consumption of space heating was 400.74 kgce, accounting for 36.88% of the total. Meanwhile, household electrical appliances consumed 113.62 kgce, accounting for a small percentage, 10.46% of the total. Energy consumed for transportation was still mainly fuel oil (including diesel, gasoline, kerosene and ethanol-added gasoline). In 2014, the consumption of fuel oil for transportation reached 121.46 kgce. If energy consumption of transportation was included, the average energy consumption per household in China in 2014 would be 1,208.03 kgce.

Concerning the energy consumption of cooking, as shown in Fig. 6, the annual energy consumption of cooking per household in China was 432.49 kgce in 2014, and the main energy consumed were biomass energy and gas. To be specific, firewood and straw consumption accounted for 46.70% of the total energy consumption of cooking, gas (including bottled LPG, pipeline natural gas and pipeline coal gas) consumption accounted for 33.5% and the energy consumption of other cooking equipment (including electric equipment and those burning coal) accounted for 19.54%, while the energy consumption of oil stoves and biogas stoves accounted for the smallest percentage. This is because of the energy consumption habits in rural and urban areas in China. In rural areas where biomass energy is more accessible and can be collected at lower cost, the energy source for cooking is mainly firewood or

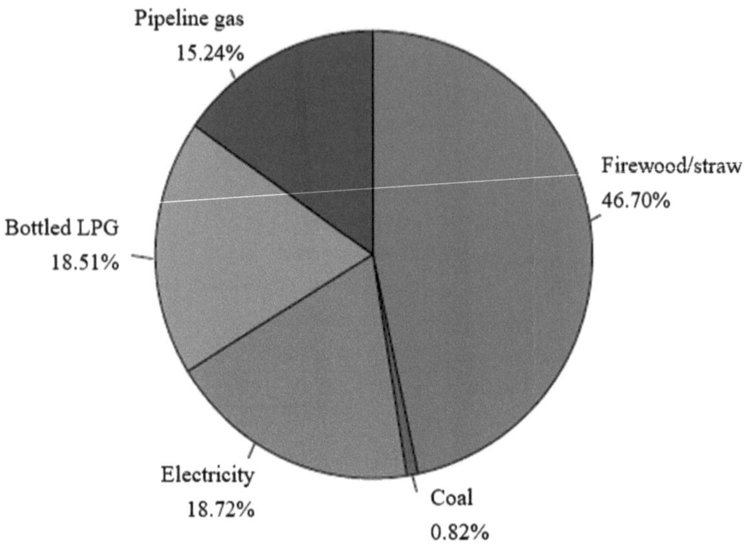


**Fig. 6** Main energy sources for cooking in standard Chinese households in 2014

straw. In urban areas, pipeline gas and bottled LPG are popular energy for cooking and electric cooking equipment is also extensively used.

The energy consumed by household electrical appliances is solely electricity, with an annual consumption of 113.62 kgce. Electricity consumers are mainly television sets, refrigerators and freezers, the electricity consumption of which accounted for 63.71%, 13.63% and 1.40% of the total energy consumption of household electrical appliances respectively. Computer was the second largest in terms of electricity consumption and its electricity consumption accounted for 10.15% of the total. Washing machines accounted for 7.29% of the total energy consumption and light bulbs accounted for 3.72% of the total energy consumption (Fig. 7). Large electrical appliances such as television sets, refrigerators and washing machines remained the main energy consumers (air conditioners are considered electric heating equipment and not included in this group).

Space heating is another major end use of energy in residential energy consumption in China, the total energy consumption of which amounted to 400.75 kgce per year. Concerning the various means of heating, district heating accounted for 54.16% of the total and household heating accounted for 46.84%. As for the fuels of household heating, firewood and straw remained dominant, accounting for 50.93% of the total, and the second largest percentage was taken up by coal, accounting for 45.14% of the total, while natural gas and electricity accounted for 1.82% and 2.11% of the total respectively (Fig. 8).

The energy consumption for water heating was similar to that of household electrical appliances. In 2014, the energy consumption for water heating of a standard Chinese household was 129.84 kgce per year. Pipeline natural gas was the primary

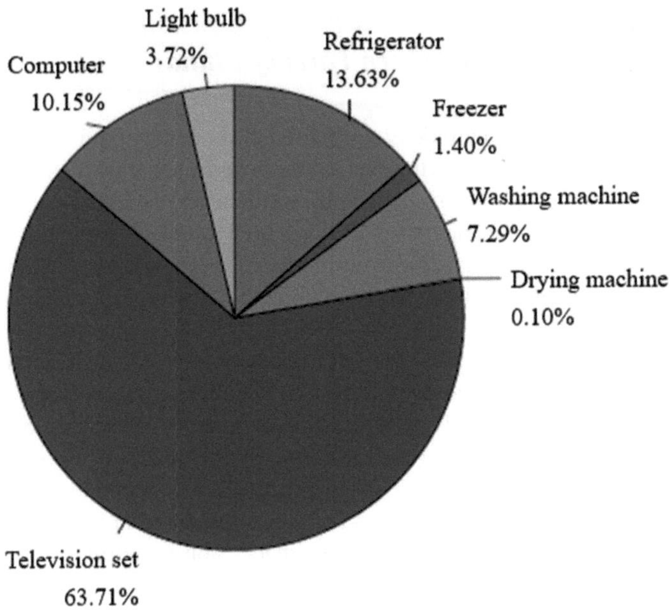


**Fig. 7** Types of energy-consuming household electrical appliances in standard Chinese households in 2014

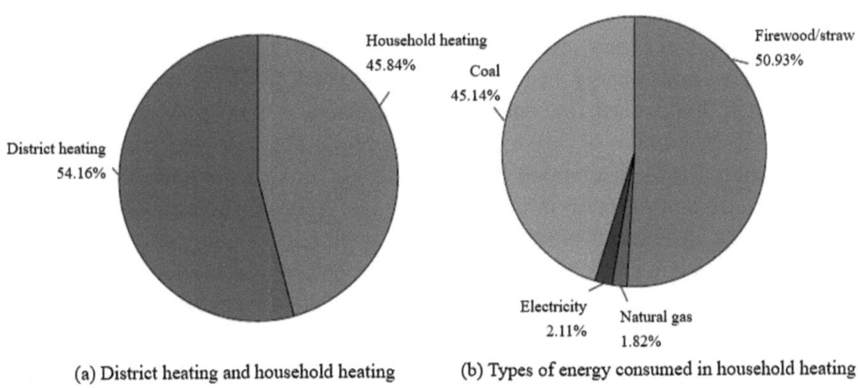


**Fig. 8** Types of energy consumed for space heating in standard Chinese households in 2014

source of energy, accounting for 43.44% of the total. Electricity, bottled LPG and solar energy accounted for 19%, 20% and 16.9% of the total respectively.

The energy consumption of transportation of a standard Chinese household in 2014 was 121.46 kgce per year. Gasoline was the main energy consumed in this regard.

### 3.2 *Comparison of Residential Energy Consumption in Northern and Southern Parts of China*

In this book, the 34° north latitude is considered the boundary between northern and southern China, which applies whenever northern and southern China is mentioned. Meanwhile, as some provinces cover both northern and southern parts of China, which causes difficulty in calculation of household numbers, while comparing the energy consumption characteristics in northern and southern parts of China, the data used was not weighted. In another word, we directly calculated the mean value based on the questionnaire data.

In the southern part of China, the total residential energy consumption (transportation excluded) per household in 2014 was 888.29 kgce per year and the energy consumption per capita was 291.35 kgce per year. In the northern part of China, the total residential energy consumption (transportation excluded) in 2014 per household was 1,615.9 kgce per year and the energy consumption per capita was 490.62 kgce per year. The residential energy consumption per household in northern China was 1.82 times the figure in the south, and the energy consumption per capita of the former was 1.68 times the figure of the latter. The additional energy consumption in the north is mainly caused by space heating in winter.

(1) South-north differences in types of energy consumed

In terms of the types of energy, electricity was the main type of energy consumed in the southern part of China, amounting to 264.1 kgce per household per year, and the second was biomass energy, the consumption of which was 218.46 kgce per household per year. In the north, the energy consumption was mainly for district heating, leading to consumption of 548 kgce per household per year, and the second was biomass energy, the consumption of which was 472.14 kgce per household per year. The electricity consumption in the north was 217 kgce per household per year. In addition to the differences in space heating in winter, the south-north differences in China mainly lied in the consumption of pipeline natural gas, bottled LPG and coal. In the south, the household consumption of pipeline natural gas was 188.61 kgce per household per year, accounting for 21.23% of the total household energy consumption, larger than the proportion (7.30%) in the north. The consumption of bottled LPG in the south was 124.6 kgce per household per year, accounting for 14.03% of the total, larger than the proportion (4.58%) in the north. Coal consumption accounted for 10.75% of the total energy consumption in the north, while the proportion of coal consumption was only 1.36% in the south (Fig. 9).

(2) South-north differences in energy demand

Considering from the perspective of end uses of energy, the southern and northern parts of China show obvious differences in proportions of energy consumption for cooking and space heating (Fig. 10).

In the south, the annual energy consumption of cooking per household was 465 kgce, accounting for 54.36% of the total household energy consumption in this

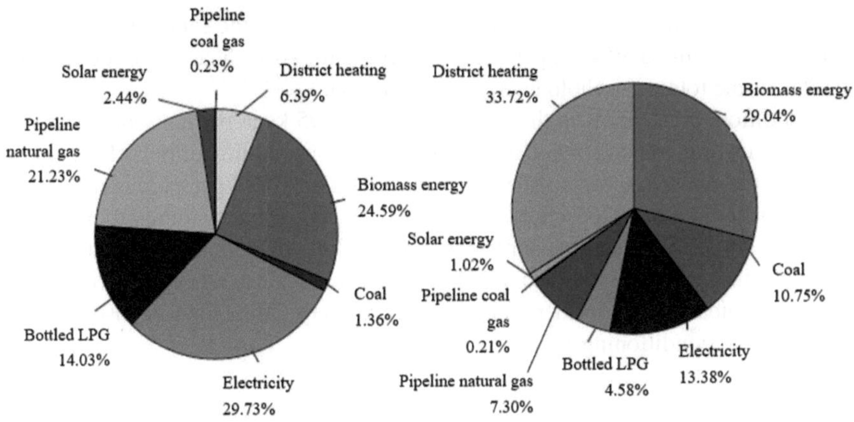


(a) Types of energy in residential energy consumption in southern China

(b) Types of energy in residential energy consumption in northern China

**Fig. 9** South-north differences in types of energy in residential energy consumption

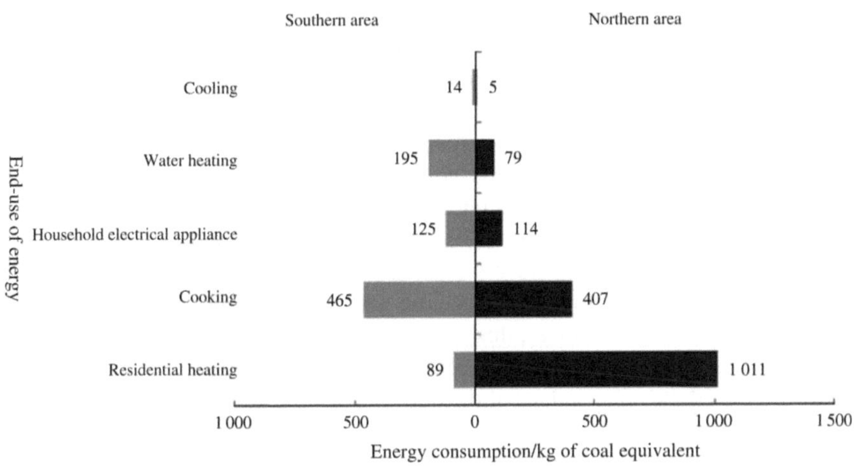


**Fig. 10** Comparison of energy consuming activities in southern and northern parts of China

area. By comparison, in the north, the annual energy consumption of cooking per household was only 407 kgce, accounting for 25.19% of the total household energy consumption in the north.

However, concerning the energy consumption of space heating, due to difference in winter temperatures between northern and southern parts of China, the energy consumption of households for space heating in the north was significantly more than in the south for the same purpose, which was about 11 times the consumption for space heating in the south. As shown in Fig. 10, in 2014, each household in the north consumed 1,011 kgce for space heating on average, accounting for 62.56%

of the total household energy consumption in the north. In the south, however, each household consumed 89 kgce per year on average for space heating, accounting for 10.02% of the total household energy consumption.

In addition, households in the south consumed 195 kgce per household per year for water heating, which is more than twice of the consumption of households in the north for the same purpose, as the latter consumed only 79 kgce per household per year for water heating. Households in the south also consumed slightly more energy for use of household electrical appliances and cooking than their counterparts in the north, but there was no significant difference in this regard, especially considering that households in both northern and southern parts of China didn't consume much energy for air conditioning.

## 3.3 Comparison of Residential Energy Consumption in Rural and Urban Areas

How to distinguish between rural and urban residents: In the survey, there are 7 types of *hukou*, household registration of respondents, i.e., agricultural *hukou*, non-agricultural *hukou*, resident (formerly agricultural) *hukou*, resident (formerly non-agricultural) *hukou*, others, military service and having no household registration. During calculation, based on information offered by the respondents, "non-agricultural *hukou*, resident (formerly non-agricultural) *hukou*, others, military service and having no household registration" were all considered urban *hukou*, resulting in 1,480 sample observations, while "agricultural *hukou* and resident (formerly agricultural) *hukou*" were considered rural *hukou*, resulting in 2,383 sample observations. Meanwhile, due to lack of accurate data about number of rural and urban households in various provinces, this book uses unweighted data for comparison of characteristics of rural and urban residential energy consumption. In another word, we directly used the mean values of the questionnaire data.

If energy consumption of transportation is considered, the annual energy consumption of urban residents per household would be 1,456.3 kgce, and the annual energy consumption of rural residents per household would be 1,248.7 kgce. If we exclude energy consumption of transportation, the annual household energy consumption of urban and rural residents would be 1,274.7 and 1,152.74 kgce, and the energy consumption per capita would be 430.5 kgce per year and 352.2 kgce per year respectively. The total household energy consumption and energy consumption per capita of urban residents were 1.11 times and 1.22 times the figures of their rural counterparts respectively.

(1) Urban-rural differences in types of energy in energy consumption

As shown in Fig. 11, in terms of the types of energy sources, the consumption of firewood and straw in rural households accounted for a large proportion, the annual per-household consumption of which reached 494.27 kgce, accounting for 42.89% of the total energy consumption. The second and third most consumed energy

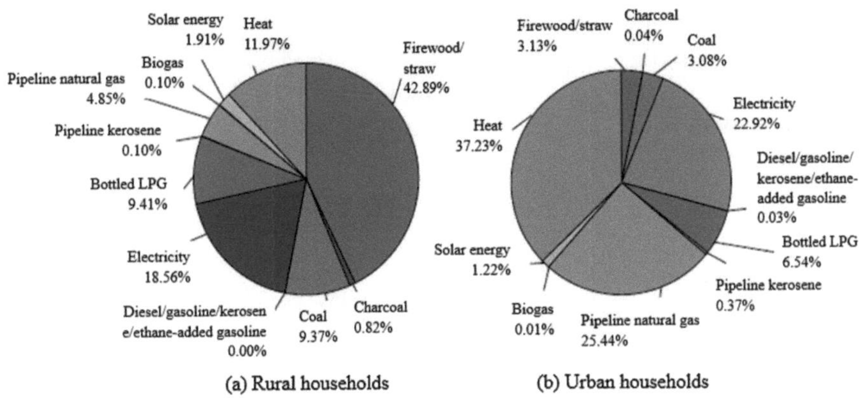


**Fig. 11** Comparison of household energy consumption in rural and urban areas (transportation excluded)

sources in rural households were electricity and heat, while the shares of solar energy and pipeline kerosene in the total were small. For the urban households, the heat consumption for district heating accounted for a large proportion, amounting to 474.51 kgce per year per household and accounting for 37.23% of the total energy consumption. The second and third most consumed energy for urban households were electricity and pipeline natural gas, both accounting for more than 20% of the total. Compared with their rural counterparts, the urban residents consumed less firewood, straw and coal, the consumption for each of which accounting for less than 5% of the annual energy consumption. Though, similar to the case of the rural households, the consumption of diesel, gasoline, kerosene and ethanol-added gasoline of urban households accounted for a very small proportion of the total.

(2) Urban-rural differences in energy demand

The differences in annual energy consumption of various equipment in rural and urban households in terms of end uses of energy are shown in Fig. 12. It can be seen that the annual energy consumption of cooking per urban household was 328.90 kgce, accounting for 25.80% of the total energy consumption per year. The annual energy consumption of cooking per rural household was 509.59 kgce, accounting for 44.21% of the total, which is much higher than the consumption for cooking in urban areas. Energy consumption of urban households mainly came from space heating, consuming 549.33 kgce per household per year and accounting for 43.10% of the annual energy consumption. Rural households consumed 442.24 kgce per household per year for space heating, 100 kg fewer than the consumption for space heating in urban areas, but it still accounted for 38.4% of the annual energy consumption of rural households. It can be seen that in both rural and urban households, energy consumption of space heating accounted for a large proportion of the total. Meanwhile, energy consumption of air conditioning and use of household electrical appliances were of small proportions in rural and urban households.

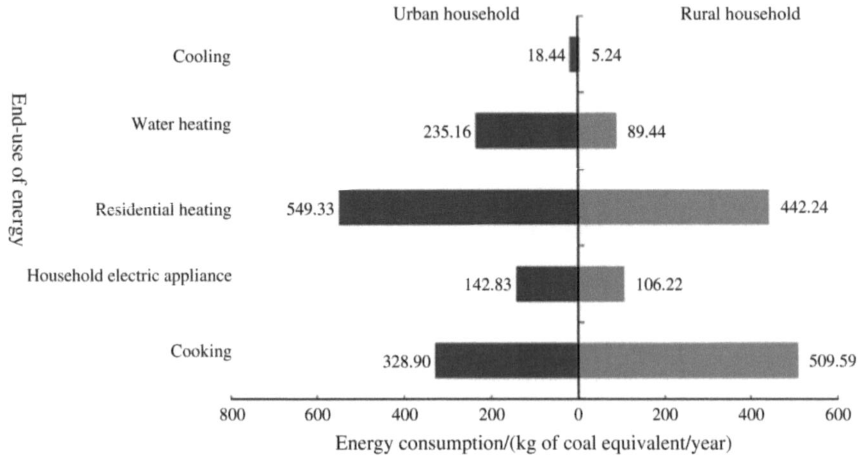


**Fig. 12** Urban-rural differences in household energy-consuming activities

Concerning the energy consumption of cooking (Fig. 13), in 2014, the annual energy consumption of cooking per household was 509.6 kgce in rural areas and 328.9 kgce in urban areas. Rural households consumed more energy for cooking than their urban counterparts, approximately 1.55 times the consumption for cooking of the latter. Concerning the type of energy consumed, biomass energy was the major energy consumed by rural households for cooking, the annual consumption of which amounted to 307.9 kgce per household, far more than their urban counterparts which consumed little biomass energy. Urban households consumed far more pipeline natural gas than rural households, as pipeline natural gas was the major energy consumed by urban households for cooking. Meanwhile, there was no significant difference in consumption of electricity and bottled LPG for cooking between rural and urban households and they both consumed a small amount of pipeline kerosene and coal for cooking. Such energy composition for cooking is due to accessibility of firewood/straw and underdeveloped infrastructure of pipeline gas in rural areas.

Concerning the energy consumption of household electrical appliances (Fig. 14), the annual energy consumption of household electrical appliances was 1,162 kWh per urban household and 864 kWh per rural household. The energy consumption of electrical appliances of urban households was 1.34 times such consumption of rural households. Considering from the perspective of specific appliances, the main energy consumer in both rural and urban households was television sets. Meanwhile, the energy consumption of bulbs, computers, television sets, washing machines and refrigerators in urban households was more than the energy consumption of such appliances in rural households.

As shown in Table 7, in winter, urban households mainly used district heating, which consumed 475.3 kgce per year per household, about 3.45 times the energy consumption of district heating for rural households. Rural households mainly used

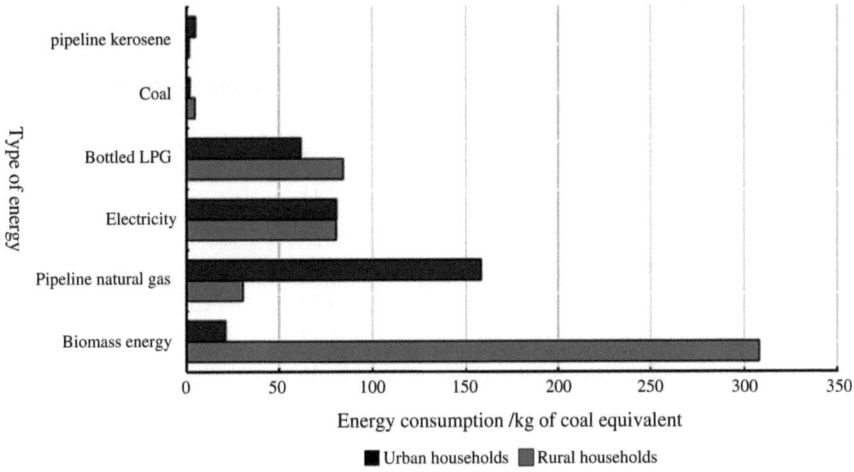


**Fig. 13** Urban-rural differences in energy consumption of cooking in standard households

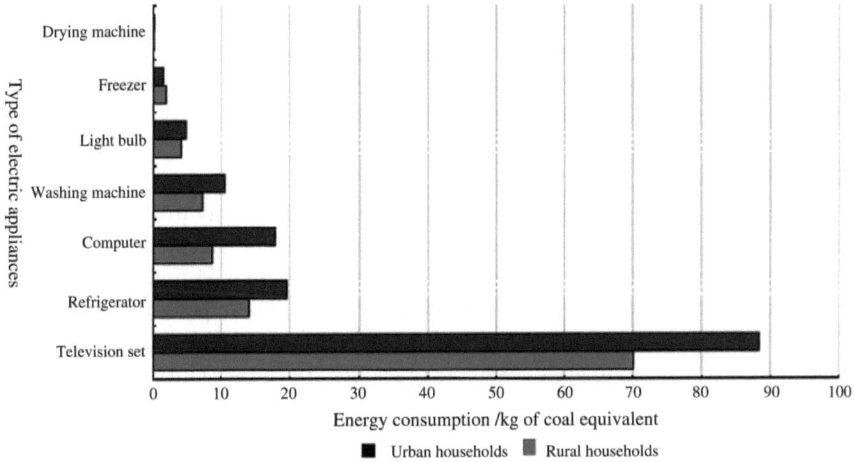


**Fig. 14** Urban-rural differences in energy consumption of household electrical appliances in standard households

household heating, which consumed 304.60 kgce per year per household, about 5.39 times the energy consumption of household heating for urban households. Among the energy for household heating of rural households, firewood/straw, charcoal and coal were the mail fuels. This is related with the residential distribution in rural and urban areas in China. Rural residences are scattered, so the efficiency of district heating through pipelines is not high. In urban areas where people in live in apartments, the efficiency of district heating through pipelines is undoubtedly much higher than in rural areas.

**Table 7** Urban-rural differences in energy consumption of space heating of standard households (Unit: kgce/year)

| End use of energy | Energy | Urban household | Rural household |
|---|---|---|---|
| District heating | Heat | 475.25 | 137.80 |
| Household heating | Electricity | 5.71 | 3.35 |
| | Natural gas | 12.11 | 0.38 |
| | Firewood/straw, charcoal, coal | 26.91 | 300.87 |
| | Sum | 56.50 | 304.60 |
| Water heating | Electricity | 128.19 | 118.83 |
| | Bottled LPG | 21.57 | 15.07 |
| | Pipeline natural gas | 153.41 | 155.04 |
| | Solar energy | 15.31 | 11.28 |
| | Sum | 318.49 | 300.23 |
| Air conditioning | Air conditioner | 18.51 | 5.22 |

Concerning supply of hot water, there is no significant difference in energy consumption in this regard between rural and urban households. The annual energy consumption of water heating was 318.49 kgce per household in urban areas and 300.23 kgce per household in rural areas. Both rural and urban households mainly used electricity and pipeline natural gas for water heating, and consumption of bottled LPG and solar energy constituted a small proportion.

For air conditioning, both rural and urban households mainly used air conditioners. The energy consumption of air conditioners was significantly higher in urban households than in rural households, with the former being 3.54 times of the latter.

Concerning transportation, the annual energy consumption per household in this regard in urban and rural areas was 182 kgce and 96 kgce respectively in 2014. Private cars were the primary consumers in energy consumption for transportation. Gasoline was still the main fuel for cars.

# 4 Analysis and Comparison of Residential Energy Cost

## *4.1 Difference in Energy Expenditure in Terms of Energy Types: Transportation Excluded*

According to the survey and calculation, in 2014, the annual income of Chinese households was RMB68,989 per household, the residential energy expenditure per capita was RMB906 and the energy expenditure per household was RMB2,341,[1]

[1] The sample size here is 3,092 (For samples which did not answer this question and which answered this question using different units, the observation was considered 0).

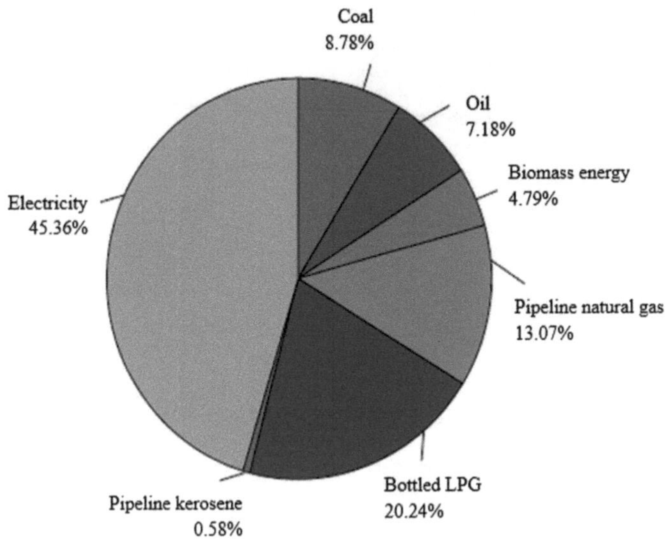


**Fig. 15** Comparison of expenditure on various energy sources by Chinese households

accounting for 3.4% of the annual household income. The mean value of residential expenditure on consumption in China was RMB35,029.23 in 2014, in which the expenditure on energy consumption accounted for 6.68%.

Comparing the expenditure on consumption of various energy sources, the annual expenditure on electricity was the highest at RMB1,061.75, accounting for 45.36% of the total energy expenditure. The second was bottled LPG at RMB474, accounting for 20.24% of the total. Expenditure on pipeline natural gas and coal was also high, amounting to RMB305 and RMB205 respectively and accounting for 13.07 and 8.78% of the total. The proportions of expenditure on various energy sources to the total are as shown in Fig. 15.

In terms of the proportions of expenditure on various energy sources to the total annual consumption expenditure of Chinese households, expenditure on electricity accounted for 3.03% of the total, followed by bottled LPG and pipeline natural gas which accounted for 1.35% and 0.87% of the total respectively. The expenditure on other types of energy accounted for no more than 1% of the total respectively (Fig. 16).

## *4.2 South-North Differences in Residential Energy Expenditure in China*

The energy expenditure per household was RMB2,592.3 per year in the south and RMB2,144.5 per year in the north. The energy expenditure per capita was

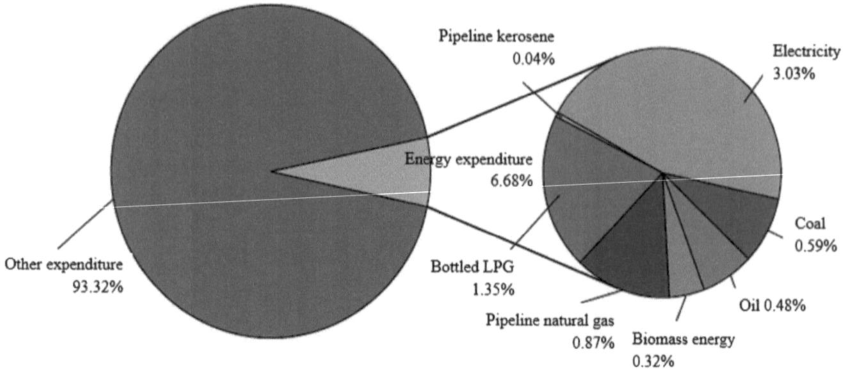


**Fig. 16** Proportions of various energy expenditure to total household consumption expenditure

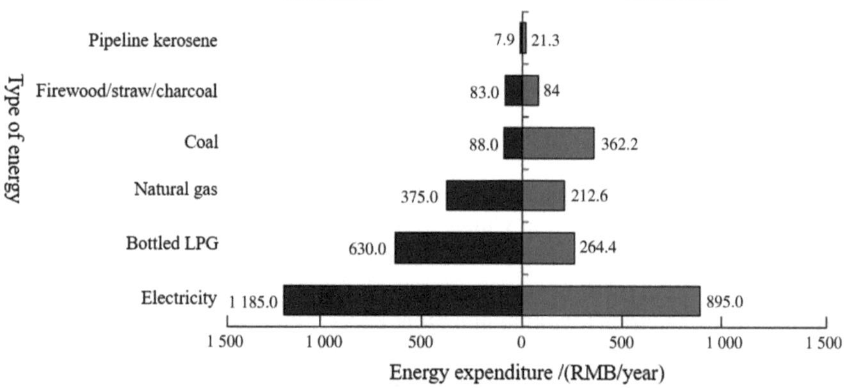


**Fig. 17** Comparison of energy expenditure of households in southern and northern parts of China

RMB1,036.9 per year in the south and RMB932.4 per year in the north. As shown in Fig. 17, in terms of the types of energy consumed, electricity consumption was dominant in residential energy consumption both in the south and in the north, which reached RMB1,185.0 per year per household in the south and RMB895.0 per year per household in the north. The annual expenditure on bottled LPG per household in the south was approximately 2.4 times the expenditure in the north, with the former being RMB630.0 per year and the latter RMB264.4 per year. The annual expenditure on pipeline natural gas per household was RMB375.0 in the south and RMB212.6 in the north. But the expenditure on coal was much higher in the north than in the south, with the former being RMB362.2 per year per household and the latter RMB88.0 per year per household.

## 4.3 Urban-Rural Differences in Residential Energy Expenditure in China

The household energy expenditure in 2014 in China was RMB2,786.7 per household for urban households and RMB2,266 for rural households. The annual energy expenditure of urban households was 1.23 times the expenditure of rural households. In terms of the types of energy consumed, a significant proportion of energy expenditure was used for electricity consumption both in the rural and urban areas. To be specific, the urban households spent RMB1,283.90 per household on electricity consumption, making up 46% of the total energy expenditure, while the rural households spent RMB923.78 per household on electricity consumption, making up 40% of the total energy expenditure. In addition, urban households spent much more than their rural counterparts on pipeline natural gas, the consumption of which was about 6 times the figure of rural households. By contrast, rural households spent more money than urban households on bottled LPG, the consumption of which was about 1.34 times the figure of urban households. Such differences are related with the development of infrastructure in rural and urban areas (Fig. 18).

Rural and urban households had no obvious difference in consumption of pipeline kerosene and firewood/straw. The consumption of biomass energy accounted for a larger proportion of rural household energy consumption, but biomass energy such as firewood is accessible free of charge and no significant cost is incurred in this regard.

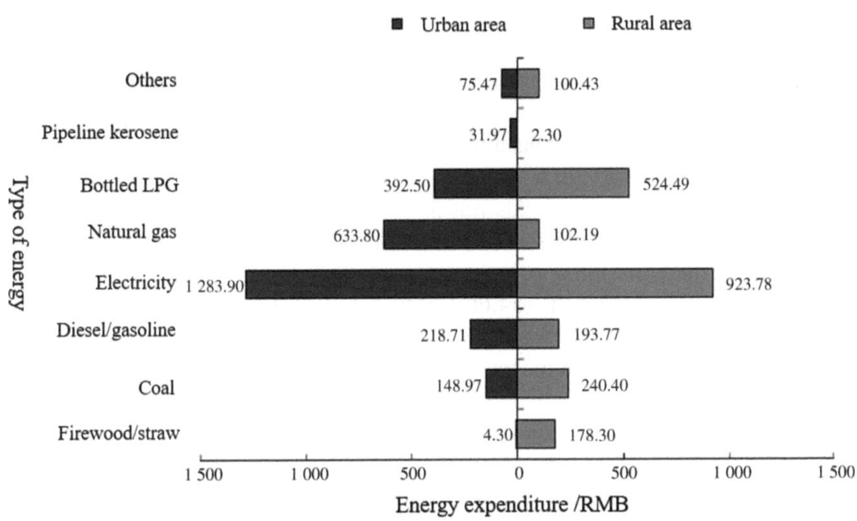


**Fig. 18** Comparison of energy expenditure in rural and urban households

# 5 Analysis and Comparison of Carbon Footprint of Households

## *5.1 Analysis of Residential Carbon Emission in China*

The carbon emission of energy was calculated according to the following factors. Carbon content and oxidation rate of carbon were cited from the *General Principles for Calculation of the Comprehensive Energy Consumption* (GB/T 2589–2008), the average lower heating value and emission factor were cited from the *Guidelines for Provincial Greenhouse Gas Inventories* (NDRC Climate [2011] No. 1041). Considering the incomplete combustion of coal in residential use, 50% of the standard factor was used in our calculation. Concerning the default value of $CO_2$ emission, for the carbon emission data of (honeycomb) briquettes, gasoline, diesel, kerosene, LPG, pipeline natural gas, pipeline coal gas, fuel oil and charcoal, the default emission factors for stationary combustion in the residential and agriculture/forestry/fishing/fishing farms categories from the *2006 IPCC Guidelines for National Greenhouse Gas Inventories* were adopted. Considering the carbon neutrality of biomass energy, its carbon emission factor was considered 0. According to the *Methods for Calculating Greenhouse Gas Emission and Reporting Guidelines for Public Building Operating Enterprises*[2] issued by the National Development and Reform Commission of China, the carbon emission of heat was considered 110,000 kg/TJ. As for electricity, the carbon emission factors in various provinces in 2010 were adopted. For details, please refer to Tables 8 and 9.

In this section, a 2D matrix consisting of carbon emission and end use of energy is created based on the above coefficients for conversion to coal equivalent. After being weighted according to the provincial household numbers, the carbon emission balance (Table 10) of residential energy consumption in China in 2014 was obtained based on calculation of coal consumption of power generation. It can be seen that the annual carbon emission of a standard household after being weighted according to provincial number of households was 3,465.70 kg (transportation excluded). The primary sources of carbon emission were electricity, heat and coal.

In terms of the emission source (transportation excluded), the carbon emission was 1,894.38 kg from electricity (54.66% of the total), 699.75 kg from district heating (20.19% of the total), 408.33 kg from coal (11.78% of the total), 264.92 kg from pipeline natural gas (7.64% of the total) and 178.8 kg from bottled LPG (5.56% of the total) (Fig. 19). Some people, according to common sense, consider that electricity is a kind of clean energy. In fact, the use of electricity is clean, but its production is not. In China, about 70% of its electricity is generated using coal. Considering the low efficiency at 30–40% of power generation units burning coal and long-distance transmission, the ultimate efficiency is even lower. Therefore, electricity itself is not low-carbon.

---

[2]http://www.ndrc.gov.cn/zcfb/zcfbtz/201511/W020151111537500738061.pdf.

**Table 8** Carbon emission factors of energy

| Energy | Carbon content/(tons of carbon/TJ) | Carbon oxidation rate | Lower bound of 95% confidence interval of emission factor | Average lower heating value (kj/kg) | Emission factor |
|---|---|---|---|---|---|
| Coal (Anthracite) | 26.37 | 0.9 | 87,300 | 20,908 | 1.8194 |
| Gasoline | 18.9 | 0.98 | 67,500 | 43,070 | 2.9251 |
| Diesel | 20.2 | 0.98 | 72,600 | 42,652 | 3.0959 |
| LPG | 17.2 | 0.98 | 61,600 | 50,179 | 3.1013 |
| Natural gas | 15.32 | 0.99 | 54,300 | 51,434 | 2.8603 |
| Coke oven gas | 13.58 | 0.98 | 37,300 | 16,726 | 0.8162 |
| Fuel oil | 21.1 | 0.98 | 75,500 | 81,816 | 3.1705 |

*Note* Fuel with lower heating value of 29,307 kJ was considered 1 kgce. The data in columns of carbon content and carbon oxidation rate were cited from the *General Principles for Calculation of the Comprehensive Energy Consumption* (GB/T 2589–2008). The data in columns of average lower heating value and carbon factor were cited from the *Guidelines for Provincial Greenhouse Gas Inventories* (NDRC Climate [2011] No. 1041). Method for calculation of $CO_2$ emission factor with raw coal as an instance: $1.9003 = 20908 \times 0.000\,000\,001 \times 26.37 \times 0.94 \times 1\,000 \times 3.666\,67$

**Table 9** Emission factors of regional power grid in 2015 (Unit: kg of $CO_2$/kWh)

| Region | Carbon emission factor of power grid |
|---|---|
| North China | 1.0416 |
| Northeast China | 1.1291 |
| East China | 0.8112 |
| Central China | 0.9515 |
| Northwest China | 0.9457 |
| South China | 0.8959 |

*Source* Baseline emission factors of regional power grid in China in 2015; Weighted average of OM 2011–2013

In terms of the end uses (Fig. 20), the largest proportion (38.87% of the total) of carbon emission came from residential heating, amounting to 1,126.77 kg. The following was household electrical appliances and cooking, the $CO_2$ emission from which accounted for similar proportions, i.e., 22.80% and 24.02% of the total emission respectively. The $CO_2$ emission from water heating accounted for 9.42% of the total. The smallest proportion (4.89% of the total) of $CO_2$ emission was from air conditioning, which was 187.08 kg.

**Table 10** Carbon emission balance of residential energy consumption weighted to provincial number of households in 2014: based on coal consumption of power generation (unit: kg of $CO_2$)

| Energy | | Firewood/straw | Charcoal | Coal | Diesel/gasoline/kerosene/ethanol-added gasoline | Electricity | Bottled LPG | Pipeline natural gas | Pipeline coal gas | Biogas | Solar energy | Heat | Sum |
|---|---|---|---|---|---|---|---|---|---|---|---|---|---|
| Cooking | Stoves burning firewood | | | | | | | | | | | | |
| | Stoves burning honeycomb briquettes | | | 18.14 | | | | | | | | | 18.14 |
| | Oil stove | | | | 0.04 | | | | | | | | 0.04 |
| | Induction cooktop | | | | | 266.93 | | | | | | | 266.93 |
| | Gas stove | | | | | | 144.5241 | 136.43 | 5.369054 | | | | 286.33 |
| | Biogas stove | | | | | | | | | | | | |
| | Electric rice cooker | | | | | 254.58 | | | | | | | 254.58 |
| | Pressure cooker | | | | | 26.25 | | | | | | | 26.25 |
| | Microwave oven | | | | | 13.01 | | | | | | | 13.01 |
| | Oven | | | | | 0.48 | | | | | | | 0.48 |
| | Solar cooker | | | | | | | | | | | | |

(continued)

**Table 10** (continued)

| Energy | | Firewood/straw | Charcoal | Coal | Diesel/gasoline/kerosene/ethanol-added gasoline | Electricity | Bottled LPG | Pipeline natural gas | Pipeline coal gas | Biogas | Solar energy | Heat | Sum |
|---|---|---|---|---|---|---|---|---|---|---|---|---|---|
| | Electric kettle | | | | | 53.25 | | | | | | | |
| | Others | | | | | | | | | | | | 53.25 |
| Electrical appliance | Refrigerator | | | | | 118.8305 | | | | | | | 118.83 |
| | Freezer | | | | | 12.90 | | | | | | | 12.90 |
| | Washing machine | | | | | 63.21 | | | | | | | 63.21 |
| | Drying machine | | | | | 0.85 | | | | | | | 0.85 |
| | Television set | | | | | 555.82 | | | | | | | 555.82 |
| | Computer | | | | | 88.37 | | | | | | | 88.37 |
| | Light bulbs | | | | | 32.28 | | | | | | | 32.28 |
| Residential heating | District heating | | | | | | | | | | | 699.75 | 699.75 |
| | Heatable brick bed | | | 46.17 | | | | | | | | | 46.17 |
| | Residential air conditioner for space heating | | | | | 6.10 | | | | | | | 6.10 |

(continued)

**Table 10** (continued)

| Energy | | Firewood/ straw | Charcoal | Coal | Diesel/gasoline/ kerosene/ ethanol-added gasoline | Electricity | Bottled LPG | Pipeline natural gas | Pipeline coal gas | Biogas | Solar energy | Heat | Sum |
|---|---|---|---|---|---|---|---|---|---|---|---|---|---|
| | Boiler pipe for space heating | | | 75.81 | 0.10 | 0.81 | | 7.19 | | | | | 83.90 |
| | Heating stove (burning wood and coal, etc.) | | | 268.21 | | | | | | | | | 268.21 |
| | Electric radiator heater | | | | | 22.65 | | | | | | | 22.65 |
| | Oil-filled radiator heater | | | | | | | | | | | | |
| | Electric heating film | | | | | | | | | | | | |
| | Others | | | | | | | | | | | | |
| Hot water | Water heater | | | | | 190.98 | 48.29 | 121.30 | | | | | 360.58 |

(continued)

**Table 10** (continued)

| Energy | | Firewood/straw | Charcoal | Coal | Diesel/gasoline/kerosene/ethanol-added gasoline | Electricity | Bottled LPG | Pipeline natural gas | Pipeline coal gas | Biogas | Solar energy | Heat | Sum |
|---|---|---|---|---|---|---|---|---|---|---|---|---|---|
| Air conditioning | Air conditioner | | | | | 187.08 | | | | | | | 187.08 |
| Total (transportation excluded) | | | | 408.33 | 0.14 | 1,894.38 | 192.82 | 264.92 | 5.37 | | | 699.75 | 3,465.70 |
| Transportation | Automobile | | | | 240.37 | | | | | | | | 240.37 |
| Total (transportation included) | | | | 408.33 | 240.51 | 1,894.38 | 192.82 | 264.92 | 5.37 | | | 699.75 | 3,706.07 |

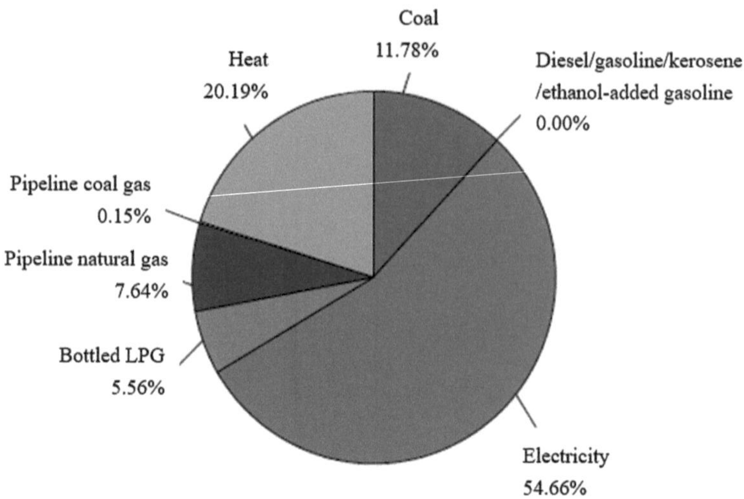


**Fig. 19** Composition of sources of carbon emission in terms of energy types

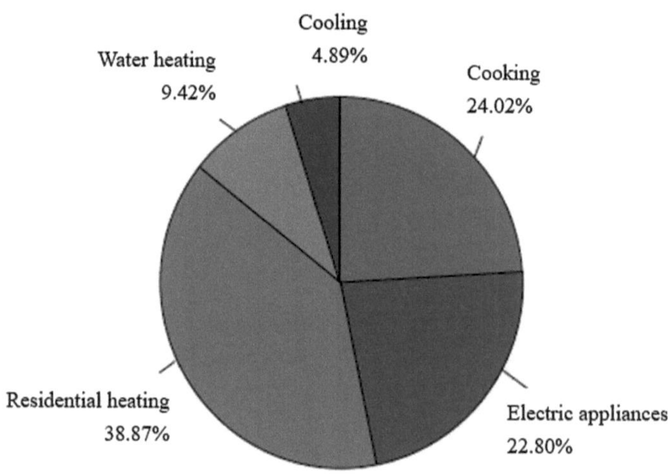


**Fig. 20** Composition of sources of carbon emission in terms of end uses

## 5.2 *South-North Differences in Residential Carbon Emission in China*

Concerning the total residential carbon emission in China, the $CO_2$ emission per household in 2014 was 3,186.2 kg in the south, mainly from cooking and use of household electrical appliances, and 5,256.7 kg in the north, more than half of which was from space heating. The annual carbon emission of households in the north was

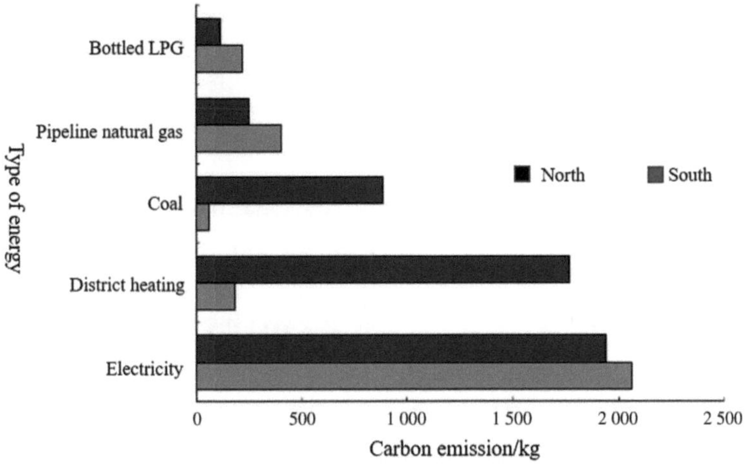


**Fig. 21** South-north differences in source of carbon emission in terms of types of energy

approximately 1.65 times the emission of households in the south. Such difference is also due to difference in space heating.

(1) South-north differences in sources of carbon emission in terms of energy types

In terms of the energy sources that cause carbon emission (Fig. 21), electricity consumption remains the primary source of carbon emission in households in the southern and northern parts of China. The carbon emission from electricity consumption was 2,064 kg per households in the south, accounting for 64% of the total household carbon emission, and 1,960 kg per household in the north, accounting for 37% of the total. The carbon emission from district heating was apparently higher in the north than in the south. The second largest south-north difference in carbon emission was most noticeable in coal consumption. The carbon emission from coal consumption per household in the north was 855 kg, about 10 times such carbon emission (88.2 kg) per household in the south. Meanwhile, households in the south produced more carbon emission than their counterparts in the north through consumption of gas (including pipeline natural gas and bottled LPG), especially use of bottled LPG, the carbon emission caused by which was about twice the emission of households in the north in this regard.

(2) South-north differences in carbon emission in terms of end uses

Concerning the sources of carbon emission, as shown in Fig. 22, households in the south produced 1,027 kg of carbon emission for cooking per household in 2014, which is slightly more than the carbon emission from cooking per household in the north and accounts for 34.91% of the annual household carbon emission. In the north, the carbon emission caused by cooking per household was 850 kg, accounting for 17.09% of the annual household carbon emission.

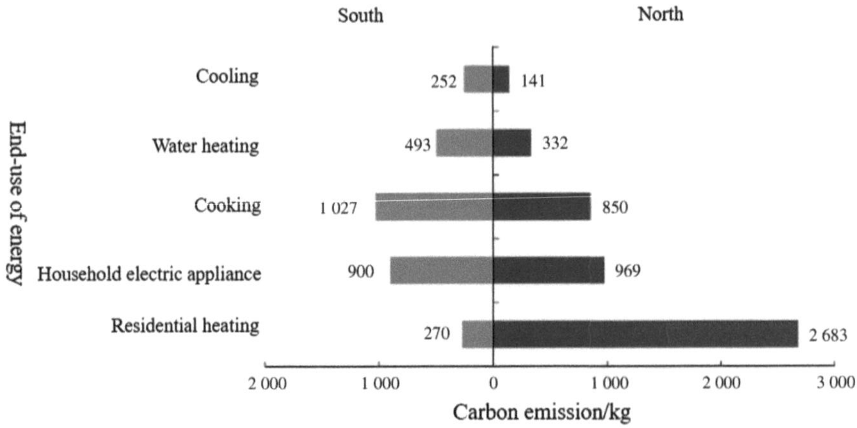


**Fig. 22** South-north differences in residential carbon emission in terms of end use

Concerning space heating, due to different temperature in the south and north, the carbon emission caused by space heating in the south was only 270 kg per household, accounting for 8% of the annual household carbon emission, while space heating was the primary cause of carbon emission in the north, which amounted to 2,685 kg per household, more than 9 times the emission of households in the south for space heating and accounted for more than half of the annual household carbon emission.

Also due to differences in temperature, households in the south produced more carbon emission than households in the north from air conditioning and water heating, 252 kg and 493 kg respectively, accounting for 8.57% and 16.76% of the annual household carbon emission respectively. The carbon emission of households in the north caused by air conditioning and water heating was 141 and 332 kg, making up 2.83 and 6.67% of the annual household carbon emission.

Concerning the carbon emission caused by household electrical appliances, households in the south and north did not have significant differences. Households in the south produced 900 kg of carbon emission from use of household electrical appliances, accounting for 30.59% of the annual household carbon emission. In the north, the carbon emission caused by use of household electrical appliances was 969 kg, accounting for 19.48% of the annual household carbon emission.

## *5.3 Urban-Rural Differences in Residential Carbon Emission in China*

The annual residential carbon emission in 2014 was 5,331 kg per household in urban areas and 2,878 kg per household in rural areas. The annual residential carbon emission of urban households was about twice the emission of rural households. Moreover, the $CO_2$ emissions caused by cooking, household electrical appliances,

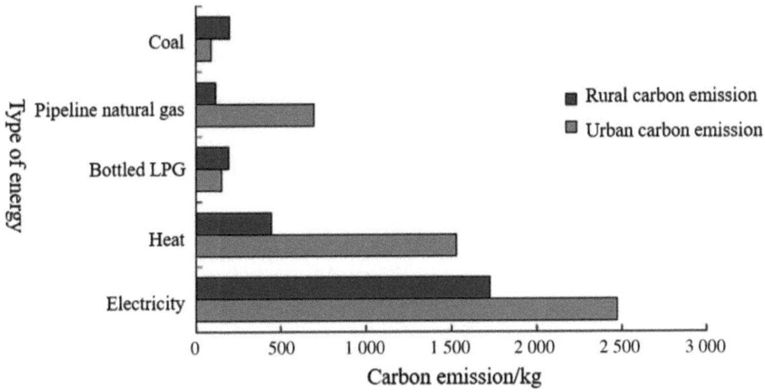


**Fig. 23** Urban-rural differences in sources of carbon emission in terms of types of energy

space heating, water heating, air conditioning and transportation were all higher in urban households than in rural households.

(1) Urban-rural differences in sources of carbon emission in terms of energy types

In terms of the energy types that cause carbon emission (Fig. 23), electricity consumption remained the primary source of carbon emission in urban and rural households in China. The annual carbon emission from electricity consumption per household was 2,474 kg and 1,724 kg for urban and rural households respectively. The carbon emission caused by electricity consumption of urban households was 1.4 times the emission in this regard of rural households. The most obvious difference in residential carbon emission between urban and rural households was caused by consumption of pipeline natural gas. The carbon emission from pipeline natural gas consumption of urban households was 5.7 times the emission of rural households in this regard. Meanwhile, significant differences also existed in terms of the carbon emission caused by consumption of bottled LPG and fuel oil.

Rural households produced more carbon emission than urban households from coal consumption. However, as most of the urban households used district heating and heat was mainly produced by burning coal or natural gas, the carbon emission in this regard cannot be accurately calculated for comparison.

(2) Urban-rural differences in sources of carbon emission in terms of end uses

In terms of the end uses of energy that cause carbon emission (Fig. 24), in 2014, the main sources of carbon emission for urban households was space heating and water heating, producing 1,790.60 kg and 724.00 kg of carbon emission respectively, while the rural households produced 999.46 kg of carbon emission from space heating and 238.34 kg of carbon emission from water heating in the same year. The carbon emissions of urban households caused by space heating and water heating were 1.79 times and 3 times the figures of the rural households. This is related with the composition of rural residential energy consumption. Biomass energy is a major

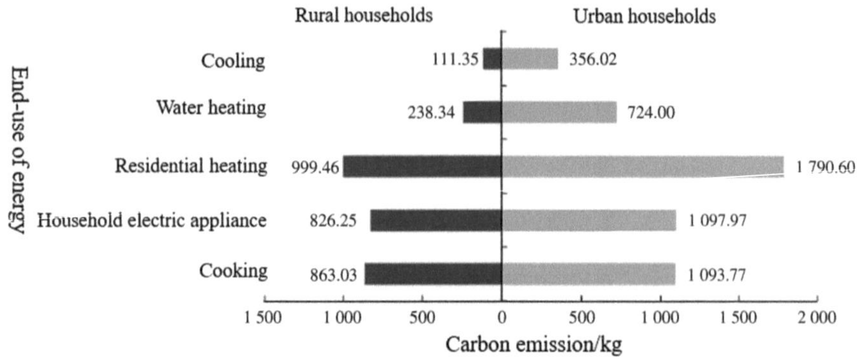


**Fig. 24** Urban-rural differences in sources of carbon emission in terms of end uses

source of energy for rural energy consumption, in which firewood accounts for the largest proportion. Due to the carbon neutrality of biomass energy, which means that the carbon in such energy comes from the nature, the carbon emission caused by burning of biomass energy doesn't change the carbon content in the atmosphere.

The urban and rural households did not have obvious differences in carbon emissions caused by cooking and household electrical appliances. In 2014, the carbon emission of urban households was 1,093.77 kg per household from cooking and 1,097.97 kg per household from household electrical appliances, while the rural households produced 863.03 kg of carbon emission per household for cooking and 826.25 kg of carbon emission per household for use of household electrical appliances. The difference in carbon emissions caused by cooking and household electrical appliances between urban and rural households were not obvious, with the former being 1.27 times and 1.3 times of the latter respectively. However, carbon emissions from cooking and household electrical appliances were main causes of rural residential carbon emission, both accounting for more than 30% of the total residential carbon emission.

# Chapter 5
# International Comparison of Residential Energy Consumption Surveys

**Yutong Zhao and Dan Wang**

**Abstract** The study of structure and amount of residential energy consumption are of great significance for improving residents' way of life, optimizing the structure of residential energy consumption and managing the residential energy supply and demand. Therefore, surveys about residential energy consumption are increasingly popular around the world, and studies in this field are receiving more and more attention. However, the situations and energy endowment vary in countries, the measurement and calculation standards are also diversified. Consequently, the reference period, content and implementation of surveys are different. Comparison and contrast of residential energy consumption in various countries are of great significance to future studies. This chapter compares the residential energy consumption in different countries, and gives a brief introduction of residential energy consumption surveys in the relevant countries.

## 1 International Comparison of Residential Energy Consumption

According to statistics of the World Bank about access to electricity in 250 countries and regions, there are still gaps between countries in this regard.[1] As shown in Fig. 1, up to 2010, only 65 countries and regions had 100% access to electricity and the global average access to electricity was 83%. In China, the access to electricity in 2010 was 99.7% in general and 98% in rural areas, ranking the 75th in the surveyed countries and regions.

The World Bank also conducted a survey about access to non-solid fuels, the result of which is shown in Fig. 2.

[1] World Bank: Sustainable Energy for All Data.

Y. Zhao · D. Wang (✉)
Renmin University of China, Beijing, China
e-mail: ynifqp502317434@126.com



X. Zheng and C. Wei (eds.), *Household Energy Consumption in China: 2016 Report*, https://doi.org/10.1007/978-981-13-7523-1_5

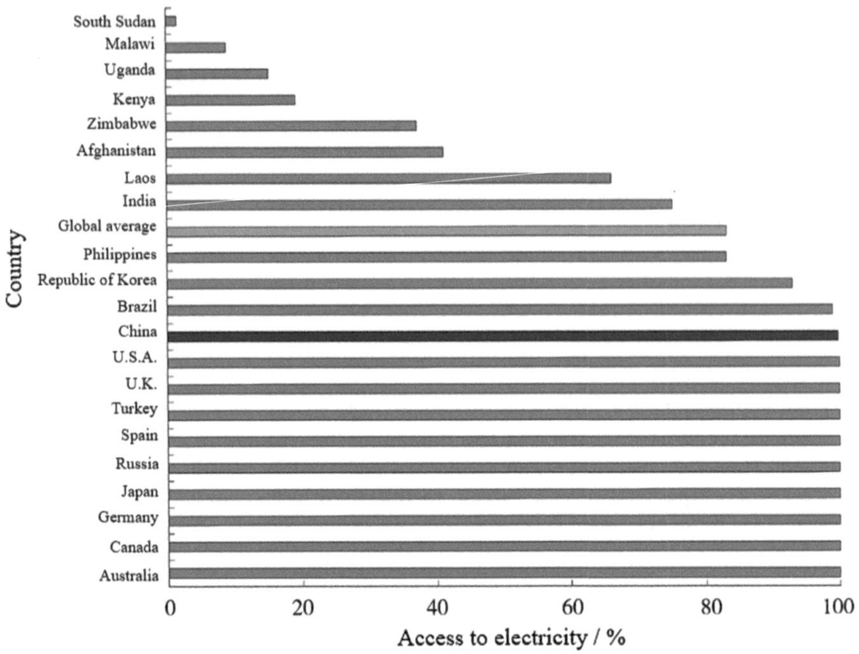


**Fig. 1** Access to electricity in different countries in 2010 the access to electricity in the above countries are as follows: South Sudan, 1.50%; Malawi, 8.70%; Uganda, 15.00%; Kenya, 19.00%; Zimbabwe, 37.00%; Afghanistan, 41.00%; Laos, 66.00%; India, 75.00%; Philippines, 83.00%; Republic of Korea, 93.00%; Brazil, 99.00%; China, 99.70%; USA, U.K., Turkey, Spain, Russia, Japan, Germany, Canada and Australia, 100%; Global average, 83.00%. *Source* World Bank: Sustainable Energy for All Data

It is obvious that certain differences exist between countries, especially between developing countries and developed countries, in terms of access to electricity and non-solid fuels, which have influences on the feasibility and implementation of residential energy consumption surveys. While reviewing and organizing the residential energy consumption survey reports of various countries, we found that developed countries and developing countries had significant differences in terms of the implementation and content of surveys as well as the ultimate completeness and reliability of data. Residential energy consumption surveys in developed countries like the United States, Canada and European countries are comparatively mature, and many studies based on the survey data may throw some light on our future surveys. In contrast, the data of developing countries are scarce and the content of surveys in developing countries is also simple, but these surveys are helpful to understand the form of surveys and the energy consumption structure in lower-income regions.

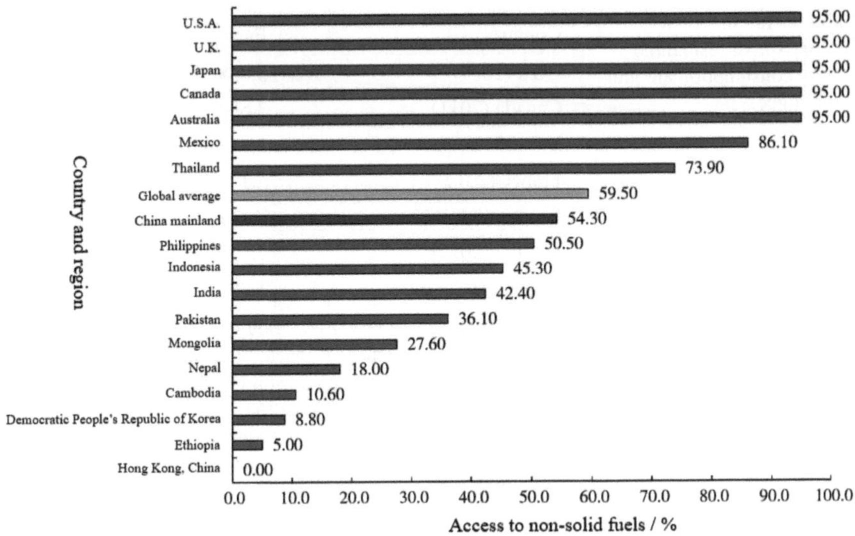


**Fig. 2** Access to non-solid fuel in different countries and regions in 2010. *Source* World Bank: Sustainable Energy for All Data

## *1.1 International Comparison of Residential Energy Consumption Amount*

Concerning the total amount of energy consumption, according to the calculation result of thermal equivalent based on the survey result which is weighted according to provincial household numbers, the average energy consumption per household in China was 1,087 kgce per year. Compared with developed countries, the residential energy consumption in China is at a lower level, as shown in Fig. 1. The residential energy consumption per household in 2014 in China is 35.8% of the consumption per household in the United States in 2009 (Table 1).

Concerning the structure of residential energy consumption (Fig. 3), according to the survey result, household consumption of biomass energy in China accounted for a larger proportion (27.8%) of the total than in other countries. Electricity and natural gas are the primary sources of energy in residential energy consumption in most countries, but in China, natural gas consumption accounted for a smaller proportion (11.3%) of the total.

Concerning the energy-consuming activities in households (Fig. 4), the primary end uses of energy in Chinese households are space heating and cooking, consuming 400.75 kgce per year per household and 432.49 kgce per year per household respectively. Meanwhile, energy consumption of residential air conditioning accounted for the smallest proportion. Unlike the residential energy consumption in most countries,

**Table 1** International comparison of residential energy consumption amount (Unit: kgce)

| Country | Energy consumption |
|---|---|
| USA (2009) | 3,038 |
| Canada (2011) | 3,679 |
| UK (2012) | 2,113 |
| France (2012) | 2,153 |
| Germany (2012) | 2,192 |
| Estonia (2012) | 3,170 |
| China (2014) | 1,087 |

*Source* USA (2009): U.S. EIA: 2009 RECS Survey Data; Canada (2011): Natural Resources Canada: Statistics Canada's Report on Energy Supply-Demand in Canada (RESD); EU-27 (2012) and its members: Electricity information 2015, IEA; Estonia (2012): 2012 Household Energy Consumption Survey Final Report, Statistics Estonia; China (2014): calculation result by RUC in Chinese residential energy consumption survey

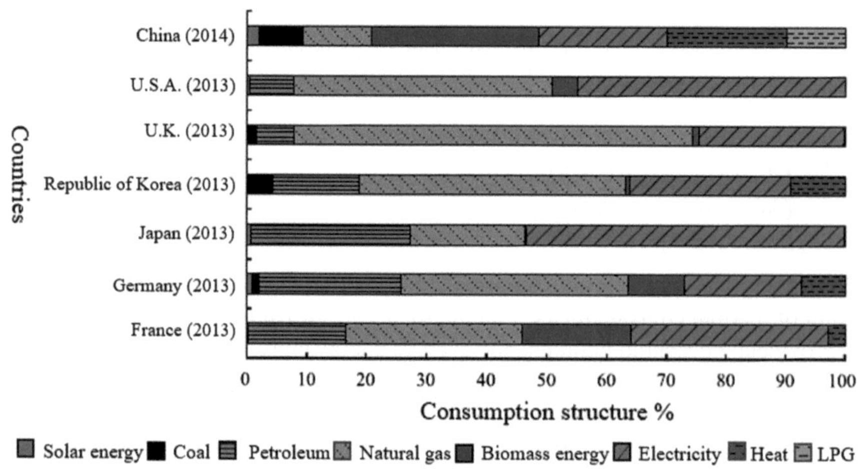


**Fig. 3** International comparison of residential energy consumption in terms of energy sources. *Source* World Bank: Sustainable Energy for All Data

energy consumption of cooking in China accounted for a large proportion, 39.8% of the total, while air conditioning accounted for only 0.91%. The energy consumption of space heating accounted for over 50% of the total residential energy consumption in other countries.

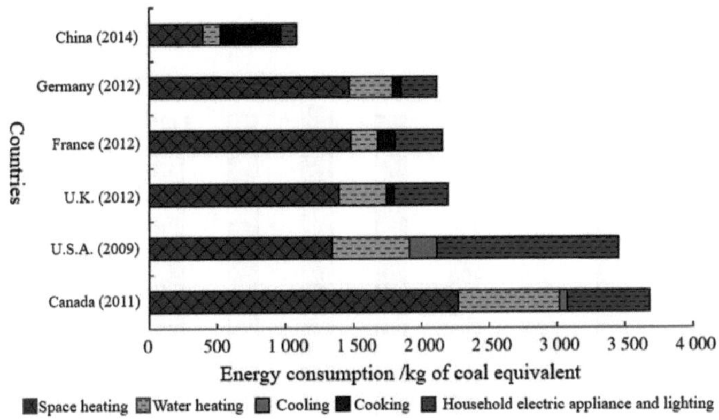


**Fig. 4** International comparison of residential energy consumption in terms of end uses. *Source* World Bank: Sustainable Energy for All Data

## *1.2 Comparison of Residential Energy Consumption in China and the United States*

It can be noted from the residential energy consumption statistics in the United States during the period from 1980 to 2009 (Fig. 5) that the consumption amount showed an overall declining trend in the ten surveys over the nearly 30 years, despite several fluctuations, which dropped from 3,869.0 kgce per year per household in 1980 to 3,038.0 kgce per year per household in 2009. With an annual decline percentage of 0.7%, there was no significant changes in general. The overall decline in residential energy consumption is related with the year-on-year increase in energy efficiency and the extensive use of energy-efficient electrical appliances. Even considering such situation, comparing with the residential energy consumption during the said period in the United States, the residential energy consumption in China is still lower. The residential energy consumption in China in 2014 was about 36% of the consumption in the United States in 2009.

The Residential Energy Consumption Survey (RECS) in the United States was first conducted in 1978, and there had been 13 such surveys up to 2009. The methodology of surveys and composition of questionnaires of the RECS are of great referential value. The results of each survey include data tables, a microdata file and a series of reports. Data tables generally consist of two parts, i.e., “household characteristics” and “consumption & expenditures”. The RECS and many supplier surveys are integral ingredients for some of EIA’s comprehensive products and reports, such as the Annual Energy Outlook (AEO) and Annual Energy Review (AER). These products can be used for broader comparisons across sectors and projections of future consumption trends. The RECS was conducted in the form of household interviews. Its scope of survey and categorization of energy sources are as shown in Table 2.

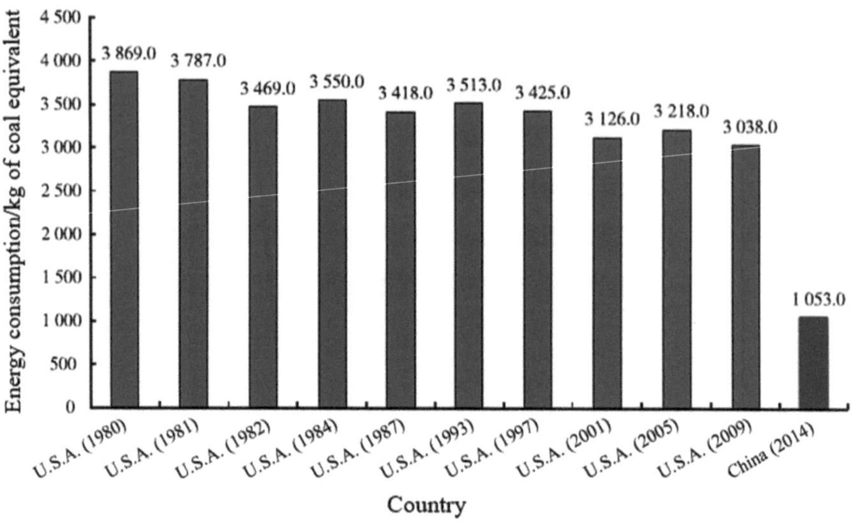


**Fig. 5** Trend of residential energy consumption in the U.S. and comparison of residential energy consumption in China and the U.S. *Source* U.S.A: EIA: 2009 RECS Survey Data; China: survey data from residential energy consumption survey by RUC

**Table 2** Energy categories in the RECS

| Energy | Description of category |
|---|---|
| Electricity | Measurement of primary electricity includes the energy used to produce and deliver the electricity. Adjusted electricity uses 1/3 of the primary electricity as conversion factor. This figure is approximated by the standard amount of energy used by steam power plants to generate electricity from fuel. The data of electricity in the calculation are adjusted electricity |
| Natural gas | A hydrocarbon gas (mostly methane) delivered as an energy source to individual buildings by pipelines from a central utility company, excluding LPG. The natural gas used by some households is supplied by private companies |
| LPG | Any flammable gas in liquid form, such as propane and butane. It is usually delivered to households by special trucks and stored near the users in a cylinder until used. The most common type of LPG used by the surveyed households is liquefied propane |
| Firewood and wood chips | The amount of wood burned in fireplaces or stoves in residences during the past 12 months. A standard cord of wood measures 4 feet by 4 feet by 8 feet (1 foot = 0.3048 m), or 128 cubic feet. To help respondents accurately report the amount of wood they burned, respondents were provided with a drawing of a person, as a point of reference, standing beside wood piles of different sizes |

**Table 3** Energy end-use categories in the RECS

| End use | |
|---|---|
| Space heating | The use of energy to generate heat in housing units using main or secondary space-heating equipment. This category does not include the use of energy by appliances (such as lights, televisions and refrigerators) that give off heat as a byproduct |
| Water heating | The use of energy to heat water, including use of hot running water, as well as on stoves and auxiliary water-heating for washing or bathing, cleaning and other non-cooking appliances. This category does not include energy used for cooking, hot drinks or swimming pools |
| Air conditioning | A refrigeration appliance that can cool and dehumidify the air using electricity or natural gas. This category does not include fans, blowers and evaporative cooling systems (swamp coolers) |
| Appliances | This category includes the home appliances and lights used by households in the past year, including those borrowed from others and frequently used. Home appliances not in use are excluded, unless they are under repair for the time being. Refrigerators are a separate category and not included in this category |
| Refrigerators | A household appliance designed for storing food at temperatures above 32° Fahrenheit (0 °C). Most refrigerators have a second compartment for freezing and storing frozen foods at temperatures of 8° Fahrenheit (−13 °C) or below |

Concerning the categorization of end uses of energy, the RECS also has clear definitions as shown in Table 3.

## 1.3 *Comparison of Energy Consumption of Cooking in Developing Countries*

(1) Survey of residential energy consumption of cooking in India

The distribution of main energy sources for cooking in rural and urban Indian households is as shown in Table 4.

During the period from 2011 to 2012, in India, more than 2/3 of urban households used LPG as the main energy source for cooking and 14.0% mainly used firewood. Comparing with their rural counterparts, urban households using firewood as the main energy source for cooking accounted for a smaller proportion, while households mainly consuming LPG accounted for a larger proportion. The energy consumption structure for cooking is significantly cleaner in urban areas than in rural areas.

According to the results of the recent five national surveys in India, compared with the data of the period from 1993 to 1994, the proportion of urban households using firewood as the main source of energy for cooking dropped by about 50%, while the proportion of households using LPG as the main source of energy for cooking

**Table 4** Distribution of percentages of energy sources for cooking in Indian households (Unit: %)

| Energy source for cooking | | Percentage of households using main energy sources for cooking | | | | |
|---|---|---|---|---|---|---|
| | | 1993–1994 | 1999–2000 | 2004–2005 | 2009–2010 | 2011–2012 |
| Rural areas | Coke/coal | 1.4 | 1.5 | 0.8 | 0.8 | 1.1 |
| | Firewood | 78.2 | 75.5 | 75 | 76.3 | 67.3 |
| | LPG | 1.9 | 5.4 | 8.6 | 11.5 | 15.0 |
| | Excrement | 11.5 | 10.6 | 9.1 | 6.3 | 9.6 |
| | Kerosene | 2.0 | 2.7 | 1.3 | 0.8 | 0.9 |
| | No cooking arrangement | 0.7 | 1.1 | 1.3 | 1.6 | 1.3 |
| | Other sources | 4.1 | 3.1 | 3.8 | 2.7 | 4.9 |
| Urban areas | Coke/coal | 5.7 | 4.1 | 2.8 | 2.3 | 2.1 |
| | Firewood | 29.9 | 22.3 | 21.7 | 17.5 | 14.0 |
| | LPG | 29.6 | 44.2 | 57.1 | 64.5 | 68.4 |
| | Excrement | 2.4 | 2.1 | 1.7 | 1.3 | 1.3 |
| | Kerosene | 23.2 | 21.7 | 10.2 | 6.5 | 5.7 |
| | No cooking arrangement | 6.3 | 4.3 | 4.9 | 6.5 | 6.9 |
| | Other sources | 3.0 | 1.3 | 1.6 | 1.5 | 1.5 |

*Source* 2011–2012 Energy Sources of Indian Households for Cooking and Lighting

showed significant increase in rural and urban areas, increasing from 1.9% during 1993–1994 to 15.0% during 2011–2012 in rural areas. In addition, the proportion of urban households using kerosene as the main source of energy for cooking declined from 23.2% during 1993–1994 to 5.7% during 2011–2012. On the other hand, for nearly 20 years, the proportion of rural households using firewood as the main source of energy for cooking remained more than 2/3 of the total, while in urban households, the nearly equivalent proportions of firewood, LPG and kerosene were replaced with the dominant position of LPG (urban households using LPG accounted for more than 2/3 of the total).

(2) Survey of residential energy consumption of cooking in Malawi

The composition of cooking fuels in urban areas of Malawi is diversified. 48.2% of urban households used charcoal as the primary cooking fuel, 37.9% used firewood (2/3 of which used commercial firewood bought on the market) and some households used electricity (Fig. 6). In rural areas, the cooking fuels were comparatively unvaried,

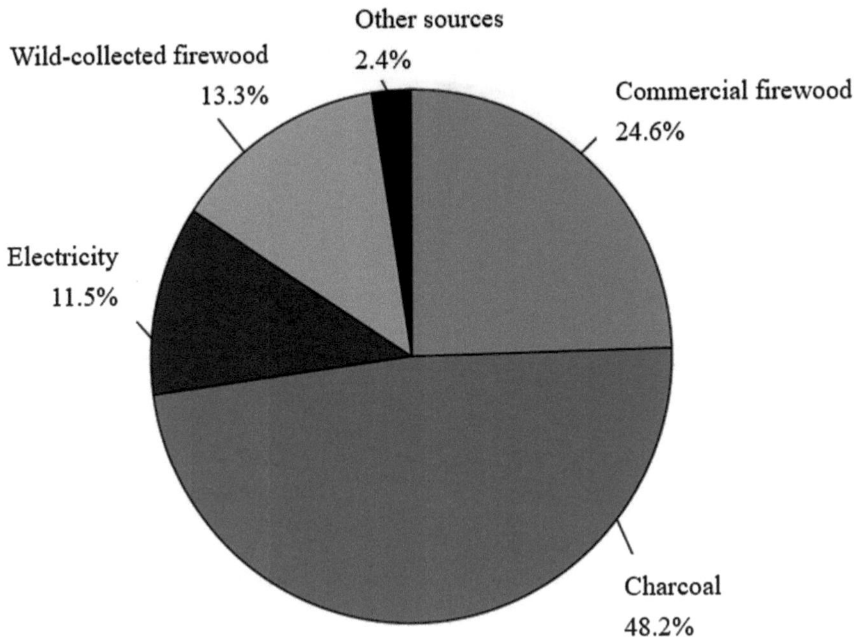


**Fig. 6** Composition of cooking fuels in urban areas of Malawi. *Source* Integrated Household Survey of Malawi

with 97% of rural households used firewood as the main cooking fuel, most of which were collected from the wild or through deforestation. The energy consuming method for cooking in rural areas is backward (Fig. 7).

## *1.4 Survey of Residential Energy Consumption of Cooking in Ethiopia*

Most Ethiopian households used firewood as the main source of energy for cooking. As shown in Fig. 8, 88% of rural households, 81% of households in small towns and 40% of households in large towns used firewood as the main cooking fuel. It is noteworthy that most of the firewood used by rural households was collected from the wild or through deforestation, while the proportion of households using commercial firewood increased with the degree of urbanization.

For Ethiopian households, firewood collection or deforestation for firewood and water fetching are important household chores. On average, each Ethiopian household spent 41.3 min collecting firewood and 37.8 min fetching water every day. In rural areas where the main source of cooking fuel is wild-collected firewood instead of commercial firewood, people spent more time, nearly one hour per day on aver-

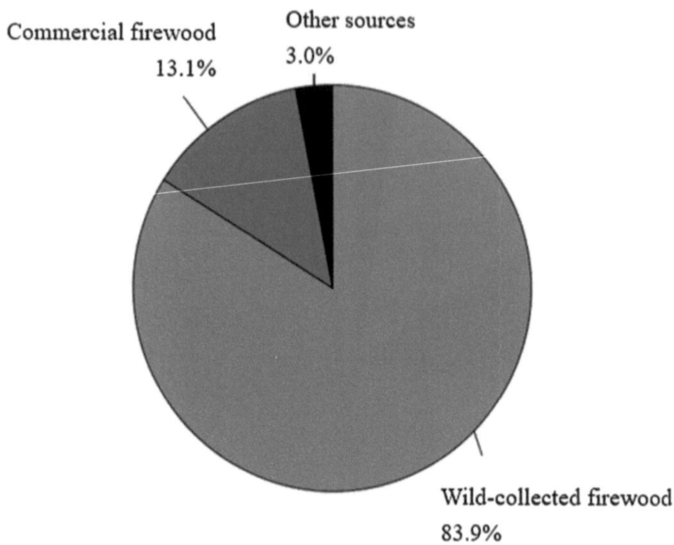


**Fig. 7** Composition of cooking fuels in rural areas of Malawi. *Source* Integrated Household Survey of Malawi

age, collecting firewood than urban residents. The annual firewood consumption per household in Ethiopia amounted to 2.45 tons, 2.88 tons in rural areas, 2.95 tons in small towns and 2.16 tons in large towns.

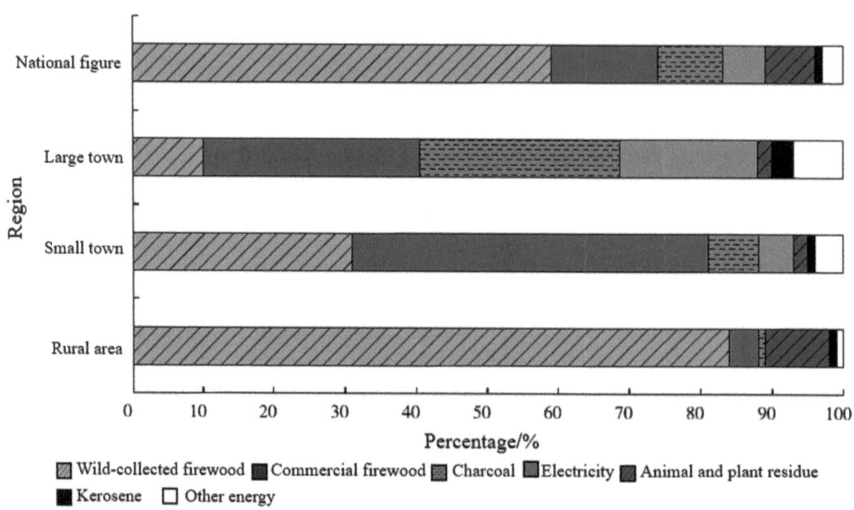


**Fig. 8** Proportion of main sources of energy for cooking used by Ethiopian households. *Source* Ethiopia Socioeconomic Survey

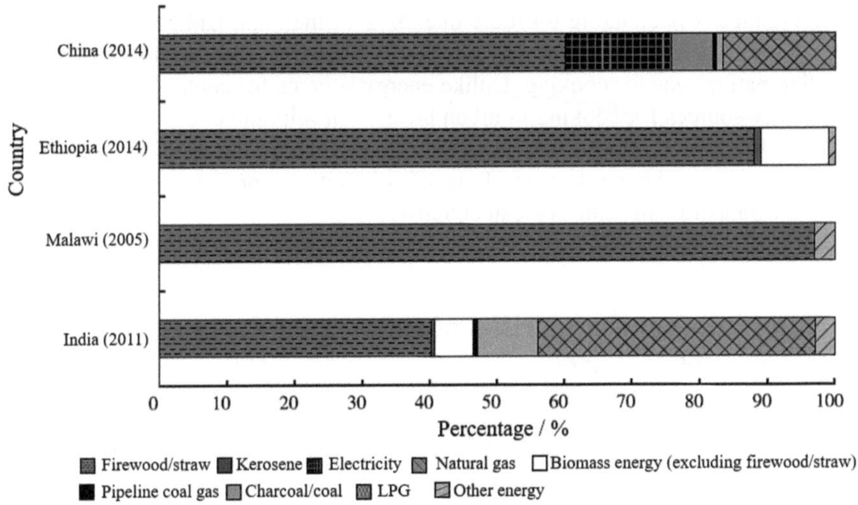


**Fig. 9** Comparison of energy consumption for cooking in rural households of developing countries

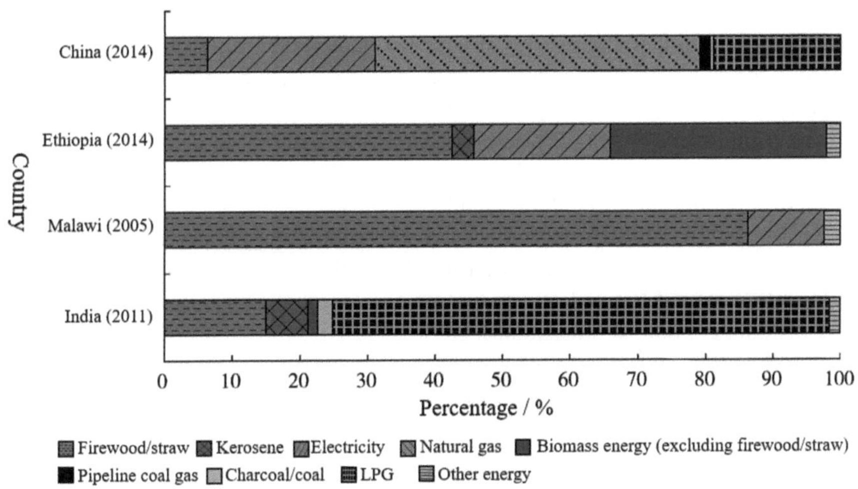


**Fig. 10** Comparison of energy consumption for cooking in urban households of developing countries. *Source* Ethiopia: Ethiopia Socioeconomic Survey (2014); Malawi: Integrated Household Survey of Malawi (2005); India: 2011–2012 Energy Sources of Indian Households for Cooking and Lighting; China: survey data from residential energy consumption survey by RUC

(3) Comparison of residential energy consumption of cooking in developing countries

The comparison of residential energy consumption of cooking in rural and urban areas of developing countries is as shown in Figs. 9 and 10. In rural areas of developing countries including China, the primary source of energy for cooking was firewood or straw, mostly accounting for more than 50% of the total. Unlike other developing countries, a large proportion of rural households in China used electricity and pipeline natural gas for cooking. Unlike energy sources for cooking in rural areas, the energy sources for cooking in urban areas of developing countries showed significant differences. The primary energy sources for cooking in urban households were electricity and natural gas in China, LPG in India according to relevant surveys and firewood/straw in some African countries.

# 2 International Comparison of Residential Energy Consumption Surveys

## *2.1 General Introduction of International Residential Energy Consumption Surveys*

Despite the increasing popularity of surveys about residential energy consumption across the world, due to different situations in countries and various standards for measurement and calculation, the surveys in countries are different in terms of the reference period, content and implementation of surveys. Table 5 presents some basic information of energy consumption surveys in several countries.

The comparison of sample sizes is as shown in Table 6. In countries with large populations such as China, the United States and India, the sample sizes accounted for a small proportion of the total populations. Wide discrepancies existed between countries in terms of the proportion of sample size to the total population, but there were no significant differences in terms of sample sizes. The survey in India for 2011–2012 covered 101,651 effective samples, more than other countries. In the said survey, India conducted household interviews in 101,651 households (59,683 rural and 41,968 urban) in 7,469 villages and 5,268 urban blocks. Though, the survey was only about energy consumption of cooking and lighting and did not cover residential energy consumption for other end uses.

## *2.2 Introduction of Residential Energy Consumption Surveys in Various Countries*

The residential energy consumption surveys in various countries include statistics about the total amount and structure of energy consumption, end uses and energy expenditures, etc. In the following section, we will give a brief introduction of some typical statistics in these countries.

**Table 5** International comparison of residential energy consumption surveys

| Country | Survey | Methodology |
|---|---|---|
| USA (2009) | The residential energy consumption | To investigate the residential energy consumption in the United States, EIA conducts periodical sample surveys, i.e., the Residential Energy Consumption Survey (RECS). The RECS is conducted by EIA to a nationally representative sample of housing units. Specially trained interviewers collect energy characteristics on the housing unit, usage patterns, and household demographics. This information is combined with data from energy suppliers to estimate energy costs and usage for heating, cooling, appliances and other end uses-information critical to meeting future energy demand and improving efficiency and building design. First conducted in 1978, the thirteenth RECS was conducted in 2009. The results of each RECS include data tables, a microdata file and a series of reports. Data tables generally consist of two parts, i.e., "Household Characteristics" and "Consumption & Expenditures". The RECS and many of the EIA supplier surveys are integral ingredients for some of EIA's more comprehensive products and reports, such as the Annual Energy Outlook and Annual Energy Review of EIA. These products allow for broader comparisons across sectors, as well as projections of future consumption trends |
| Canada (2011) | Households and the environment: energy use | Administered by Statistics Canada, this survey mainly consisted of two parts: one is heating equipment, heating fuel, (total and average) household energy use and household energy use by size of heated area, dwelling type, dwelling tenure (owned or rented), dwelling construction period, household income and education level; the other is statistics about energy-saving use in households including energy-saving methods. The survey was conducted in two phases. The first phase was brief phone interviews as supplement to the Canadian Community Health Survey, and the second phase was household energy use survey, for which the questionnaires were delivered and received in the form of mails and e-mails. Respondents were samples responding to the phone interview in the first phase. The phone interviews focus on household behaviors relating to the environment |
| Estonia (2012) | Household energy consumption survey | The survey is conducted by statistics Estonia in cooperation with the Ministry of Economic Affairs and Communications of Estonia. The sampling was based on an address list obtained from the Estonian Land Board for the purposes of carrying out the 2011 Population and Housing Census. The interviewers carried out personal interviews in households to collect data about household energy consumption in 2010. The survey was conducted in the form of household interviews, the data and results of which were recorded in computers by interviewers and in rare cases, paper questionnaires were used for interview. The survey content was designed in accordance with the Eurostat recommendations and the questionnaire consisted of 13 topical sections with 117 questions about housing stock characteristics, household characteristics, energy consumption (by type of fuels and energy), space heating, domestic hot water, use of air-conditioning and other electrical appliances, efficient use of energy and utilization of renewable energy sources. The sample was selected from across the country, including 15 counties and Tallinn, the capital. The inclusion probabilities were all between 0.008 and 0.010 to ensure the even distribution of the sample. The sample was selected using stratified systematic sampling design. Samples were randomly selected in accordance with three levels of codes within each secondary unit, and the selected samples were independent of each other. To ensure a geographically even distribution of the sample, addresses were subject to stratified systematic sampling: first by the county code; within the county, by the rural municipality code; within the rural municipality, by the village municipality code |

(continued)

**Table 5** (continued)

| Country | Survey | Methodology |
|---|---|---|
| India (2011) | Energy sources of Indian households for cooking and lighting | The national sample survey office (NSSO) of India conducts national sample surveys every year and surveys on household consumer expenditure with large sample size of households quinquennially. Since the 27th national sample survey (the first survey on household consumer expenditure) from October 1972 to September 1973, 9 surveys on household consumer expenditure were conducted in the 32nd, 38th, 43rd, 50th, 55th, 61st, 66th and 68th national samples survey. Energy sources of indian households for cooking and lighting, 2011–12 is one of the six reports on the 9th survey on household consumer expenditure, which analyzes the percentages of energy sources of Indian households for cooking and lighting |
| | | There are seven sources of energy for cooking and lighting in households of India, namely, firewood, LPG, dung cake, kerosene, coke/coal, biogas, charcoal and electricity. NSSO enquired the households about their major source of energy during the 30 days preceding the date of enquiry, which was considered the primary source of energy. Statistics and reports were prepared based on the unit of household |
| Ethiopia (2013–2014) | Ethiopia socioeconomic survey | The Ethiopia socioeconomic survey was a collaborative project between the central statistics agency of Ethiopia and the world bank living standards measurement study-integrated surveys on agriculture (LSMS-ISA) team, which was conducted from 2013 to 2014. Through two-stage sampling, the survey covered 5,469 households across the country, and the ultimate effective sample size was 5,262 households responding to interviews. The samples were selected from 11 administrative regions, including 3,323 from rural areas, 453 from small towns and 1,486 from large towns |
| Malawi (2004–2005) | Integrated household survey | The second integrated household survey in Malawi was conducted by the Malawi national statistics office from 2004 to 2005. Through household interviews, the survey obtained data of 11,280 sample households. The samples were selected from three regions of the country, i.e., the southern part, the northern part and the central part, including 4 urban areas and 26 rural areas. The three regions were further divided into 564 sub-regions, including 72 urban areas and 492 rural areas<br>The fieldwork was conducted from March 8, 2014 to April 6, 2015. The survey team consisted of zone supervisors, field supervisors and enumerators. Zone supervisors supervised the field supervisors and enumerators, ensured the consistency of questionnaires, observed interviews and questionnaires, conduced on-site review, ensured that housings were vacant or closed, visited refusing households and motivated their cooperation, motivated enumerators, ensured that field supervisors and enumerators had all the necessary material. Field supervisors supervised 2–3 enumerators, ensured the consistency of questionnaires, observed interviews and arranged revisits to ensure quality of enumeration, conducted on-site review of questionnaires and managed the questionnaires of the neighborhood. Enumerators assisted the calculators with calculation |

(1) Use of renewable energy sources in Estonia

The renewable energy sources in Estonia includes biomass energy as the primary source as well as some hydro and solar energy and heat pumps. In 2010, biomass energy accounted for 14.1% of the total supply of fuels, which is attributed to the abundant forest resources in Estonia. The primary source of energy in households was wood fuels, which accounted for 40.2% of non-motor energy consumption, reaching even 68.2% in rural areas. Firewood was the primary source of wood fuel, accounting

**Table 6** Comparison of sample sizes for residential energy consumption surveys in countries

| Country | Sample size | Proportion of sample size to the total population/$10^{-4}$ |
|---|---|---|
| USA (2009) | 12,083 | 0.39 |
| Canada (2011) | 11,241 | 3.27 |
| Australia (2012) | 15,797 | 6.95 |
| Estonia (2012) | 3,690 | 27.90 |
| India (2011) | 101,651 | 0.82 |
| Ethiopia (2013) | 5,469 | 0.58 |
| Malawi (2004) | 11,280 | 9.10 |
| China (2014) | 3,863 | 0.03 |

*Source* The data of sample sizes are from residential energy consumption surveys of the above countries, and the population data are cited from data of the World Bank

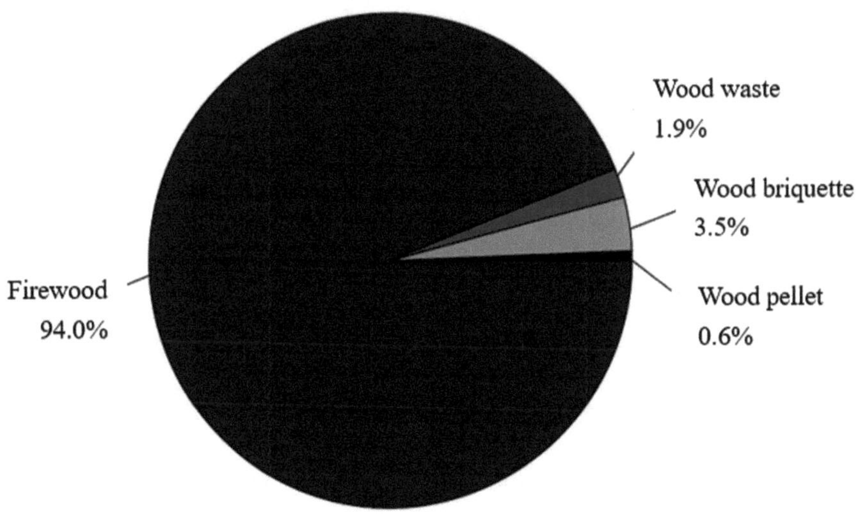


**Fig. 11** Proportions of wood fuels in residential energy consumption in Estonia

for 94.0% of the wood fuel consumption (Fig. 11). Use of hydro and solar energy was scarce in households at $10^{-4}$. Heat pumps, a new energy technology, is gradually popular in Estonia. 3.5% of households in Estonia have installed heat pumps and the share is still growing.

(2) Statistics about energy consumption of lighting in India

The primary sources of energy for lighting in India households are kerosene and electricity: electricity has always been the primary energy source for lighting in urban areas, while in rural areas, the dominant position of kerosene as energy source

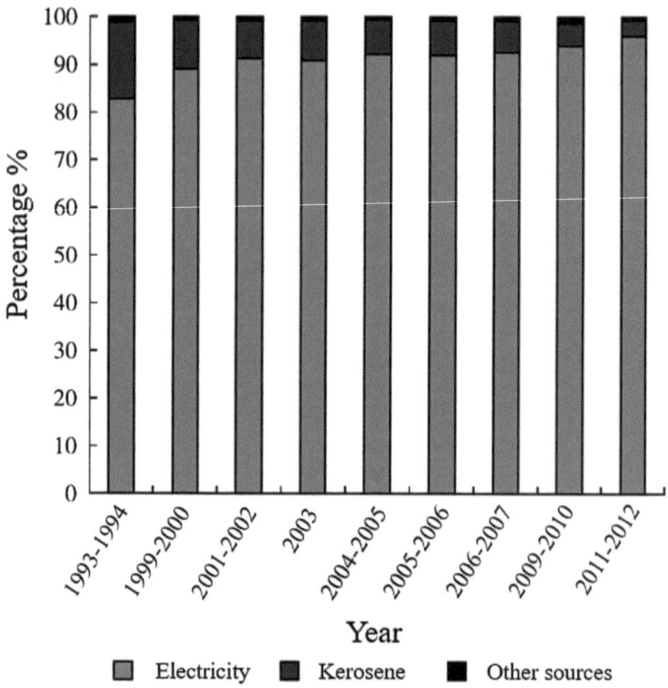


**Fig. 12** Change of percentages of households using energy sources for lighting in urban India. *Source* Energy Sources of India Households for Cooking and Lighting

for lighting is gradually replaced by electricity. For nearly 20 years, percentages of households using electricity as the primary source of energy for lighting in rural and urban areas of India have been on the rise (Figs. 12 and 13), increasing from 82.8% during 1993–1994 to 96.1% during 2011–2012 in urban areas and from 37.1% during 1993–1994 to 72.7% during 2011–2012. Meanwhile, percentages of households mainly consuming kerosene for lighting have been declining.

(3) Access to electricity in Malawi

The access to electricity in Malawi was very low, with only 30.4% of households in Lilongwe, 35.2% in other urban areas and 2% of rural households connected to the national electrical grid (Fig. 14). Moreover, in urban areas of Lilongwe, 30.6% of households were not connected to the national electrical grid within 100 meters, and the percentage reached 57.1% in other urban areas.

Some households in Malawi were not connected to the electrical grid despite the possibility of connection because of high cost of electricity consumption. Underdeveloped industry, reliance on importation for most electrical appliances and inadequate transportation as an inland country contributes to high prices of electrical appliances in Malawi. In addition, Malawian households used traditional and even backward housing structures and roofs, which had to be transformed to connect to

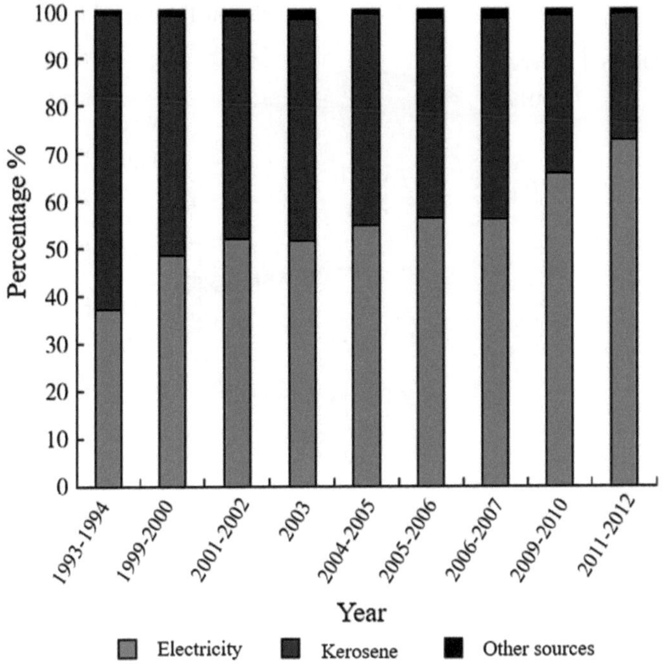


**Fig. 13** Change of percentages of households using energy sources for lighting in urban India. *Source* Energy Sources of India Households for Cooking and Lighting

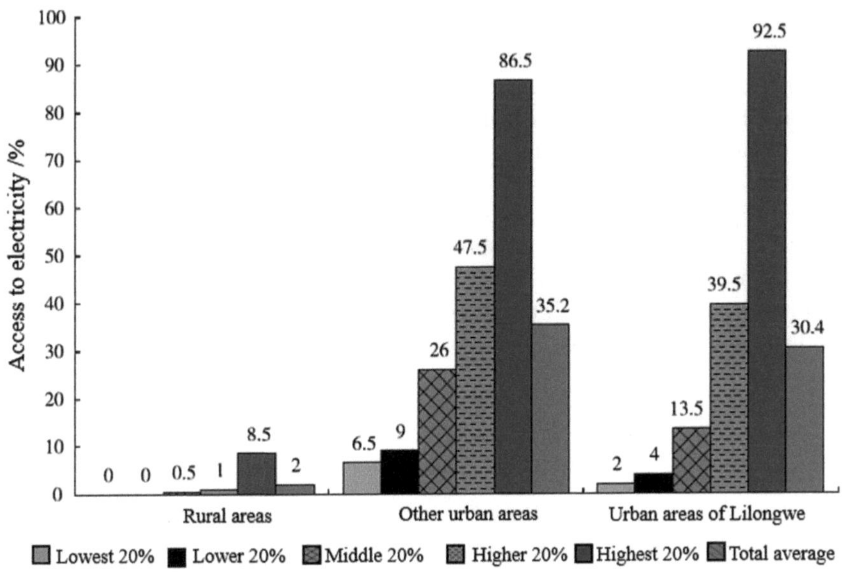


**Fig. 14** Access to electricity in households by income levels and regions. *Source* Integrated Household Survey of Malawi

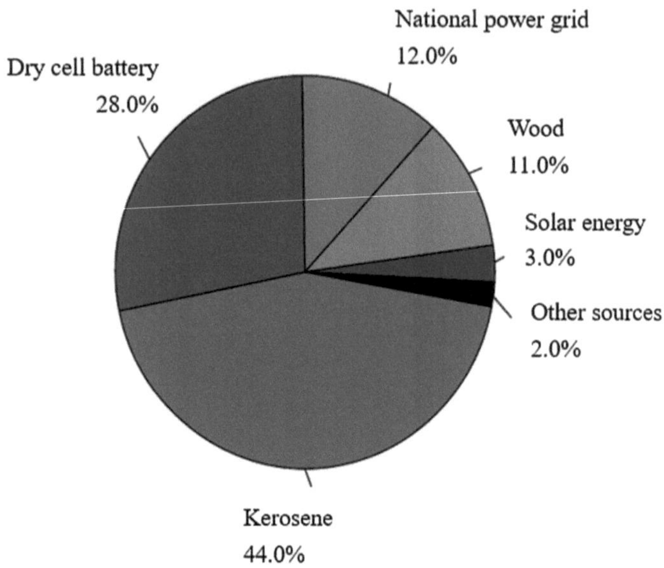


**Fig. 15** Percentages of households using various energy sources in rural areas of Ethiopia

the grid. Due to cost of residence transformation and electric cable arrangement, many households chose not to connect to the grid.

(4) Statistics about residential lighting in Ethiopia

In rural areas of Ethiopia, only a small proportion of households had electricity and use of electric lights was not feasible. So, kerosene was mainly used for lighting in rural areas. In urban areas, since households were connected to the national electrical grids or had their own generators, they had better fuels for lighting than kerosene. Therefore, the main use of kerosene in urban areas was not for lighting. As shown in Figs. 15, 16 and 17, kerosene was the main source of energy for lighting in 44.0% of rural households, while the proportions were 6.0% and 2.0% in small towns and large towns respectively. Only 12.0% of rural households had lighting powered by national electrical grids, while the proportions were 82.0% and 96.0% in small towns and large towns respectively.

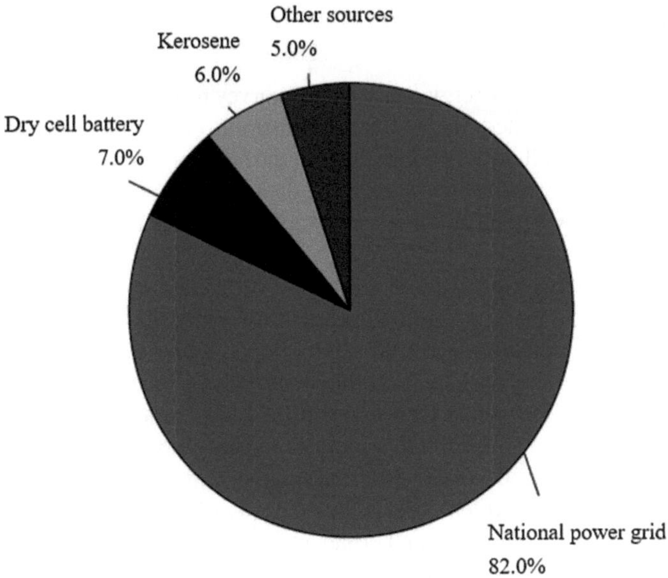


**Fig. 16** Percentages of households using various energy sources in small towns in Ethiopia

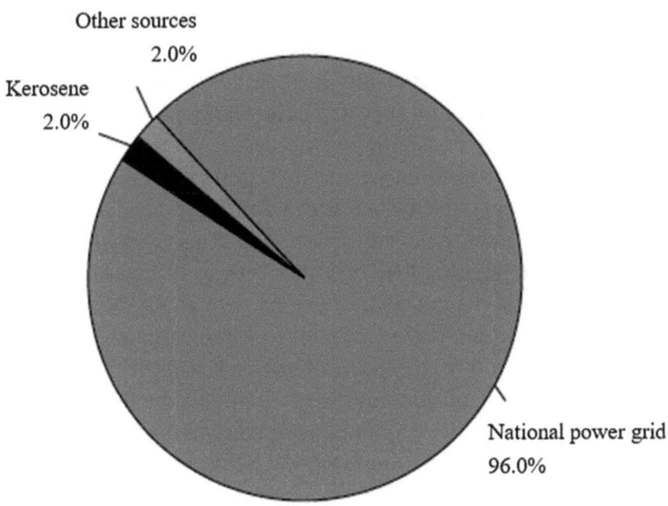


**Fig. 17** Percentages of households using various energy sources in large towns in Ethiopia. *Source* Ethiopia Socioeconomic Survey

## 3 Summary

Reviewing the residential energy consumption survey reports of developed countries such as Canada, the United States, UK and Australia, etc., we note that the relevant surveys have been well developed in these countries after implementation for many years. The surveys have formed systems. The data transparency is better in developed countries than in developing countries, and the scope and content of surveys are more extensive.

Most of the energy consumption surveys in developed countries are conducted through household interview and independent algorithm. In terms of energy consumption, a significant difference between developed countries and developing countries is 100% access to electricity. In addition, developed countries have efficient use of natural gas and LPG, while China consumes a large amount of diesel and coal. In general, the energy consumption structures in rural and urban areas do not have significant differences, but certain differences existed in terms of the percentages of various energy sources, which is related to the way of life, living habits and availability of energy sources in rural and urban areas. In terms of the end uses of energy, space heating and air conditioning are primary end uses of energy in households of developed countries, and the substantial use of electrical appliances is also an important characteristics of residential energy consumption in developed countries. What's more, many developed countries have conducted in-depth surveys and studies on the basis of residential energy consumption survey reports. For example, the United States once included a survey about low-income household assistance program in its residential energy consumption survey. These studies may serve as references for our future residential energy consumption surveys.

Reviewing the energy consumption survey reports of developing countries, we note that most developing countries face more difficulties than developed countries in data collection, while the data transparency and accuracy of surveys are also inferior. India, for example, only listed the percentages of households using certain energy sources in the reports, but did not collect data about the specific amount of consumption. In addition, we find it difficult to locate data about specific amount of consumption or expenditure in reports of African countries. Due to underdeveloped economy, the energy consumption is to a large extent dependent on regional energy endowment. Meanwhile, economic inequality and urban-rural gap also lead to significant differences in energy consumption between different regions of developing countries. It can be seen from the reports of various countries that cooking and lighting are the primary end uses of energy in less developed countries, which are also focuses in energy consumption surveys in developing countries. In terms of end uses of energy, the most obvious difference between some developing countries and developed countries and even China is their frequent use of firewood, paraffin wax and candles. Low access to electricity and low efficiency in energy use are pressing issues concerning residential energy consumption in less developed regions.

# Chapter 6
# Comparison of Residential Energy Consumption in Urban and Rural Areas

**Xie Lunyu and Zhang Shuhan**

In this chapter, we analyze the difference between urban and rural residents in amount and structure of energy consumption based on the survey data from the CRECS 2015. An advantage of the data from this survey is that the energy consumption data of urban and rural households are from the same year, eliminating the possible interannual differences in comparison of urban and rural energy consumption. In addition, in this chapter, we use econometric models to conduct quantitative analysis of factors leading to differences in urban and rural energy consumption. The effective samples in this survey are 3,863 households, which are divided into urban households and rural households according to the household registration location of respondents.[1] The effective samples include 1,480 urban households and 2,383 rural households. The questionnaire included energy consumption amount and expenditure offered by households and power and frequency of use of household electrical appliances as well as usage and frequency of use of other energy-consuming equipment in households. We consider both information provided by households and the usage of energy-consuming equipment to address the issue of missing data in respondent-provided information and to avoid confusing missing data and no use.

[1] Since the classification of urban and rural residents are based on household registration locations, the comparison in this chapter is comparing energy consumption of residents of urban and rural household registration. In the Chinese Household Energy Consumption Report 2015, urban and rural residents were classified depending on where they lived instead of household registration location. Therefore, this chapter shall not be compared directly with the said report.

X. Lunyu (✉) · Z. Shuhan
Renmin University of China, Beijing, China
e-mail: lunyuxie@ruc.edu.cn



X. Zheng and C. Wei (eds.), *Household Energy Consumption in China: 2016 Report*, https://doi.org/10.1007/978-981-13-7523-1_6

# 1 Comparison of Residential Energy Consumption in Urban and Rural Areas

In this section, we compare the total amount of energy consumption and total energy expenditure as well as the consumption amount and expenditure (energy consumption structure) of various energy sources in households of urban and rural household registration. The energy consumption structures are different in urban and rural areas, with significant differences in end-use efficiency (for example, when firewood is burnt for cooking, only a small proportion of the heat from combustion is used by cooking utensils) and prices of various energy sources. Therefore, it is possible that rural households may consume more energy despite lower energy expenditure than urban households. We will comment on this issue in detail in the following section.

## *1.1 Access to Various Sources of Energy*

Table 1 compares access to various sources of energy in urban and rural areas, the effective samples for which consist of 1,472 urban households and 2,353 rural households. In general, both urban and rural areas had 100% access to electricity, urban households had better access to district heating, natural gas and pipeline kerosene, a larger proportion of rural households used coal and biomass energy, but there was no apparent urban-rural difference in consumption of biogas and solar energy, which accounted for small proportions in urban and rural areas.

Concerning the specific data of samples, households consuming electricity accounted for nearly 100% of the total in both urban and rural areas, 32.1% of urban households and less than 8% of rural households used district heating, mainly because of inadequate infrastructure of district heating in rural areas. Consumption of pipeline kerosene was also affected by infrastructure development: 49.9% of urban

**Table 1** Access to various energy sources in urban and rural areas (Unit: %)

| Source of energy | Urban areas | Rural areas |
|---|---|---|
| Electricity | 100 | 100 |
| District heating | 32.1 | 7.3 |
| Natural gas | 49.9 | 8.3 |
| LPG | 27.1 | 36.3 |
| Pipeline kerosene | 6.3 | 1.6 |
| Diesel | 0.1 | 0.2 |
| Coal | 6.9 | 20.5 |
| Biomass energy | 4.5 | 40.4 |
| Biogas | 0.1 | 1.2 |
| Solar energy | 1.8 | 1.5 |

households and 8.3% of rural households used natural gas, 6.3% of urban households and 1.6% of rural households used pipeline kerosene. The proportions of rural households using coal, LPG and biomass energy were significantly higher than that of urban households: 20.5% of rural households used coal as energy source for daily life, while only 6.9% of urban households used coal; 36.3% of rural households and 27.1% of urban households used LPG, 40.4% of rural households and 4.5% of urban households used biomass energy. Use of biogas and solar energy are scarce in China: in urban areas, there was nearly no households using biogas, and in urban areas, only about 1.2% of households used biogas. Only 1–2% of households used solar energy in rural and urban areas.

## 1.2 *Amount of Energy Consumption*

Table 2 and Fig. 1 show comparison of the total amount of energy consumption and the consumption amount by energy sources in urban and rural households. For calculation of the total amount of energy consumption, the consumption amount of each energy source has been converted to kgce. The "consumption proportion" in Table 2 refers to the household average by energy sources. The proportions of energy sources in Fig. 1 is household consumption amount by energy sources divided by average of total energy consumption amount. The difference between the two calculation methods is that the former gives each household the same weight while the latter gives more weight to households consuming more energy.

It can be seen from the above table and figure that urban households had a higher amount of energy consumption than rural households. Among the various energy

**Table 2** Comparison of energy consumption in urban and rural areas in kgce

| Variable | Consumption amount/kgce | | Consumption proportion/% | |
|---|---|---|---|---|
| | Urban areas | Rural areas | Urban areas | Rural areas |
| Energy consumption in kgce | 1,274.65 | 1,152.7 | | |
| Electricity | 292.21 | 213.96 | 22.92 | 18.56 |
| District heating | 474.51 | 137.95 | 37.23 | 11.97 |
| Natural gas | 324.27 | 55.92 | 25.44 | 4.85 |
| LPG | 83.33 | 108.50 | 6.54 | 9.41 |
| Pipeline kerosene | 4.71 | 1.30 | 0.37 | 0.11 |
| Diesel | 0.37 | 0.04 | 0.03 | 0.00 |
| Coal | 39.23 | 108.04 | 3.08 | 9.37 |
| Biomass energy | 40.39 | 503.72 | 3.17 | 43.70 |
| Biogas | 0.08 | 1.14 | 0.01 | 0.10 |
| Solar energy | 15.55 | 21.97 | 1.22 | 1.91 |

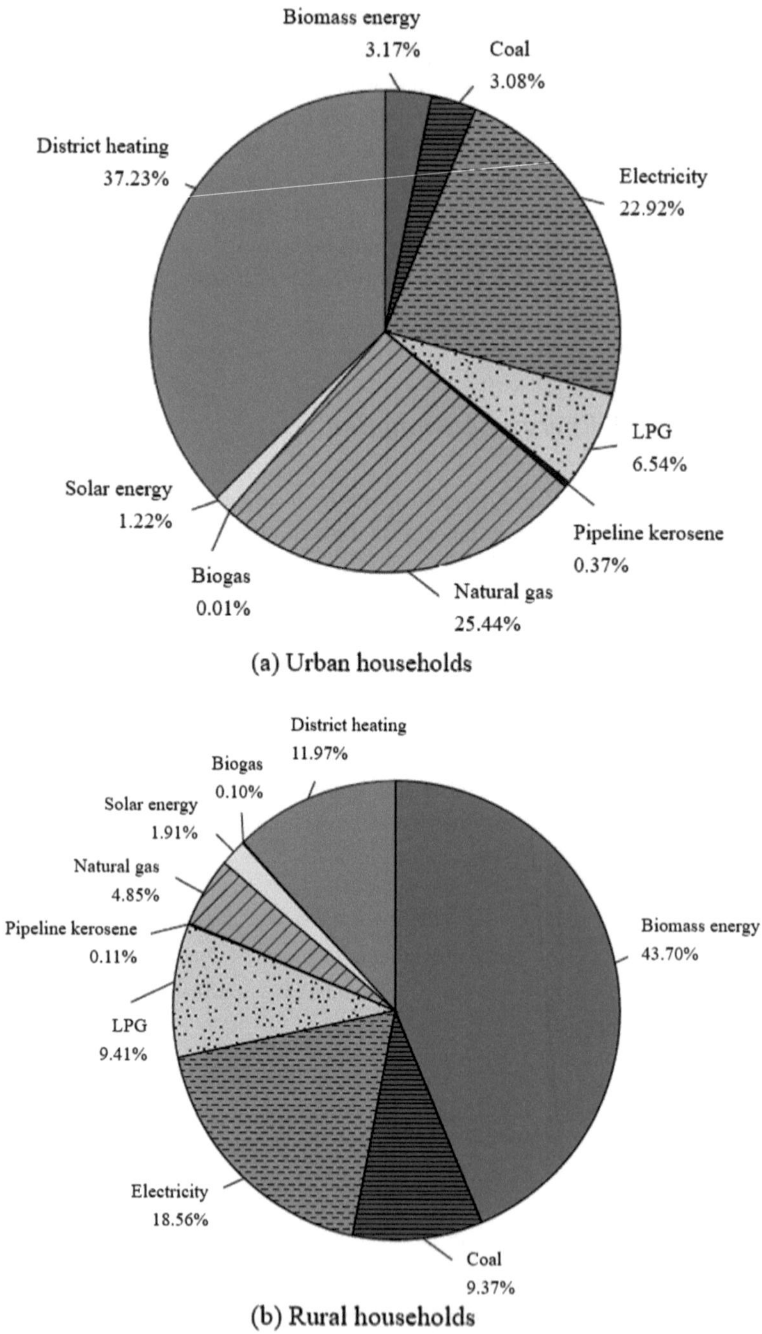


**Fig. 1** Comparison of energy consumption structure in rural and urban areas

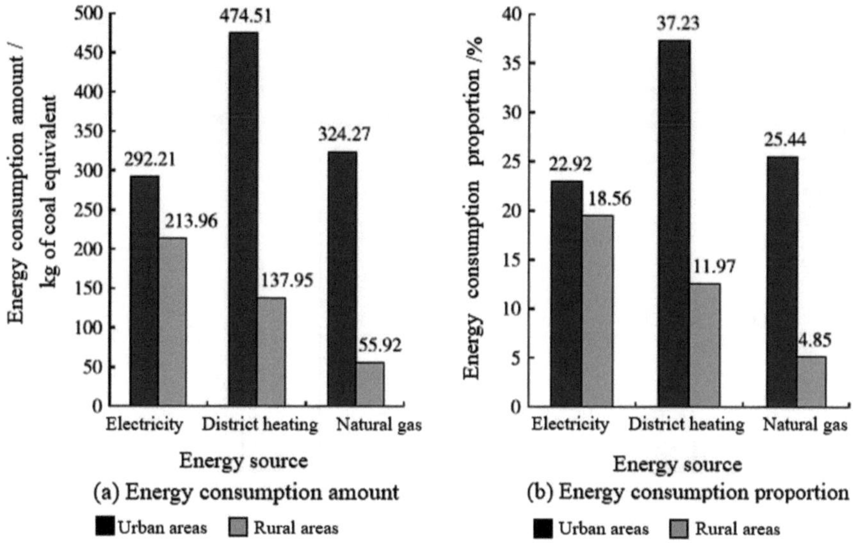


**Fig. 2** Comparison of consumption of electricity, district heating and natural gas in rural and urban areas

sources, the leading sources of energy were district heating, natural gas and electricity for urban households and biomass energy, electricity and district heating for rural households.

(1) Urban households consumed a large amount of electricity, district heating and natural gas

Concerning the energy consumption structure, the leading sources of energy for urban households were district heating, natural gas and electricity, the consumption amount and proportion in the total of which were both higher than in rural areas (Fig. 2). On average, the electricity consumption was 292.21 kgce per year per urban household, accounting for 22.92% of the total energy consumption of urban households, and 213.96 kgce per year per rural household, accounting for 18.56% of the total. The energy consumption for district heating was 474.51 kgce per year per urban household, accounting for 37.23% of the total, while each rural household consumed 137.95 kgce per year for district heating, accounting for 11.97% of the total. The natural gas consumption was 324.27 kgce per year per urban household, accounting for 25.44% of the total, and 55.92 kgce per year, per rural household accounting for 4.85% of the total.

(2) Rural households consumed a large amount of biomass energy and coal

The consumption amount and proportions in the total of biomass energy and coal were higher in rural households than in urban households (Fig. 3). According to the survey data, for rural households, the biomass energy consumption was 503.72 kgce per household per year, accounting for 43.70% of the total energy consumption of

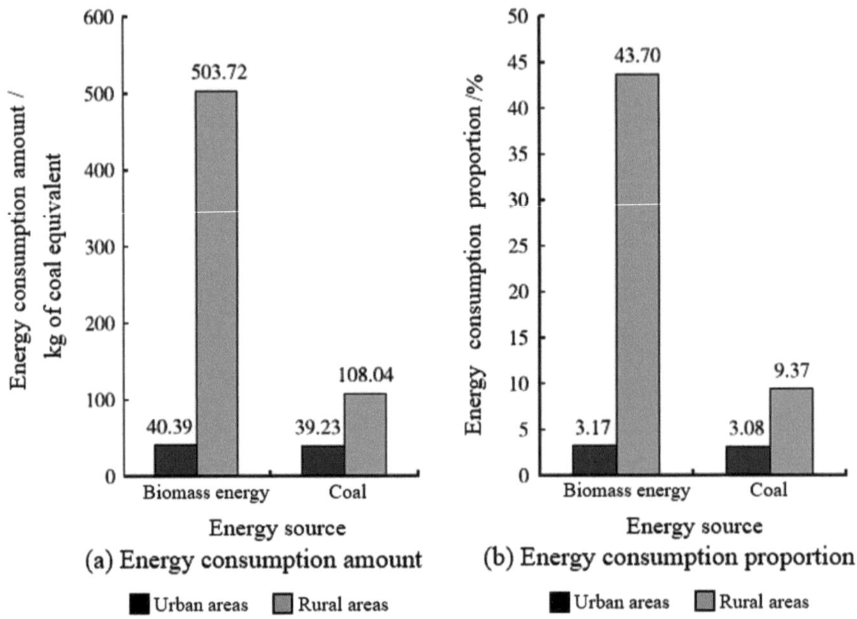


**Fig. 3** Comparison of biomass energy and coal consumption in rural and urban areas

rural households, the coal consumption was 108.04 kgce per household per year, accounting for 9.37% of the total. For urban households, the consumption amount of biomass energy and coal was 40.39 kgce and 39.23 kgce respectively, accounting for 3.17 and 3.08% of the total, much lower than the consumption amount and proportions in the total of these energy sources for rural households.

(3) There were no significant differences between urban and rural areas in use of LPG, diesel, biogas and solar energy

Urban and rural households did not have significant differences in use of LPG, diesel, biogas and solar energy (Fig. 4). Among these energy sources, consumption of LPG was larger, and rural households consumed slightly more LPG than urban households, with the former at 108.50 kgce and the latter at 83.33 kgce. Both rural and urban households consumed a small amount of diesel, biogas and solar energy.

## *1.3 Energy Expenditure*

Table 3 and Fig. 5 show comparison of energy expenditure of urban and rural households, covering 1,480 urban samples and 2,383 rural samples. Similar to energy consumption proportions, the proportion in Fig. 6 is average household expenditure by energy sources divided by average of total energy expenditure and the proportion

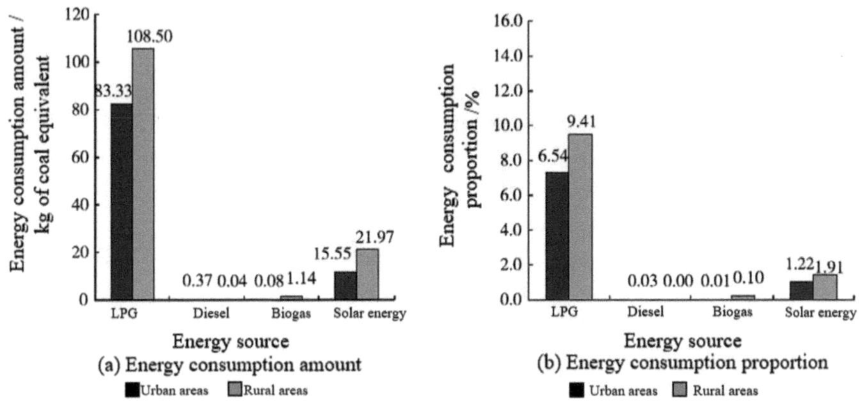


**Fig. 4** Comparison of consumption of LPG, diesel, biogas and solar energy in rural and urban areas

**Table 3** Comparison of energy expenditure in rural and urban areas

| Variable | Expenditure/RMB | | Expenditure proportion/% | |
|---|---|---|---|---|
| | Urban areas | Rural areas | Urban areas | Rural areas |
| Total energy expenditure | 2,786.7 | 2,266.1 | | |
| Electricity | 1,283.9 | 923.8 | 46.10 | 40.84 |
| Natural gas | 633.8 | 102.2 | 22.70 | 4.50 |
| LPG | 392.5 | 524.5 | 14.10 | 23.12 |
| Pipeline kerosene | 32.0 | 2.3 | 1.10 | 0.10 |
| Diesel | 25.6 | 41.8 | 0.90 | 1.80 |
| Gasoline | 191.0 | 152.4 | 6.90 | 6.71 |
| Coal | 148.9 | 240.4 | 5.30 | 10.61 |
| Biomass energy | 4.3 | 178.3 | 0.20 | 7.91 |
| Other sources | 74.7 | 100.4 | 2.70 | 4.40 |

of expenditure in Table 3 is the mean value of household expenditure proportions. The total annual energy expenditure of urban households on average was RMB2,786.7 per household, far more than the energy expenditure of rural households (RMB2,266.1 per household). But it is noteworthy that the energy expenditure of rural households was 40% higher than the same in the CRECS 2013, possibly due to increase in per capita income in rural areas (Comparison of data from 2014 to 2013 shows an increase of 43% in per capita income in rural areas). In terms of the proportions of expenditure on various energy sources in the total, the primary source of energy expenditure for urban households was electricity, accounting for more than 45% of the total, followed by natural gas which accounted for about 23% of the total and LPG which accounted for 14.10% of the total. For urban households, expenditure on gasoline and coal accounted for similar proportions (about 6%) of the total, while expenditure on other energy sources accounted for small proportions. For rural households,

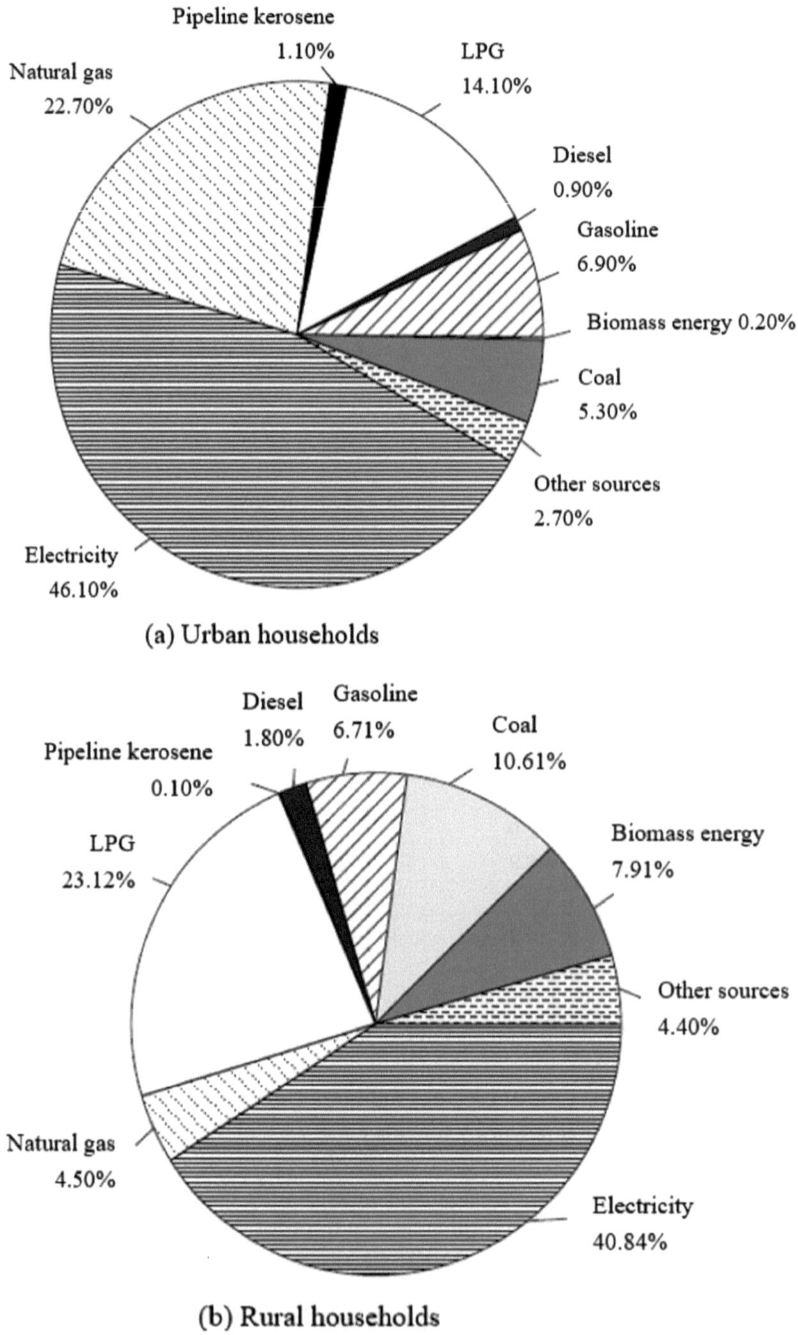


**Fig. 5** Comparison of energy expenditure structure in rural and urban areas

electricity also accounted for the largest proportion of energy expenditure, followed by LPG, coal and biomass energy.

(1) Electricity was the primary source of energy expenditure both in rural and urban households.

Electricity expenditure accounted for the largest proportion in terms of consumption amount and proportion in the total in energy consumption structures of urban and rural households. Therefore, at present, electricity is the primary source of energy and energy expenditure in the residential sector in China. Figure 6 presents the use of electricity in urban and rural areas: The electricity expenditure of urban households was significantly more than that of rural households, but there was no major difference between urban and rural households in terms of the proportion of electricity expenditure in the total, both accounting for more than 40%. The main reasons are that the total energy consumption of rural households was less than that of urban households and that a considerable portion of energy sources in energy consumption structure of rural households, such as firewood and straw, was very cheap and even free.

(2) Urban households spent more on natural gas, gasoline and pipeline kerosene than rural households.

As shown in Fig. 7, the expenditure on natural gas per year per household was RMB633.8 in urban households, accounting for 22.70% of the total, and RMB102.2 in rural households, accounting for 4.50% of the total. It can be seen that natural gas is an important source of energy for urban households, but rural households had low access to natural gas, mainly because of inadequate infrastructure in rural areas. Concerning the expenditure on gasoline, the proportions were similar in urban and rural households, both accounting for less than 7% of the total, but the expenditure was much higher in urban households than in rural households: RMB191.0 per urban household and RMB152.4 per rural household. Concerning the expenditure on pipeline kerosene, the average expenditure was RMB32.0 per urban household, accounting for 1.10% of the energy expenditure, and RMB2.3 per urban household, accounting for 0.10% of the total.

(3) Rural households spent more on coal, biomass energy and bottled LPG than urban households

Coal and biomass energy are extensively used for cooking and space heating in rural areas. The expenditure of rural households on these energy sources was significantly more than that of urban households. As shown in Fig. 8, the average coal expenditure was RMB148.9 per urban household, accounting for 5.30% of the energy expenditure, and RMB240.4 per rural household, accounting for 10.61% of the total. Concerning the expenditure on biomass energy, it was RMB4.3 per urban household, accounting for 0.20% of the total, and RMB178.3 per rural household, accounting for 7.91% of the total. The expenditure on biomass energy and its proportion in total energy expenditure were significantly more in rural households than urban households. The expenditure on bottled LPG was also more in rural households than urban households, with the former at RMB524.4, accounting for 23.12% of the total, and the latter at RMB392.5, accounting for 14.10% of the total.

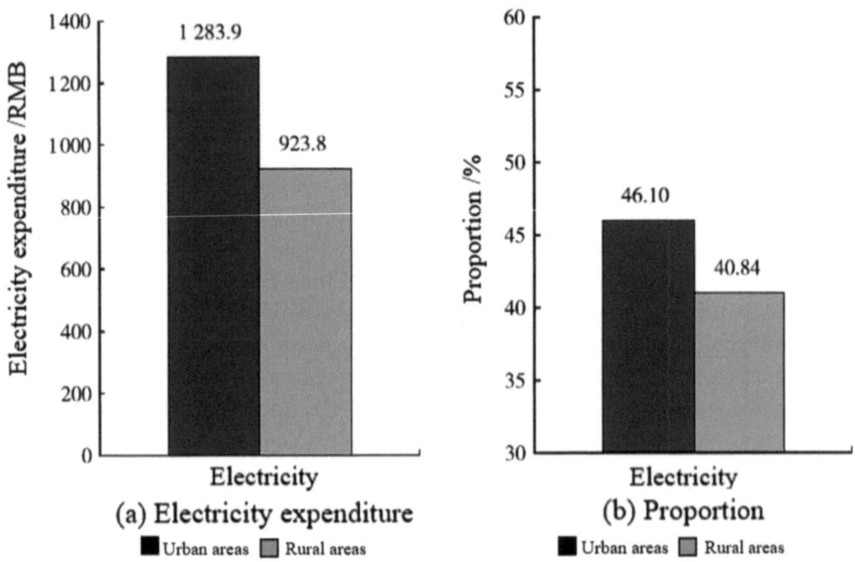


**Fig. 6** Comparison of electricity expenditure in rural and urban areas

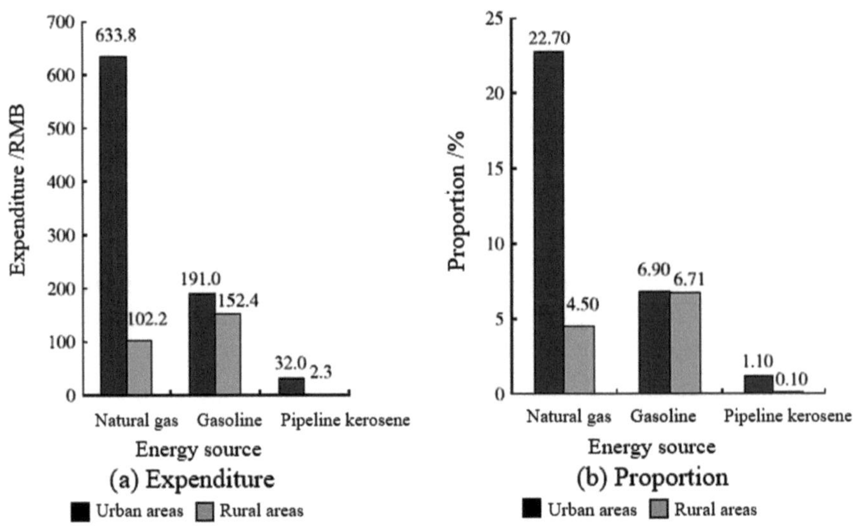


**Fig. 7** Comparison of expenditure on natural gas, gasoline and pipeline kerosene in urban and rural areas

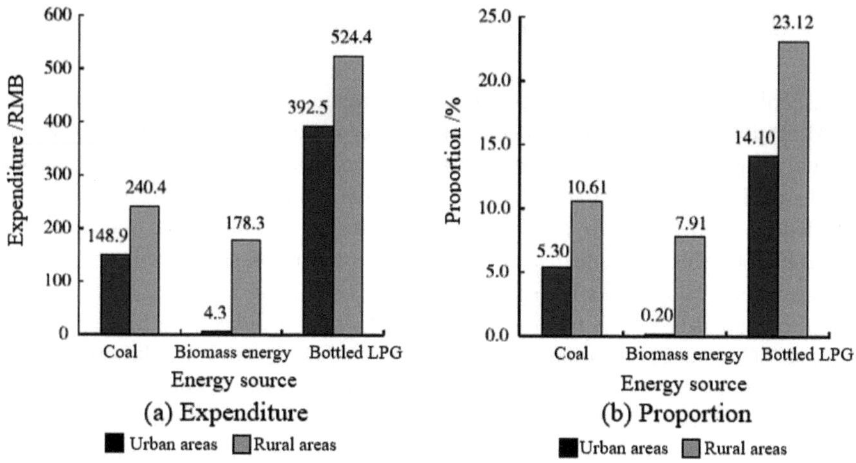


**Fig. 8** Comparison of expenditure on coal, biomass energy and bottled LPG in urban and rural areas

## 2 Comparison of Influential Factors

Based on review of literature about influential factors of the amount and structure of residential energy consumption, the main factors affecting the residential energy consumption include household characteristics, income level, energy price, location and energy consumption awareness, etc. According to the survey data, we select variables as shown in Table 4 and compare the differences between urban and rural residents in terms of these variables to identify the possible factors in urbanization that may affect residents' energy-consuming behavior.

**Table 4** Comparison of influential factors in urban and rural areas

| Variable | Urban areas | | Rural areas | |
|---|---|---|---|---|
| | Sample size | Mean value | Sample size | Mean value |
| Annual income per capita/RMB | 1,359 | 43,989.55 | 2,175 | 20,791.5 |
| Number of permanent residents in household/person | 1,480 | 2.04 | 2,383 | 2.7 |
| Time spent at home per capita/(day/year) | 1,480 | 349.3 | 2,383 | 348.4 |
| Average age of household members | 1,480 | 42.1 | 2,179 | 36 |
| Year of construction of residence | 1,335 | 1994 | 2,179 | 1996 |
| Usable area of residence/m$^2$ | 1,480 | 92.5 | 2,382 | 130.9 |
| Sunshine duration of residence in winter/hour | 1,434 | 4.6 | 2,293 | 5.4 |
| Sunshine duration of residence in summer/hour | 1,434 | 5.9 | 2,383 | 6.7 |

## 2.1 Household Characteristics

Household characteristics include annual income per capita, number of permanent residents in households, time spent at home per capita, average age of household members and education level of respondents. A wide gap existed between urban and rural areas in terms of annual income per capita: the annual income per capita of urban residents was RMB43,900, but for rural residents, the annual income per capita was RMB20,700, which was much lower than that of urban residents. Concerning number of permanent residents per households, there was no major difference between rural and urban areas, with the former (2.7 persons) slightly higher than the latter (2.04 persons). Concerning the time spent at home per capita, it was 349.3 days per year in urban areas and 348.4 days per year in rural areas, both close to 12 months, suggesting little mobility of permanent residents. As for the average age of household members, it was larger in urban households (about 42 years old) than in rural households (about 36 years old).

## 2.2 Characteristics of Residence

Characteristics of residence include the year of construction, usable area of residences and sunshine duration in summer and winter. The average year of construction was 1994 in urban areas and 1996 in rural areas. Concerning the usable area of residences, a wide gap existed between urban and rural areas: the average usable area was 92.5 $m^2$ per household in urban areas and 130.9 $m^2$ per household in rural areas. The sunshine duration was generally longer in rural residences than urban ones. The sunshine duration in winter was 4.6 h per day for urban residences and 5.4 h per day for rural residences, and the sunshine duration in summer was 5.9 h per day for urban residences and 6.7 h per day for rural residences. As China is in the North Hemisphere, the sunshine duration in winter is shorter than in summer. Due to high density of buildings in urban areas and larger usable areas of residences in rural areas, the sunshine duration of rural residences is longer than in urban residences.

# 3 Quantitative Analysis

In this section, we use the method of least squares in econometrics for quantitative estimation of the influence of the above factors on residential energy consumption amount and energy expenditure. To minimize the influence of extreme values on the estimation, the energy consumption amount and energy expenditure as dependent variables are both in the form of logarithmic, and the household income and housing area as independent variables are also in the form of logarithmic. Concerning education level, some groups that were similar in nature and accounted for small proportions were combined. For example, adult education for bachelor degree and adult education for associate degree were considered a group, while general education for associate degree, degrees of bachelor, master and above were considered a group. The results of regression are as shown in Table 5.

**Table 5** Analysis of influential factors in residential energy consumption amount and energy expenditure

| Dependent variable | Log (energy consumption amount) | Log (energy expenditure) | Log (energy consumption amount) | Log (energy expenditure) |
|---|---|---|---|---|
| | (1) | (2) | (3) | (4) |
| Urban dummy variable | | | 0.235***<br>(0.045) | 0.399***<br>(0.045) |
| Log (annual income of household) | 0.071***<br>(0.019) | 0.283***<br>(0.019) | 0.042**<br>(0.019) | 0.234***<br>(0.019) |
| Number of permanent residents in household | 0.089***<br>(0.015) | 0.175***<br>(0.015) | 0.086***<br>(0.015) | 0.169***<br>(0.015) |
| Respondent' s age | 0.002<br>(0.001) | 0.000<br>(0.001) | 0.001<br>(0.001) | −0.001<br>(0.001) |
| *Education level* | | | | |
| Primary or middle school education | 0.184***<br>(0.058) | 0.289***<br>(0.058) | 0.159***<br>(0.058) | 0.246***<br>(0.057) |
| High school | 0.299***<br>(0.069) | 0.467***<br>(0.069) | 0.225***<br>(0.071) | 0.340***<br>(0.070) |
| Adult education for associate and bachelor degrees | 0.327***<br>(0.105) | 0.376***<br>(0.105) | 0.216**<br>(0.107) | 0.185*<br>(0.106) |
| General education for associate and bachelor degrees and above | 0.514***<br>(0.080) | 0.433***<br>(0.079) | 0.411***<br>(0.082) | 0.259***<br>(0.080) |
| Age of residence | −0.001<br>(0.001) | −0.004***<br>(0.001) | −0.001<br>(0.001) | −0.004***<br>(0.001) |
| Log (housing area) | 0.012<br>(0.033) | 0.059*<br>(0.033) | 0.045<br>(0.033) | 0.114***<br>(0.033) |
| Sunshine duration in winter | −0.002<br>(0.014) | −0.013<br>(0.014) | 0.001<br>(0.014) | −0.008<br>(0.014) |
| Sunshine duration in summer | −0.004<br>(0.014) | −0.010<br>(0.014) | −0.002<br>(0.014) | −0.006<br>(0.014) |
| Constant term | 5.499***<br>(0.266) | 3.802***<br>(0.265) | 5.588***<br>(0.266) | 3.957***<br>(0.262) |
| $R^2$ | 2868 | 2873 | 2868 | 2873 |
| Observation | 0.042 | 0.159 | 0.051 | 0.182 |

***, ** and * means significance at the level of 1%, 5% and 10% respectively
*Note* Value in brackets is *P* value

The dependent variable is the energy consumption amount in column (1) and energy expenditure in column (2). The regression results show that annual income of households, household size and education level of household members have significant influences on the residential energy consumption amount and energy expenditure. On average, 1% rise in income leads to 7.1% increase in energy consumption amount and 28.3% increase in energy expenditure, while each additional household member leads to 8% increase in energy consumption amount and 18% increase in energy expenditure. Education level is positively correlated with the energy consumption amount and energy expenditure. Meanwhile, age of residence and housing area do not have significant influences on energy consumption amount, but have significant influences on household energy expenditure. The age of residence is negatively correlated with energy expenditure, which is due to the influence of insulating performance of residences and energy-consuming behavior of households. We do not identify significant influences on energy consumption amount and energy expenditure from other independent variables such as average age of household members and sunshine duration in summer and winter.

In column (3) and (4), the urban dummy variable is added on the basis of column (1) and (2). This dummy variable shows that excluding the difference between urban and rural residents in household characteristics and housing characteristics, they may have different energy-consuming behaviors due to differences in energy-saving awareness and living habits. According to the results, with the same household characteristics and housing characteristics, the energy consumption of urban households is 23.5% more than that of rural households, and the energy expenditure of urban households is 39.9% more than that of rural households. Comparing column (3) with column (1) and column (4) with column (2), the results show that with the urban dummy variable, the influences of annual income of households and education level on energy consumption amount and energy expenditure has reduced, which is consistent with the observation that income and education level of rural households are generally inferior to urban residents.

# 4 Summary

By comparison of energy consumption amount, energy consumption structure and energy expenditure of urban and rural households, in this chapter, we compare the household and housing characteristics of urban and rural areas, analyze the influences of urbanization on energy-consuming behaviors in households and identify the mechanism of such influences. Study shows that if, after urbanization, the energy-consuming behavior of new urban residents is the same as the former urban residents, the energy consumption of these new urban households will undergo the following changes: electricity consumption and energy expenditure will double; there will be little use of coal and consumption of biomass energy will decline to a great extent; district heating or electric heating equipment will be used for space heating; natural gas or electricity will be sources of energy for cooking.

Through data analysis, we note that the main observable factors of differences between urban and rural energy consumption are urban-rural differences in annual income of households, household size and education level. Non-observable factors such as difference in energy-saving awareness and living habits also lead to different energy consumption in urban and rural areas. Rural households become urban households in urbanization, the income and housing conditions of which will change accordingly. The energy-consuming behavior of these households will also change, with increase in energy consumption and energy expenditure. In the long run, the convergence of rural and urban residents in energy-saving awareness and living habits will lead to further increase in energy consumption and energy expenditure. Therefore, the increase in demand for energy caused by urbanization will remain for a long period.

# Chapter 7
# Household Appliance Ownership and Income Inequality

**Xiaobing Zhang, Ping Qin, Naiyuan Hu and Qitong Wang**

## 1 Research Background

Energy consumption forecast has always been a critical concern to energy economists and the energy industry. Considering from the perspective of growth in energy demand, the growth of energy consumption in European countries and the United States is slowing down, and the future growth in energy demand will mainly come from developing countries. China, among the developing countries, shows the most significant increase in energy demand. This is not only because of the giant base figure of energy consumption in China, but also because of the long-term high growth rate of energy consumption in China (Wang and Wei 2014) caused by urbanization and industrialization. The total energy consumption in China amounted to 786,000,000 tons of oil equivalent in 2000 and rose to 1,988,000,000 tons of oil equivalent in 2014, increasing by nearly 150%. Meanwhile, with rapid economic development and increase in income, energy consumption in the residential sector in China has witnessed substantial and rapid increase. The energy consumption in the residential sector in China increased on a year-on-year basis from 2000 to 2014, making it the second largest energy-consuming sector. In 2014, the energy consumption of the residential sector (excluding energy consumption of personal transportation) in China was 406,640,000 tons of oil equivalent, accounting for 20.46% of the national energy consumption. Take electricity consumption as an example. From 2000 to 2014, the residential electricity consumption increased from 145,200 to 717,700 GWh, increasing by nearly 4 times with an annual growth rate of 12.1%. For the foreseeable future, energy consumption in the residential sector in China will continue to grow. At present, there is still a wide gap between China and developed countries in terms of per-capita energy consumption. But as China is currently going through industrialization, to meet people's ever-increasing expectation for life, the

X. Zhang (✉) · P. Qin · N. Hu · Q. Wang
Renmin University of China, Beijing, China
e-mail: xiaobing.zhang@ruc.edu.cn



X. Zheng and C. Wei (eds.), *Household Energy Consumption in China: 2016 Report*, https://doi.org/10.1007/978-981-13-7523-1_7

residential energy consumption is expected to continue to grow. Meanwhile, with the advancement of urbanization, the urban-rural gap in China continues to widen. Large-scale population mobility and settlement change the structure of residential energy consumption, with consumption of some biomass energy replaced by modern energy sources. This process will also witness increase in the residential energy consumption (Wei et al. 2016). Therefore, an accurate understanding of the development trends of residential energy consumption is helpful to energy consumption forecast in China and formulation of relevant plans.

For a long period, the energy consumption in the residential sector is mainly for space heating. However, the proportion of energy consumption by household electrical appliances increased apparently in recent years. Take the United States as an example. The proportion of energy consumption for space heating in the residential sector dropped from 53.1% in 1993 to 41.5% in 2009, while the energy consumption proportion of household electrical appliances increased from 24.0 to 34.6% during this period. Consistent with this phenomenon, the appliance ownership of urban residents in China increased dramatically. The air conditioner ownership per 100 households in urban areas of China, for example, increased from 8 in 1995 to 106 in 2009 (Auffhammer 2014).

Farrell (1954) stated in his study of residential consumption of durable goods that an S-shaped curve was observed when household income level was the horizontal axis and ownership of energy-using durable goods was the vertical axis. The shape of the S-shaped curve shows that the penetration of household durable goods stays at a low level until the household income rises above a certain acquisition threshold, but the penetration increases rapidly once the household income passes the threshold level. Farrell studied the penetration of motor cars in the United States, based on which he forecasted the equilibrium price of motor cars. An S-shaped curve is also observed in growth of household electrical appliance ownership when McCarthy and Ryan (1974) analyzed the penetration of television in Ireland. Many studies used data at the macro level to analyze influential factors of energy-consuming goods ownership in the residential sector. For example, low-income households are not likely to spend their income on purchase of electrical appliances. However, when the household income rises above a certain threshold, households are more likely to spend their income on refrigerators, cars and electric kettles, though such ownership growth tends to slow down after the income level rises above the second threshold (Gertler et al. 2013). When income of low-income households passes the threshold, the purchase decisions are mostly made because purchase of electrical appliances at this stage may significantly improve the household welfare. With a refrigerator, people may spend less time traveling between stores and their residences. Refrigerator ownership may also affect nutrition and diet patterns and improve health conditions (Tobergte and Curtis 2013). Many additional factors are considered in studies of household appliance ownership. McNeil and Letschert (2010) used macro data of many countries to study the influences of household income, urbanization level and electrification level on household appliance ownership. Liu et al. (2016) used the price deflator model to analyze the macro data of 30 provinces in China from 1995 to 2012 and examined how electricity consumption in the residential sector changed with rising income, who pointed out that the government shall introduce higher standards of energy efficiency and improve people's income to ensure sustainable development of the electric power industry in China.

During recent years, micro data has been used in more and more studies of residential energy consumption, especially electricity consumption. Leahy and Lyons (2010) estimated the influential factors of household appliance ownership for Irish residents based on micro data, and calculated the energy consumption level in the residential sector in Ireland. Wijaya and Tezuka (2013), in a study of characteristics of residential electricity consumption in Indonesia, found that cities of different cultural backgrounds had different energy consumption habits. To be specific, according to their study, education level and time spent at home had significant positive effect on household energy consumption in Bandung, but in Yogyakarta, these two variables had significant negative effect on electricity bills. Therefore, Wijaya and Tezuka proposed that local characteristics shall be considered in promotion of energy conservation policies to ensure better implementation of such policies. Zhou and Teng (2013) used micro data of cities in China from 2007 to 2009 to study the income and price elasticities of residential electricity demand in Sichuan, China. Matsumoto (2016) studied the influential factors of household appliance ownership based on micro data of Japanese households, focusing on influences of household income on household appliance ownership. Belaïd (2016) used data of France and studied the factors of residential energy consumption, from which he found that the dominant factors were energy price and socioeconomic variables of households: for example, when housing characteristics are under control, characteristics of house owners have significant influences.

Auffhammer and Wolfram (2014) pointed out that the current studies focused only on economic growth, but ignored the influences of income distribution on home appliance ownership. In fact, in most cases, income distribution is biased. Studies about Kuznets curve show that income inequality may first increase and then decrease with economic growth. So, Auffhammer and Wolfram studied the province-level panel data in China and found that when influences of income was under control, on the macro level, the share of population living under the poverty line had decisive influences on household appliance holdings. However, as mentioned above, more and more researches are using micro data to study the influential factors of household appliance ownership, but no research on the micro level has considered the influence of regional income distribution on appliance ownership. In such cases, this book seeks to fill the gap by using micro data to analyze the influential factors of household appliance ownership while considering the influence of regional income inequality. To be specific, the main contribution of this chapter is to study the correlation between income inequality and household appliance ownership using simple inequality indexes of income distribution in various provinces based on micro data, and analyze the influences of factors such as socioeconomic variables and dwelling characteristics, etc. of households (Jones et al. 2015). This will help optimize the current forecast of residential energy consumption and facilitate the formulation of relevant plans.

## 2 Data Specifications

### 2.1 *Source of Data*

The data used in this chapter is from the CRECS 2014, consisting of 9 parts, i.e., household income and expenditure, housing characteristics, kitchen equipment and household electrical appliances, space heating and air conditioning data, means of transportation, energy acquisition and consumption, peak-valley electricity pricing, basic information of electricity consumption and tiered electricity pricing. Kitchen equipment and household electrical appliances cover 6 types of electrical appliances. Since ownership of freezer and dryer is extremely lower than other electrical appliances, in this chapter, we use data about ownership of air conditioners, televisions, refrigerators and washing machines. This chapter focuses on the correlation between income distribution and household appliance ownership. Therefore, samples with missing value for main variables were removed and ultimately 3,137 samples were used for econometric analysis.

### 2.2 *Main Variables*

(1) Appliance ownership

Table 1 presents the household appliance ownership: The average television ownership per household was 1.17, registering a penetration rate of 95.54%. The average washing machine ownership per household was 0.82, registering a penetration rate of 79.95%. The average ownership of refrigerators per household was also 0.82, with a penetration rate of 79.98%. The general air conditioner ownership was low at 0.68 per household. Households with at least one air conditioner accounted for 43.99% of the total samples.

(2) Income inequality index

To study the income distribution, this chapter uses the income data from the survey to simulate the relative standard deviation and construct four indexes for depiction of household income inequality in different provinces and municipalities. Gini

**Table 1** Household ownership of main appliances

| Household appliance ownership | | Observation: 3,137 | | |
|---|---|---|---|---|
| Statistics | Air conditioner | Television | Washing machine | Refrigerator |
| Share/% | 43.99 | 95.54 | 79.95 | 79.98 |
| Average/piece | 0.68 | 1.17 | 0.82 | 0.82 |
| Maximum/piece | 5 | 5 | 3 | 4 |
| Minimum/piece | 0 | 0 | 0 | 0 |

coefficient is usually used in study of income distribution and inequality. Xie and Zhou (2014) used micro survey data in China for calculation of Gini coefficient to describe the income inequality in China. However, for calculation of Gini coefficient, the income of regions under study shall be arranged in sequence and integral shall be used to approximate area for calculation of the coefficient. Among the data used in this chapter, this method is not appropriate for the sample sizes by region and approximation may have major errors. Besides, it is not rare in studies to construct indexes that can reflect income inequality. In a macro-level study of income inequality and appliance ownership, Auffhammer and Wolfram (2014) used the share of households with annual income of less than RMB3,000 in provincial household number to reflect the degree of income inequality of a province. Therefore, in this chapter, we construct four indexes to reflect the provincial income inequality, namely, Ineq_1a Ineq_1b, Ineq_2a and Ineq_2b.

$$\text{Ineq\_1a}_i = \frac{\sqrt{\frac{1}{N_i}\sum_j (\text{income}_{j,i} - \mu_i)^2}}{\mu_i}$$

$$\text{Ineq\_1b}_i = \frac{\sqrt{\frac{1}{M_{1i}}\sum_j (\chi_{<\mu_i}(\text{income}_{j,i}) - \mu_i)^2}}{\mu_i}$$

$$\text{Ineq\_2a}_i = \frac{\sqrt{\frac{1}{N_i}\sum_j (\text{income}_{j,i} - \text{Med}_i)^2}}{\text{Med}_i}$$

$$\text{Ineq\_2b}_i = \frac{\sqrt{\frac{1}{M_{2i}}\sum_j (\chi_{<\text{med}_i}(\text{income}_{j,i}) - \text{Med}_i)^2}}{\text{Med}_i}$$

In the above formulas, $\text{income}_{j,i}$ is the household income of the $j$th household in the $i$th province; $\mu_i$ is the mean value of household income of the $i$th province; $N_i$ is the sample size of the $i$th province; $\chi_{<\mu_i}$ ($\text{income}_{j,i}$) is samples with household income below the provincial mean value ($M_{1i}$ is total samples satisfying the requirement); $\chi_{<\text{Med}i}$ ($\text{income}_{j,i}$) is samples with household income below the provincial median value ($M_{2i}$ is total samples satisfying the requirement); $\text{Med}_i$ is median value of household income of the $i$th province; $i = 1, 2, 3 \ldots, 27, 28$.

Such method for construction of inequality indexes is different from use of variance alone to describe sample differences. Ineq_1a obtained from the variance-to-mean ratio is the relative standard deviation in a standard circumstance. Ineq_1a and Ineq_2a reflect the income difference in a province. The index we construct grows with the income gap within the province. The two indexes are different in that Ineq_1a used mean value of household income in the province as deviation model while Ineq_2a used median value of household income in the province as deviation model. Under some circumstances, median values may better describe the whole than mean values. What's more, Ineq_1b and Ineq_2b were constructed using some of the samples. Ineq_1b was constructed using samples with household income below the provincial mean value to calculate the relative deviation from the mean value of all

**Table 2** Income inequality in provinces, municipalities and autonomous regions

| Inequality index | Observation: 28 provinces | | | |
|---|---|---|---|---|
| Statistics | Ineq_1a | Ineq_1b | Ineq_2a | Ineq_2b |
| Mean value | 0.89 | 0.56 | 1.26 | 0.57 |
| Maximum value | 1.45 | 0.70 | 2.64 | 0.70 |
| | Gansu | Guangxi | Gansu | Guangxi |
| Minimum value | 0.56 | 0.42 | 0.60 | 0.43 |
| | Tianjin | Tianjin | Tianjin | Beijing |

samples, while Ineq_2b was constructed using samples with household income below the provincial median value. Therefore, the value of Ineq_1b (Ineq_2b) increases with the deviation of lower-income households in a province from the provincial mean value (median value). The values of the four indexes increases with the degree of income inequality.

It can be seen from Table 2 that in measurement based on different indexes, the provinces and municipalities with the maximum and minimum value of inequality do not show much change. For example, Tianjin has the lowest inequality in measurement based on three indexes.

(3) Other controlled variables

In this chapter, the following variables that may have influences on household appliance ownership are controlled.

## 2.3 *Housing Characteristics*

Housing characteristics are considered crucial in studies of household energy use (Druckman and Jackson 2008; Jones et al. 2015). Therefore, this chapter includes the following variables to describe various housing characteristics: location of sample (urban/rural area), year of construction of residence, permanent resident in household and floor space of residence.

(1) Location of sample (urban/rural areas): This variable is introduced to see if there are significant differences between urban and rural areas in household appliance ownership. Generally, urban areas have better infrastructure and better access to electricity, therefore, it is foreseeable that urban areas have higher level of appliance ownership than rural areas. We used dummy variable (urban area = 1, rural area = 0) for econometric analysis in the research.
(2) Location of sample (north/south): Among the surveyed electrical appliances, air conditioner ownership is to a great extent correlated with the climate of the sample's location. Summer in North China is not so hot as in the south, leading to lower demand for air conditioners in the north. Accordingly, it is foreseeable that the location of residences in the north/south has influences on air conditioner

ownership, and we expect lower level of air conditioner ownership in North China. In our research of air conditioner ownership, we used dummy variable (North = 1, South = 0) for econometric analysis.

(3) Year of construction of residence: Most researchers wanted to introduce the variable of year of construction, but the data they used did not include information in this regard. Therefore, researchers tended to abandon this explanatory variable or seek substitutes. People living in recently-built residences may have a stronger tendency to purchase more household electrical appliances, while those living in older residences may own old and low-efficiency appliances (Leahy and Lyons 2010). In our research, we used dummy variable (residence constructed after 2000 = 1, otherwise = 0) for econometric analysis.

(4) Permanent resident in household: The number of permanent residents in a household has great influences on household energy consumption. To be specific, more residents in a household mean higher energy demand. Zhou and Teng (2013) studied the residential electricity demand based on data of Sichuan, China from 2007 to 2009 and found scale effect of household size on electricity consumption. However, specific analysis is required concerning whether more permanent residents in a household may lead to a tendency to own more appliances. We used continuous variable of permanent residents for econometric analysis.

(5) Floor space of residence: Floor space of residence also affects appliance ownership in a household. With larger floor space, more air conditioners may be required for air conditioning, more televisions may be needed for entertainment and more refrigerators may be needed for food storage or distributed storage. Therefore, we introduced the continuous variable of floor space of residence.

## 2.4 Household Income

Household income is considered an important influential factor of appliance ownership. McNeil and Letschert (2010) studied the appliance ownership in many developing countries and found an S-shaped correlation between economic growth and appliance ownership. The appliance ownership rate is low in developing countries, but it rises rapidly with economic growth, and such increase of appliance ownership will slow down when most households own at least one piece of a type of electrical appliance. Considerable increase in appliance ownership leads to considerable increase in electricity consumption. Meanwhile, when a household owns basic electrical appliances, we consider that they have entered the middle class, which will lead to more electricity consumption (Auffhammer and Wolfram 2014). We used annual income of households (log value) to control the influences of household income on appliance ownership.

## 2.5 Respondents' Information

In view of the sampling method used in the survey, the respondent of each household was randomly selected. Their characteristics reflect the household information to a certain extent, so, we can use these variables to control the influences of characteristics of household members on appliance ownership. In this chapter, we mainly control the age, employment status and education level of the respondents. For respondent's age, continuous variable was used. Respondent's employment status was divided into employed and unemployed. Respondent's education level was divided into primary education and below, middle school, college and above.

(1) Age: Age of household members is considered a significant influential factor of electricity consumption in previous studies, according to which people of 50–65 years of age have higher electricity consumption, while people below 50 and above 65 consume less electricity. The higher electricity consumption of people between 50 and 65 is mainly because that they have retired and spend more time at home (Jones et al. 2015). Consequently, we assume that this group of people may have greater demand for electrical appliances and have higher appliance ownership.
(2) Employment status: Studies about influences of employment status on appliance ownership do not reach consistent conclusions, but most studies show that there is no significant correlation between employment status and electricity consumption. In another word, unemployed people do not have more electricity consumption. The influences of employment status on appliance ownership remain unclear.
(3) Education level: In a study of influential factors about household energy consumption in Sichuan, China, Zhou and Teng (2013) found that people who received no further education beyond primary education had more electricity consumption. Leahy and Lyons (2010) found from micro data of Ireland that people of lower education level had lower possibilities of owning a certain type of electrical appliance than those of higher education level. We expect that education level may have positive effect on household appliance ownership.

## 2.6 Descriptive Statistical Analysis

Table 3 is a summary of the socioeconomic variables used in this chapter. Table 4 presents the differences between urban and rural areas in terms of appliance ownership.

The mean value of annual household income of the samples was RMB57,858.86. Residences constructed after 2000 accounted for 45% of the total. The average floor space of residences was 120.45 m$^2$. 55% of the residences of the samples were in urban areas and 45% in rural areas. The average age of the respondents was 50.18, the youngest being 17 and the eldest being 92. 37% of the respondents received primary

**Table 3** Descriptive statistics of basic variables

| Variable | Sample size: 3,137 | | | | |
|---|---|---|---|---|---|
| | Unit | Mean value or share | Standard deviation | Minimum value | Maximum value |
| *Household income* | | | | | |
| Total household income | RMB/year | 57,858.86 | 56,272.79 | 200 | 400,000 |
| *Housing characteristics* | | | | | |
| Location of residence (urban/rural areas) | Dummy variable | 0.55 | | 0 | 1 |
| Location of residence (north/south) | Dummy variable | 0.44 | | 0 | 1 |
| Floor space of residence | $m^2$ | 120.45 | 89.43 | 5 | 1,050 |
| Year of construction (after 2000) | Dummy variable | 0.45 | | 0 | 1 |
| Permanent resident in household | Person | 2.90 | 1.39 | 1 | 14 |
| *Respondent's characteristics* | | | | | |
| Age | years | 50.18 | 16.29 | 17 | 92 |
| Primary education and below (REF) | Dummy variable | 0.37 | | | |
| Middle school | Dummy variable | 0.47 | | 0 | 1 |
| College and above | Dummy variable | 0.16 | | 0 | 1 |
| Employed | Dummy variable | 0.58 | | 0 | 1 |

**Table 4** Urban-rural differences (Unit: piece)

| Area | Television | | Refrigerator | | Washing machine | | Air conditioner | |
|---|---|---|---|---|---|---|---|---|
| | Mean value | Standard deviation | Mean value | Standard deviation | Mean value | Standard deviation | Mean value | Standard deviation |
| Urban | 1.24 | 0.57 | 0.94 | 0.34 | 0.91 | 0.35 | 1.05 | 1.05 |
| Rural | 1.12 | 0.52 | 0.72 | 0.48 | 0.74 | 0.48 | 0.36 | 0.71 |

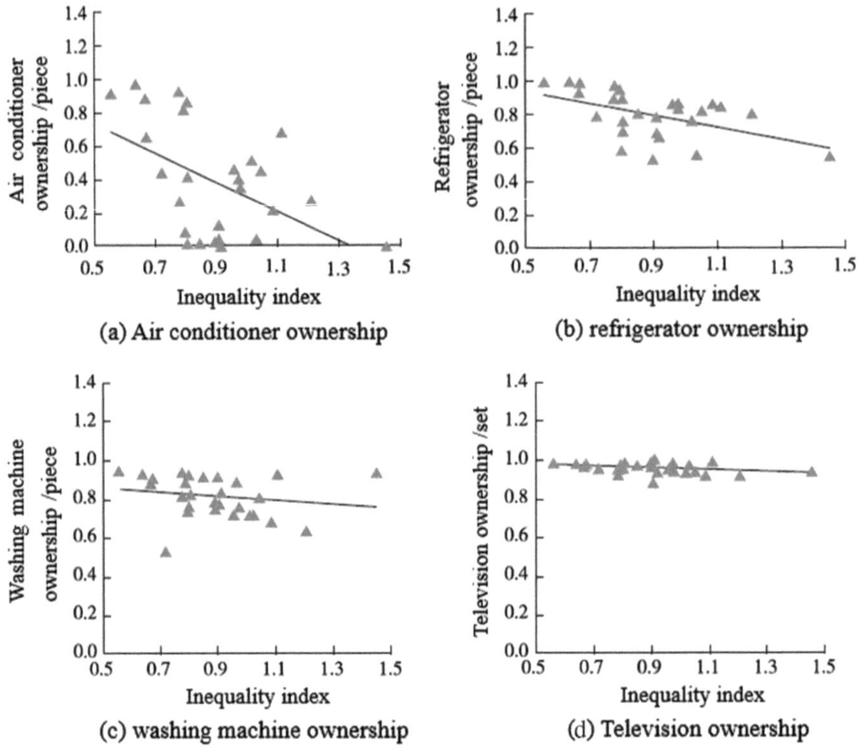


**Fig. 1** Income inequality and appliance ownership

education at the best, 47% received middle school education and 16% received college and better education. Unemployed respondents accounted for 42% of the total.

It can be seen from Table 4 that the location of samples has influences on mean values of ownership of different appliances. The mean values of appliance ownership are higher in urban areas than in rural areas. The most obvious difference between urban and rural areas lies in air conditioner ownership, with urban ownership per household at 1.05 pieces and rural ownership per household at 0.36 piece. Figure 1 presents the correlation between inequality index and appliance ownership in difference provinces., which shows that provinces with lower degree of inequality have higher appliance ownership.

# 3 Econometric Models

This chapter mainly uses two econometric models, bivariate regression model and count variable regression model, to analyze the influential factors of appliance ownership.

## 3.1 Bivariate Regression Model

In this chapter, we first use the Logit model to analyze the factors that may influence whether a household owns a specific type of electrical appliance. We choose this model because we seek to identify the determinant factors of resident's desire or ability to purchase electrical appliances by reviewing the influences of different factors on resident's ownership of a specific type of appliance.

In Logit regression, the probability of household's ownership of a specific type of appliance is calculated according to cumulative distribution function of standard logistic distribution:

$$\Pr(Y = 1X) = F(AX_{\mathrm{i}})$$

$F$ in the above formula is cumulative probability function of standard logistic distribution:

$$F(AX_i) = \frac{1}{1 + \mathrm{e}^{-(AX_i)}}$$

$$X_i = \begin{pmatrix} \text{Inequality}_i,\ \text{citytown}_i,\ \text{Build Age}_i,\ \text{Family Size}_i,\ \text{Floor Space}_i, \\ \text{Income}_i,\ \text{Age}_i,\ \text{Employment}_i,\ \text{Education}_i,\ \text{North}_i \end{pmatrix}$$

In the above formula, $X_i$ is dependent variable matrix; Income is the total household income (natural log); Inequality is the degree of inequality; city town is the location of households; Floor Space is the floor space of residence; Family Size is the number of household members; Build Age is the year of construction of residence; Age is the respondent's age; Employment is the employment status of respondent; Education is the education level of respondent; $\text{North}_{\mathrm{i}}$ is the location of households in North (or South) China in analysis of air conditioner ownership (climate has great influences on air conditioner ownership); $A$ is coefficient matrix.

### 3.2 Count Variable Regression Model

Matsumoto (2016) used the Poisson model to analyze the penetration of household electrical appliances in Japan and obtained satisfactory results. Considering the characteristics of the data we used, we used the Poisson model to analyze the influential factors of household appliance ownership in China.

We assume that the probability of household $i$ owning $y_i$ pieces of a type of appliance is calculated according to Poisson's equation:

$$\text{Prob}(\text{Y} = y_i | \boldsymbol{X}_i = \frac{(\boldsymbol{AX})^{yi} \exp(-\boldsymbol{AX})}{y_i!}$$

$$X_i = \begin{pmatrix} \text{Inequality}_i,\ \text{citytown}_i,\ \text{Build Age}_i,\ \text{Family Size}_i,\ \text{Floor Space}_i, \\ \text{Income}_i, \text{Age}_i,\ \text{Employment}_i,\ \text{Education}_i,\ \text{North}_i \end{pmatrix}$$

Poisson model is commonly used for estimation. This estimation method allows for better simulation of ownership of several appliances of a type. O'Doherty et al. (2008) used the Poisson counting model to analyze the penetration of energy-saving equipment in Irish households, and mentioned the extensive use of Poisson model in analysis of counting data. Compared with the multinomial logistic model, the Poisson model allows more accurate depiction of the process of owning several appliances of a type.

## 4 Results of Empirical Analysis

We used two models to conduct econometric analysis of household appliance ownership and used two types of inequality indexes in regression. By so doing, we aim to test whether there is any difference between Ineq_1a for measuring overall inequality and Ineq_1b for measuring inequality in lower-income population in terms of their influences on household's desire to purchase appliances and household appliance ownership. Results also show the estimated coefficients of the models and the marginal effects of variables based on the models.

### 4.1 Logit Model

Tables 5 and 6 present the regression analysis results of ownership of television, refrigerator, washing machine and air conditioner in respondents' households using the Logit model. As the Logit model is nonlinear, we mainly explained and analyzed through the marginal effects (Table 6) of explanatory variables when other variables were fixed at the mean value. The value of marginal effects represents the change in probability of the household owning the specified appliance corresponding to increase of the variable by each unit. For dummy variables, the values in Tables 5 and 6 represents the change in probability of the household owning the specified appliance corresponding to the change of dummy variables from 0 to 1.

Statistics in Table 6 show that the probabilities of households owning four types of appliances increase significantly with the increase in household income. For example, in regression using Ineq_1a, with each unit of increase in household income (log value), the probability of the household owning television increased by 0.0132, the probability of owning refrigerator increased by 0.0548, the probability of owning washing machine increased by 0.0578 and the probability of owning air conditioner increased by 0.158.

Results in Table 6 show that the income inequality index of the province where the household is located had significant negative influences on the household's probability of owning the specified appliance in terms of statistics, although such influence is not significant in terms of the probability of television ownership. McNeil and Letschert (2010) mentioned in their research that television is a common appliance in modern households, and in most cases, television is the first household electrical appliance that residents may consider to purchase once they have enough income. Though their conclusion is based on study of the United States, we believe it also applies to China. The penetration rate of television of our samples reached over 95%. So, in population with income lower than the mean value and among the entirety, income distribution (inequality) does not have significant influences on household ownership of television. Meanwhile, it is worth mentioning that the probability of owning washing machines decreases with rising Ineq_1b, but increase in Ineq_1a does not have significant influences on such probability. It shows that washing machine ownership of households does not have a significant correlation with the general income inequality of the province where the household is located, but has significant negative correlation with the income inequality of lower-income population of the province.

In addition, urban residents have larger probabilities of owning the specified appliance. Increase in number of permanent residents in a household also leads to rising probabilities of households owning the specified appliance. Previous studies wanted to introduce year of construction of residence as a variable, but our research shows that it does not have significant influences on household appliance ownership. Employment status of respondents does not have significant influences either. However, respondent's age has significant influences on the probability of household owning a certain appliance, which shows an inflection, as probabilities of owning the appliances in question decrease when respondent is over 60. Meanwhile, if respondent received secondary or tertiary education, the corresponding household has larger probabilities of owning washing machines and air conditioners. Ownership of air conditioner, the use of which is closely related with climate, is likely to have correlation with the respondent's location. The analysis results proved our assumption: respondents living in North China is less likely to own air conditioners.

**Table 5** Logit model regression results

| Variable | Using Ineq_1a | | | | Using Ineq_1b | | | |
|---|---|---|---|---|---|---|---|---|
| | Television | Refrigerator | Washing machine | Air conditioner | Television | Refrigerator | Washing machine | Air conditioner |
| Household income | 0.483***<br>(0.0867) | 0.410***<br>(0.0493) | 0.422***<br>(0.0511) | 0.652***<br>(0.0588) | 0.467***<br>(0.0853) | 0.373***<br>(0.0500) | 0.357***<br>(0.0516) | 0.580***<br>(0.0595) |
| Ineq_1a | −0.387<br>(0.522) | −0.966***<br>(0.281) | 0.327<br>(0.302) | −3.052***<br>(0.277) | | | | |
| Ineq_1b | | | | | −1.902<br>(1.719) | −5.205***<br>(0.914) | −4.528***<br>(0.976) | −10.83***<br>(0.863) |
| Urban or rural | 0.651**<br>(0.260) | 1.167***<br>(0.142) | 0.859***<br>(0.132) | 0.859***<br>(0.1000) | 0.632**<br>(0.262) | 1.119***<br>(0.141) | 0.724***<br>(0.128) | 0.795***<br>(0.102) |
| Floor space of residence | 0.00368*<br>(0.00199) | 0.00305***<br>(0.000809) | 0.00356***<br>(0.000865) | 0.00117**<br>(0.000569) | 0.00398*<br>(0.00204) | 0.00362***<br>(0.000874) | 0.00424***<br>(0.000949) | 0.00181***<br>(0.000600) |
| Permanent resident in household | 0.409***<br>(0.119) | 0.116***<br>(0.0424) | 0.185***<br>(0.0434) | 0.0452<br>(0.0337) | 0.414***<br>(0.120) | 0.125***<br>(0.0429) | 0.197***<br>(0.0439) | 0.0684**<br>(0.0347) |
| Year of construction (after 2000) | 0.213<br>(0.189) | 0.145<br>(0.101) | 0.182*<br>(0.104) | 0.0121<br>(0.0898) | 0.218<br>(0.190) | 0.152<br>(0.102) | 0.212**<br>(0.103) | 0.0195<br>(0.0906) |
| Employment status | −0.358*<br>(0.201) | −0.0838<br>(0.110) | −0.266**<br>(0.112) | −0.196**<br>(0.0992) | −0.349*<br>(0.201) | −0.0583<br>(0.111) | −0.226**<br>(0.112) | −0.141<br>(0.0994) |
| Age | 0.120***<br>(0.0283) | 0.0575***<br>(0.0171) | 0.0432**<br>(0.0173) | 0.0327**<br>(0.0150) | 0.117***<br>(0.0284) | 0.0525***<br>(0.0173) | 0.0415**<br>(0.0177) | 0.0236<br>(0.0155) |
| $Age^2$ | −0.103***<br>(0.0282) | −0.0512***<br>(0.0165) | −0.0456***<br>(0.0165) | −0.0301**<br>(0.0148) | −0.100***<br>(0.0284) | −0.0467***<br>(0.0167) | −0.0449***<br>(0.0170) | −0.0223<br>(0.0153) |

(continued)

**Table 5** (continued)

| Variable | Using Ineq_1a | | | | Using Ineq_1b | | | |
|---|---|---|---|---|---|---|---|---|
| | Television | Refrigerator | Washing machine | Air conditioner | Television | Refrigerator | Washing machine | Air conditioner |
| Secondary education | −0.0631<br>(0.236) | 0.387***<br>(0.119) | 0.370***<br>(0.120) | 0.629***<br>(0.108) | −0.0695<br>(0.235) | 0.370***<br>(0.119) | 0.347***<br>(0.120) | 0.590***<br>(0.109) |
| Tertiary education | −0.811**<br>(0.362) | 0.314<br>(0.210) | 0.716***<br>(0.223) | 0.895***<br>(0.173) | −0.837**<br>(0.362) | 0.247<br>(0.210) | 0.646***<br>(0.224) | 0.799***<br>(0.175) |
| North | | | | −0.620***<br>(0.0880) | | | | −0.781***<br>(0.0906) |
| Constant term | −6.000***<br>(1.150) | −4.725***<br>(0.746) | −5.552***<br>(0.771) | −6.000***<br>(0.775) | −5.073***<br>(1.466) | −2.292**<br>(0.912) | −2.014**<br>(0.979) | −1.625*<br>(0.944) |
| Sample size | 3,137 | 3,137 | 3,137 | 3,137 | 3,137 | 3,137 | 3,137 | 3,137 |

***, ** and * means significance at the level of 1%, 5% and 10% respectively

*Note* In the brackets are robust standard deviations

**Table 6** Logit regression marginal effects

| Variable | Television | | Refrigerator | | Washing machine | | Air conditioner | |
|---|---|---|---|---|---|---|---|---|
| Household income | 0.0132*** (0.00259) | 0.0127*** (0.00256) | 0.0548*** (0.00672) | 0.0492*** (0.00668) | 0.0578*** (0.00712) | 0.0483*** (0.00705) | 0.158*** (0.0140) | 0.141*** (0.0143) |
| Ineq_1a | −0.0106 (0.0141) | | −0.129*** (0.0377) | | 0.0449 (0.0413) | | −0.738*** (0.0665) | |
| Ineq_1b | | −0.0516 (0.0458) | | −0.663*** (0.121) | | −0.612*** (0.131) | | −2.632*** (0.208) |
| Urban or rural | 0.0177** (0.00690) | 0.0171** (0.00696) | 0.156*** (0.0179) | 0.148*** (0.0176) | 0.118*** (0.0177) | 0.0978*** (0.0171) | 0.208*** (0.0241) | 0.193*** (0.0247) |
| Floor space of residence | 0.000100* (0.0000541) | 0.000108** (0.0000548) | 0.000407*** (0.000106) | 0.000477*** (0.000113) | 0.000489*** (0.000117) | 0.000573*** (0.000126) | 0.000284** (0.000138) | 0.000439*** (0.000146) |
| Permanent resident in household | 0.0111*** (0.00279) | 0.0112*** (0.00279) | 0.0155*** (0.00562) | 0.0165*** (0.00560) | 0.0254*** (0.00589) | 0.0267*** (0.00588) | 0.0109 (0.00815) | 0.0166** (0.00844) |
| Year of construction (after 2000) | 0.00581 (0.00509) | 0.00591 (0.00508) | 0.0194 (0.0136) | 0.0201 (0.0134) | 0.0250* (0.0142) | 0.0286** (0.0140) | 0.00293 (0.0217) | 0.00473 (0.0220) |
| Employment status | −0.00974* (0.00544) | −0.00947* (0.00543) | −0.0112 (0.0148) | −0.00769 (0.0146) | −0.0365** (0.0153) | −0.0306** (0.0151) | −0.0473** (0.0240) | −0.0342 (0.0241) |
| Age | 0.00326*** (0.000769) | 0.00318*** (0.000778) | 0.00769*** (0.00227) | 0.00693*** (0.00228) | 0.00592** (0.00237) | 0.00561** (0.00240) | 0.00792** (0.00363) | 0.00575 (0.00376) |
| $Age^2$ | −0.00280*** (0.000764) | −0.00272*** (0.000773) | −0.00684*** (0.00219) | −0.00616*** (0.00220) | −0.00626*** (0.00226) | −0.00607*** (0.00230) | −0.00728** (0.00359) | −0.00542 (0.00372) |
| Secondary education | −0.00155 (0.00572) | −0.00169 (0.00566) | 0.0532*** (0.0169) | 0.0500*** (0.0166) | 0.0541*** (0.0182) | 0.0498*** (0.0178) | 0.147*** (0.0244) | 0.140*** (0.0251) |

(continued)

**Table 6** (continued)

| Variable | Television | | Refrigerator | | Washing machine | | Air conditioner | |
|---|---|---|---|---|---|---|---|---|
| Tertiary education | −0.0288*<br>(0.0150) | −0.0299**<br>(0.0151) | 0.0442<br>(0.0284) | 0.0348<br>(0.0285) | 0.0937***<br>(0.0262) | 0.0840***<br>(0.0264) | 0.214***<br>(0.0414) | 0.192***<br>(0.0422) |
| North | | | | | | | −0.150***<br>(0.0212) | −0.190***<br>(0.0219) |
| Sample size | 3,137 | 3,137 | 3,137 | 3,137 | 3,137 | 3,137 | 3,137 | 3,137 |

***, ** and * means significance at the level of 1%, 5% and 10% respectively
*Note* In the brackets are robust standard deviations

## 4.2 Poisson Model

Tables 7 and 8 present the regression analysis results of household ownership of television, refrigerator, washing machine and air conditioner using the Poisson model. The Poisson model is also nonlinear, so, we also focused on analysis of the marginal effects of explanatory variables, which represent the influences of each unit of change of specified variables on expected appliance ownership when other variables remain at the mean value.

It can be seen from Table 8 that the household income of respondents has significant positive influences on appliance ownership. For example, in regression using Ineq_1a, with each unit of increase (log value) in household income, the expected television ownership increased by 0.104, the expected refrigerator ownership increased by 0.0821, the expected washing machine ownership increased by 0.0904 and the expected air conditioner ownership increased by 0.213.

The result of the Poisson model also shows a significant negative correlation between income inequality of the province where the respondent is located and the household appliance ownership. Different from the results of Logit regression, household television ownership is subject to significant influences of income inequality. It's also worth mentioning that the correlation between washing machine ownership and Ineq_1a is not significant at the significance level of 5%, but washing machine ownership and Ineq_1b have a significant negative correlation.

A possible explanation for the negative correlation between income inequality and household appliance ownership is that there is a nonlinear correlation between household appliance ownership and household income, leading to minor influences of population with extremely low and high income on appliance ownership. Main consumers of electrical appliances are the middle class. So, in cases of high income inequality, there are many people of extreme income and appliance ownership is low. Another possible explanation is that rising income inequality results in higher savings rate among high-income population and lower consumption capability of low-income population (Kumhof and Rancière 2010). This is especially the case in China. Due to underdeveloped financial market in China, income inequality cannot be reduced by appropriate financial behaviors. On the contrary, because high-income population owns a large amount of wealth, their rising savings rate may have great influences on consumption in the market. In addition, uncertainties in society caused by income inequality lead to even higher savings rate, which may possibly further curb residential consumption of electrical appliances (Chan et al. 2016).

In addition, urban respondents own more household electrical appliances. Floor space of residence and number of permanent residents in household also have significant influences on appliance ownership. Households with respondents who have received secondary or tertiary education tend to purchase more washing machines and air conditioners. Respondents in the north have less air conditioners in households.

**Table 7** Poisson regression results

| Variable | Using Ineq_1a | | | | Using Ineq_1b | | | |
|---|---|---|---|---|---|---|---|---|
| | Television | Refrigerator | Washing machine | Air conditioner | Television | Refrigerator | Washing machine | Air conditioner |
| Household income | 0.0898***<br>(0.00988) | 0.102***<br>(0.0122) | 0.113***<br>(0.0124) | 0.441***<br>(0.0322) | 0.0854***<br>(0.00991) | 0.0962***<br>(0.0123) | 0.0985***<br>(0.0125) | 0.397***<br>(0.0324) |
| Ineq_1a | −0.241***<br>(0.0548) | −0.181***<br>(0.0558) | 0.106*<br>(0.0556) | −1.450***<br>(0.152) | | | | |
| Ineq_1b | | | | | −0.765***<br>(0.151) | −0.727***<br>(0.143) | −0.631***<br>(0.154) | −4.723***<br>(0.435) |
| Urban or rural | 0.0553***<br>(0.0203) | 0.190***<br>(0.0240) | 0.133***<br>(0.0220) | 0.546***<br>(0.0600) | 0.0517**<br>(0.0205) | 0.183***<br>(0.0241) | 0.110***<br>(0.0221) | 0.508***<br>(0.0606) |
| Floor space of residence | 0.000484***<br>(0.0000929) | 0.000490***<br>(0.0000962) | 0.000582***<br>(0.000108) | 0.000879***<br>(0.000267) | 0.000532***<br>(0.000097) | 0.000543***<br>(0.0000977) | 0.000647***<br>(0.000110) | 0.00117***<br>(0.000273) |
| Permanent resident in household | 0.0565***<br>(0.00693) | 0.0328***<br>(0.00817) | 0.0405***<br>(0.00739) | 0.0744***<br>(0.0172) | 0.0577***<br>(0.00695) | 0.0343***<br>(0.00818) | 0.0423***<br>(0.00732) | 0.0862***<br>(0.0170) |
| Year of construction (after 2000) | −0.00115<br>(0.0169) | 0.0345*<br>(0.0189) | 0.0276<br>(0.0187) | 0.103**<br>(0.0447) | −0.00110<br>(0.0169) | 0.0359*<br>(0.0188) | 0.0366*<br>(0.0187) | 0.113**<br>(0.0443) |
| Employment status | −0.000544<br>(0.0179) | −0.0133<br>(0.0212) | −0.0654***<br>(0.0207) | −0.128**<br>(0.0503) | 0.00349<br>(0.0179) | −0.00888<br>(0.0212) | −0.0591***<br>(0.0208) | −0.0994**<br>(0.0497) |
| Age | 0.00953***<br>(0.00300) | 0.00863***<br>(0.00322) | 0.00797**<br>(0.00319) | 0.0150**<br>(0.00714) | 0.00859***<br>(0.00300) | 0.00778**<br>(0.00322) | 0.00746**<br>(0.00321) | 0.0100<br>(0.00712) |
| $Age^2$ | −0.00711**<br>(0.00289) | −0.00792**<br>(0.00316) | −0.00900***<br>(0.00323) | −0.0137*<br>(0.00706) | −0.00627**<br>(0.00289) | −0.00720**<br>(0.00316) | −0.00872***<br>(0.00325) | −0.00957<br>(0.00702) |

(continued)

**Table 7** (continued)

| Variable | Using Ineq_1a | | | | Using Ineq_1b | | | |
|---|---|---|---|---|---|---|---|---|
| | Television | Refrigerator | Washing machine | Air conditioner | Television | Refrigerator | Washing machine | Air conditioner |
| Secondary education | 0.00825 (0.0202) | 0.0914*** (0.0249) | 0.0907*** (0.0255) | 0.323*** (0.0672) | 0.00388 (0.0203) | 0.0870*** (0.0249) | 0.0864*** (0.0255) | 0.291*** (0.0672) |
| Tertiary education | −0.0619* (0.0337) | 0.0388 (0.0326) | 0.0936*** (0.0337) | 0.393*** (0.0859) | −0.0732** (0.0338) | 0.0273 (0.0327) | 0.0803** (0.0339) | 0.327*** (0.0867) |
| North | | | | −0.291*** (0.0449) | | | | −0.369*** (0.0437) |
| Constant term | −1.105*** (0.143) | −1.642*** (0.168) | −1.927*** (0.162) | −5.069*** (0.416) | −0.824*** (0.165) | −1.314*** (0.187) | −1.317*** (0.188) | −3.101*** (0.512) |
| Sample size | 3,137 | 3,137 | 3,137 | 3,137 | 3,137 | 3,137 | 3,137 | 3,137 |

***, ** and * means significance at the level of 1%, 5% and 10% respectively

*Note* In the brackets are robust standard deviations

**Table 8** Poisson regression marginal effect

| Variable | Television | | Refrigerator | | Washing machine | | Air conditioner | |
|---|---|---|---|---|---|---|---|---|
| Household income | 0.104***<br>(0.0115) | 0.0989***<br>(0.0115) | 0.0821***<br>(0.00960) | 0.0773***<br>(0.00971) | 0.0904***<br>(0.00972) | 0.0790***<br>(0.00981) | 0.213***<br>(0.0147) | 0.191***<br>(0.0150) |
| Ineq_1a | −0.279***<br>(0.0636) | | −0.145***<br>(0.0448) | | 0.0848*<br>(0.0446) | | −0.698***<br>(0.0720) | |
| Ineq_1b | | −0.886***<br>(0.175) | | −0.584***<br>(0.114) | | −0.506***<br>(0.123) | | −2.271***<br>(0.206) |
| Urban or rural | 0.0640***<br>(0.0235) | 0.0599**<br>(0.0238) | 0.152***<br>(0.0189) | 0.147***<br>(0.0191) | 0.107***<br>(0.0174) | 0.0881***<br>(0.0176) | 0.263***<br>(0.0284) | 0.244***<br>(0.0286) |
| Floor space of residence | 0.000560***<br>(0.000108) | 0.000616***<br>(0.000113) | 0.000394***<br>(0.0000769) | 0.000436***<br>(0.000078) | 0.000467***<br>(0.0000862) | 0.000519***<br>(0.0000879) | 0.000423***<br>(0.000129) | 0.000561***<br>(0.000132) |
| Permanent resident in household | 0.0654***<br>(0.00806) | 0.0669***<br>(0.00809) | 0.0264***<br>(0.00657) | 0.0275***<br>(0.00658) | 0.0325***<br>(0.00590) | 0.0340***<br>(0.00583) | 0.0358***<br>(0.00833) | 0.0414***<br>(0.00822) |
| Year of construction (after 2000) | −0.00133<br>(0.0195) | −0.00127<br>(0.0196) | 0.0277*<br>(0.0152) | 0.0288*<br>(0.0151) | 0.0222<br>(0.0150) | 0.0293*<br>(0.0150) | 0.0497**<br>(0.0216) | 0.0545**<br>(0.0214) |
| Employment status | −0.000630<br>(0.0207) | 0.00405<br>(0.0207) | −0.0107<br>(0.0170) | −0.00713<br>(0.0171) | −0.0525***<br>(0.0166) | −0.0474***<br>(0.0166) | −0.0618**<br>(0.0240) | −0.0478**<br>(0.0238) |
| Age | 0.0110***<br>(0.00347) | 0.00994***<br>(0.00347) | 0.00693***<br>(0.00258) | 0.00625**<br>(0.00258) | 0.00639**<br>(0.00256) | 0.00598**<br>(0.00257) | 0.00722**<br>(0.00345) | 0.00482<br>(0.00343) |
| $Age^2$ | −0.00823**<br>(0.00334) | −0.00725**<br>(0.00334) | −0.00636**<br>(0.00254) | −0.00578**<br>(0.00253) | −0.00722***<br>(0.00259) | −0.00700***<br>(0.00260) | −0.00659*<br>(0.00340) | −0.00460<br>(0.00338) |
| Secondary education | 0.00963<br>(0.0236) | 0.00454<br>(0.0238) | 0.0731***<br>(0.0197) | 0.0697***<br>(0.0197) | 0.0719***<br>(0.0199) | 0.0686***<br>(0.0200) | 0.148***<br>(0.0295) | 0.135***<br>(0.0298) |

(continued)

**Table 8** (continued)

| Variable | Television | | Refrigerator | | Washing machine | | Air conditioner | |
|---|---|---|---|---|---|---|---|---|
| Tertiary education | −0.0698*<br>(0.0375) | −0.0824**<br>(0.0375) | 0.0302<br>(0.0255) | 0.0212<br>(0.0254) | 0.0743***<br>(0.0269) | 0.0635**<br>(0.0270) | 0.187***<br>(0.0427) | 0.154***<br>(0.0423) |
| North | | | | | | | −0.140***<br>(0.0218) | −0.177***<br>(0.0212) |
| Sample size | 3,137 | 3,137 | 3,137 | 3,137 | 3,137 | 3,137 | 3,137 | 3,137 |

***, ** and * means significance at the level of 1%, 5% and 10% respectively

*Note* In the brackets are robust standard deviations

## 5 Summary

Energy consumption forecast has always been a critical concern for energy economists and the energy industry. Growth in energy consumption slows down in European countries and the United States, while developing countries become the main source of growth in energy consumption, and China will play an important role in such growth. A better understanding of the influential factors of residential energy consumption and especially appliance ownership in China is helpful to optimize the existing models for residential energy consumption forecast in China, thus facilitating formulation of relevant plans.

This chapter seeks to use micro data to study the correlation between income inequality and appliance ownership, trying to fill the gap in relevant studies. We used data from the household survey of the CGSS 2015 to construct statistics about income distribution in provinces and study the influences of income inequality on household appliance ownership. We also conducted systematic studies of factors that may have influences on household appliance ownership from the perspectives of ownership and number of appliances owned.

Results of the empirical study show that in most cases (except for television), income inequality has negative influences on household appliance ownership. This is probably due to the nonlinear correlation between household appliance ownership and household income, while population of extremely high and low income has minor influences on appliance ownership. Main consumers of electrical appliances are the middle class. Therefore, when income inequality is high, there is a large population with extremely high or low income, and household appliance ownership is low. Another possible reason is that high income inequality leads to rising savings rate among high-income population and excessively low disposable income for low-income population, thus resulting in decreasing consumption.

In addition, our study shows that even with controlled income distribution, respondent's personal and household characteristics still have significant influences on household appliance ownership. Such characteristics include location of household, year of construction of residence, number of permanent residents in household, floor space of residence, disposable income of household and education level. They all have significant positive influences on household appliance ownership.

# Chapter 8
# Rural Resident's Choice of Water Heater in China

**Yihua Yu and Ben Ma**

This chapter studies the patterns in choice of water heaters in developing countries based on micro-level personal data, with focus on decision-making process and influential factors relating to purchase of water heaters in rural households in China. Results show that in addition to sociodemographic characteristics such as income, household size and age, information accessibility is a significant determinant in household's decision-making process to purchase water heaters, while electricity price and subsidy policies in the "Home Appliances Going to the Countryside" program do not have much effect in promoting solar water heaters in rural China. Accordingly, we propose that subsidy policies in China shall focus on energy-saving or low-carbon water heaters, provide financial incentives to rural residents to encourage use of low-carbon products and improve product information disclosure.

## 1 Research Background

Climate change is a common challenge today for humanity. Carbon emission reduction is one of the most critical environmental issues confronting the international community. It is recognized worldwide that to protect the ecological environment, slow down global warming and seek sustainable development of humanity, great efforts shall be made to utilize renewable energy sources and reduce consumption of fossil energy. Energy demand and supply and ecological environment protection in rural areas of developing countries are important components of the global strategy for sustainable energy development. As the largest developing country with a population of over 1.3 billion, growth in residential energy consumption, especially growth in energy consumption and carbon emission caused by rural residents which account for over 2/3 of the national population, is turning into new areas of growth

Y. Yu (✉) · B. Ma
Renmin University of China, Beijing, China
e-mail: yihua.yu@ruc.edu.cn



X. Zheng and C. Wei (eds.), *Household Energy Consumption in China: 2016 Report*, https://doi.org/10.1007/978-981-13-7523-1_8

of energy consumption and carbon emission in China. However, for a long period, studies on carbon emission focused on the industry, transportation and other fields, but ignored the residential energy consumption. In fact, households are not only the ultimate units of consumption, but also a driving force of production. Due to the urban-rural dualism in China, there are significant differences between urban and rural residents in energy demand and residential energy consumption structure, which lead to urban-rural dualism in energy consumption.

Residential energy consumption in rural areas mainly refers to energy consumption in daily life of rural areas, including energy consumed for lighting, cooking, space heating, water heating and electrical appliances, etc. China is a developing country. Rural areas in China have long relied on biomass energy (straw, firewood, biogas, etc.) as the primary source of energy for daily life,[1] with low access to clean and high-efficiency energy sources. Solar water heater is common for households in urban areas and towns near to urban areas, but it is still not in extensive use in rural areas, especially in remote mountainous regions. As a kind of clean renewable energy source, solar energy has many unparalleled advantages.[2] According to Article 17 of the *Renewable Energy Law of the People's Republic of China*, "the state encourages entities and individuals to install and use solar water heating systems, solar space heating and refrigeration systems and solar photovoltaic electricity generation systems". Considering the global gasoline and electricity shortage as well as the global environmental pollution, to encourage and promote solar water heaters in rural China is of vital significance to energy conservation, carbon emission reduction, ecology protection, economic development and to improve rural residents' quality of life.[3]

In the context of China, this chapter seeks to study the choice of water heaters of rural households in developing countries, especially their decision-making process and influential factors relating to purchase of solar water heaters. We aim to provide references and advice to the government concerning improving policies of energy conservation, emission reduction, guiding residents on change of consumption behavior and way of life, optimizing residential energy consumption structure in rural areas, slowing down climate change and achieving emission targets.

---

[1] As revealed in the survey data of *Chinese Household Energy Consumption Report 2015*.

[2] It is calculated that compared with coal burning, a 2-$m^2$ solar water heater, in its 15 years of service, can reduce $CO_2$ emission by 26 tons, Co emission by 136 tons, dust pollution by 1,120 tons, $SO_2$ by 352 tons and Nitrogen and hydrogen compounds by 908 tons. Meanwhile, installation of solar water heater is easy and its use is subject to few limitations. It works throughout the year wherever the sun shines.

[3] On behalf of China, Premier Li Keqiang announced to the international community in 2015 that according to the Enhanced Actions on Climate Change: China's Intended Nationally Determined Contributions, by 2030, carbon dioxide emissions per unit of GDP in China will lower by 60 to 65% from the 2005 level. Beijing 2022 Winter Olympics Bidding Committee also undertook that the $PM_{2.5}$ density will lower by about 45% from the 2012 level before the 2022 Winter Olympics. According to the National Plan on Climate Change (2014–2020) issued by the National Development and Reform Commission of China, the target for installed capacity of solar power by 2020 is 100 GW.

## 2 Literature Review

Extensive studies on rural energy issues in foreign countries started in the twentieth century and obtained fruitful results. In China, studies on rural energy consumption also began to grow in recent years. However, no study focused on use of water heaters in rural China. Foreign studies mainly include two categories, i.e., to prove or test the choice of appliances and energy sources of rural residents at the national, state or local level by theories or empirical studies.

A main topic in study of household appliance choice is consumer's choice of space heating equipment, but few studies focus on water heating systems in households. Goto et al. (2011) used mixed and nested Logit models to examine how consumers select ecologically efficient water heaters in Japan. They found that energy price was an important determinant in consumer's choice of energy-saving appliances. Wasi and Carson (2013) used discrete choice experiments to study resident's shift from electrical water heaters toward more climate-friendly water heaters (e.g., solar water heaters) in New South Wales, and evaluated the effectiveness of subsidy programs aiming to encourage use of solar water heaters.

Another important topic is household appliance choice. Most of the existing literature in this regard are about household appliance choice in developed countries, especially in Germany (Braun 2010; Decker and Menrad 2015; Michelsen and Madlener 2016; Scarpa and Willis 2010). Solar water heater, commercial application of renewable energy technologies (Chang et al. 2009; Han et al. 2010), becomes a hot topic for studies and its use ranks the first across the world. These studies focus on different aspects of water heaters, such as social acceptance and public awareness of water heaters (Yuan et al. 2011), analysis of economic feasibility of diffusion of solar water heaters (Han et al. 2010; Li et al. 2013; Ma et al. 2014), institutional economic analysis of successful cases (Li et al. 2013; Goess et al. 2015) and analysis of influential factors and policy effectiveness (Chang et al. 2011, 2016; Ma et al. 2014). Studies in China mostly focus on certain regions, such as studies on characteristics, structure and influential factors of rural energy consumption based on samples in Jiangsu, Shandong and Tibetan ethnic areas (Lu and Lu 2006; Xu 2014; Han et al. 2014; Yao et al. 2015; Sun et al. 2015). Wang et al. (2014) conducted household surveys covering 1,440 households in counties of 8 major economic zones in China, and based on the survey data, they considered that rural households generally used both traditional biomass energy and commercial energy, but there were apparent differences between regions in energy consumption structures. Qiu et al. (2015) analyzed the consumption of renewable energy in rural China and the influential factors. Li et al. (2013) studied the influences of carbon tax and energy subsidies on rural energy consumption in China. The existing studies may help us learn about the overall rural household energy consumption, but there have not been many studies on solar water heaters. In recent years, Ma et al. (2012) analyzed the cost and economic feasibility of household solar water heaters at the micro level in China. Zhang et al. (2012) and Ma et al. (2015) studied the income effect and word-of-mouth effect of application and diffusion of solar water heaters in rural China. However, up to now, there is no study on Chinese household's discrete choice of water heaters.

# 3 Brief Introduction of Data

## 3.1 *Questionnaire Design*

The questionnaire design was mainly based on the CRECS 2013. The questionnaire included 324 questions in 6 main areas: household characteristics, dwelling characteristics, household appliances, space heating and cooling, patterns of personal transportation, and electricity pricing, metering and pricing options. Generally, we believe that four types of factors ($x$) may have influences on respondent's choice of water heaters (y). The first type is sociodemographic characteristics of the individual, such as age, sex, per-capita income and education level. The second type is price of each energy source, such as electricity, LPG and other fossil fuels. The third type is dwelling characteristics, such as location of the respondent's residence. The fourth type is incentive policies, especially those promoting low-carbon water heaters (e.g., solar water heaters).

Due to some market and nonmarket barriers such as lack of information about availability of technologies and limitations on access to capital, the energy efficiency gap takes the form of underinvestment in energy efficiency relative to the socially optimal level of energy efficiency (Allcott and Greenstone 2012; Gillingham et al. 2009). For example, insufficient information, high risks and excessively high up-front cost may hinder use of solar water heaters in rural China. The questionnaire included six types of explanatory variables: sociodemographic characteristics, information exchange, living habit, natural resource, energy price and policy variable.

## 3.2 *The Implementation Process*

Samples in the CRECS 2013 were selected by probability proportional sampling (PPS) and multistage random sampling. The sampling was conducted in four stages. First, prefectures (prefecture-level cities, province capitals, municipalities and their suburban areas) and counties were selected as the primary sampling unit. Second, residential districts, villages and towns were selected as the secondary sampling unit. Third, neighborhood committees and village committees were selected as the tertiary sampling units. Fourth, an individual from each household was selected as the last level of sampling unit.

In the CRECS 2013, 12 provinces were selected from four administrative regions (coastal areas, central areas, western areas and northeastern areas) in China, and 60 villages were selected from the 62 primary sampling units of the 12 provinces, making 4,140 samples. The selected provinces were Hebei, Heilongjiang, Jiangsu, Zhejiang, Fujian, Hubei, Hunan, Guangdong, Sichuan, Yunnan, Shaanxi and Gansu. As the questionnaire had 324 questions in 6 areas, the average time spent for interview per person was 1–1.5 h. Afterwards, we removed the observations of samples (as a whole) with one and more missing independent variables, since data of these samples contained errors. Ultimately, we had 3,404 effective observations.

### 3.3 Data Description

Table 1 presents a list of the variables and the descriptive statistics of sampling. Yuan et al. (2011) conducted a survey in Jinan, Shandong in 2010 and found that acceptance of solar water heaters was much lower in people over 60 years old than in other age groups. Therefore, we used a dummy variable: the value of the dummy variable was set as 1 if the household owner was over 60 years old. Concerning energy conservation awareness, if a household used at least one low-efficiency incandescent light bulb, we used a binary variable and set its value as 1. The basic logic is that use of incandescent light bulb when fluorescent lamps or energy-efficient lights are in extensive use in rural China reveals the household's low awareness of energy conservation. For household owners with no formal education, we set the value of the variable of education level as 1 in a binary system. We also introduced a dummy variable to represent the going-out frequency of a household. If the frequency was between 1 and 5, the dummy variable value was set as 1. Likewise, the variable value for households within 1 km from the downtown area was set as 1 and otherwise 0.

China has an abundant supply of solar energy, with about 67% of its territory enjoying 2,200 sunshine hours per year (Liu et al. 2010). In this book, a dummy variable is used to represent the solar energy received by each household. Concerning subsidies for on-grid tariff of photovoltaic power generation (The National Development and Reform Commission 2013), according to the grading of solar irradiance, we set the value as 1 if a household was in Grade I or Grade II (suggesting abundant solar irradiance) and otherwise as 0. For policy variable, its value was set as 1 if the household received subsidies while purchasing water heaters. Subsidies to rural residents in China mainly refer to the "Home Appliances Going to the Countryside" policy from 2009 to early 2013.

## 4 Empirical Results

First, we used the multinomial Logit model to test the determinants in rural residents' buying decision process of water heaters in China. Independent variables included sociodemographic characteristics, information exchange, living habit, natural resource, energy price and policy variable. As shown in Table 2, we focused on three types of water heaters, i.e., electrical water heaters, LPG water heaters and solar water heaters. Households without water heaters are considered the basic category, and the estimation results are as shown in the 3rd to 5th column of Table 2. In the 6th to 8th column, households with electrical water heaters (the 6th and 7th column) and households with LPG water heaters (the 8th column) are considered the basic category.

Among the sociodemographic characteristics, we found that income, household size and age of household owner had obvious effect on household's buying decision of water heaters. Household income per capita had significant positive influences

**Table 1** Descriptive statistics of variables

| Variable | Type of variable | Item | Observation | Share (%) |
|---|---|---|---|---|
| Water heater | Multinomial | No use | 2,245 | 65.95 |
| | | Electric water heater | 389 | 11.43 |
| | | LPG water heater | 146 | 4.29 |
| | | Solar water heater | 576 | 16.92 |
| | | Other types | 48 | 1.41 |
| Income (RMB1,000/person) | Continuous value | (0, 4) | 665 | 30.37 |
| | | (4, 8) | 543 | 24.79 |
| | | More than 8 | 982 | 44.84 |
| Household size | Discrete value | 1 | 269 | 8.29 |
| | | 2 | 1,231 | 37.95 |
| | | 3 | 676 | 20.84 |
| | | 4 | 524 | 16.15 |
| | | More than 4 | 544 | 16.77 |
| Age of household owner | Binary | 60 and above (=1) | 1341 | 39.39 |
| | | Below 60 (=0) | 2,063 | 60.61 |
| Energy conservation awareness | Binary | Use incandescent lamp (=1) | 1,197 | 35.16 |
| | | Otherwise (=0) | 2,207 | 64.84 |
| Education level of household owner | Binary | Illiterate (=1) | 374 | 11.83 |
| | | Other (=0) | 2,787 | 88.17 |
| Frequency of going out per year | Binary | [1, 5] (=1) | 835 | 24.53 |
| | | Other (=0) | 2,569 | 75.47 |
| Distance from the nearest downtown area (km) | Binary | [0, 1](=1) | 595 | 18.73 |
| | | Other (=0) | 2,582 | 81.27 |
| Average temperature (°C) | Continuous value | Below 15 °C | 1,595 | 47.04 |
| | | 15 °C and above | 1,796 | 52.96 |
| Solar irradiance | Binary | Abundant area (=1) | 1,527 | 44.86 |
| | | Otherwise (=0) | 1,877 | 55.14 |
| Electricity price (RMB0.01/kWh) | Continuous value | [45, 55] | 2,401 | 70.53 |
| | | (55, 82) | 1,003 | 29.47 |
| LPG price (RMB/kg) | Continuous value | [4, 8.5] | 1,694 | 55.78 |
| | | [8.5, 11.5] | 1,343 | 44.22 |
| Subsidy | Binary | With subsidy (=1) | 468 | 13.75 |
| | | Otherwise (=0) | 2,936 | 86.25 |
| Total observation | | | 3,404 | 100 |

**Table 2** Parameter estimation of multinomial Logit model

| Model | | ML-1 (Basic model: no water heater) | | | ML-2 (Basic model: electrical water heater) | | ML-3 (Basic model: LPG water heater) |
|---|---|---|---|---|---|---|---|
| | | Electrical water heater | LPG water heater | Solar water heater | LPG water heater | Solar water heater | Solar water heater |
| Sociodemographic characteristics | Income | 0.0285*** (0.00945) | 0.0653*** (0.0161) | 0.0237*** (0.00805) | 0.0369** (0.0157) | −0.00475 (0.00842) | −0.0416*** (0.0158) |
| | Household size | 0.256*** (0.0597) | 0.477*** (0.107) | 0.232*** (0.0493) | 0.221* (0.114) | −0.0242 (0.0587) | −0.245** (0.111) |
| | Household owner age | −0.318 (0.203) | −1.028*** (0.391) | −0.414** (0.166) | −0.710* (0.418) | −0.0965 (0.204) | 0.613 (0.410) |
| | Energy conservation awareness | −0.0176 (0.191) | 0.141 (0.357) | 0.248 (0.162) | 0.158 (0.380) | 0.266 (0.192) | 0.108 (0.374) |
| | Education level | −0.262 (0.348) | −0.120 (0.647) | −0.143 (0.275) | 0.142 (0.695) | 0.120 (0.362) | −0.0228 (0.677) |
| Information exchange | Going-out frequency | 0.342* (0.200) | 0.299 (0.382) | 0.269 (0.166) | −0.0431 (0.403) | −0.0738 (0.195) | −0.0306 (0.396) |
| | Distance | 0.461* (0.236) | 0.430 (0.673) | 0.726*** (0.176) | −0.0308 (0.687) | 0.265 (0.231) | 0.296 (0.678) |
| Living habits | Temperature | 0.114*** (0.0326) | 0.566*** (0.115) | 0.0793*** (0.0238) | 0.451*** (0.115) | −0.0349 (0.0323) | −0.486*** (0.115) |
| Natural resource | Solar irradiance | −0.942*** (0.240) | −13.90 (585.6) | −0.426** (0.177) | −12.95 (585.6) | 0.516** (0.240) | 13.47 (585.6) |

(continued)

**Table 2** (continued)

| Model | | ML-1 (Basic model: no water heater) | | | ML-2 (Basic model: electrical water heater) | | ML-3 (Basic model: LPG water heater) |
|---|---|---|---|---|---|---|---|
| | | Electrical water heater | LPG water heater | Solar water heater | LPG water heater | Solar water heater | Solar water heater |
| Energy price | Electricity price | $-0.0889^{***}$ (0.0316) | $0.110^{**}$ (0.0508) | $-0.115^{***}$ (0.0286) | $0.199^{***}$ (0.0543) | −0.0260 (0.0330) | $-0.225^{***}$ (0.0541) |
| | LPG price | −0.124 (0.0816) | −0.251 (0.201) | $-0.258^{***}$ (0.0604) | −0.127 (0.210) | −0.134 (0.0820) | −0.00681 (0.206) |
| Policy variable | Subsidy | 20.48 (7352) | 18.89 (7352) | 19.88 (7352) | $-1.596^{***}$ (0.465) | $-0.599^{***}$ (0.185) | $0.997^{**}$ (0.467) |
| Constant term | | 0.972 (1.710) | $-20.00^{***}$ (3.388) | $4.462^{***}$ (1.509) | $-20.97^{***}$ (3.610) | $3.490^{*}$ (1.783) | $24.46^{***}$ (3.580) |
| Observation | | 1,757 | | | 1,757 | | 1,757 |
| Adjusted $R^2$ | | 0.342 | | | 0.342 | | 0.342 |
| Likelihood function | | −1,164.1 | | | −1,164.1 | | −1,164.1 |
| Degree of freedom | | 36 | | | 36 | | 36 |

***, ** and * means significance at the level of 1%, 5% and 10% respectively

*Note* Value in brackets is standard error. Since option A based on option B and option A based on option A are opposite to each other, we do not contain the other group of coefficients on rural household's decision to install water heaters. The income coefficients for three types of water heaters were all positive, which shows that the probability of using any type of water heaters may increase with the rising household income. To be specific, when household income increased by RMB1,000, the log odds ratio of LPG water heaters relative to the basic category (e.g., the category without water heaters) increased by 6.53%. The coefficients for electrical and solar water heaters were 2.85% and 2.37% respectively, much smaller than the coefficient for LPG water heaters. For households with electrical water heaters, higher income led to increased chances of using LPG water heaters, but no increase in probability of using solar water heaters. The significance level of coefficient for household size was like that of income. With each additional household member, the log odds ratio of LPG water heaters relative to no installation of LPG water heaters increased by 47.7%. The ratios for electrical and solar water heaters relative to no installation of LPG water heaters were 25.6% and 23.2% respectively, showing the influences of scale economy on rural household's choice of water heaters. The age coefficient, however, was quite different. When the household owner was over 60 years old, the probability of installing LPG and solar water heaters decreased significantly, the coefficients for which were −1.028 and −0.414 respectively. Energy conservation awareness and education level did not have significant influences on purchase of water heaters.

Information exchange is also correlated with rural resident's buying decision of water heaters. Compared with households having no water heaters, households had a stronger tendency to install electrical water heaters if household members went to urban areas several times each year. However, it seems that the going-out frequency was not correlated with use of LPG or solar water heaters. Concerning the influences of household location, rural residents were more likely to install an electrical or solar water heater when they were within 1 km from the nearest downtown area.

Concerning living habit, we found that temperature was a significant determinant. Compared with households having neither of the three types of water heaters, rural residents living in higher average temperature tended to install more water heaters. Among the three types, LPG water heater is a better choice for rural residents living in high temperature.

Residents living in areas with abundant solar irradiance did not show a strong desire to purchase solar water heaters. It means that advantages in energy resource did not have a decisive role in household's choice of water heaters, which is out of our expectation.

For households with no water heaters, high electricity price reduced the probability of installing electrical water heaters in households. This is understandable, as high electricity price increases the cost of using electrical water heaters. We further realized that high electricity price increased the probability of using LPG water heaters in households, but did not increase the probability of using solar water heaters, which shows that LPG water heater is a better choice than electrical ones. The coefficient of LPG price was not significant, suggesting that LPG price is not an important factor in rural resident's choice of water heaters.

Concerning the policy variable, with households having no water heaters as the control group, the coefficient of policy variable was usually not significant. However, the probability of installing electrical water heaters was better improved than LPG or solar water heaters by subsidies in the "Home Appliances Going to the Countryside" policy. The coefficients of influence of the said policy on LPG and solar water heaters were $-1.596$ and $-0.599$ respectively, with more significant effects on solar water heaters than LPG water heaters. This suggests that the government's energy conservation subsidies effectively facilitate the development of solar water heater market.

To guarantee validity of the empirical study based on multinomial Logit model, assumption of independence of irrelevant alternatives (IIA assumption) shall be maintained. The assumption makes the possibility of choosing an alternative independent of other alternatives. We used both Hausman-McFadden test and Small-Hsiao test to test the IIA assumption relative to each category that might be ignored. At a normal 5% significance level, the Hausman-McFadden test showed that the possibility of the four alternatives was dependent of other alternatives (including no water heaters, electrical water heaters, LPG water heaters and solar water heaters). However, the Small-Hsiao test verified the independence of no water heaters, electrical water heaters and solar water heaters, while the independence of LPG water heaters was shown to be dependent of other alternatives.

Consequently, due to the following reasons, it is necessary to further run the nested Logit model. First, nested Logit model relaxes the strict assumption that each choice is independent of each other. Second, the choice of water heaters of rural residents in China has an obvious two-stage structure. To complete the entire decision-making process, rural residents first decide whether to buy water heaters, and then choose one of the three types of water heaters. Third, if the estimation results obtained by multinomial and nested Logit models are consistent, such cross-validation strategy can confirm the robustness of our main conclusions.

We first divided all explanatory variables into two groups. The first group included main factors that determine whether a household will install a water heater, and the second group included factors that affect household's choice of a specific type of water heater. Explanatory variables at the first stage included income, household size, age of household owner, frequency of going out, distance and temperature. The other variables were used at the second stage (NL-1 in Table 3). Considering that some variables may have influences at both stages, we exchanged income, frequency of going out and distance with electricity price, LPG price and subsidies at the two stages (NL-2 in Table 3). The estimation results are as shown in Table 3.

Results of the first stage showed that variables including income, household size, age of household owner, frequency of going out, distance, temperature and LPG price had influences on the buying decision, which is consistent with the results of multinomial Logit model which showed that income, household size, frequency of going out, distance and temperature had positive effects on rural resident's use of water heaters. To put it more accurately, when income increased by RMB1,000, the log odds ratio increased by 2.82%. With each additional household member, the probability of installing water heaters increased significantly by 26.5%. These findings are consistent with popularization of solar water heaters in Taiwan. Economic condition (disposable income and incentives) and demographic characteristics (household

**Table 3** Nested Logit model parameter estimation

| Model | | NL-1 | | | NL-2 | | |
|---|---|---|---|---|---|---|---|
| 1st stage | | Installation (basic model: no installation) | | | Installation (basic model: no installation) | | |
| Sociodemographic characteristics | Income | | $0.0282^{***}$ (0.00743) | | | | $0.0282^{***}$ (0.00743) |
| | Household size | | $0.265^{***}$ (0.0432) | | | $0.277^{***}$ (0.0428) | $0.265^{***}$ (0.0432) |
| | Age of household owner | | $-0.436^{***}$ (0.146) | | | $-0.413^{***}$ (0.145) | $-0.436^{***}$ (0.146) |
| Information exchange | Going-out frequency | | $0.287^{*}$ (0.147) | | | | $0.287^{*}$ (0.147) |
| | Distance | | $0.636^{***}$ (0.164) | | | | $0.636^{***}$ (0.164) |
| Living habit | Temperature | | $0.0958^{***}$ (0.0223) | | | $0.0795^{***}$ (0.0230) | $0.0958^{***}$ (0.0223) |
| Energy price | Electricity price | | | | | 0.0178 (0.0193) | |
| | LPG price | | | | | $-0.223^{***}$ (0.0560) | |
| Policy variable | Subsidy | | | | | 21.58 (1,591) | |
| 2nd stage | | LPG water heater (basic model: electrical water heater) | Solar water heater (basic model: electrical water heater) | Solar water heater (basic model: LPG water heater) | LPG water heater (basic model: electrical water heater) | Solar water heater (basic model: electrical water heater) | Solar water heater (basic model: LPG water heater) |

(continued)

**Table 3** (continued)

| Model | | NL-1 | | | NL-2 | | |
|---|---|---|---|---|---|---|---|
| Sociodemographic characteristics | Income | | | | 0.0124 (0.0518) | −0.0147 (0.0337) | −0.0270 (0.0448) |
| | Energy conservation awareness | 0.169 (0.324) | 0.239 (0.183) | 0.0701 (0.323) | 0.524 (1.197) | 1.324 (0.914) | 0.800 (0.960) |
| | Education level | 0.142 (0.570) | 0.0754 (0.307) | −0.0665 (0.551) | 0.838 (1.959) | 1.039 (1.470) | 0.201 (1.564) |
| Information exchange | Going-out frequency | | | | −0.995 (1.281) | −1.111 (0.972) | −0.114 (1.125) |
| | Distance | | | | $-5.792^{**}$ (2.855) | $2.209^{**}$ (1.061) | $7.999^{***}$ (3.073) |
| Natural resource | Solar irradiance | −14.26 (2,190) | $0.464^{*}$ (0.251) | 14.79 (2,272) | −69.77 (2,237) | $2.621^{**}$ (1.293) | 73.07 (2,416) |
| Energy price | Electricity price | $0.324^{***}$ (0.0981) | $-0.0459^{*}$ (0.0263) | $-0.370^{***}$ (0.109) | | | |
| | LPG price | −0.113 (0.173) | $-0.166^{**}$ (0.0795) | −0.0531 (0.172) | | | |
| Policy variable | Subsidy | $-1.423^{***}$ (0.548) | $-0.526^{**}$ (0.236) | $0.896^{**}$ (0.447) | | | |
| Constant term | | $-18.90^{***}$ (6.134) | $4.145^{**}$ (1.732) | $23.04^{***}$ (7.117) | $-3.315^{*}$ (1.966) | 0.137 (0.833) | $3.450^{*}$ (2.090) |
| Observation | | | 7,028 | | | 7,028 | |

(continued)

**Table 3** (continued)

| Model | | NL-1 | | | NL-2 | | |
|---|---|---|---|---|---|---|---|
| Household number | | | 1,757 | | | 1,757 | |
| Likelihood | | | −1,180.8 | | | −1,315.0 | |
| Degree of freedom | | | 24 | | | 24 | |

***, ** and * means significance at the level of 1%, 5% and 10% respectively

*Note* Value in brackets is the standard error. Since option A based on option B and option A based on option A are opposite to each other, we do not contain the other group of coefficients size) in Taiwan were proved to be major barriers to household's decision to install water heaters (Chang et al. 2009). Ma et al. (2014, 2015) also found that increase in net income led to significant increase in use of solar water heaters among rural residents.

Information exchange is another significant factor in buying decision process of rural residents, the influence of which is caused by the variables of going-out frequency and distance, coefficients of which were 0.287 and 0.636 respectively. Living habit represented in temperature is also an important factor. The estimation results were consistent in NL-1 and NL-2. According to Han et al. (2010), solar water heaters cannot serve as channel of water when temperature is below 8 °C, otherwise water may freeze. Like multinomial estimation, the coefficient of LPG price was unexpected. When consumers purchase a water heater burning fossil fuel, though energy price is theoretically an important factor (Michelsen and Madlener 2016), electricity price and subsidy policy were not significant factors during the first stage of the buying decision process.

During the second stage, sociodemographic characteristics such as income, energy conservation awareness and education level were not important, which means that income level determines the purchasing behavior alone, but cannot determine the type of water heaters to be purchased. This is consistent with the findings of Goto et al. (2011), as they found that to purchase a high- or low-efficiency water heater was not correlated with household income in Japan. Though, the situation in Spain and Tunisia is different. Ramos et al. (2016) conducted a survey in Spain, which showed that households with higher level of income and education were more likely to make investment to improve energy efficiency. Based on survey data from Tunisia, Jridi et al. (2015) found that unlike use of traditional water heaters, use of solar water heaters were subject to positive influences from income and education level.

Among the explanatory variables, distance, solar irradiance, electricity price and subsidy had effects on specific type of water heaters to be purchased. Here are some interesting findings. First, if a rural household is near to the downtown area, it has significantly higher possibility of installing a solar water heater than an electrical or LPG one. In China, solar water heaters are first used by urban residents and then introduced to rural areas (Zheng et al. 2014). Rural households near to downtown areas have advantages in accessibility of information, especially information about solar water heaters, because they can easily see application of the new technology on roofs. Other relevant studies also proved information accessibility as an important factor. For example, in Germany, Goto et al. (2011) and Michelsen and Madlener (2016) found that better informed household owners were more likely to replace traditional heating systems with renewable ones. This further illustrates the importance of information accessibility (e.g., expected energy-saving effect, technological reliability and advice on technical specifications) in buying process of solar water heaters.

Second, in regions with the most abundant solar irradiance, residents are more likely to purchase solar water heaters rather than electrical ones. This does not come as a surprise. Meanwhile, it is more reasonable than coefficients obtained from multinomial Logit model and justifies the use of nested Logit model.

Third, high electricity price promotes replacement of LPG water heaters with electrical ones. However, the coefficient of electricity price relative to solar water heaters was negative, and the coefficients of electricity price relative to electrical or LPG solar waters were −0.0459 and −0.370 respectively. It is surprising to observe such results in an industrial country, and it is contradictory to basic demand theories and the current situation. For example, Goto et al. (2011) and Michelsen and Madlener (2016) found that increase in energy prices led to rising probabilities of using energy-efficient water heaters in Germany and Japan, since consumers had better energy conservation awareness because of higher prices. When energy-efficient household appliances are used, cost reduction in energy consumption is inevitable. A possible reason of the unexpected symbols of coefficients is government's strict control of terminal electricity price in China. Rural areas are usually in remote regions, so, more investment is required to provide rural residents with access to electricity than urban residents. Due to government control of electricity price, the residential electricity price is too low to reflect the actual cost in this regard in rural China.

Fourth, compared with the influence of price subsidies on solar and LPG water heaters, the 13% price subsidy was most effective for electrical water heaters. Meanwhile, price subsidies had larger influences on solar water heaters than LPG water heaters. In Japan, when consumers knew accessibility of financial subsidies from the government, their probability of buying energy-efficient water heaters with high up-front cost increased significantly (Goto et al. 2011). However, in China, rural residents tend to have a stronger tendency to obtain government subsidies while purchasing electrical water heaters. With a free ride, more rural residents decide to purchase electrical water heaters in advance and obtain subsidies when available.

## 5 Summary

Buying decisions relating to durable goods such as water heaters, etc. are important, because they may fix the energy consumption type and pattern of a household relating to water heaters in the several or a dozen years to come. Once a household decides to use a solar water heater instead of those powered by traditional fuels, its low-carbon consumption will maintain for a long period. Use of solar water heaters not only reduces consumption of fossil fuels and household energy cost, but also reduces $CO_2$ emission from households. Starting from this key factor of growth in residential energy consumption, we conducted an on-site survey about household's choice of water heaters, with focus on the buying decision process of rural households in China relating to solar water heaters. The conclusions of empirical study are of great significance to formulate relevant energy policies, encourage resident's use of energy-efficient products and achieve goals of energy conservation and emission reduction.

By empirical analysis of micro-level personal data (the data is from the questionnaire survey designed by the research group of this book), we found that rural residents had different preferences for specific type of water heaters, and the importance of key determinants also varied. It means that the decision process to purchase water heaters is a complex one. Results revealed the different driving forces behind the choice of water heaters, which are summarized as follows:

(1) Demographic variables have significant effects during the first stage of resident's choice of water heaters (whether to buy water heaters), but have no effect on choice during the second stage (what type of water heater to buy).
(2) In addition to sociodemographic characteristics (such as income, household size and household owner's age), we found that information accessibility is a significant determinant in the decision-making process of households to purchase water heaters. Information exchange is important in both the first and second stage. Households near downtown areas are more likely to install solar water heaters.
(3) A novel finding in this chapter is that income, household size and age of household owner can only determine whether to install water heaters in households, but cannot determine the type of water heater to be installed. In rural China where electricity price is under strict control, electricity price does not have a significant role in accelerating the green transformation of the energy system.
(4) Concerning promotion of solar water heaters in rural China, the subsidy policy in the "Home Appliances Going to the Countryside" program does not have any effect at the first stage, and the influence is larger on choice of electrical water heaters than solar water heaters at the second stage. This result suggests that government subsidies have not achieved the desired results. The government shall be more cautious to formulate further policies to promote the use of low-carbon solar water heaters and green transformation of the energy system.

Based on our study in this chapter, the following three policy implications can be drawn:

First, the government shall provide rural residents with subsidies for high-efficiency and low-carbon products like solar water heaters.

Compared with water heaters powered by traditional energy sources, solar water heater is a low-carbon product and stronger policy support shall be given to it. Possible policy interventions to promote the use of solar water heaters include measures to increase energy conservation awareness, command and control instruments as well as market-based instruments (investment support and operating support) (Scarpa and Willis 2010). However, the changes needed for consumption behavior to shift to sustainable consumption are normally not enforced, but only with a kind of voluntary approach such as information provision policies or monetary incentives (Shen and Saijo 2009).

It requires financial incentive polices to accelerate the diffusion of solar water heaters in rural China. For rational individuals, to decide whether to make an energy-saving investment, they will first weigh the initial cost and expected savings (Gillingham et al. 2009; Wasi and Carson 2013). A survey in Zhejiang, China showed that the up-front cost of a solar water heater (average price and pipeline expenditure) was around RMB2,250, which is much more expensive than buying an electrical water heater (average price: RMB833) or LPG water heater (average price: RMB560)

(Han et al. 2010). In China, economic factor is considered the most important in resident's choice of solar water heaters (Yuan et al. 2011). However, at present, there is no incentive policy in China aiming at disposition of low-carbon products (Li et al. 2013). The four-year subsidy policy in the "Home Appliances Going to the Countryside" program came to an end in early 2013 (Ma et al. 2014). This policy is not exclusively for promotion of solar water heaters in rural China. The 13% price subsidy also applies to electrical and LPG water heaters. Compared with other alternatives, the higher up-front cost of solar water heaters remains a barrier to rural resident's investment on low-carbon products. According to the empirical results in Tables 2 and 3, the subsidy policy seems to be more effective to electrical water heaters than solar water heaters. Considering the limited purchasing capability of rural residents, the higher up-front cost of solar water heaters may be a key factor. Subsidy policies in China shall be improved by focusing on energy-saving or low-carbon water heaters. As Ma et al. (2014) advised, China shall start a new program (possibly a subsidy policy) exclusively for promotion of solar water heaters in rural areas and provide financial incentives to rural residents for use of low-carbon products.

Second, disclosure of information about product quality, expected energy-saving effect, technological reliability and technical specifications of solar waters shall be improved. Consumers in urgent need of water heaters may not be able to collect enough information due to limited time and knowledge, which may result in low-efficiency investment decisions. The best policy is to improve information accessible to consumers who purchase water heaters in an emergency (Wasi and Carson 2013). According to empirical results in this chapter, income is one of the key factors determining the use of water heaters in rural China, but it cannot determine which type of water heater to buy. In China, there are more than 5,000 solar water heater manufacturers, most of which have limited production capacity and product quality (Han et al. 2010). To survive in the fierce market competition, they sell low-quality solar water heaters at very low prices, which disrupts the market. All these highlight the importance of providing information on solar water heaters. To correct information failure in the market, it is necessary to provide information about product quality, expected energy-saving effect, technological reliability and technical specifications. These measures can accelerate the transformation to low-carbon energy consumption of rural households in China.

Third, China started a new round of electricity pricing reform in 2015. A key objective of the electricity pricing reform is to shift from a highly regulated pricing mechanism to a market-based pricing mechanism (Zeng et al. 2016). If the terminal residential electricity price can reflect its actual cost and external environmental damage, the market incentives for investment in solar water heaters will likely promote the use of low-carbon products more effectively.

# Chapter 9
# Does Air Pollution Reduce Residents' Happiness?

**Ping Qin, Wenjie Miao, Yang Zhang and Shuai Chen**

## 1 Introduction

Economic growth in China has long been heavily dependent on investment in non-renewable fossil energy, characterized by high investment, high energy consumption, high emission and low output. It causes giant pressure on the ecological environment in China. With economic development, rapid expansion of urban areas and fast-growing vehicle ownership cause irreversible damages to the ecological environment. Due to frequent and long-lasting heavy smog in recent years, air pollution has become a major concern of the public, media and the government.

According to the *2015 Report on Air Qualities in Cities* issued by the Ministry of Ecology and Environment of the People's Republic of China which covered 74 cities, including cities in the Beijing-Tianjin-Hebei region, the Yangtze River Delta, the Pearl River delta and municipalities directly under the central government, province capitals and municipalities cities specially designated in the state plan, the average density of $PM_{2.5}$ in these cities was 55 $\mu g/m^3$, down by 14.1% compared with the previous year, and the average density of $PM_{10}$ was 93 $\mu g/m^3$, down by 11.4%. However, air pollution remains a serious concern in some regions, especially in Beijing. With surging vehicle ownership and increasing traffic congestion, the average AQI[1]

[1] Air quality was measured by air pollution index (API) before 2013, which was obtained by computing concentration of three major air pollutants: $SO_2$, $NO_x$ and TSP. After 2013, a new AQI for measuring air quality was adopted. AQI is obtained by computing concentration of six major air pollutants. According to the *Technical Regulation on Ambient Air Quality Index* (*on trial*) (*HJH 633-2012*), air quality is classified into six levels: AQI between 0 and 50 is excellent (level 1), AQI between 51 and 100 is good (level 2), AQI above 100 is defined as air pollution, including 101–150 as light pollution (level 3), 151–200 as moderate pollution (level 4), 201–300 as heavy pollution (level 5) and above 300 as severe pollution (level 6). The maximum AQI is 500. So, when it is over 500, it cannot be measured in AQI.

P. Qin (✉) · W. Miao · Y. Zhang · S. Chen
Renmin University of China, Beijing, China
e-mail: Pingqin@ruc.edu.cn



X. Zheng and C. Wei (eds.), *Household Energy Consumption in China: 2016 Report*, https://doi.org/10.1007/978-981-13-7523-1_9

in Beijing from 2000 to 2014 was 96.8. In another word, Beijing met the air quality standard (AQI < 100) only in about half of the 15 years, while in the remaining days, Beijing was lightly polluted at the best (AQI $\geq$ 100), and the pollution in heating seasons in winter was even worse. For example, in 2013, Beijing met the air quality standard (AQI < 100) only in 48% of the year, and was heavily polluted (AQI > 200) in 15% of the year. Concerning the specific pollutants, take $PM_{2.5}$ as an example. The average density of $PM_{2.5}$ in Beijing in 2013 was 89.5 $\mu g/m^3$, which is 2.5 times higher than the national air quality standard in China and around 9 times the WHO standard. According to the 2014 version of WHO's Ambient Air Pollution database, Haikou had the best air quality in China, but it only ranked the 674th in 1,626 cities across the world. That's to say, over 2/3 of the cities in the world had better air quality than China. How to improve urban air quality in China has increasingly become a major concern for Chinese society.

Meanwhile, with increase in income, people gradually realize that economic growth is not the sole objective of economic development. Happiness has gradually become another important goal pursued by individuals, households and the society. The state is also gradually considering happiness of residents as an important factor in policy making. Many factors may have influences on happiness. In addition to traditionally recognized factors such as income, marriage and health, etc., environmental quality is considered in many studies an important social factor of residents' happiness. Based on literature review, this book matches hourly data of urban air pollution and the micro survey data about personal happiness in the CGSS 2015, and uses instrumental variables and other econometric approaches to conduct an empirical study of the correlation between air pollution and happiness of rural and urban residents.

There have been many studies about air pollution in China, but the focus has been influences of air pollution on health and economic cost of air pollution. The correlation between air quality and happiness has not drawn much attention from researchers until recent years. There are two main reasons for such phenomenon. First, happiness is about subjective feelings and there are no criteria for objective assessment. Second, China does not have a comprehensive mechanism for real-time publication of major air pollutants until recent years. The openness and transparency of data allows for more rigorous empirical studies.

## 2 Literature Review

Since the Industrial Revolution, fossil fuels have been in increasingly extensive use in human life and production. While experiencing unprecedented economic development, countries are also confronted with the challenge of air pollution. Emerging economies witnessed rapid economic development in recent years, but such extensive growth have various negative effects. Air pollution is attracting more and more attention from the society. Under these circumstances, there are many studies on air pollution in China and foreign countries.

The *Global Burden of Disease 2010* (GBD 2010) issued by the WHO in 2012 is one of the most authoritative studies about effects of air pollution on human health. GBD 2010 uses unified and comparable methods for comprehensive analysis of the disease and death data of different genders and age groups in 187 countries and 21 regions from 1990 to 2010, and evaluated the effects of ambient air pollution on human health using migration models and satellite-based observations of aerosol optical depth. According to estimates in GBD 2010, each year, the ambient air pollution in the form of fine particles caused 3.2 million premature deaths and 76 million lost years of healthy life across the world. Of the total, 2.2 million premature deaths in China were caused by air pollution, accounting for 1/3 of the global deaths.

Researches at home and abroad usually use stated preference and revealed preference to study the environmental value of air quality improvement. Due to limitations of observations, most studies use stated preference such as contingent valuation to estimate the economic cost that residents are willing to bear in exchange for better air quality. Hammitt and Zhou (2006) conducted a questionnaire survey covering 3,700 households in Beijing, Anqing (Anhui) and the rural areas near Anqing using contingent valuation method, results of which showed that the average willingness to pay (WTP) to prevent an episode of cold of the samples ranged between USD3 and USD6, and the average WTP to prevent chronic bronchitis ranged between USD500 and USD1,000. In the same year, Li et al. used contingent valuation method to study the WTP for treatment of air pollution of Beijing residents, covering 1,371 households in 8 districts of Beijing. Results showed that the average WTP per household to lower the density of air pollutants in Beijing by 50% was RMB143/year, accounting for 0.7% of the annual household income in Beijing. Wang and Mullahy (2006) conducted a sample survey of 500 households to study the health effects of air quality improvement in Chongqing, which showed that the WTP of Chongqing residents to save one statistical life was USD34,458. By using contingent valuation method, researchers simulate the market and directly ask respondents about their WTP for certain improvement of air quality. The biggest problem with this method is that the scenario is hypothetical, so, the respondents are likely to overestimate or underestimate their WTP and result in hypothetical bias. Therefore, the shortcoming of this method may cause major errors in residents' WTP for air quality.

The revealed preference method is generally considered to be able to overcome the shortcoming of stated preference method, because the revealed preference method uses data from market observations rather than stated preference data provided by residents. Zhang and Mu (2016) estimated the residents' WTP for defense against air pollution based on the sales data on Taobao and Tmall of particulate-filtering masks in 316 cities in China from February 2013 to April 2014. Results showed that each 100-point increase in Air Quality Index (AQI) led to increase in consumption of particulate-filtering masks by 54.5% and anti-$PM_{2.5}$ masks by 70.6%. According to their estimation, if heavily polluted days (AQI > 201) decreased by 10%, the savings on particulate-filtering masks alone in China would be USD187 million. In addition, Ito and Zhang (2016) estimated the WTP for clean air of Chinese residents based on sales data of air purifiers in 82 cities in China from January 2006 to December 2012. Results showed that the residents' WTP for reducing 1 $\mu g/m^3$ of $PM_{10}$ was

USD1.52/year, far more than they had expected. This suggests that improvement on air management in China is required to satisfy residents' requirement.

With more attention on happiness in recent years, more and more researchers are working on effects of air pollution on people's mental health and happiness index, while further estimating the happiness cost of air pollution and obtaining residents' WTP for reduced air pollution through marginal transformation of income and pollutants. Foreign studies in this area started earlier. Menz (2011) conducted analysis of data about air pollution and happiness in 48 countries from 1990 to 2006 using life satisfaction approach (LSA) and concluded that air pollution significantly reduced residents' happiness. Welsch (2006) also found negative correlation between happiness and air pollution in study of panel data of ten European countries from 1990 to 1997. MacKerron and Mourato (2009) conducted a survey among 400 residents in London about their happiness and matched air pollution data according to the geographic information system, after which they also found significant negative correlation between air pollution and happiness. With implementation of large-scale surveys by universities and research institutions in China and further publication of air pollution data by the government, there have been many studies in this area in recent years. Zhang et al. (2015) studied the correlation between air quality and happiness based on relevant depression scales in the China Family Panel Studies in 2010 and 2012 and the air pollution index in the same period. Li (2015) used the ordered Probit model to analyze the absolute and relative deprivation effects of environmental pollution on residents' happiness based on data of the CGSS 2008. Yang and Zhang (2014) studied the correlation between air pollution and residents' happiness based on data of the CGSS 2010 and estimated the average WTP for reduction of air pollution of Chinese residents using LSA. The above studies reached similar conclusions that poor air quality had significant negative influences on residents' happiness. In addition, such influences may have major differences depending on the individual's age, income and health, etc.

Compared with the above similar studies, the main contribution and characteristics of our study are as follows:

1. It covers a broader scope of samples. Data used in this chapter are 1/5 of the samples are randomly-selected samples from the CGSS 2015, including 3,863 respondents in 28 provincial administrative regions.
2. Many pollutants are covered in the research. Pollutant data covered in this chapter include hourly density of $PM_{2.5}$, $O_3$, $PM_{10}$, $SO_2$, $NO_2$ and CO as well as the comprehensive AQI. So, this chapter studies the different influences of pollutants on happiness.
3. The key variables are more accurately matched in terms of time and space. First, the air pollution data used in this chapter is matched to the time of interview (precise time down to the hour), rather than the annual average or daily average in most studies. Second, the climate, pollution and surveyed region (center point in county) are matched according to the principle of the shortest distance in space to ensure spatial matching.

4. Respondents are divided into groups based on specific characteristics. This chapter conducts regression in groups according to the age, gender and other characteristics of the respondents, and analyzes whether the other characteristics of the respondents may affect the correlation between air pollution and happiness of urban and rural residents.
5. Instrumental variable is used. This chapter uses the maximum wind speed on the day of interview as an instrumental variable for air pollution to eliminate the possible estimation errors caused by missing variables and two-way causality.

## 3 Statistical Description of Data

### *3.1 Data Sources*

This chapter uses four types of variables and data: micro data of happiness and self-evaluation of health, variable of respondent's characteristics, hourly air pollution data and climate data per day.

Happiness and self-evaluation of health of urban and rural residents are main variables in this chapter. Both variables are from the CGSS 2015 conducted by RUC. The questions, both about subjective evaluation of the respondent, are: "How do you describe your overall happiness?" and "How do you think of your current health?". With a rating scale from 1 to 5, high values represent high happiness and evaluation of health.

Air pollution is the core independent variable in this chapter. Pollutants covered in this chapter include $PM_{2.5}$, $O_3$, $PM_{10}$, $SO_2$, $NO_2$ and CO as well as AQI. Since data from the CGSS 2015 contain information about the specific time (precise time down to the hour) of interview, we were able to match the respondent's happiness and self-evaluation of health with the air pollution in the corresponding time precise down to the hour. Meanwhile, concerning space matching, air pollution data were matched with climate data and surveyed region (center point in county) according to the principle of the shortest distance in space, i.e., the longest distance between air pollution station and the respondent was 100 km. If the distance between a respondent and a weather station or air pollution monitoring station was over 100 km, the climate or air pollution data was considered missing in the interview and such samples were not subject to regression (This case was only found in one county). Air pollution data are from real-time publication of national air quality issued by China National Environmental Monitoring Centre.[2]

The meteorological data used in this chapter include temperature, precipitation, sunshine hours and maximum wind speed. Temperature, precipitation and sunshine hours use daily data, while wind speed as an instrumental variable uses the maximum wind speed of the day of interview. The logic is: if there is a strong wind at certain

[2]http://www.cnemc.cn/.

time on the day of interview, the air pollution of that day may not be very heavy. High wind speed facilitates diffusion and dilution of air pollutants. Meteorological data are from the daily meteorological statistics V3.0 of China Meteorological Data Network.[3]

## 3.2 Statistical Description

Table 1 is a statistical description of the above four types of variables, showing name, definition and basic statistical characteristics such as mean value and variance, etc. of the variables.

According to the results of statistical description, the mean value of subjective well-being of the samples was 3.87. Yang and Zhang (2014), Lu and Yang (2016) used the data of the CGSS 2012 and CGSS 2013 respectively in their studies, and the mean values of subjective well-being of their samples were 3.79 and 3.751 respectively,

**Table 1** Statistical description of variables

| Variable | Definition | Mean value | Variance | Minimum value | Maximum value | Sample size |
|---|---|---|---|---|---|---|
| *Dependent variable* | | | | | | |
| Self-evaluation of health | 1-unhealthy to 5-healthy | 3.595 | 1.069 | 1 | 5 | 3,860 |
| Subjective well-being | 1-unhappy to 5-happy | 3.867 | 0.817 | 1 | 5 | 3,855 |
| *Air pollution variables* | | | | | | |
| AQI | (hourly record) | 64.53 | 48.12 | 9 | 410 | 3,479 |
| $PM_{2.5}$ | μg/m$^3$ (hourly record) | 40.57 | 41.52 | 1 | 364 | 3,479 |
| $O_3$ | μg/m$^3$ (hourly record) | 82.19 | 51.02 | 1 | 374 | 3,461 |
| $PM_{10}$ | μg/m$^3$ (hourly record) | 66.40 | 48.30 | 4 | 410 | 3,085 |
| $SO_2$ | μg/m$^3$ (hourly record) | 14.61 | 17.35 | 1 | 436 | 3,472 |
| $NO_2$ | μg/m$^3$ (hourly record) | 22.70 | 17.74 | 1 | 149 | 3,474 |
| CO | mg/m$^3$ (hourly record) | 0.875 | 0.568 | 0.057 | 5.889 | 3,465 |

(continued)

[3]http://data.cma.cn/.

**Table 1** (continued)

| Variable | Definition | Mean value | Variance | Minimum value | Maximum value | Sample size |
|---|---|---|---|---|---|---|
| *Social characteristics* | | | | | | |
| Gender | 1-male, 0-female | 0.47 | 0.499 | 0 | 1 | 3,863 |
| Residence | 1-urban, 0-rural | 0.27 | 0.446 | 0 | 1 | 3,863 |
| Marriage | 1-yes, 0-no | 0.79 | 0.410 | 0 | 1 | 3,863 |
| Age | Years | 50.64 | 16.78 | 18 | 93 | 3,863 |
| Education level | Level 1 to13 | 4.97 | 3.148 | 1 | 13 | 3,849 |
| Minority (yes/no) | 1-yes, 0-no | 0.08 | 0.268 | 0 | 1 | 3,863 |
| Religion (yes/no) | 1-yes, 0-no | 0.125 | 0.330 | 0 | 1 | 3,863 |
| Annual income per capita | RMB10,000 | 3.068 | 9.824 | 0 | 500 | 3,640 |
| *Household characteristics* | | | | | | |
| Living space | $m^2$ | 116.4 | 86.61 | 0 | 1050 | 3,863 |
| Household size | | 2.883 | 1.408 | 1 | 14 | 3,852 |
| *Meteorological variables* | | | | | | |
| Temperature | 0.1 °C (daily average) | 244.8 | 45.80 | 58 | 330 | 3,863 |
| Precipitation | 0.1 mm (8:00–20:00 accumulated precipitation) | 25.68 | 87.14 | 0 | 1173 | 3,863 |
| Sunshine | 0.1 h (daily total) | 57.76 | 41.58 | 0 | 134 | 3,863 |
| *Instrumental variable* | | | | | | |
| Wind speed | 0.1 m/s (hourly record) | 20.68 | 12.41 | 3 | 134 | 3,863 |

with no major difference from the mean value of subjective well-being of the samples in this chapter. Concerning the social characteristics of the samples, 47% of the respondents were male, 27% were from urban areas and about 80% were married. The average of age of the samples was 51 and the average education period was about 5 years. In addition, the average annual income of the respondents was RMB30,680 yuan, higher than RMB21,966 in the survey data of the National Bureau of Statistics concerning the per-capita disposable income of residents in China in 2015.

## 4 Equation Setting and Empirical Analysis

### *4.1 Equation Setting*

This chapter examines the effects of air pollution on urban and rural residents' happiness and self-evaluation of health. To eliminate the influences of missing variables and two-way causality on the estimation results, this chapter uses the instrumental variable (IV) method and uses the maximum wind speed on the day the sample was interviewed as the instrumental variable of the dependent variable of air pollutant density.

The two-stage regression equation for influences of air quality on self-evaluation of health is set as follows:

$$\text{Poll}_{jmdh} = \alpha_0 + \alpha_1 \text{Wind}_{jmd} + X_{ij}\pi + W_{jd}\omega + \delta_j + \eta_m + \theta_h + \varepsilon_{ijt} \quad (1)$$

$$\ln \text{Heal}_{ij} = \beta_0 + \beta_1 \widehat{\text{Poll}_{jmdh}} + X_{ij}\gamma + W_{jd}\tau + \delta_j + \eta_m + \theta_h + v_{ijt} \quad (2)$$

In the above equations, $i$ and $j$ represent the $i$th person and the $j$th region respectively; $m$, $d$, and $h$ represent the $m$th month, the $d$th day and the $h$th hour. In equation of the first stage (1), Poll represents the hourly density of air pollutants in region $j$. Wind is the instrumental variable representing the maximum wind speed in region $j$ on the day of interview; $X$ is the controlled variable representing respondent's characteristic variables with influences on self-evaluation of health, such as gender, ager, ethnic group, education level, marital status, religion and annual income, etc.; $W$ represents weather variables with influences on respondent's self-evaluation of health, such as temperature, precipitation and sunshine hours, etc.; $\delta$ represents fixed effect of the sample region; $\eta$ represents monthly fixed effect; $\theta$ represents hourly fixed effect; $\varepsilon$ represents random error term. In equation of the second stage (2), ln Heal represents the self-evaluation of health reported by resident, while the other exogenous variables are the same as in the first stage.

The higher the maximum wind speed on the day of interview, the better air quality due to dilution and diffusion of air pollutants. Therefore, the instrumental variable Wind has a strong correlation with Poll the density of air pollutants. In regression of Eq. (1), if the coefficient before the instrumental variable is significant, it suggests a strong correlation between Wind the instrumental variable and Poll the density of air pollutants. In addition, through analysis, it is easy to note that there is no correlation between the maximum wind speed on the day of interview and other factors that may affect the respondents' self-evaluation of health including income, gender, age, education level and marital status, etc., guaranteeing the exogenous nature of the instrumental variable.

The two-stage regression equation for influences of air quality on happiness is set as follows:

$$\mathrm{Poll}_{jmdh} = \alpha_0 + \alpha_1\,\mathrm{Wind}_{jmd} + X_{ij}\pi + W_{jd}\omega + \delta_j + \eta_m + \theta_h + \varepsilon_{ijt} \tag{3}$$

$$\ln \mathrm{Happ}_{ij} = \beta_0 + \beta_1 \bar{\mathrm{p}}\mathrm{oll}_{jmdh} + X_{ij}\gamma + W_{jd}\tau + \delta_j + \eta_m + \theta_h + v_{ijt} \tag{4}$$

In the above equations, $i$ and $j$ represent the $i$th person and the $j$th region respectively; *m, d, and h* represent the $m$th month, the $d$th day and the $h$th hour. In equation of the first stage (3), Poll represents the hourly density of air pollutants in region $j$. Wind is the instrumental variable representing the maximum wind speed in region $j$ on the day of interview; $X$ is the controlled variable representing respondent's characteristic variables with influences on *subjective well-being*, such as gender, ager, ethnic group, education level, marital status, religion and annual income, etc.; $W$ represents weather variables with influences on respondent's self-evaluation of health, such as temperature, precipitation and sunshine hours, etc.; δ represents fixed effect of the sample region; $\eta$ represents monthly fixed effect; $\theta$ represents hourly fixed effect; $\varepsilon$ represents random error term. In equation of the second stage (4), ln Happ represents the happiness reported by resident, while the other exogenous variables are the same as in the first stage.

## 4.2 *Empirical Analysis*

Based on the regression Eqs. (1)–(4), this section uses the instrumental variable method to estimate the influences of different air pollutants including $PM_{2.5}$, $O_3$, $PM_{10}$, $SO_2$, $NO_2$, CO and AQI on self-evaluation of health and happiness. $PM_{2.5}$ is very harmful to public health, and is drawing more and more attention. Therefore, we first study the influences of $PM_{2.5}$ on residents' self-evaluation of health and happiness.

Tables 2 and 3 present the results of two-stage regression of the influences of $PM_{2.5}$ on residents' self-evaluation of health and happiness. It can be seen from the results of the first-stage regression that with the other exogenous variables under control, the maximum wind speed on the day of interview has significant negative influences on the density of $PM_{2.5}$.

**Table 2** Two-stage estimation of influences of $PM_{2.5}$ on self-evaluation of health (1)

| Variable | 1st stage $PM_{2.5}$ | (2) ln Heal | (3) ln Heal | (4) ln Heal | (5) ln Heal |
|---|---|---|---|---|---|
| PM2.5 | | $-0.0037^{***}$ (−4.13) | $-0.0036^{***}$ (−4.04) | $-0.0036^{***}$ (−3.97) | $-0.0035^{***}$ (−3.66) |
| Wind speed | $-0.4241^{***}$ (−6.83) | | | | |
| Gender | −1.5788 (−1.36) | | $0.0472^{**}$ (2.13) | $0.0466^{**}$ (2.15) | 0.0299 (1.17) |
| Age | 0.0879 (0.62) | | $-0.0091^{***}$ (−4.30) | $-0.0112^{***}$ (−5.31) | $-0.0126^{***}$ (−6.43) |
| Age_sq | −0.0008 (−0.69) | | 0.0000 (1.33) | $0.0000^{**}$ (2.28) | $0.0001^{***}$ (3.12) |
| Edu | −0.6910 (−0.49) | | $0.0423^{***}$ (5.08) | $0.0401^{***}$ (4.25) | $0.0380^{***}$ (3.56) |
| Edu_sq | 0.0280 (0.30) | | $-0.0024^{***}$ (−4.68) | $-0.0022^{***}$ (−4.13) | $-0.0024^{***}$ (−3.97) |
| Resid | 1.0046 (0.29) | | | 0.0040 (0.23) | −0.0016 (−0.11) |
| Marriage | −0.1067 (−0.05) | | | $0.0392^{***}$ (3.66) | 0.0182 (1.45) |
| Minority | 3.1879 (1.06) | | | −0.0043 (−0.17) | −0.0061 (−0.21) |
| Religion | −1.7785 (−1.37) | | | −0.0064 (−0.46) | −0.0074 (−0.57) |
| Ln(yearinc) | 0.6370 (0.82) | | | | $0.0675^{***}$ (5.06) |
| Living space | 0.0099 (1.54) | | | | $0.0002^{*}$ (1.78) |
| Family-num | −0.0501 (−0.11) | | | | 0.0062 (1.11) |
| Imonth_FE | Yes | Yes | Yes | Yes | Yes |
| Ihour_FE | Yes | Yes | Yes | Yes | Yes |
| Icity_FE | Yes | Yes | Yes | Yes | Yes |
| Weather | Yes | Yes | Yes | Yes | Yes |
| N | 3246 | 3477 | 3465 | 3465 | 3246 |
| $R^2$ | | 0.065 | 0.074 | 0.075 | 0.097 |

***, ** and * mean significance at the level of 1%, 5% and 10% respectively

*Note* Value in the bracket is the t statistic. Robust estimation and clustered standard error are used

**Table 3** Two-stage estimation of influences of $PM_{2.5}$ on happiness (2)

| | 1st-stage | (2) | (3) | (4) | (5) |
|---|---|---|---|---|---|
| | $PM_{2.5}$ | ln Happ | ln Happ | ln Happ | ln Happ |
| $PM_{2.5}$ | | −0.0020* (−1.95) | −0.0020* (−1.94) | −0.0020** (−2.12) | −0.0023*** (−2.65) |
| Wind speed | −0.4244*** (−6.80) | | | | |
| Gender | −1.5674 (−1.35) | | −0.0151 (−1.63) | −0.0154** (−2.49) | −0.0232*** (−2.76) |
| Age | 0.0918 (0.66) | | −0.0048*** (−3.21) | −0.0101*** (−4.57) | −0.0098*** (−3.92) |
| Age_sq | −0.0009 (−0.74) | | 0.0001*** (3.78) | 0.0001*** (4.88) | 0.0001*** (4.21) |
| Edu | −0.6637 (−0.47) | | 0.0189** (2.10) | 0.0159* (1.82) | 0.0128 (1.39) |
| Edu_sq | 0.0261 (0.27) | | −0.0007 (−1.05) | −0.0004 (−0.70) | −0.0003 (−0.58) |
| Resid | 0.9680 (0.28) | | | −0.0105 (−0.79) | −0.0125 (−0.97) |
| Marriage | −0.0779 (−0.04) | | | 0.0965*** (7.11) | 0.0815*** (6.83) |
| Minority | 3.2189 (1.06) | | | 0.0210 (1.14) | 0.0211 (1.21) |
| Religion | −1.9515 (−1.54) | | | 0.0065 (0.48) | 0.0084 (0.58) |
| Ln(yearinc) | 0.6462 (0.82) | | | | 0.0270*** (2.93) |
| Living space | 0.0099 (1.53) | | | | 0.0002*** (4.42) |
| Family-num | −0.0792 (−0.18) | | | | 0.0103*** (5.02) |
| Imonth_FE | Yes | Yes | Yes | Yes | Yes |
| Ihour_FE | Yes | Yes | Yes | Yes | Yes |
| Icity_FE | Yes | Yes | Yes | Yes | Yes |
| Weather | Yes | Yes | Yes | Yes | Yes |
| N | 3,243 | 3,471 | 3,459 | 3,459 | 3,243 |
| $R^2$ | | 0.010 | 0.025 | 0.043 | 0.037 |

***, ** and * mean significance at the level of 1%, 5% and 10% respectively

*Note* Value in the bracket is the t statistic. Robust estimation and clustered standard error are used

The t statistics of Tables 4 and 5 are 6.83 and 6.80 respectively, suggesting that the chosen instrumental variable, the maximum wind speed, has a strong correlation with the density of $PM_{2.5}$.

In regression of the second stage, as shown in Tables 6 and 7, $PM_{2.5}$ alone is added in model (2), respondent's gender, age and education level are added in model (3), respondent's location, marital status, ethnic group and religion are further added in model (4) and respondent's annual income, living space, household size and respondent's other characteristic variables in model (4) are included in model (5). Climate and fixed effects of time and location are controlled in the above models.

It can be seen from the results of models in Table 2 that $PM_{2.5,}$ the regression coefficients of which remain between −0.0037 and −0.0035 from model (2) to model (5), has stable influences on self-evaluation of health. Model (5) containing all the possible controlled variables is used as the benchmark model. Results show that each increase of 10 units (μg/m$^3$) in $PM_{2.5}$ density leads to reduction by 3.5% in the resident's self-evaluation of health. $PM_{2.5}$ density has a significant correlation with age and education level, but the influences are nonlinear. In addition, we found that respondents with higher income level had higher self-evaluation of health.

It can be seen from the results of models in Table 3 that $PM_{2.5}$ has significant influences on residents' happiness. With each increase of 10 units (μg/m$^3$) in PM2.5 density, the resident's happiness reduces by about 2.3%. Happiness is also influenced by factors like income, marital status, dwelling condition and household size: married

**Table 4** Two-stage estimation of influences of other air pollutants on self-evaluation of health

| Dep. Var: ln Heal | (1) | (2) | (3) | (4) | (5) | (6) | (7) |
|---|---|---|---|---|---|---|---|
| AQI | −0.0032*** (−3.61) | | | | | | |
| $PM_{2.5}$ | | −0.0035*** (−3.66) | | | | | |
| $O_3$ | | | −0.0066** (−2.12) | | | | |
| $PM_{10}$ | | | | −0.0026*** (−4.10) | | | |
| $SO_2$ | | | | | −0.0100*** (−4.23) | | |
| $NO_2$ | | | | | | −0.0067*** (−3.91) | |
| CO | | | | | | | −0.2582*** (−4.35) |
| N | 3246 | 3246 | 3230 | 2884 | 3239 | 3241 | 3232 |
| $R^2$ | 0.085 | 0.097 | 0.179 | 0.141 | 0.055 | 0.157 | 0.137 |

***, ** and * mean significance at the level of 1%, 5% and 10% respectively

*Note* The other controlled variables are the same as in the regression model of $PM_{2.5}$. Value in the bracket is t statistic. Robust and clustered standard error are used

**Table 5** Two-stage estimation of influences of other air pollutants on happiness

| Dep. Var: ln Happ | (1) | (2) | (3) | (4) | (5) | (6) | (7) |
|---|---|---|---|---|---|---|---|
| AQI | −0.0021*** (−2.68) | | | | | | |
| $PM_{2.5}$ | | −0.0023*** (−2.65) | | | | | |
| $O_3$ | | | −0.0039* (−1.82) | | | | |
| $PM_{10}$ | | | | −0.0014* (−1.87) | | | |
| $SO_2$ | | | | | −0.0062*** (−3.14) | | |
| $NO_2$ | | | | | | −0.0044** (−2.19) | |
| CO | | | | | | | −0.1588*** (−2.83) |
| N | 3243 | 3243 | 3227 | 2882 | 3236 | 3238 | 3229 |
| $R^2$ | 0.025 | 0.037 | −0.189 | 0.073 | −0.009 | 0.075 | 0.071 |

***, ** and * mean significance at the level of 1%, 5% and 10% respectively
*Note* The other controlled variables are the same as in the regression model of $PM_{2.5}$. Value in the bracket is t statistic. Robust and clustered standard error are used

**Table 6** Grouped regression of influences of air pollution on self-evaluation of health

| Dep. Var: ln Heal | (1) | (2) | (3) | (4) | (5) | (6) | (7) |
|---|---|---|---|---|---|---|---|
| | Male | Female | Age < 30 | Age [30–60] | Age > 60 | Urban | Rural |
| AQI | −0.0040** (−2.14) | −0.0023 (−1.14) | −0.0053 (−1.51) | −0.0041*** (−4.25) | −0.0017 (−0.66) | −0.0029* (−1.90) | −0.0032** (−2.57) |
| N | 1,537 | 1,709 | 424 | 2,252 | 994 | 863 | 2,383 |
| $PM_{2.5}$ | −0.0048** (−1.98) | −0.0022 (−1.15) | −0.0060 (−1.21) | −0.0045*** (−4.38) | −0.0017 (−0.64) | −0.0035* (−1.78) | −0.0033*** (−2.63) |
| N | 1,537 | 1,709 | 424 | 2,252 | 994 | 863 | 2,383 |

***, ** and * mean significance at the level of 1%, 5% and 10% respectively
*Note* The other controlled variables are the same as in the regression model of $PM_{2.5}$. Value in the bracket is t statistic. Robust and clustered standard error are used

respondents and those with higher income level, good dwelling condition and large household size are happier.

Through estimation in Tables 4 and 5, we estimated the influences of other air pollutants on self-evaluation of health and happiness. Based on comparative analysis, we come to the following conclusions:

1. With each increase of 10 units in AQI, resident's self-evaluation of health reduces by 3.2% and subjective well-being reduces by 2.1%. The results are close to the regression results of $PM_{2.5}$.

**Table 7** Grouped regression of influences of air pollution on happiness

| Dep. Var: ln Happ | (1) Male | (2) Female | (3) Age < 30 | (4) Age [30–60] | (5) Age > 60 | (6) Urban | (7) Rural |
|---|---|---|---|---|---|---|---|
| AQI | −0.0004 (−0.64) | −0.0039*** (−3.18) | 0.0002 (0.23) | −0.0025*** (−3.02) | −0.0011 (−0.83) | −0.0023** (−1.98) | −0.0016** (−2.10) |
| N | 1536 | 1707 | 422 | 2249 | 994 | 861 | 2382 |
| $PM_{2.5}$ | −0.0005 (−0.64) | −0.0038*** (−3.03) | 0.0003 (0.23) | −0.0028*** (−2.96) | −0.0011 (−0.81) | −0.0028* (−1.90) | −0.0017** (−2.08) |
| N | 1,536 | 1,707 | 422 | 2,249 | 994 | 861 | 2,382 |

***, ** and * mean significance at the level of 1%, 5% and 10% respectively

*Note* The other controlled variables are the same as in the regression model of PM2.5. Value in the bracket is t statistic. Robust and clustered standard error are used

2. All air pollutants have significant negative influences on residents' self-evaluation of health and happiness. In another word, when the density of whatever air pollutant is higher, the residents' self-evaluation of health and happiness becomes lower.
3. The negative correlations between $O_3$, $PM_{10}$ and the dependent variables are obviously of low significance, while the correlation between the dependent variables and common pollutants such as $PM_{2.5}$, AQI, $SO_2$, etc. show high significance. This is possibly due to more attention on $PM_{2.5}$, the main indicator of smog, and $SO_2$, the main component of acid rain. It may also be attributed to people's different perception of different pollutants.

In addition, we conduct grouped regression of the samples by gender, age and location in urban or rural areas and further studied the heterogeneity of influences of air pollution on different groups. Tables 6 and 7 present the regression results of self-evaluation of health and subjective well-being, in which the AQI and $PM_{2.5}$ are used as the air pollutant indexes.

The regression results show significant heterogeneity in influences of the density of air pollutants on public health. For the male population, air pollution had a significant negative correlation with self-evaluation of health, but such negative correlation was not significant for the female population. For the samples grouped by age, we did not notice any significant negative correlation between air pollution and self-evaluation of health in groups aged below 30 and above 60. For the samples grouped by location in rural or urban areas, rural residents' self-evaluation of health was apparently subject to the influences of air pollution, but such negative correlation was not significant among the urban residents.

The influences of the density of air pollutants on public happiness also show heterogeneity. The subjective well-being of the female population had a significant negative correlation with air pollution, suggesting that their happiness is more likely to be affected by air pollution. For the samples grouped by age, we observed significant reduction in subjective well-being caused by air pollution in samples aged between 30 and 60, but we did not notice any significant correlation between air pollution and subjective well-being. For the samples grouped by location in urban or rural areas, their happiness showed a significant negative correlation with air pollution, but the regression coefficients showed that air pollution had more influences on urban residents' happiness than on rural residents' happiness.

# 5 Summary

Based on the data about respondents' subjective well-being and self-evaluation of health of the CGSS 2015, this chapter matches such data with the hourly air pollution data at the time of interview, and uses the maximum wind speed on the day of interview as an instrumental variable to conduct an in-depth study of the correlation between air pollution and the self-evaluation of health and happiness of urban and rural residents.

Results show that air pollution significantly reduces the subjective well-being and self-evaluation of health of urban and rural residents. To be specific, when AQI increases by 10 units, residents' self-evaluation of health decreases by 3.2% and subjective well-being decreases by 2.1%. When $PM_{2.5}$ density increases by 10 units ($\mu g/m^3$), residents' self-evaluation of health decreases by about 3.5% and subjective well-being decreases by 2.3%. However, the influences of different pollutants on people's subjective well-being are different. The negative correlation between common pollution indicators such as $PM_{2.5}$ density, AQI, $SO_2$ density and happiness is particularly significant. In addition, the influences of air pollution on residents' self-evaluation of health and subjective well-being varies among residents of different income levels, genders and in urban and rural areas.

This chapter uses rigorous econometric analysis to study the influences of air pollution on happiness of urban and rural residents from multiple perspectives. Air pollution not only affects people's health, but also reduces residents' happiness by affecting their subjective feelings. Based on detailed and accurate data and rigorous empirical analysis, our research enriches the existing literature on study of happiness in China and enhances people's understanding of air pollution. We also note that the Chinese government made unprecedented efforts to tackle environmental pollution in recent years. We hope that in the near future, "APEC blue" and "Parade blue" will be common in our life.

# Chapter 10
# Study of Residential Demand-Side Management

**Feng Song and Jieqi Wu**

## 1 Introduction

### *1.1 Research Background*

Residential energy consumption is an important component of terminal energy consumption in China. The terminal energy consumption in the residential sector in China was 455 million tons of coal equivalent in 2013, accounting for 11.3% of the total. At present, the residential energy consumption in China is at a lower level in the world (about half of the residential energy consumption in OECD countries), but with further urbanization and improvement of people's life, the energy demand in the residential sector will grow gradually. In the 1990s, China issued the *Energy Conversation Law of the People's Republic of China* (Energy Conservation Law), which required lower energy consumption and waste reduction during the process of energy exploitation and utilization. It also proposed that the residential terminal shall use high-efficiency electricity-consuming appliances and that measures shall be taken to manage energy efficiency labels. The Energy Conservation Law may be considered the beginning of residential demand-side management in China.

Demand-side management refers to the scheme where the government, with cooperation of the energy supplying sectors, intermediate service sectors, suppliers of energy-saving products and end users, uses effective guiding and incentive measures to improve the terminal energy consumption efficiency or energy consumption behavior to achieve the goals of energy conservation and load adjustment while satisfying the energy demand (Luo 2007). Residential demand-side management is application of such energy management concept in the residential sector.

Compared with the industrial sector, the energy consumption of residential sector accounts for a smaller proportion of the total. It is comparatively independent of

F. Song (✉) · J. Wu
Renmin University of China, Beijing, China
e-mail: songfeng@ruc.edu.cn



X. Zheng and C. Wei (eds.), *Household Energy Consumption in China: 2016 Report*, https://doi.org/10.1007/978-981-13-7523-1_10

the energy consumption system and dispersed. The development of energy-saving technologies relating to demand side of the residential sector has been slow, which hinders the implementation of residential demand-side management. However, with continuous growth in residential energy demand, the high carbon emission in the residential sector causes great pressure on energy security, economic development and ecological environment in China. In such cases, it is especially necessary to understand the characteristics of residential energy consumption and advance the demand-side management in the residential sector. In the *Several Opinions on Further Deepening Electricity System Reform* [(2015) No. 9] issued in 2015, the Chinese government emphasized the importance of demand-side management in the electricity system reform and issued supporting policies. This marks an unprecedentedly important opportunity to the reform in demand-side management in China.

In the following sections, we will introduce the relevant techniques of demand-side management in China and conduct a brief review of the studies at home and abroad. We will explore the potentials of residential demand-side management in China, review the relevant policies and measures and analyze the chances and challenges in residential demand-side management in China considering the new electricity system reform. The conclusions and projection are at the end.

## 1.2 Techniques of Residential Demand-Side Management

In the dynamical system, the power demand-side management is well developed with advanced techniques. The demand-side management mentioned in relevant literature usually refers to demand-side management in the electricity market. The general framework of power demand-side management in the residential sector is as shown in Fig. 1.

The demand-side management in the power sector consists of energy efficiency management and load management, and the latter is generally implemented through demand-side response. The objects of energy efficiency management are terminal energy-consuming products. Concerning the energy efficiency management in households, it refers to energy-saving improvement of household appliances. Household electrical appliances such as air conditioners, refrigerators/freezers, electrical rice cookers and televisions are main consumers of electricity in the residential sector. So, to encourage and guide residents to make investment in energy conversation by purchasing household appliances of higher energy efficiency is a crucial measure to promote energy conservation on the demand side. Concerning load management, the residential demand-side management in China mainly uses direct control measures like TOU pricing system, peak-load shifting or reduction and power rationing. Overall, energy efficiency management requires scientific and effective management mechanism of energy efficiency labels in the household appliance market and effective promotion of energy-saving products. The government's strict supervision and reasonable subsidies relating to the household appliance market have a significant role in this area. The system of demand-side response is more complicated, as it

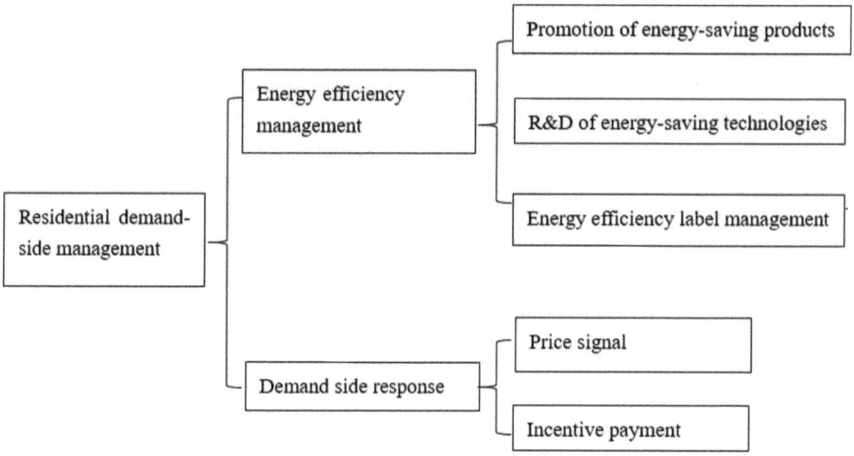


**Fig. 1** Framework of residential power demand-side management

requires not only accurate load curves from power companies and effective pricing or incentive mechanisms for automatic load reduction, but also well-developed power information transmission to guarantee the effective operation of the market. At present, China is still making attempts in both areas, especially in relation to demand-side response techniques. China did not start the peak-valley pricing system for residential electricity across the country until the end of 2015, the effect of which remains to be tested.

## *1.3 Literature Review*

Foreign studies on demand-side management mainly focus on the following points:

(1) Influences of electricity price on demand. Covino (1999) simulated the residential response to real-time electricity price using computer simulation technology and made deductions using mathematical models. Biewald and Woolf (1997) described the response mechanism between demand and price through modeling based on data of the American electric industry.
(2) Effect verification of demand-side management. Nadel and Eric (2004) summarized and analyzed the demand-side management in the United States since the 1980s, reviewed the major achievements in demand-side management in various energy-consuming sectors in the United States and made some predictions. Clark (2007) used mathematical models to study how demand-side management influences the electricity consumers and verified using empirical data of European countries and the United States.

(3) Demand-side incentive mechanisms (incentives for power companies/users). Bachrach (2003) summarized the experience in electricity reform in California and proposed that financial incentives shall be provided to utilities based on their energy-efficiency management performance. King and Cronin (1998) studied the existing performance management mechanisms based on various policy goals and user preferences and proposed that performance management goals shall be based on policies of various states. Hagler and Bailly (2000) reviewed the subsidies, loans and lower tariffs for use of energy-efficient equipment and other financial measures to stimulate the end users based on the demand-side management market in Australia.

Studies in China on demand-side management start later and the existing analyzable empirical material is limited. Yang et al. (2002) claimed that the government shall play a more active role in demand-side management and take effective measures to promote energy conservation, while using the relevant techniques of demand-side management in energy conservation practice. Duan et al. (2005) proposed that the power grid may serve as a major player in demand-side management at the current stage. Zhu and Xu (1999) claimed that instead of considering orderly use of electricity as the only focus in demand-side management, great efforts shall be made to improve energy efficiency management while optimizing resource distribution. Zhu (2005) proposed that to establish a long-standing mechanism of demand-side management, efforts shall be made in multiple aspects including electricity pricing reform, better-developed regulations, financial incentives, comprehensive planning and project financing, etc. Concerning incentives for the power grid, Zeng et al. (2003) proposed that long-term investment in demand-side management projects may be considered as investment in fixed assets the cost of which is to be gradually recovered and may gain profits as is appropriate. Ou et al. (2005) proposed that power companies are only motivated to conduct demand-side management when the profit rate of demand-side management projects is not lower than that of power supply development projects.

## 2 Analysis of Potentials in Residential Demand-Side Management in China

### 2.1 *General Characteristics of Residential Energy Demand*

(1) The energy consumption grows.

The residential sector in China is only second to the industrial sector in energy consumption. The share of residential energy consumption in the total remains 11–12%, and the absolute amount showed significant growth in recent years. The residential energy consumption in 2013 was 1.73 times more than the consumption in 2000 (Fig. 2). In the same year, the share of average household energy consumption in

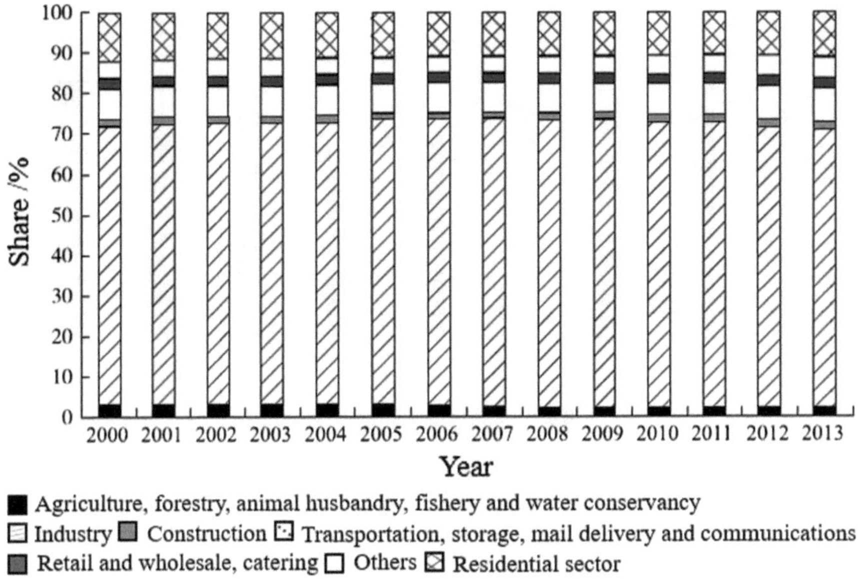


**Fig. 2** Terminal energy consumption in various sectors in China from 2000 to 2013

**Table 1** Comparison of terminal energy consumption distribution in 2013: China, OECD countries and other non-OECD countries (Unit: %)

| Terminal | OECD countries | Other non-OECD countries | China |
|---|---|---|---|
| Residential sector | 20 | 23 | 11 |
| Industrial sector | 31 | 37 | 69 |
| Transportation sector | 33 | 28 | 9 |
| Service sector | 13 | 8 | 3 |
| Others | 3 | 4 | 8 |

the total terminal energy consumption was 23% in non-OECD countries and 20% in OECD countries, but the share was only 11% in China, about half of the share in OECD countries (Table 1). Considering the stages in social development and industrial upgrading, with intensive development and high-efficiency in the industrial sector and industrial restructuring in China, the share of industrial energy consumption in the total will decrease, while the energy consumption in the service and residential sectors will account for larger percentages.

(2) Gap between urban and rural areas is narrowed.

Due to long-standing differences between urban and rural areas in China, the overall energy consumption of urban residents is higher than that of rural residents. With

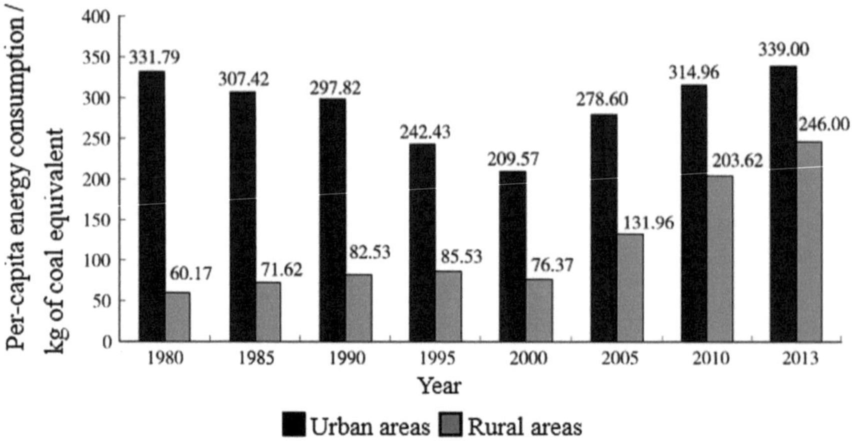


**Fig. 3** A comparison of energy consumption per capita between urban and rural residents in China from 1980 to 2014

development of the rural economy, the per-capita energy consumption in rural areas has been growing significantly, while the urban energy consumption of urban residents has fluctuations. Therefore, the gap between urban and rural areas are narrowing in general. In 2013, the ratio of per-capita energy consumption in urban and rural areas was 5:3, while the per-capita energy consumption in rural areas accounted for about 18% of the per-capita energy consumption of urban residents in 1980 (Fig. 3).

(3) Electricity consumption grows obviously.

With rapid development of household appliances and continuous increase in per-capita income, there are more and more types of electrical appliances in households. The durable goods ownership per household increases, and electricity accounts for an increasingly larger share in residential energy consumption. Electricity consumption accounted for 18.9% of the total residential energy consumption in 2013, up by 8.2% from the level of 2000 (Fig. 4). The residential electricity consumption in China amounted to 692,800 GWh in 2014, which is 23.18 times more than the consumption in 1990 and 3.14 times more than the consumption in 2000. The share of residential electricity consumption on the total electricity consumption has generally been on the rise, despite certain fluctuations after 2000, and maintained at about 12% in recent years (Fig. 5). The increase in electricity demand leads to significant increase in residential energy consumption. Electricity conservation and optimization of residents' electricity-consuming behavior are focuses in residential demand-side management in various countries. This chapter analyzes the potential of residential demand-side management in China from the perspectives of energy efficiency management and electricity price management.

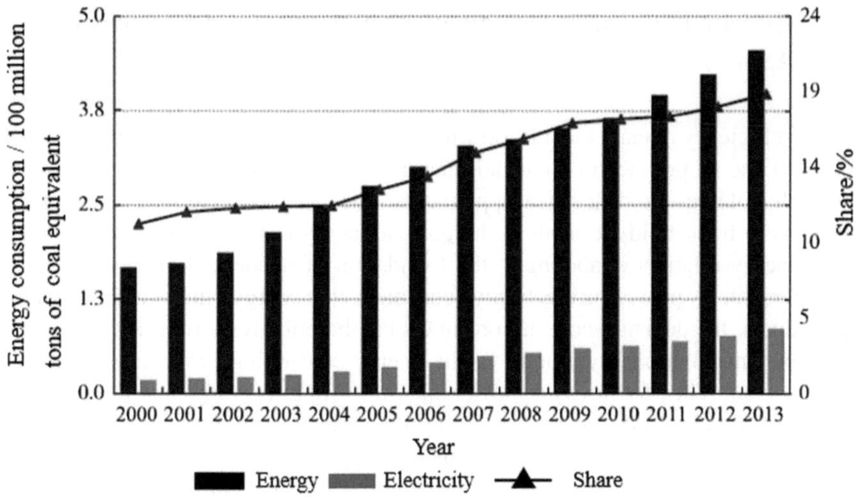


**Fig. 4** Residential electricity consumption and total energy consumption and share of the former in the latter in China from 2000 to 2013

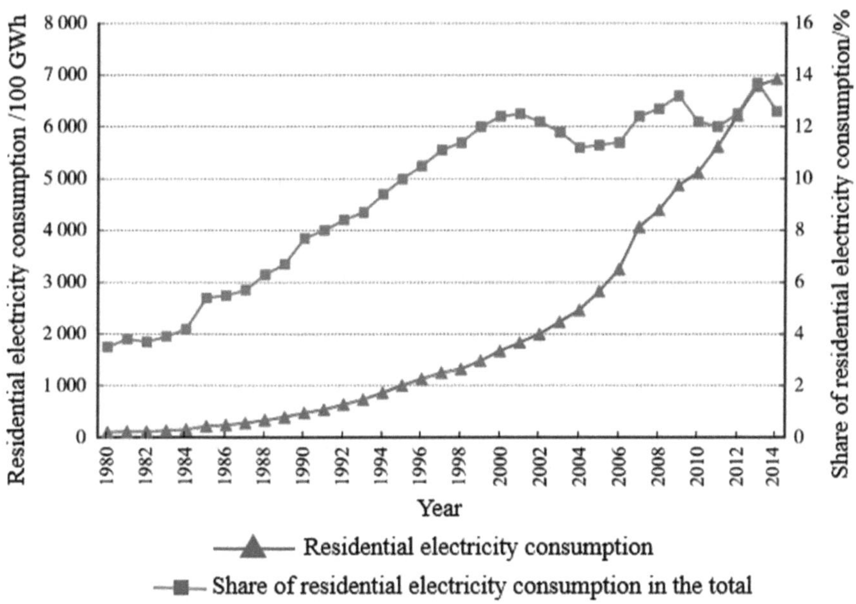


**Fig. 5** Residential electricity consumption and its share in the total electricity consumption in China from 1980 to 2014

## 2.2 Energy Efficiency Management of Household Electrical Appliances

Energy efficiency management is a key measure of demand-side management, which refers to use of policies or financial measures based on purchasing behavior and ownership of household electrical appliances to encourage purchase of energy-saving products in households to achieve the goal of energy conservation on the demand side. Energy efficiency labeling is the foundation of residential energy efficiency management. By providing electricity consumers with energy efficiency information of products, the decision cost of consumers can be effectively reduced, which can eliminate information asymmetry in the energy-consuming products market to a certain extent. The *Measures for the Administration of Energy Efficiency Labels* took effect in China in 2005 determined uniformly applicable product energy efficiency standards, implementation rules, specimen and specifications of energy efficiency labels for widely used products with great potential in energy conservation. It covered 33 types of products including multiple household appliances. This chapter analyzes the energy efficiency labeling and usage of residential durable goods based on the survey results of the CRECS 2014 and further explores the energy conservation potentials of Chinese households in energy efficiency management.

The household electrical appliances with energy efficiency labels covered in the CRECS 2014 were mainly refrigerators, washing machines, water heaters and air conditioners, the energy efficiency distribution of which is as shown in Figs. 6 and 7. In both urban and rural households, a considerable proportion of household electrical appliances did not have any energy efficiency label. Over half of the washing machines and water heaters did not have energy efficiency labels. Among the appliances with energy efficiency labels, refrigerators of Grade-1 energy efficiency had the largest share of 34.7% in urban households, and the share in rural households was 50%. The share of the other three types of appliances of Grade-1 energy efficiency was around 20% respectively.

Statistical results show that even with measures for administration of energy efficiency labels, a considerable proportion of household electrical appliances did not follow the regulation to mark their energy efficiency grades. Meanwhile, products of high energy efficiency accounted for a small proportion of the total, suggesting that the promotion of energy-saving products did not achieve the desired effect. On one hand, this is because the energy efficiency labeling mechanism in China is still at an early stage. Without well-developed corresponding regulations and laws, it does not have much binding effect on enterprises. The corresponding supervision system is not complete, either. On the other hand, considering from the perspectives of ethology and economics, this phenomenon reflects consumers' inattention on energy efficiency of products, which is referred to as "rational inattention" by some researchers (Levy 2005; Sallee et al. 2016). While making purchase decisions, if a certain characteristic of a product has minor influences on the overall cost or if high cost is involved to understand such information, consumers tend to ignore such cost.

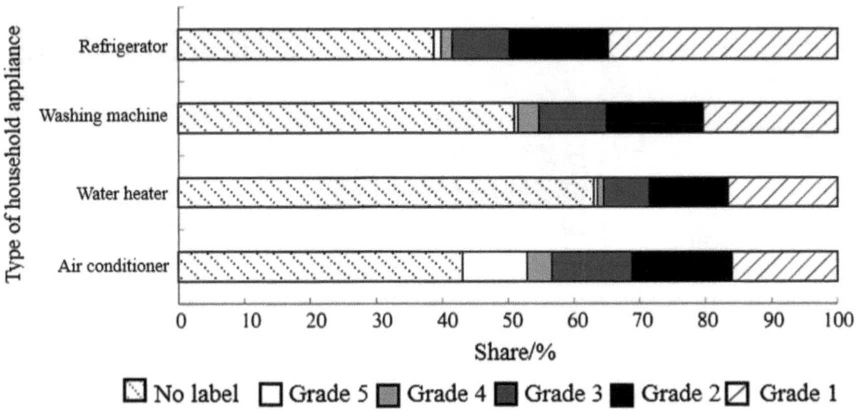


**Fig. 6** Energy efficiency distribution of household electrical appliances in urban areas in China in 2014

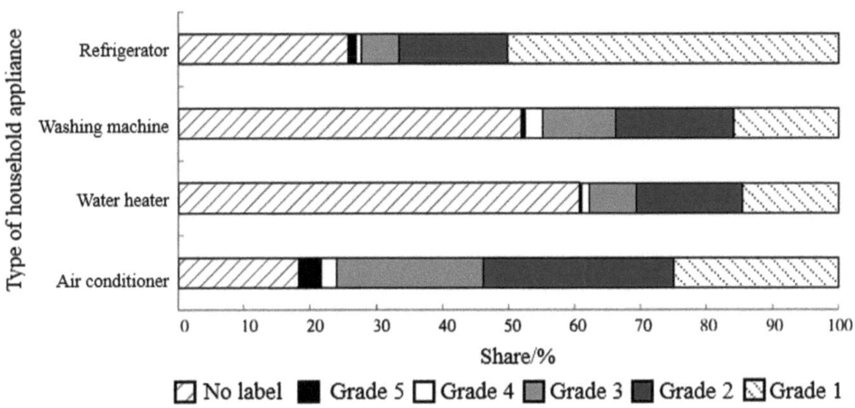


**Fig. 7** Energy efficiency distribution of household electrical appliances in rural areas in China in 2014

The energy consumption level of products contained in energy efficiency labels has direct influences on whether consumers have "rational inattention". As shown in Fig. 8, energy efficiency labels in China contain only simple information about product's energy efficiency grade and electricity consumption per day. In Australia, energy efficiency labels contain not only product's energy efficiency grade, but also its annual electricity consumption in a certain standard context. In addition to such information, energy efficiency labels in the United States contain operating cost based on electricity price and the maximum and minimum electricity consumption per year in different conditions. By comparison, energy efficiency labels in the United States contain more indexes and enable consumers to compare different products. When energy consumption is expressed in the form of specific expenditure, the

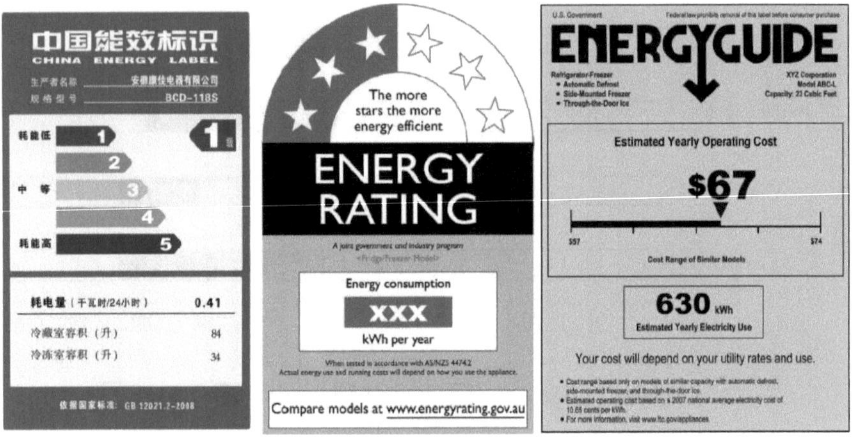


**Fig. 8** Energy efficiency labels in China, Australia and the United States

decision-making cost of consumers in selection of energy-consuming products is further reduced.

To analyze the energy-saving effects and economic influences of products of various energy efficiency grades in a visual manner, this chapter studies the differences in annual electricity consumption and electricity expenditure between products of the same type but of different energy efficiency grades, using the refrigerators of a model of a Chinese brand as examples. The results are as shown in Table 2. Under the same conditions, the electricity consumption of the refrigerators of the lowest energy efficiency was 80% higher than that of the highest efficiency. Supposing that the refrigerator is in service every day throughout a year, the electricity expenditure incurred by a refrigerator of Grade-1 energy efficiency is RMB69.9 lower than the same model of Grade-5 energy efficiency and RMB17.5 lower than the same model of Grade-2 energy efficiency. Supposing that a refrigerator is in service for 6 months in a year, the maximum electricity cost saved is RMB34.4 if the refrigerator is of Grade-1 energy efficiency.

Following the principle of minimum cost, in rational choice of energy-saving products, consumers need to know the energy cost. For products with larger baseline energy consumption and higher use frequency, consumers tend to buy those of better energy efficiency. Improvement of energy efficiency labels is helpful to eliminate information asymmetry concerning energy cost in the market of household electrical appliances. Combined with reasonable pricing of products and energy sources, it can effectively promote the use of energy-saving products in households and help achieve the goal of energy conservation on the demand side.

Tables 3, 4, 5, 6, 7 and 8 show electricity consumption distribution of different types of household electrical appliances of various energy efficiency grades. Depending on the baseline electricity consumption and use frequency, theoretically, the replacement of lowest-energy-efficiency appliance with a highest-energy-efficiency

**Table 2** Annual electricity consumption and electricity expenditure of double-door refrigerators of different energy efficiency grades

| 186 L Double-door refrigerators | | | | | | | | | | |
|---|---|---|---|---|---|---|---|---|---|---|
| Baseline electricity consumption (kWh) | 0.98 | | | | | | | | | |
| Energy efficiency grade | 1 | | 2 | | 3 | | 4 | | 5 | |
| Corresponding index | 0.5 | | 0.6 | | 0.7 | | 0.8 | | 0.9 | |
| Daily consumption(kWh/day) | 0.5 | | 0.6 | | 0.7 | | 0.8 | | 0.9 | |
| Days of effective service (day) | 180.0 | 365.0 | 180.0 | 365.0 | 180.0 | 365.0 | 180.0 | 365.0 | 180.0 | 365.0 |
| Annual consumption (kWh/year) | 88.2 | 178.9 | 105.8 | 214.6 | 123.5 | 250.4 | 141.1 | 286.2 | 158.8 | 321.9 |
| Electricity price (RMB/kWh) | 0.5 | | | | | | | | | |
| Electricity cost (RMB/year) | 43.1 | 87.3 | 51.7 | 104.8 | 60.3 | 122.3 | 68.9 | 139.7 | 77.5 | 157.2 |

**Table 3** Annual electricity consumption of triple-door refrigerators of various energy efficiency grades

| 216 L Triple-door refrigerators | | | | | | | | | | |
|---|---|---|---|---|---|---|---|---|---|---|
| Baseline electricity consumption (kWh) | 1.12 | | | | | | | | | |
| Energy efficiency grade | 1 | | 2 | | 3 | | 4 | | 5 | |
| Corresponding index | 0.5 | | 0.6 | | 0.7 | | 0.8 | | 0.9 | |
| Annual consumption (kWh/day) | 0.56 | | 0.672 | | 0.784 | | 0.896 | | 1.008 | |
| Days of effective service (day) | 180 | 365 | 180 | 365 | 180 | 365 | 180 | 365 | 180 | 365 |
| Annual consumption (kWh/year) | 100.80 | 204.4 | 120.96 | 245.28 | 141.12 | 286.16 | 161.28 | 327.04 | 181.44 | 367.92 |

**Table 4** Annual electricity consumption of wall-mounted air conditioners of various energy efficiency grades

| 1.5 hp Wall-mounted air conditioners | | | | | | |
|---|---|---|---|---|---|---|
| hp | 1.5 | | | | | |
| Corresponding refrigerating capacity (w) | 3500 | | | | | |
| Energy efficiency grade | 1 | | 2 | | 3 | |
| Corresponding energy efficiency ratio | 3.6 | | 3.4 | | 3.2 | |
| Refrigeration power (w) | 972.22 | | 1029.41 | | 1093.75 | |
| Variable frequency/Fixed frequency | Variable frequency | Fixed frequency | Variable frequency | Fixed frequency | Variable frequency | Fixed frequency |
| Adjustment coefficient of fixed and variable frequencies | 0.7 | 1 | 0.7 | 1 | 0.7 | 1 |
| Number of hours in service (h/day) | 8 | | | | | |
| Number of days in service (day/year) | 40 | | | | | |
| Annual electricity consumption (kWh/year) | 217.78 | 311.11 | 230.59 | 329.41 | 245.00 | 350.00 |

one leads to an annual reduction of 10.300 kWh in electricity consumption. Considering the extensive use of low-efficiency household electrical appliances in Chinese households as revealed in the CRECS, there is a very large space for improvement of residential energy efficiency management in China.

### 2.3 *Management of Electric Load and Residential Electricity Price*

Besides energy efficiency management, an important measure of demand-side management is to optimize residents' electricity consumption behavior through scien-

**Table 5** Annual electricity consumption of floor standing air conditioners of various energy efficiency grades

| 1.5 hp Floor standing air conditioners | | | | | | |
|---|---|---|---|---|---|---|
| hp | 2 | | | | | |
| Corresponding refrigerating capacity (w) | 5250 | | | | | |
| Energy efficiency grade | 1 | | 2 | | 3 | |
| Corresponding energy efficiency ratio | 3.6 | | 3.4 | | 3.2 | |
| Refrigeration power (w) | 1,458.33 | | 1,544.12 | | 1640.63 | |
| Variable frequency/Fixed frequency | Variable frequency | Fixed frequency | Variable frequency | Fixed frequency | Variable frequency | Fixed frequency |
| Adjustment coefficient of fixed and variable frequencies | 0.7 | 1 | 0.7 | 1 | 0.7 | 1 |
| Number of hours in service (h/day) | 8 | | | | | |
| Number of days in service (day/year) | 40 | | | | | |
| Annual electricity consumption (kWh/year) | 326.67 | 466.67 | 345.88 | 494.12 | 367.50 | 525.00 |

tifically arranged electricity price, which can improve the electricity consumption efficiency, thus alleviating the tension in electricity supply and demand during peak hours and reducing the load of the power grid.

As residential electricity consumption is closely related with residents' daily routine and the temperature, residential electrical load shows apparent peaks and valleys and varies in seasons. According to the survey results of the CRECS, the residential electricity consumption per household in China had two peaks in summer and winter in 2012, with the maximum load in August when the temperature was the highest, but in spring and autumn, there was obvious decline in residential electric load (Fig. 9). Considering from the perspective of residents' electricity consumption behavior, the main end uses of residential electricity consumption are cooking, daily life, lighting, space heating and air conditioning, entertainment and work, etc. The influences of

**Table 6** Annual electricity consumption of electrical water heaters of various energy efficiency grades

| 60 L Electrical water heaters | | | | | | | | | | |
|---|---|---|---|---|---|---|---|---|---|---|
| Energy efficiency grade | 1 | | 2 | | 3 | | 4 | | 5 | |
| 24 hours Intrinsic energy consumption coefficient | 0.6 | | 0.7 | | 0.8 | | 0.9 | | 1 | |
| Hot water output rate (%) | ≥70 | | ≥60 | | ≥55 | | ≥55 | | ≥50 | |
| National standard | 1.7 | | | | | | | | | |
| Daily electricity consumption (kWh/day) | 1.02 | | 1.19 | | 1.36 | | 1.53 | | 1.7 | |
| Days of effective service (day) | 180 | 365 | 180 | 365 | 180 | 365 | 180 | 365 | 180 | 365 |
| Annual consumption (kWh/year) | 183.60 | 372.30 | 214.20 | 434.35 | 244.80 | 496.40 | 275.40 | 558.45 | 306.00 | 620.50 |

**Table 7** Annual electricity consumption of front-load washing machines of various energy efficiency grades

| Front-load washing machines | | | | | | | | | | |
|---|---|---|---|---|---|---|---|---|---|---|
| Energy efficiency grade | 1 | | 2 | | 3 | | 4 | | 5 | |
| Electricity consumption per load (kWh/kg) | 0.11 | | 0.13 | | 0.15 | | 0.17 | | 0.19 | |
| Capacity (kg) | 5 | | | | | | | | | |
| Frequency of use (time/year) | 180 | 365 | 180 | 365 | 180 | 365 | 180 | 365 | 180 | 365 |
| Annual consumption (kWh/year) | 99.00 | 200.75 | 117.00 | 237.25 | 135.00 | 273.75 | 153.00 | 310.25 | 171.00 | 346.75 |

**Table 8** Annual electricity consumption of top-load washing machines of various energy efficiency grades

| Top-load washing machines | | | | | | | | | | |
|---|---|---|---|---|---|---|---|---|---|---|
| Energy efficiency grade | 1 | | 2 | | 3 | | 4 | | 5 | |
| Electricity consumption per load (kWh/kg) | 0.011 | | 0.012 | | 0.015 | | 0.017 | | 0.022 | |
| Capacity (kg) | 5 | | | | | | | | | |
| Frequency of use (time/year) | 180 | 365 | 180 | 365 | 180 | 365 | 180 | 365 | 180 | 365 |
| Annual consumption (kWh/year) | 9.90 | 20.08 | 10.80 | 21.90 | 13.50 | 27.38 | 15.30 | 31.03 | 19.80 | 40.15 |

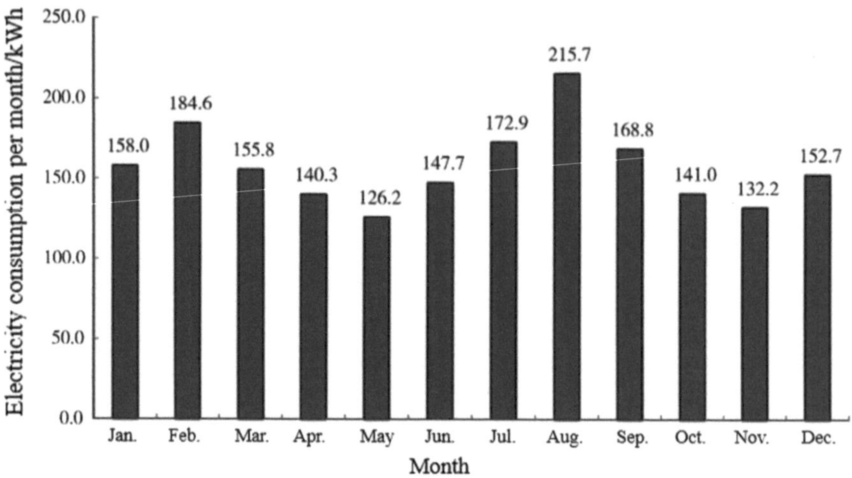


**Fig. 9** Distribution of monthly residential electricity consumption in China in 2012

refrigerators and storage water heaters on daily and seasonal load are stable, and they may operate during off-peak hours. Other home appliances (excluding air conditioners) have certain influences on the daily load curve, but have minor influences on the seasonal load.

As shown in Fig. 10, air conditioner ranks the first in household electrical appliances in terms of average power, and its average power is far higher than other appliances. Usage of air conditioners varies with the temperature, and it is the main contributor of peak load in summer and winter. Generally, when the indoor temperature is above 26 °C in July and August or below 12 °C in January and February, the frequency of residential use of air conditioners goes up, leading to peak load. Due to the characteristics of the power of air conditioners and the stable frequency of use of other appliances, in hot or cold days, usage of air conditioners has a decisive role in the peak load of residential electricity consumption [During peak hours, the cooling load may account for 40% of the total and the heating load may account for about 20% of the total (Hu et al. 1998)].

As shown in Fig. 11, during the period from 2000 to 2012, the air conditioner ownership per household had varying growth rates in urban and rural areas, and the growth was especially rapid in urban households. Due to strong similarity in seasons and periods of using air conditioners among households in a region, the increase in air conditioner ownership means heavier load on the regional grid during peak hours of electricity use. The government may optimize the electricity load curve from the demand side through pricing measures, which can reduce the residents' electricity expenditure and the supplier's investment in power plants and primary energy. It is a multi-win solution for residents, power companies and the society in terms of economic development and environmental protection.

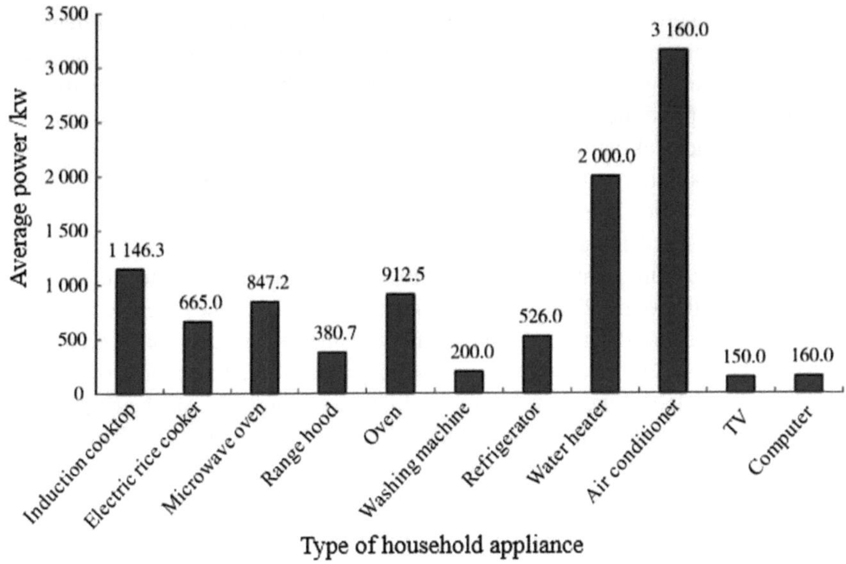


**Fig. 10** Distribution of average power of household appliances in China in 2012

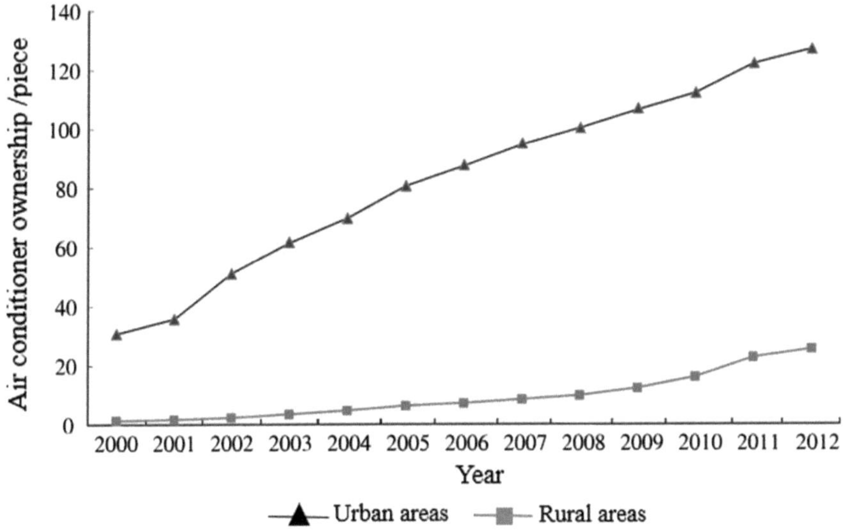


**Fig. 11** Variation in air conditioner ownership per 100 households in urban and rural areas in China

At present, there are two main residential electricity pricing policies for demand-side management, namely tiered pricing and peak-valley TOU pricing. In the tiered electricity pricing system, electricity prices are tiered based on the electricity consumed and the price increases to a higher level with the increase in electricity consumption. In the peak-valley TOU electricity pricing, each day is divided to several sections of peak hours and valley hours with varying prices: high during peak hours and low during valley hours.

The CRECS 2014 contained a survey about residents' knowledge of the two electricity pricing systems. Statistical results show that 38% of the respondents knew the peak-valley TOU policy, 27% knew such policy in the region they were located, and 13% had received notifications from power companies about such policy. Compared with peak-valley TOU electricity pricing policy, residents had a better knowledge of tiered pricing. 41% of the samples adopted tiered pricing. 57% of the respondents heard of tiered pricing, 48% had knowledge about such policy, and 27% had received notifications from power companies about such policy. There are potentials in China to further promote and optimize the tiered electricity pricing and peak-valley TOU electricity pricing. Considering the achievements of developed countries during the recent decades through peak-load shifting, we expect that promotion of residential electricity price management in China will lead to considerable economic and social benefits.

## 3 Status-Quo of Residential Demand-Side Management in China

Since the relevant concept was introduced to China in the 1990s, researchers and policy makers have been pressing forward with demand-side management in study of theories and practice. The potentials of demand-side management in energy conservation, distribution optimization and pollution reduction are gradually untapped. In view of the proportions of terminal energy consumption of various sectors in the total, the industrial sector has long been the focus in demand-side management in China and played a vital role in demand-side energy conservation and peak-load regulating. Multiple techniques are used for demand-side management in the industrial sector, including installation of load controller and energy storage devices, application of energy-efficient production lines, promotion of alternative energy and use of high-efficiency insulation technologies and thermal insulation materials. In the residential sector, the main techniques are household appliance energy efficiency management and electricity pricing management. For comprehensive analysis of the status-quo of residential demand-side management in China, this section will review the relevant policies and corresponding measures in China for residential demand-side management.

## 3.1 Policy Framework

The *Energy Conservation Law* in China was issued in 1997, which required that the energy-consuming process shall be better managed to reduce loss and waste. A series of energy-saving measures were taken from the perspectives of technologies, equipment and promotion. The energy efficiency labeling policy was adopted for household appliances, and relevant catalogues and energy efficiency standards were issued based on practical application and technical standards. According to the *Measures for Administration of Electricity Conservation* issued in 2000, for electricity load control, focus shall be on another key measure of demand-side management, i.e., electricity pricing. It required that the peak-valley TOU pricing shall be optimized and promoted. The *Guiding Opinions on Strengthening the Electrical Power Demand-Side Management* issued in 2004 contained a comprehensive list of relevant measures for demand-side management, specifying the entities responsible for promotion, supervision and implementation of the policies and requiring that the electricity power saved by demand-side management shall be included in regional planning, thus determining the position of such measure in regional policies. The *Measures for the Electricity Demand-Side Management* issued in 2010 improved the existing measures, and further collected and analyzed energy consumption data to provide users with targeted energy service. It also learned from the international experience and encouraged third-party organizations to verify the amounts of conserved electricity, involving more parties in the demand-side management (Table 9). The continuous optimization and development of smart grids allows for delicacy demand-side management. According to the *12th Five-year Plan for Energy Development* in China, further efforts shall be made to advance the construction of smart grids and formulation of corresponding pricing policies, and pilot projects of demand-side management shall be conducted in several cities. In the new electricity system reform started in 2015, in addition to relaxing regulations on power retailing, power retailing companies are encouraged to provide users with comprehensive, differentiated energy conservation services. The Plan proposes the concept of demand-side response and users in pilot cities are encouraged to participate in peak regulation. Users will have access to real-time electricity consumption data and other technical support. It also provides financial support to demand-side management projects.

## 3.2 Residential Demand-Side Management Measures

Within the existing policy framework (Table 9), currently, the main types of measures for residential demand-side management include economic, administrative, technical and incentive ones, covering the following specific measures (Table 10).

Different types of demand-side management measures are closely related. The implementation of all such measures is dependent on technological progress, while technological development requires the support of corresponding financial incentive

**Table 9** Documents about residential demand-side management and relevant content

| Year of taking effect | Document | Relevant content |
|---|---|---|
| 1997 | Energy Conversation Law of the People's Republic of China (amended in 2007) | • The state supports the development and promotion of energy conversation technologies by tax preferences, energy conservation subsidies and other financial measures;<br>• The state makes efforts to publicize the importance of energy conservation;<br>• Energy efficiency labeling is adopted for widely used and highly energy-consuming products;<br>• A certification system is established for energy-saving products |
| 2000 | Measures for Administration of Electricity Conservation | • Set a maximum power consumption per unit product for highly power-consuming products;<br>• Electrical power during off-peak hours may be effectively utilized by intermittent load and direct load control of terminal users;<br>• Expand the use of two-part power pricing system;<br>• Accelerate the promotion of peak-valley TOU electricity pricing and varying electricity rates in abundant water period and drought period |
| 2004 | Guiding Opinions on Strengthening the Electrical Power Demand-Side Management | • The government takes charge of leading and promoting the power demand-side management, electricity regulatory authorities enforces effective regulation, electric grid operators are the main implementors and large electricity consumers are major participants;<br>• Electrical power saved through demand-side management is included in regional energy sources and economic development planning as a type of resource;<br>• Direct users to use electricity in a rational way through financial incentive measures;<br>• Strongly promote technical measures for energy storage;<br>• In the case of short supply of electric power, implement peak load shifting schemes;<br>• Economic subsidies and preferential loan policies for energy conservation technologies;<br>• Promote energy efficiency standards of energy-consuming equipment and energy-saving design standards of buildings |
| 2010 | Measures for the Electricity Demand-Side Management | • Promote and improve the peak-valley TOU pricing, encourage off-peak energy storage;<br>• In regions where conditions permit, implement seasonal power pricing, high-reliability power pricing and intermittent load power pricing;<br>• Power-grid enterprises shall strengthen the collection and analysis of information on users' electricity consumption, and provide technical support for users of demand-side management;<br>• Power-grid enterprises are encouraged to use energy-saving power transformers, rationally lower the radius of power supply, enhance reactive power management and steadily reduce the transmission line loss-rate;<br>• Encourage third-party organizations to verify the amounts of conserved electricity |

(continued)

**Table 9** (continued)

| Year of taking effect | Document | Relevant content |
|---|---|---|
| 2012 | Interim Measures for Management over Funds of the Central Government Finance for Cities with Pilot Programs of Electrical Power Demand-Side Management | Finance is provided to the following demand-side management work:<br>• Management platform of electrical power service;<br>• Efficiency power plant;<br>• Peak-load shifting technologies;<br>• Relevant scientific studies, promotion and training, review and assessment |
| 2013 | 12th five-year plan for energy development | • Press ahead with construction of smart grids and implementation of corresponding electricity pricing;<br>• Conduct comprehensive pilot programs of demand-side management in cities;<br>• Expand public procurement of energy-saving products and implement projects of energy-saving products to benefit the people |
| 2015 | Several Opinions on Further Deepening Electricity System Reform | • Use modern information technology to develop electrical power service and implement demand-side response;<br>• Encourage power transaction enterprises to develop innovative services and provide users with value-added services including energy performance contracting, comprehensive energy conservation and energy consumption consulting, etc.<br>• Eliminate restrictions on the user-side distributed power sources |
| | Notice of the National Development and Reform Commission and the Ministry of Finance on Comprehensive Pilot Programs in Cities concerning Improving Power Emergency Mechanism and Electrical Power Demand-Side Management | • Press ahead with 4 pilot programs of demand-side management and 1 pilot program of demand-side response;<br>• Improve peak electricity pricing or seasonal electricity pricing, encouraging users to reduce peak load;<br>• Encourage and support electrical power service industry;<br>• Monitor the electricity consumption of users and join the same in the national platform (Users connected with the national platform and voluntarily participating in demand-side response are in principle not subject to power rationing) |

**Table 10** Residential demand-side management measures

| Type | | Measure | Content |
|---|---|---|---|
| Economic measures | Pricing policy | Tiered electricity pricing | Electricity consumption is graded into several tiers and the electricity price increases in tiers, encouraging residents to save energy in a rational scope |
| | | Peak-valley TOU electricity pricing | A price discrimination strategy based on time of use. Electricity price is high during peak hours and low during off-peak hours, encouraging residents to use electricity during off-peak hours and enabling balance in electricity supply and demand |
| | Financial policy | Subsidies for energy-saving household appliances | Provided subsidies to residents for purchasing high-efficiency home appliances. Residents receive subsidies while purchasing air conditioners, FPD televisions, refrigerators, washing machines and water heaters of Grade-2 and Grade-1 energy efficiency (This measure is valid till June 2013) |
| | | Subsidies for energy conservation technologies | Provide subsidies to enterprises manufacturing energy-saving products |
| | | Tax preference for organizations engaged in development of energy conservation technologies | Provide tax reference for organizations engaged in development of energy conservation technologies |
| Administrative measures | | Administration of energy efficiency labels | The products are graded in different energy efficiency grades based on energy-saving performance and the energy efficiency information is attached to products on labels |

(continued)

**Table 10** (continued)

| Type | Measure | Content |
|---|---|---|
| | Compulsory elimination of highly energy-consuming household appliances | Highly energy-consuming products are eliminated in accordance with the maximum energy consumption standard |
| Technological measures | Energy conservation technologies of household appliances | Promote and encourage the development of high-efficiency home appliances |
| | Building energy conservation technologies | Optimize the insulation and lighting performance, etc. of buildings to reduce energy consumption of space heating and lamps |
| | Alternative energy technologies | Develop alternative energy sources, e.g., design high-efficiency solar water heaters, etc. |
| | Smart grid technologies | Promote the smart grid technologies and realize two-way flow of electricity consumption at each node |
| Incentive measures | Publicity of energy conservation knowledge | Publicize knowledge about energy conservation in communities, directing residents to save energy |
| | Information disclosure | Disclose information about residential energy consumption and energy efficiency of products, reducing information asymmetry and directing residents to be more rational in decision-making concerning energy consumption |

**Table 11** Obstacles in residential demand-side management

| Type | Obstacle | Description of obstacle |
|---|---|---|
| System | Energy efficiency regulation | At present, the energy efficiency regulations of energy-saving products in China are not well developed, and there are misstatements of energy efficiency or energy-consuming goods without energy efficiency labels in the market |
| | Electricity price regulation | The residential electricity price in China is under control and the electricity price cannot reflect the cost in an accurate manner |
| Market mal-function | Cross subsidization | Cross subsidies to residential electricity price from the industrial and commercial sectors result in price distortion |
| | Information asymmetry | There is severe information asymmetry in the electricity market. The residents have difficulties having real-time knowledge of electricity cost, which negatively affects their decision to minimize the cost |
| | Negative externality | The retail price of electricity cannot accurately reflect the negative external cost of power generation |
| Market barriers | Energy conservation subsidies | The residential electricity price is low while the cost to purchase high-efficiency electricity-consuming appliances is high, so, the residents need enough subsidies to purchase energy-saving appliances |
| | Opportunity cost | The residents need to make considerable efforts to obtain a complete understanding of a product's energy consumption information and its implicit cost |
| Behavior choice | Rational inattention | If great effort is required to fully understand the energy consumption cost of a product or if the energy consumption cost accounts for a tiny proportion of the total cost of decision making, consumers may choose to rationally ignore such cost |
| | Energy conservation awareness | The energy conservation awareness of Chinese households shall be further improved |

measures. Meanwhile, the residential energy-saving demand released through economic, administrative and incentive measures may also promote the development of technologies. In fact, residential demand-management has been in constant development through use of multiple measures, while assisted by reasonable policies and regulations. Though China has started the residential demand-side management, it is worth mentioning that it still faces many obstacles in this area at the current stage. There is a wide gap between China and the developed countries in demand-side management in terms of the system, market structure, technologies and awareness. The existing obstacles in residential demand-side management in China are listed as follows in Table 11. In Sect. 4 of this chapter, we will, in view of the new electricity system reform, analyze the chances and challenges in the residential demand-side management in China.

# 4 Chances and Challenges in Residential Demand-Side Management in the Context of the New Electricity System Reform

Further promotion of demand-side management is one of the core tasks in the new electricity system reform. The *Several Opinions on Further Deepening Electricity System Reform* [(2015) No. 9] issued in 2015 highlighted the importance of demand-side management in maintaining supply-demand balance and facilitating energy conservation and emission reduction. In the Opinions, demand-side management was included in the five basic principles, and supporting policies about demand-side management were also issued. The said Opinions proposed three key measures, "utilization of modern information technology", "development of electrical power service" and "implementation of demand-side response", providing guidance for future reform of demand-side management from the perspectives of electrical technologies, market structure and market concepts. We expect that the new electricity system reform will help advance the reform of demand-side management to a new level. This section focuses on the articles about residential demand-side management in the *Several Opinions on Further Deepening Electricity System Reform* [(2015) No. 9] and the supporting policies to explore the chances and challenges in the process of advancing residential demand-side management in China.

## *4.1 Chances*

(1) Perfection of electrical and information technologies

Information asymmetry in the electricity market has been a major barrier to the implementation of residential demand-side management. Both energy efficiency management and electricity price management are based on the "rationality" of consumers, which affects the consumers' cost function and subsequently their electricity consumption behavior. In the case of major information asymmetry in the market, consumers tend to make "irrational" decisions, resulting in the so-called "market malfunction". The *Several Opinions on Further Deepening Electricity System* Reform [(2015) No. 9] proposed to fully develop and apply electrical and information technologies, and one of the focuses is to provide consumers with technical support to enable consumers' reasonable management of the electricity cost.

One of the objectives of smart grid development is "smart interaction". Based on two-way flow of information and electrical power, users may have real-time access to electricity consumption information and cut down the electricity cost by optimizing their electricity consumption behavior. The State Grid Corporation of China announced the smart grid development plan for the first time in 2009. During the 12th Five-Year Plan period, China built pilot smart grids in several cities, and continuously improved the electrical and information technologies through development of intelligent buildings, communities and parks, etc.

Smart grid technology is more mature in developed countries such as European countries and the United States than in China, and the residential demand-side management based on such technology has advanced significantly in these countries. The Ontario Energy Board conducted an empirical study of residential smart power consumption from 2006 to 2007, supported by several organizations, which proved that smart power consumption and TOU pricing significantly improved the users' cost control: the power consumption of users during the summer peak period was down by 25% on average. In the energy feedback carried out by the British government in 2007, by using smart meters and communication technologies for feedback on energy consumption to users, without any compensation mechanism or price incentive, the total energy consumption was down by 2.3% in one year, and the peak load was significantly shifted.

Considering the continuous development of electrical and information technologies, China can learn from the developed countries in terms of regulations, technologies and application and develop channels for interaction between residents and power grids relating to energy consumption to further implement the demand-side management.

(2) Diversification of electrical power services

The core of the new electricity system reform is to build an effective electricity market. Restrictions on electricity distribution and retailing will be lifted in sequence to involve more parties and increase competition in the market, so that the electricity price can reflect the cost of power generation. To this end, the government encourages "qualified social capital, energy conservation service enterprises, power generation enterprises, etc." to engage in electricity retailing and establish independent electricity retailing companies. In another word, in the future market of electricity retailing, the monopoly of a single power grid will be replaced by competition between multiple entities. To gain more competitive advantages, electricity retailing companies are motivated to provide differentiated services to power users. Since the power itself is homogeneous, the electricity retailing companies are more likely to foster innovation on trading methods and energy conservation services. With the electricity retailing companies providing energy conservation consulting and plans, the feasibility of energy conservation and off-peak power consumption on the residential demand-side will be significantly enhanced.

The practice of power companies in Japan may be helpful in providing energy conservation services to residents. Although electricity retailing in Japan is monopolized in regions, due to national strategies, the power companies are still motivated to provide energy conservation services to residents. In addition to the traditional tiered electricity pricing, the power companies in Japan offers a variety of power billing packages depending on residents' preferences. For example, the time-of-use electricity pricing package of Tokyo Electric Power Company allows the households to pay a fixed monthly fee to consume electricity at a lower rate (about half of the price during daytime) during valley hours (23:00 to 7:00 the next day). This billing system is well received, not only because it reduces residents' electricity cost, but also because it encourages residents to consume power during off-peak hours while the power company's upfront investment is also recovered through the fixed payment.

With more entities engaged in electricity retailing and diversification of electrical power services, the Chinese residents will have more options in power consumption, and the potentials of residential demand-side management will be better utilized.

(3) Demand-side response

As one of the instruments for demand-side management, demand-side response refers to the scheme where power suppliers use higher electricity price or other compensation, which is delivered to the power users through effective conduction mechanisms, to change the users' power consumption behavior and reduce or shift the electric load. The government's choice of instruments for demand-side response depends on the role of market forces in the electricity market. If the electricity market is well developed, real-time electricity pricing can dynamically reflect the cost of power generation, and there is good information exchange between the power suppliers and demanders, then the demand-side response can be realized through price signals. If the electricity market is not fully developed, the demand-side response requires the government or the power grid company to implement incentive payments or even administrative control.

Considering the unique characteristics of residential electricity consumption, to implement demand-side response in the residential sector, the following basic factors shall be available: 1. Professional load integrators. Since residents as power users are small in scale and dispersed, power companies bear high cost to provide electrical power services for residents. Via load integrators, small users are integrated as groups to participate in the demand-side response. Load integrators also provide relevant power management services. It not only reduces the cost, but also enhances the household's capacity to participate in the demand-side response. 2. Electrical and information technologies. Good information exchange between the suppliers and demanders makes it possible for the demand side to dynamically optimize its electricity consumption behavior based on incentives or price signals. 3. Dynamic electricity pricing system. The TOU electricity price is a main instrument for demand-side response. Power companies set different electricity prices in phases with different loads to affect the electricity consumption cost of residents, thus achieving the goal of load reduction.

The new electricity system reform in China aims to further open the electricity market and introduce competition to enable more efficient electricity distribution under the influence of market forces. Ideally, the new players in future electricity market include electricity retailing companies that offer differentiated services, load integrators that implements demand-side response in the residential sector and small-scale power generation and distribution systems such as microgrids with regional characteristics. This creates opportunities for the implementation of demand-side response. China has launched a pilot project of demand-side response in Shanghai. In the assessment report issued in August 2015, the direct load control project in relation to residential air conditioners accounted for 23–33% of the expected market potential of the demand-side response project. It is expected that by 2030, the demand-side management of residential air conditioners alone can reduce the peak load in Shanghai by 800,000 kWh.

## *4.2 Challenges*

(1) Cross subsidization

According to the *Several Opinions on Further Deepening Electricity System Reform* [(2015) No. 9], the pricing of power generation and retailing shall be reformed, and the electricity price shall be determined by market forces while the prices for power transmission and distribution are separated from the prices for power generation and retailing. The reform is mainly targeted at power users in the industrial and commercial sectors and large-scale power users, but excludes the residential sector. The residential electricity price is still to be determined by the government. Regulation of residential electricity price leads to inflexible price which cannot reflect the electricity cost in real time. Meanwhile, the long-standing problem of cross subsidization in the electricity market in China remains unsettled.

Cross subsidization to residents from the industrial and commercial users has long existed in the electricity market in China. The residential cost of electricity consumption is relatively low, about 1/2 of that in OECD countries. Cross subsidization itself reflects the distortion of the market, suggesting the disconnection between price and cost and resulting in the transfer of benefits between different entities and unfair distribution. As far as demand-side management is concerned, cross subsidization creates certain obstacles to its implementation in the residential sector. First, the excessively low electricity price in the residential sector encourages residents to use more electricity than needed, resulting in inefficient use or waste of electricity. Second, low electricity price increases the relative cost of purchasing high-efficiency home appliances, and residents' purchase decisions of electricity-consuming appliances based on their own minimum cost may deviate from the social optimum. Third, due to low cost of electricity consumption, the government needs to provide more subsidies to promote energy-efficient home appliances, which causes price distortion in the home appliances market.

In order not to raise the living cost of residents, the new electricity system reform does not cancel the cross subsidies, and only proposes to recover the cross subsidies through prices of power transmission and distribution. A major challenge for future demand-side management in China is how to address the cross-subsidization problem gradually and properly in the process of electricity system reform, so that the residential electricity price can accurately reflect the cost of electricity consumption.

(2) Lack of attention on the residential sector

In China, the potential of the residential demand-side management has not received enough attention from the government or the households. The industrial sector is the main target in the *Several Opinions on Further Deepening Electricity System Reform* [(2015) No. 9] and the previous documents related to demand-side management, and there are few articles about the residential sector. This is in part due to the energy consumption structure in China, as the industrial sector is the major energy consumer in China, and it has more potential in demand-side management than other sectors. Meanwhile, the underdeveloped electricity market and the complicated residential electricity consumption in China make it difficult to implement residential demand-side management. However, in the longitudinal analysis of residential energy consumption in China and the horizontal comparison with the developed countries, it is not difficult to find that the residential sector in China plays an increasingly prominent role in terminal use of energy, showing a further upward trend with the improvement of living standard. To press ahead with the residential demand-side management in China, more attention shall be paid to this area by developing relevant electrical and information technologies and fostering electrical power service enterprises to provide service to the residential sector. Meanwhile, the residents' energy conservation awareness and ability shall be improved through publicity and training.

## 5 Summary

With the rising share of residential energy consumption in China, the residential demand-side management is also becoming increasingly important. China is in the initial stage of demand-side management, and there is room for further improvement in terms of regulations, technologies and public awareness. In the context of the new electricity system reform, China faces brand-new chances and challenges in residential demand-side management. The government shall make full use of the opportunity of the new electricity system reform to promote the reform of residential demand-side management in China, thus improving energy conservation in China and alleviating the tension between supply and demand during period of peak load.

Demand-side management includes energy efficiency management and demand-side response. Concerning energy efficiency management, the measures for management of energy efficiency labeling and promotion of energy-efficient products in China need to be improved. Concerning demand-side response, the government shall foster load integrators and electrical power service entities to provide service to the residential sector, further develop and promote electrical and information technologies, and develop effective TOU electricity price for peak-load shifting.

The *Several Opinions on Further Deepening Electricity System Reform* [(2015) No. 9] contained specific requirements for fostering new players in the electricity market, optimizing electrical and information technologies and advancing the implementation of demand-side response. This is a great opportunity for the residential demand-side management in China. However, the problem of cross subsidization which has been a long-standing issue in the electricity market in China is not completely solved in the electricity system reform. In addition, the strategic importance of the potential of the residential demand-side management in China does not attract enough attention. They are two barriers to development that shall be removed through further efforts in the future.

# Bibliography


Allcott, H., & Greenstone, M. (2012). Is there an energy efficiency gap? *Journal of Economic Perspectives, 26*(1), 3–28.

Armstrong, P. R., Dixon, D. R., Richman, E. E., & Rowley, S. E. (1994). *Demand-side management implementation and verification at Fort Drum, New York*. Richland, WA, USA: Pacific Northwest Lab.

Auffhammer, M. (2014). Cooling China: The weather dependence of air conditioner adoption. *Frontiers of Economics in China, 9*(1), 70–84.

Auffhammer, M., & Wolfram, C. D. (2014). Powering up China: Income distributions and residential electricity consumption. *The American Economic Review, 104*(5), 575–580.

Aunan, K. (2004). Exposure-response functions for health effects of ambient air pollution applicable for China-a meta-analysis. *Science of The Total Environment, 3,* 3–16.

Bachrach, D. (2003). Energy efficiency leadership in California: Preventing the next crisis. *The Electricity Journal, 16*(6), 37–47.

Belaïd, F. (2016). Understanding the spectrum of domestic energy consumption: Empirical evidence from France. *Energy Policy, 92,* 220–233.

Biewald, B., Woolf, T., Bradford P., Chernick, P., Geller, S., & Oppenheim, J. (1997). *Performance-based regulation in a restructured electric industry*. Prepared for the National Association of Regulatory Utility Commissioners. Cambridge.

Biewald, B., & Woolf, T. (1997). *Performance-based regulation in a restructured electric industry*. Cambridge: Synapse Energy Economics Inc.

Braun, F. G. (2010). Determinants of households' space heating type: A discrete choice analysis for German households. *Energy Policy, 38*(10), 5493–5503.

Cai, C. G., & Zheng, X. Y. (2007). Research on willingness to pay for reduction of health loss caused by air pollution. *Economic Science, 1,* 107–115 (In Chinese).

Cao, N., & Wang, R. H. (2009). Implementation summarization of China energy efficiency labeling system. *Refrigeration and Air-Conditioning, 9*(1), 9–14 (In Chinese).

CGSS Project Group. (2009). *The Chinese general social survey report (2003–2008)*. Beijing: China Social Press.

Chan, K. S., Dang, V. Q. T., Li, T., & So, J. Y. C. (2016). Under-consumption, trade surplus, and income inequality in China. *International Review of Economics & Finance, 43,* 241–256.

Chang, K. C., Lin, W. M., Li, T., & Chung, K. M. (2009). Local market of solar water heaters in Taiwan: Review and perspectives. *Renewable & Sustainable Energy Reviews, 13*(9), 2605–2612.

Chang, K. C., Lin, W. M., Lee, T. S., & Chung, K. M. (2011). Subsidy programs on diffusion of solar water heaters: Taiwan's experience. *Energy Policy, 39*(2), 563–567.




X. Zheng and C. Wei (eds.), *Household Energy Consumption in China: 2016 Report*, https://doi.org/10.1007/978-981-13-7523-1

Chang, K. C., Lin, W. M., Leu, T. S., & Chung, K. M. (2016). Perspectives for solar thermal applications in Taiwan. *Energy Policy, 94*(1), 25–28.

Chen, G., & Li, S. (2012). How can government make people happy?—An empirical study of the impact of government quality on residents' happiness. *Management World, 8,* 55–67 (In Chinese).

Chen, R. J., & Kan, H. D. (2013). Haze/fog and human health: A literature review. *Chinese Journal of Nature, 35*(5), 342–344 (In Chinese).

Covino, S. (2003). *Demand side response 21st century style*. Power Engineering Society General Meeting. IEEE.

Decker, T., & Menrad, K. (2015). House owners' perceptions and factors influencing their choice of specific heating systems in Germany. *Energy Policy, 85*(1), 150–161.

Donald, C. (1997). *US electric utility demand-side management: Trends and analysis*. US Department of Energy.

Druckman, A., & Jackson, T. (2008). Household energy consumption in the UK: A highly geographically and socio-economically disaggregated model. *Energy Policy, 36*(8), 3167–3182.

Duan, R., Zhang, C. Q., & Liu, A. F. (2005). Cost-benefit analysis model of DSM in power market and its optimization. *East China Electric Power, 33*(4), 7–10 (In Chinese).

Dubin, J. A., & McFadden, D. (1984). An econometric analysis of residential electric appliance holdings and consumption. *Econometrica, 52*(2), 345–367.

Eto, J. (1996). *The past, present, and future of US utility demand-side management programs*. CA: Lawrence Berkeley National Lab.

Farrell, M. J. (1954). The demand for motor-cars in the united states. *Journal of the Royal Statistical Society, 145*(3), 171–201.

Gerarden, T., Newell, R. G., & Stavins, R. N. (2015). Deconstructing the energy-efficiency gap: Conceptual frameworks and evidence. *The American Economic Review, 105*(5), 183–186.

Gertler, P., Shelef, O., & Wolfram, C. (2011). *Poverty, growth and the demand for energy*. SIEPR: Stanford Institute for Economic Policy Research.

Gill, N. J., Osman, P., Head, L., Voyer, M., Harada, T., Waitt, G. R., et al. (2015). Looking beyond installation: Why households struggle to make the most of solar hot water systems. *Energy Policy, 87*(1), 83–94.

Gillingham, K., & Palmer, K. L. (2013). *Bridging the energy efficiency gap*. Resources for the future discussion paper, 13-02.

Gillingham, K., Newell, R. G., & Palmer, K. L. (2009). Energy efficiency economics and policy. *Annual Review of Resource Economics, 1*(1), 597–620.

Goess, S., De Jong, M., & Ravesteijn, W. (2015). What makes renewable energy successful in China? The case of the Shandong province solar water heater innovation system. *Energy Policy, 86*(1), 684–696.

Gong, G. F. (2003). Analysis of trial point conditions for management at demand side of residential quarters. *Shanghai Electric Power, 5,* 414–417 (In Chinese).

Goto, H., Goto, M., & Sueyoshi, T. (2011). Consumer choice on ecologically efficient water heaters: Marketing strategy and policy implications in Japan. *Energy Economics, 33*(2), 195–208.

Graziano, M., & Gillingham, K. (2015). Spatial patterns of solar photovoltaic system adoption: The influence of neighbors and the built environment. *Journal of Economic Geography, 15*(4), 815–839.

Greene, W. (2011). *Econometric analysis* (7th ed.). NY: Pearson.

Greenstone, M., & Hanna, R. (2014). Environmental regulations, air and water pollution, and infant mortality in India. *The American Economic Review, 104*(10), 3038–3072.

Hammitt, J. K., & Zhou, Y. (2006). The economic value of air-pollution-related health risks in China: A contingent valuation study. *Environmental and Resource Economics, 33*(3), 399–423.

Han, J., Mol, A. P., & Lu, Y. (2010). Solar water heaters in China: A new day dawning. *Energy Policy, 38*(1), 383–391.

Han, Y., Wang, D. L., & Bi, Y. Y. (2014). Analysis of influencing factors of rural household energy consumption: An empirical study in Tancheng, Shandong province. *Management for Economy in Agricultural Scientific Research, 1,* 10–16 (In Chinese).

Haney, A. B., Jamasb, T., Platchkov, L. M., & Pollitt, M. G. (2011). Demand-side management strategies and the residential sector: Lessons from the international experience. In *The future of electricity demand: Customers, citizens and loads* (Vol. 69, p. 337).

Hausman, J. A., & McFadden, D. (1984). Specification tests for the multinomial logit model. *Econometrica, 52*(5), 1219–1240.

Hirst, E., Cavanagh, R., & Miller, P. (1996). The future of DSM in a restructured US electricity industry. *Energy Policy, 24*(4), 303–315.

Hu, Z. G., Ji, H., & Zhao, L. (1998). Application of demand side management to peak load leveling in Beijing. *Electric Power, 31*(9), 37–40 (In Chinese).

Hu, Z. G., Yang, Z. R., Li, W. Z., Zhou, F. Q., & Barbara, F. (2002). Suggestions on policies to promote power demand side management in China. *Power Demand Side Management, 4*(4), 4–6 (In Chinese).

Inglehart, R., Foa, R., Peterson, C., & Welzel, C. (2008). Development, freedom, and rising happiness: A global perspective (1981–2007). *Perspectives on Psychological Science, 3*(4), 264–285.

Ito, K., & Zhang, S. (2016). *Willingness to pay for clean air: Evidence from air purifier markets in China* (Vol. 3, pp. 3–16). Social Science Electronic Publishing.

Jones, R. V., Fuertes, A., & Lomas, K. J. (2015). The socio-economic, dwelling and appliance related factors affecting electricity consumption in domestic buildings. *Renewable & Sustainable Energy Reviews, 43,* 901–917.

Jridi, O., Bargaoui, S. A., & Nouri, F. Z. (2015). Household preferences for energy saving measures: Approach of discrete choice models. *Energy and Buildings, 103*(1), 38–47.

Kan, H. D. (2004). Economic assessment of health impact due to particulate air pollution in urban areas of Shanghai. *Environmental Science, 9,* 71–79 (In Chinese).

King, M., & Cronin, F. (1998, October 29). *Performance-based ratemaking educational seminar.* https://www.oeb.ca/documents/cases/RP-1999-0034/October_29_educational_seminar.PDF.

Kumhof, M., & Ranciere, R. (2010). *Inequality, leverage and crises.* IMF working paper, 10/268.

Leahy, E., & Lyons, S. (2010). Energy use and appliance ownership in Ireland. *Energy Policy, 38* (8), 4265–4279.

Lee, W. (2004). US lessons for energy industry restructuring: Based on natural gas and California electricity incidences. *Energy Policy, 32*(2), 237–259.

Levy, S. J. (2005). The evolution of qualitative research in consumer behavior. *Journal of Business Research, 58*(3), 341–347.

Li, C. R., & Gao, J. (2012). Energy conservation measures in tiered electricity pricing in various countries. *State Grid, 6,* 52–54 (In Chinese).

Li, J. R., & Ji, H. (1999). Research and application of demand side management in Beijing region. *Power System Technology, 23*(2), 19–21 (In Chinese).

Li, M. J. (2015). Environmental pollution, government regulation and residents' happiness-empirical analysis based on microdata of the CGSS (2008). *Modern Economic Science, 37*(5), 59–68 (In Chinese).

Li, W., Rubin, T. H., & Onyina, P. A. (2013). Comparing solar water heater popularization policies in China, Israel and Australia: The roles of governments in adopting green innovations. *Sustainable Development, 21*(3), 160–170.

Li, Y. Y., Zhao, X. L., & Lu, M. (2013). Analysis on carbon tax and energy subsidies for rural energy consumption in China. *Issues in Agricultural Economy, 34*(8), 100–104 (In Chinese).

Li, Y., Bai, M., Zhang, W., Yang, K. Z., & Wang, X. J. (2002). Analysis on the influential factors of residents' willingness to pay for improving air quality in Beijing. *China Population, Resources and Environment, 12*(6), 321–324 (In Chinese).

Liang, L. (2013). *Research on the effects and countermeasures of tiered electricity pricing for residents in Beijing*. Unpublished doctoral dissertation, North China Electric Power University, Beijing (In Chinese).

Liao, H., & Chang, T. (2002). Space-heating and water-heating energy demands of the aged in the US. *Energy Economics, 24*(3), 267–284.

Lin, W. M., Chang, K., & Chung, K. M. (2015). Payback period for residential solar water heaters in Taiwan. *Renewable & Sustainable Energy Reviews, 41*(1), 901–906.

Liu, J. D. (2013). *Benefit assessment and characteristics analysis of demand response*. Unpublished doctoral dissertation, Shandong University, Jinan (In Chinese).

Liu, M. P. (2015). Core, focus and influences of the new electricity system reform. *Macroeconomic Management, 6*, 20–22 (In Chinese).

Liu, L., Wang, Z., Zhang, H., & Xue, Y. (2010). Solar energy development in China—A review. *Renewable & Sustainable Energy Reviews, 14*(1), 301–311.

Liu, Y., Gao, Y., Hao, Y., & Liao, H. (2016). The relationship between residential electricity consumption and income: A piecewise linear model with panel data. *Energies, 9*(10), 831.

Lu, H., & Lu, Li. (2006). An empirical analysis of the impact of farmers' income level on the household energy consumption structure in the countryside. *Finance and Trade Research, 17* (3), 28–34 (In Chinese).

Lu, J. L., & Yang, G. R. (2016). Study of clean air pricing from the perspective of happiness. *Public Economics and Policy Studies, 1*, 118–133 (In Chinese).

Luo, L. H. (2007). *Research on the system of power demand side management market*. Unpublished master's thesis, Hunan University, Changsha (In Chinese).

Ma, B., Song, G., Smardon, R., & Chen, J. (2014). Diffusion of solar water heaters in regional China: Economic feasibility and policy effectiveness evaluation. *Energy Policy, 72*(1), 23–34.

Ma, B., Song, G. J., & Du, Q. Q. (2012). Cost analysis method and its application for domestic solar water heater in China. *China Population, Resources and Environment, 22*(11), 150–156 (In Chinese).

Ma, B., Du, Q. Q., & Fang, G. B. (2015). Non-linear income effect of low-carbon products application in China: Taking solar water heater in rural areas as an example. *Acta Agriculturae Zhejiangensis, 27*(3), 484–489 (In Chinese).

Mabahwi, N. A., Leh, O. L., & Omar, D. (2015). Urban air quality and human health effects in Selangor, Malaysia. *Procedia-Social and Behavioral Sciences, 170*, 282–291.

MacKerron, G., & Mourato, S. (2009). Life satisfaction and air quality in London. *Ecological Economics, 68*, 1441–1453.

Manski, C. F. (1993). Identification of endogenous social effects: The reflection problem. *The Review of Economic Studies, 60*(3), 531–542.

Matsumoto, S. (2016). Household income structure and electrical appliance ownership: Evidence from Japanese National Household Survey. *International Journal of Energy Economics and Policy, 6*(1), 14–19.

Mauritzen, J. (2015). How price spikes can help overcome the energy efficiency gap. *Economics Letters, 134*, 114–117.

McCarthy, C., & Ryan, J. (1974). An econometric-model of television ownership. *Economic & Social Review, 7*(3), 265–288.

McFadden, D. (1978). Modelling the choice of residential location. *Transportation Research Record*. In A. Karlqvist, L. Lundqvist, F. Snickars & J. W. Weibull (Eds.), *Spatial interaction theory and planning models* (pp. 75–96). Amsterdam: North-Holland Publishing Company.

McNeil, M. A., & Letschert, V. (2010). Modeling diffusion of electrical appliances in the residential sector. *Energy and Buildings, 42*(6), 783–790.

Menz, T. (2011). Do people habituate to air pollution? Evidence from international life satisfaction data. *Ecological Economics, 71*, 211–219.

Michelsen, C. C., & Madlener, R. (2012). Homeowners' preferences for adopting innovative residential heating systems: A discrete choice analysis for Germany. *Energy Economics, 34*(5), 1271–1283.

Michelsen, C. C., & Madlener, R. (2013). Motivational factors influencing the homeowners' decisions between residential heating systems: An empirical analysis for Germany. *Energy Policy, 57*(1), 221–233.

Michelsen, C. C., & Madlener, R. (2016). Switching from fossil fuel to renewables in residential heating systems: An empirical study of homeowners' decisions in Germany. *Energy Policy, 89* (1), 95–105.

Mu, H. Z., & Fan, H. M. (2014). Urbanization and residents' willing to pay for tackling air pollution. *Journal of Chinese Academy of Governance, 6,* 81–85 (In Chinese).

Nadel, S., & Geller, H. (1996). Utility DSM: What have we learned? Where are we going? *Energy Policy, 24*(4), 289–302.

National Development and Reform Commission. (2013). *Notice of the National Development and Reform Commission on utilizing pricing leverage for healthy development of the photovoltaic industry* (No. 1638). Beijing (In Chinese).

Niu, S., Zhang, X., Zhao, C., & Niu, Y. (2012). Variations in energy consumption and survival status between rural and urban households: A case study of the Western Loess Plateau, China. *Energy Policy, 49*(10), 515–527.

Niu, Y. Z., Niu, S. W., Zhang, X., & Zhao, C. S. (2013). Policy options on fuel use, energy conservation and emission reduction in household sector. *China Soft Science, 5,* 45–55 (In Chinese).

O'Doherty, J., Lyons, S., & Tol, R. S. (2008). Energy-using appliances and energy-saving features: Determinants of ownership in Ireland. *Applied Energy, 85*(7), 650–662.

Ou, B. C., Li, H. Q., & Huo, X. S. (2005). On power demand side management strategies. *Modern Management Science, 4,* 54–55 (In Chinese).

Palmer, K. L., & Walls, M. (2015). Limited attention and the residential energy efficiency gap. *The American Economic Review, 105*(5), 192–195.

Pan, X. H., Wang, B. B., & Li, Y. (2013). Demand response technology abroad and its practice. *Power Demand Side Management, 15*(1), 58–62 (In Chinese).

PHB Hagler Bailly. (2000). *Survey of demand-side participation in the national market.* Canberra: National Electricity Code Administrator.

Qiu, H. G., Yan, J. B., & Jiang, Y. (2015). Renewable energy consumption in rural China: Current situation and major driven factors. *Journal of Beijing Institute of Technology (Social Sciences Edition), 17*(3), 10–15 (In Chinese).

Ramos, A., Labandeira, X., & Loschel, A. (2016). Pro-environmental households and energy efficiency in Spain. *Environmental and Resource Economics, 63*(2), 367–393.

Research Group of Jiangxi Development and Reform Commission. (2012). Tiered residential electricity prices in the US, Japan and ROK and enlightenment to China. *Prices Monthly, 11,* 23–28 (In Chinese).

Rode, J., & Weber, A. (2016). Does localized imitation drive technology adoption? A case study on rooftop photovoltaic systems in Germany. *Journal of Environmental Economics and Management, 78*(1), 38–48.

Ruan, W. J., Wang, B. B., Li, Y., & Yang, S. C. (2012). Customer response behavior in time-of-use price. *Power System Technology, 36*(7), 86–93 (In Chinese).

Ruokamo, E. (2016). Household preferences of hybrid home heating systems—A choice experiment application. *Energy Policy, 95*(2), 224–237.

Sallee, J. M., West, S. E., & Fan, W. (2016). Do consumers recognize the value of fuel economy? Evidence from used car prices and gasoline price fluctuations. *Journal of Public Economics, 135,* 61–73.

Sappington, D. E. M., Pfeifenberger, J. P., Hanser, P., & Basheda, G. N. (2001). The state of performance-based regulation in the US electric utility industry. *The Electricity Journal, 14*(8), 71–79.

Sartor, D., & Munn, M. (1998). *Lessons learned in implementing a demand side management contract at the presidio of San Francisco*. CA: Lawrence Berkeley National Lab.

Scarpa, R., & Willis, K. G. (2010). Willingness-to-pay for renewable energy: Primary and discretionary choice of British households for micro-generation technologies. *Energy Economics, 32*(1), 129–136.

Shen, J., & Saijo, T. (2009). Does an energy efficiency label alter consumers' purchasing decisions? A latent class approach based on a stated choice experiment in Shanghai. *Journal of Environmental Management, 90*(11), 3561–3573.

Small, K. A., & Hsiao, C. (1985). Multinomial logit specification tests. *International Economic Review, 26*(3), 619–627.

Sun, Y. L., Niu, S. W., Hu, Y. Y., & Qi, J. H. (2015). The characteristics and influencing factors of rural household energy consumption in alpine Tibetan area—A case study of Gannan Plateau. *Journal of Natural Resources, 30*(4), 569–579 (In Chinese).

Tian, S. M., Wang, B. B., & Zhang, J. (2014). Key technologies for demand response in smart grid. *Proceedings of the CSEE, 34*(22), 3576–3589 (In Chinese).

Tobergte, D. R., & Curtis, S. (2013). How will energy demand develop in the developing world? *Journal of Chemical Information and Modeling, 53*(9), 1689–1699.

Towe, C., & Lawley, C. (2013). The contagion effect of neighboring foreclosures. *American Economic Journal: Economic Policy, 5*(2), 313–335.

Train, K. (2009). *Discrete choice methods with simulation*. Cambridge: Cambridge University Press.

Urban, F., Geall, S., & Wang, Y. (2016). Solar PV and solar water heaters in China: Different pathways to low carbon energy. *Renewable & Sustainable Energy Reviews, 64*(1), 531–542.

Vogelsang, I. (2002). Incentive regulation and competition in public utility markets: A 20-year perspective. *Journal of Regulatory Economics, 22*(1), 5–27.

Wang, H., & Mullahy, J. (2006). Willingness to pay for reducing fatal risk by improving air quality: A contingent valuation study in Chongqing, China. *Science of The Total Environment, 367*, 50–57.

Wang, L., & Wei, H. K. (2014). The impacts of Chinese urbanization on energy consumption. *Resources Science, 36*(6), 1235–1243 (In Chinese).

Wang, M. L. (2011). *Research on demand side management*. Beijing: Beijing Jiaotong University (In Chinese).

Wang, X. H., & Wu, Z. M. (1999). On estimation methods of rural residential energy consumption. *Renewable Energy Resources, 4*, 1–3 (In Chinese).

Wang, X. H., & Di, C. L. (2002). On rural energy consumption with sustainable development in Jiangsu province of China. *China Population, Resources and Environment, 12*(5), 98–100 (In Chinese).

Wang, X. H., & Hu, X. Y. (2010). Factors influencing rural household energy consumption. *Transactions of the Chinese Society of Agricultural Engineering, 26*(3), 294–297 (In Chinese).

Wang, X. H. (2012). Study on rural household energy consumption in Jiangsu province. *Chinese Agricultural Science Bulletin, 28*(26), 196–200 (In Chinese).

Wang, X. H., Hao, X. R., & Jin, L. (2014). Study on rural household energy consumption in China based on household investigation from typical counties. *Transactions of the Chinese Society of Agricultural Engineering, 30*(14), 206–212 (In Chinese).

Wasi, N., & Carson, R. T. (2013). The influence of rebate programs on the demand for water heaters: The case of New South Wales. *Energy Economics, 40*(1), 645–656.

Wei, C., Qing, P., Song, F., Zheng, X., Yu, Y., & Guo, J. (2016). China's energy efficiency and conservation. In *Springer briefs in environment, security, development and peace* (Vol. 31, pp. 5–22).

Welsch, H. (2006). Environment and happiness: Valuation of air pollution using life satisfaction data. *Ecological Economics, 58*, 801–813.

Wijaya, M. E., & Tezuka, T. (2013). A comparative study of households' electricity consumption characteristics in Indonesia: A techno-socioeconomic analysis. *Energy for Sustainable Development, 17*(6), 596–604.

Wiser, R., Bachrach, D., Bolinger, M., & Golove, W. (2004). Comparing the risk profiles of renewable and natural gas-fired electricity contracts: A summary of the California department of water resources contracts. *Renewable & Sustainable Energy Reviews, 8*(4), 335–363.

Xiao, Y., Wang, H. S., & Yang, J. B. (2009). Analysis of Shanghai residents' electric consumption and demand-side management measures. *Journal of Shanghai University of Electric Power, 25* (6), 614–618 (In Chinese).

Xie, Y., & Zhou, X. (2014). Income inequality in today's China. *Proceedings of the National Academy of Sciences of the United States of America, 111*(19), 2–3.

Xu, G. J., Zhang, X. F., Shi, K., & Wang, H. (2013). An empirical study of smart power consumption of users in buildings. In *Proceedings from the Electrical and Communication management & Smart Grid Communication Technology Forum.*

Xu, Y. (2014). Empirical analysis of rural resident energy consumption of China under the background of low carbon based on micro data in 7 provinces. *Journal of Anhui Agricultural Sciences, 42*(16), 5171–5174 (In Chinese).

Yang, J. D., & Zhang, Y. R. (2014). Cost of air pollution: Analysis based on happiness data. *The Journal of World Economy, 12,* 162–188 (In Chinese).

Yang, Z. R., Hu, Z. G., Zhou, F. Q., & Li, W. Z. (2002). Governmental behavior in demand side management. *Power Demand Side Management, 4*(1), 1–4 (In Chinese).

Yang, Z. R. (2003). Analysis of the evolution of demand side management. *Energy of China, 25* (4), 22–26 (In Chinese).

Yao, J. P., Wang, S., & Liu, X. D. (2015). The functional analysis of rural household energy use: An empirical study on three villages in Gansu province. *Journal of North China Electric Power University, 1,* 1–10 (In Chinese).

Yu, Y., & Guo, J. (2016). Identifying electricity-saving potential in rural china: Empirical evidence from a household survey. *Energy Policy, 94*(1), 1–9.

Yuan, X., Jian, Z., & Ma, C. (2011). Social acceptance of solar energy technologies in china-end users' perspective. *Energy Policy, 39*(3), 1031–1036.

Zeng, M., Sun, X., Zhang, Q. P., Lu, Z. M., & Li, T. (2003). The stimulating system and policy analysis and research on PDSM. *Power Demand Side Management, 5*(2), 3–6 (In Chinese).

Zeng, M., Yang, Y., Wang, L., & Sun, J. (2016). The power industry reform in China 2015: Policies, evaluations and solutions. *Renewable & Sustainable Energy Reviews, 57*(1), 94–110.

Zhang, J., & Mu, Q. (2016). *Air pollution and defensive expenditures: Evidence from particulate-filtering facemasks*. SSRN working paper.

Zhang, L., Jiang, J. X., Gao, W., & Li, C. H. (2012). Study on word-of-mouth in the diffusion of low-carbon energy technology in rural areas-taking the solar water heater as the example. *Soft Science, 26*(4), 39–43 (In Chinese).

Zhang, X., Zhang, X., & Chen, X. (2017). *Happiness in the air: How does a dirty sky affect mental health and subjective well-being?* IFPRI discussion paper.

Zheng, X., Wei, C., Qin, P., Guo, J., Yu, Y., Song, F., et al. (2014). Characteristics of residential energy consumption in China: Findings from a household survey. *Energy Policy, 75*(1), 126–135.

Zhang, Y. F. (2006). *Research on demand side management incentive theories*. Beijing: North China Electric Power University (In Chinese).

Zhao, Y., Yu, W. H., Pang, J. D., Shen, S. L., Li, G. P., & Wu, K. (2012). Residential demand-side valuation of interruptible load management for air conditioner. *Power System Technology, 36* (11), 71–76 (In Chinese).

Zhou, H., & Zhang, Y. J. (2015). The energy efficiency gap in household energy conservation investment. *China Population, Resources and Environment, 25*(4), 132–140 (In Chinese).

Zhou, S., & Teng, F. (2013). Estimation of urban residential electricity demand in China using household survey data. *Energy Policy, 61,* 394–402.

Zhu, C. Z., & Xu, R. W. (1999). *Demand-side management*. Beijing: China Electric Power Press (In Chinese).

Zhu, C. Z. (2005). On equal importance of power demand-side management and power supply development. *Distribution and Utilization, 3,* 1–3 (In Chinese).

MIX
Papier aus verantwortungsvollen Quellen
Paper from responsible sources
FSC® C105338

If you have any concerns about our products,
you can contact us on
**ProductSafety@springernature.com**

In case Publisher is established outside the EU,
the EU authorized representative is:
**Springer Nature Customer Service Center GmbH**
**Europaplatz 3, 69115 Heidelberg, Germany**

Printed by Libri Plureos GmbH
in Hamburg, Germany